COLLEGE EDITION

ENGLISH 3200

THIRD EDITION
with INDEX

English **2200**

English **2600**

English **3200**

Tests for English 2200

Tests for English 2600

Tests for English 3200

Alternate Tests for
English 3200

ANSWER KEY
FOR EACH TEST BOOK

About
the Author

Joseph C. Blumenthal received his A.B. and A.M. degrees from the University of Michigan. He also did graduate work at the University of Chicago and at Columbia University. From 1938 to 1959 he was head of the English Department at Mackenzie High School in Detroit. Among his writings are the *Common Sense English* series, the *English Workshop* series (with John F. Warriner and others), and *The English Language* series (with Louis Zahner and others).

About
the Fifth Edition

This edition retains the index that is intended to make *English 2600* more useful to students and instructors by giving them ready access to the entire body of material treated in the text. Each entry is indexed by frame and page numbers to facilitate reference.

The
Test Booklet

The 64-page test booklet designed for use with *English 2600* consists of a Pre-Test, two parallel tests for each of the twelve units, two Halfway Tests, and a Final Test.

Preface

English 2200, English 2600, and *English 3200* are the original programed courses in grammar, usage, sentence-building, capitalization, and punctuation. Since the introduction of the series in colleges in 1963, it has proved effective in teaching the elements of English to more than a million students of all abilities in a wide range of institutions: state and private universities, community, junior, and four-year colleges, vocational and technical institutes, and business colleges.

The Self-Teaching Method

Like their predecessors, the 1981 College Editions of the series are self-pacing, self-correcting, thorough, and flexible. They are programed to make the learning of grammar and usage a positive, success-oriented experience. Each lesson in *English 2200, English 2600,* and *English 3200* contains twenty to forty sequential learning "frames." Each frame has three elements: an easy-to-understand explanation of a small but significant step in the mastery of the lesson topic; a question or statement about the topic to which the student must respond; and the answer to the preceding frame's question. Students perform and correct their work individually, at their own pace. Correct responses are immediately reinforced and incorrect responses are corrected at once. This step-by-step format, based on decades of in-class testing and refinement, provides the immediate positive reinforcement and encouragement students need to maximize learning.

Three Parallel, Graduated Programs

English 2200, English 2600, and *English 3200* are parallel in approach and design and may therefore be used cumulatively. As their titles indicate, they vary in length according to the number of frames, and they vary in emphasis. *English 2200* and *English 2600* focus on the parts of speech and how they are combined into correctly punctuated sentences. In *English 2200,* students are introduced to words that make up and enrich sentences. In *English 2600,* they expand on this knowledge by studying the function of verbs, subjects, and modifiers, as well as the patterns of simple sentences. *English 3200* guides students directly from one unit on the simple sentence to six units on more sophisticated ways of handling sentences. It treats compound and complex sentences, devices of subordination, and techniques for writing sentences with variety and smoothness.

Pedagogical Flexibility

College instructors have found that the cumulative programed format of the series offers an extraordinary degree of pedagogical flexibility. They have used the same book as a basic text for an entire class, as an independent course of study for individuals, as a review for groups outside the classroom, and as a remedial text for individuals or groups. These last two uses have made the series especially attractive to writing laboratories and learning centers. Further, because the three programs in the series cover the same principles of grammar and usage, they may be used sequentially in three graduated courses or even together in a single class. For example, using the results of the diagnostic Pre-Test for *English 2600,* instructors may assign students either *English 2200, English 2600,* or *English 3200.* Instead of spending many class hours on details of grammar and usage, instructors assigning these self-teaching programs are free to devote more time to the teaching of writing, vocabulary, spelling, and other skills.

Indexes

A detailed index, useful to both instructors and students, follows each programed course. Every entry in the index is followed by the frame number and

the page, in parentheses, on which the frame appears. The frames indexed are those containing key concepts, definitions, or illustrations. For example, under the entry "fragment" in the index to *English 3200* are eleven sub-entries; these entries direct students to various kinds of fragments, as well as to methods for correcting them. Students may turn to particular entries to answer their own questions about specific points of grammar and usage. Besides offering a handy reference, however, the index is a useful aid for planning remedial and review exercises. When students reveal that they have not yet mastered a particular concept, the instructor, by consulting the index, can guide them to review the appropriate frames. Students who require help in correcting specific errors when revising a composition may be alerted to frames that show them how to identify and remedy those errors.

Test Booklets and Answer Keys

A 60- or 64-page test booklet for each volume in the series is provided free to college instructors in class quantities, one booklet for each textbook ordered. Additional copies of the test booklets are sold separately and may be ordered from the publisher. An alternate test booklet, parallel in form and content to the original, is available for *English 3200*. When placing orders for *English 3200*, instructors should indicate whether they wish the original or the alternate test booklets. In addition, an Answer Key for each of the test booklets is available to instructors.

Each test booklet contains a diagnostic Pre-Test, two parallel Mastery Tests (labeled A and B) for each unit in the textbook, two parallel Halfway Tests, and a Final Test.

This testing apparatus considerably enhances the flexibility of the series. Whether a test is given to individual students or to an entire class at the same time depends on how the textbook itself is used. If students proceed at their own rate until they complete the entire book, individual testing will be necessary. If the class waits until all students complete a given unit before proceeding to the next unit, the class may be tested simultaneously. The Pre-Test enables instructors to determine a student's overall grasp of fundamentals, to identify his or her strengths and weaknesses, and to plan an individualized program while avoiding material the student has already mastered.

The inclusion of parallel Mastery Tests offers flexibility in meeting the needs of a specific class and in providing for various classroom situations. For example:

1. Test A may be used as a pre-test for every unit and Test B as a final test.

2. Test A may serve as a practice test and Test B as the official test.

3. Test A or B may be used as a makeup test for students who did not achieve satisfactory scores on their first test.

4. Tests A and B may be used with different classes or with alternate rows in the same classroom.

No matter how the tests are used, one idea, basic to the method of programed learning, should be kept in mind: a response should have an immediate reinforcement.

To the Student

English 3200, Third Edition with Index, is a programed course in grammar, sentence-building, usage, and punctuation designed to provide a quick recapitulation of the elements of language. A very substantial part of this programed text deals with devices of sentence construction and types of subordination. The book also has lessons on the placing of modifiers, dangling construction, parallelism, the reference of pronouns, and other grammatical concepts.

If this should be your first experience with a programed textbook, you will be interested in knowing why programed instruction is regarded as a major advance in education. Programed texts are making rapid headway as a teaching method for the following reasons:

1. When a course is programed, it is broken down into very minute and carefully arranged steps—approximately 3,200 in the case of the present book—through which you reason your way, one small step at a time. There is no separation, as in conventional textbooks, between explanation and exercises; the two are woven tightly together. Every step—or frame—calls for a written response, which requires both *thinking* and *concentration*. Thinking your way, step by step, through a program is like following a very gradual path up a steep mountain. Without becoming winded or losing your footing, you suddenly discover that you have reached the top.

2. Programs are constructed on the principle of "errorless learning." The steps are so small and their order is so logical that, with reasonable concentration, you are not likely to make many mistakes. Should you, now and then, write the wrong answer, you are corrected immediately—before the error can become established. It is as though a watchful teacher were constantly looking

over your shoulder, ready to put you back on the track the moment you wander off. Using a programed textbook is the nearest approach to having a private tutor.

3. With the usual language textbook, you first study the explanation, which you may or may not understand thoroughly. Next, you apply what you have studied to the exercises in the text—often with a feeling of uncertainty. Usually, it is not until the next day that you discover whether or not you did the exercises correctly.

With *English 3200*, however, as soon as you turn the page you find out whether your reasoning was right. At this point something very important happens. The instant you find out that your answer is right, all doubt disappears and the idea "takes root," so to speak, in your brain.

The psychologists who developed programing call this *reinforcement*, and it is a most important factor in learning. The more often reinforcement takes place and the more quickly it follows the writing of your answer, the better you learn.

4. With programed instruction, you can progress at your own best rate. Many students have completed entire courses in a fraction of the time required by the traditional textbook method and have demonstrated a better mastery of the subject matter. With programed instruction, your mind is constantly in high gear. You lose no time waiting for other students to recite, correcting other students' papers, or listening to a discussion of other students' mistakes. In the rapidly developing world of today, education is becoming a longer and longer road. The time you save by this new scientific method can be used to advance yourself in literature, composition skills, discussion, and creative activities.

—

Each step, or frame, requires that you perform some operation. For example, in many of the frames, you will do one of two things:

1. If there is a blank line, write in the missing word or letter.

Example: Jones is the name of a *person*.

2. If there are two or more words or letters in parentheses, underline the correct answer.

Example: Jones is the name of a (*person, place*).

(Note: Your instructor will tell you whether to write your answers in the book or to write them in a separate notebook or on separate sheets of paper.)

The first work frame is Frame 2 (on page 3). After you complete Frame 2, turn to Frame 3, *in the same position* on the next *right-hand* page (page 5). In the column to the left of Frame 3, you will find the correct answer to Frame 2. If your answer is not correct, turn back and correct it before doing Frame 3. You will always find the answer to a frame in the column to the left of the frame that you are to do next. Thus, you find the answer to Frame 3 to the left of Frame 4, the answer to Frame 4 to the left of Frame 5, and so on.

Go completely through the book, taking only the top colored frame on each *right-hand* page (3, 5, 7, 9, 11, and so on) until you reach the end. When you reach the end of the book, turn back to page 1 and follow the second band—a white one—through the book, still working only on the *right-hand* pages. Then proceed to the third horizontal band, which is colored, going through all the *right-hand* pages. Continue in this way through the fourth, fifth, and sixth bands. When you come to the last white band on the last *right-hand* page (frame 1620), turn back to page 2 and start reading the colored bands at the top of the *left-hand* pages. Continue following each horizontal band through the *left-hand* pages. The last frame is 3232 on page 534.

The alternating colored and white bands will make it easy for you to stay on the same horizontal band as you advance through the book. Since both frame and answer are numbered (each in the lower right corner), you will always know where you are and where to go next.

Getting the Most from English 3200

1. Whenever you are puzzled for the correct answer to a frame, read the frame very carefully again. Many of the frames contain clues that guide you to the right answer, although the clues gradually diminish as the lesson advances. You are not likely to make a mistake very often. When you do, look back a few frames and try to straighten out your thinking. When you can't

help yourself, consult your instructor. With an ordinary textbook, it is difficult for your instructor to discover where your thinking jumped the track. With a programed text, your instructor can help you immediately at the precise point where you need assistance.

2. Take as much time as you need in figuring out your answer. But once you write your answer, *lose no time* in turning to the next frame to check its correctness. Scientific experiment has proved that the quicker you check your answer, the better you learn. *Even the lapse of a few seconds makes a big difference.*

3. *English 3200* is designed for students mature enough to want to improve their minds by thinking things through for themselves—the most effective way of learning and remembering. No student has paid a greater compliment to this book than the one who said, "It makes me think too much." Exercising your brain, like exercising your muscles, is sometimes a bit strenuous. But it is this effort that will develop your power to think systematically and to reason logically.

If you use *English 3200* in a mature way, you may discover that you have acquired a better knowledge of grammar and usage—and in a fraction of the usual time. You may find, too, that you have developed your ability to think and to concentrate in a way that will be useful to you in all your studies. You will have profited by the latest and most exciting discoveries of science about how people learn!

Contents

ENGLISH 3200

THIRD EDITION
with INDEX

Lesson 1 The Subject and Verb in the Simple Sentence

[Frames 2–42]

---

adverb

270

In the following frames, each sentence contains two prepositional phrases in various combinations—two adjective phrases, two adverb phrases, or one of each. Before classifying each phrase, ask yourself, "Does this phrase describe a noun or pronoun, or does it answer a question about the verb?" (*Turn to the next frame.*)

271

---

b

540

I have a friend *who raises tropical fish.*

The adjective clause *who raises tropical fish* modifies the noun _____.

541

---

b

810

Put a comma after any participial phrase that comes at the beginning of a sentence.

   a. *Thinking the paint was dry* **I sat on the bench.**
   b. **We removed the tree** *shading the flower beds.*

Which sentence requires a comma? _____

811

---

before

1080

a. **His** *strong, calloused* **hands were no strangers to work.**
b. **His hands,** *strong* **and** *calloused,* **were no strangers to work.**

In which sentence are the italicized adjectives given more emphasis? _____

1081

---

pulp. High-grade
or
pulp; high-grade

1350

It was a wonderful party   **the best I have ever attended.**

_____

1351

---

similar

1620

Try to apply parallel construction whenever you use the co-ordinating conjunctions **and, but,** and **or,** which generally connect words or word groups of the same type.

Edison paid little attention to *what he ate* **or** *his clothes.*

In this sentence does the conjunction **or** connect parallel word groups? (*Yes, No*)

1621

One

1889

Underline the correct verb:

One of these steaks (*is, are*) **enough for a meal.**

1890

---

cards

2158

The dishes *were laid* **on the sink.**

What *were laid* on the sink? _____

2159

Yes

2427

GOOD and *WELL*

Always use the adverb **well**—never the adjective **good**—to describe an action. A person eats *well*, plays *well*, or works *well*.

    a. **This pen writes** *well.*   b. **This pen writes** *good.*

Which sentence is correct? _____

2428

---

their

2696

From here on, write in the pronoun that is appropriate for formal usage:

Nobody was ever more confused about _____ **rela-tives than I.**

2697

---

items:

2965

The Student Council makes suggestions in regard to such matters as lockers, the lunchroom, and homework   and Mrs. Roska, the principal, discusses these suggestions with the faculty.

2966

A sentence is a group of words that gives us a sense of completeness.

> a. **The barking dog**
> b. **The dog is barking.**

Which group of words is a sentence—*a* or *b?* _____

2

This TV program brings the services (*a*) *of a great university* (*b*) *into your home.*

After each letter, indicate whether the corresponding phrase is an *adjective* or an *adverb* phrase. (Notice that only one of these phrases can be moved to another position.)

(a) _____ *phrase;* (b) _____ *phrase.*   272

---

friend

541

I have a friend *who raises tropical fish.*

An adjective clause signal is nearly always a *pronoun*. This pronoun stands for the noun that the entire clause modifies.

In the above sentence, the pronoun *who* stands for the noun _____.

542

---

a

811

Put a comma after any participial phrase that comes at the beginning of a sentence.

a. **We noticed a small dog** *crossing the busy highway.*
b. *Attempting to start a conversation* **I made some remark about the weather.**

Which sentence requires a comma? _____

812

---

b

1081

a. **His** *strong, calloused* **hands were no strangers to work.**
b. **His hands,** *strong* **and** *calloused,* **were no strangers to work.**

The italicized adjectives in sentence *b* are given more emphasis because they (*are, are not*) in their usual position.

1082

---

party, the

1351

There were Mother's sketches   scattered all over the yard and covered with mud.

_____

1352

No

1621

a. **Edison paid little attention to** *what he ate* **or** *his clothes.*
b. **Edison paid little attention to** *what he ate* **or** *what he wore.*

In which sentence does the conjunction **or** connect parallel word groups? _____

1622

---

is

1890

Once you state your subject, keep your mind on it until you select your verb. Don't let a noun in a prepositional phrase run away with your verb.

Our supply of scientific books (*was, were*) **inadequate.**

The noun **supply** is singular; the noun **books** is plural. We choose the verb _____ to agree with the subject _____.

1891

---

dishes

2159

PRESENT	PAST	PAST PARTICIPLE
lie (to rest)	**lay**	**(have) lain**
lay (to put)	**laid**	**(have) laid**

Laid is never a form of **lie.**

Would you ever use **laid** when you mean **rested**? (*Yes, No*)

2160

---

a

2428

WRONG: **This pen writes** *good.*

This sentence is wrong because the adjective *good* cannot modify the verb _____.

2429

---

his

2697

Almost anyone can increase _____ reading rate considerably.

2698

---

homework;

2966

Somebody   maybe it was Lenore   had let the cat out of the bag.

2967

page 4

The dog is barking.

b

This group of words is a sentence because it gives us a sense of (*completeness, incompleteness*).

2

3

Our mayor is a person (*a*) *with a reputation* (*b*) *for great honesty.*

(a) adjective
(b)   adverb

After each letter, indicate whether the corresponding phrase is an *adjective* or an *adverb* phrase:

(a) _____ *phrase;* (b) _____ *phrase*

272

273

I have a friend *who raises tropical fish.*

friend

The noun that the adjective clause modifies and the noun that the pronoun *who* stands for are (*the same word, different words*).

542

543

When a participial phrase ends a sentence, look for the word it modifies. If it modifies the subject at the other end of the sentence, set it off with a comma.

b

　a. **We found Mr. Ling** *hoeing his garden.*
　b. **Mr. Ling was in the back yard** *hoeing his garden.*

Which sentence requires a comma? _____

812

813

---

　a. **The team,** *tired* **and** *discouraged,* **trudged back to the locker room.**
　b. **The** *tired* **and** *discouraged* **team trudged back to the locker room.**

are not

In which sentence are the italicized adjectives given more emphasis? _____

1082

1083

The return on a stock is called a dividend   the return on a bond is called interest.

sketches (,)
covered

_____

1352

1353

b

1622

Ray's trouble is not *that he doesn't earn enough money* **but** *spending it foolishly.*

Does the conjunction **but** connect parallel word groups? (*Yes, No*)

1623

(verb) was
(subject) supply

1891

Several pieces of the puzzle (*was, were*) **missing.**

The noun **pieces** is plural, but the noun **puzzle** is singular. We choose the verb _____ to agree with the subject _____.

1892

No

2160

Underline the correct words. (*Note:* These two sentences are parallel and require the same verb.)

  a. **The tired travelers** (*lay, laid*) **in bed all morning.**
  b. **My missing wallet** (*lay, laid*) **in the snow all winter.**

2161

---

writes

2429

Underline the correct word:

Brush your clothes (*good, well*) **before putting them away.**

2430

---

his

2698

Both women made the welfare of children _____ **chief concern in life.**

2699

Somebody—
Lenore—

2967

Murray is allergic to several foods   for example, eggs and chocolate.

2968

completeness 3	**The dog is barking.** This group of words gives us a sense of completeness because it (1) *names* what we are talking about, and (2) *tells* something about it. Which two words belong to the *naming part* of the sentence? _____ _____ 4
(a) adjective (b) adjective 273	(*a*) *In several states,* **the smoke** (*b*) *from this forest fire* **could be clearly seen.** (a) _____ *phrase;* (b) _____ *phrase* 274
the same word 543	**I have a friend** *who raises tropical fish.* The pronouns that start adjective clauses are called **relative pronouns** because they *relate* (or *connect*) the adjective clause to the sentence. The clause signal *who* in the above sentence is called a _____ *pronoun.* 544
b 813	a. **The director took us through the museum** *explaining all the important pictures.* b. **The museum sold a guidebook** *explaining all the important pictures.* Which sentence requires a comma because the participial phrase that ends the sentence modifies the subject? _____ 814
a 1083	Underline the word or phrase which is emphasized by a change from its normal position: **For fifty years Grandmother attended the same church.** 1084
dividend. The *or* dividend; the 1353	**Ships are like people each having its own personality.** _____ 1354

No

1623

a. **Ray's trouble is not** *that he doesn't earn enough money* **but** *that he spends it foolishly.*
b. **Ray's trouble is not** *that he doesn't earn enough money* **but** *spending it foolishly.*

In which sentence does the conjunction **but** connect parallel word groups? _____

1624

(verb) were
(subject) pieces

1892

People frequently make errors in subject-verb agreement because they have the mistaken idea that adding an *s* to a verb in the present tense makes it plural.

My shoe hurts.

The subject **shoe** is singular, and the verb **hurts** is singular. The word that ends in *s* is the (*subject, verb*).

1893

---

lay

2161

Fill in the missing forms:

PRESENT	PAST	PAST PARTICIPLE
lay (to put)	_____	**(have)** _____

2162

---

well

2430

Although **good** should not be used as an adverb, **well** may be used as an adjective to mean *in good health, of good appearance,* or *satisfactory.*

     a. **Stir the paint** *well* **before using it.**
     b. **Our dog is now** *well* **again.**

Well is used as an adjective in sentence (*a, b*).

2431

---

their

2699

Everyone has _____ **own ideas about what constitutes success in life.**

2700

---

foods;
or
foods—

2968

Your letter of application should state these facts   your age, education, and experience.

(Note that this series is preceded by a grammatically complete statement.)

2969

The dog is barking.

The dog

Which two words *tell* something about **the dog** and therefore belong to the *telling part* of the sentence?

_____ _____

4
5

(a) adverb
(b) adjective

The invention (*a*) *of the automobile* **has changed American life** (*b*) *in many ways.*

(a) _____ *phrase;* (b) _____ *phrase*

274
275

I have a friend *who raises tropical fish.*

relative

The relative pronoun *who* starts the adjective clause. It also stands for the noun _____, which the clause modifies.

544
545

---

a

In this and the following frames, combine each pair of sentences by changing the italicized sentence to a participial phrase. Insert a comma wherever needed.

I read the list of winners. *I hoped to see my name.*

_____

_____

814
815

For fifty years

Underline the word or phrase which is emphasized by a change from its normal position:

Resign he will not.

1084
1085

---

people, each

O. J. trudged to the sideline   **wiping the mud from his face.**

_____

1354
1355

a 1624	Parallel construction is also needed when you use the words **than, as,** and **as well as** to make comparisons. *Writing* **is faster than** *to print.* Are the italicized words parallel? (*Yes, No*) <div align="right">1625</div>
verb 1893	<div align="center">**My <u>shoes</u> <u>hurt</u>.**</div>Now the subject **shoes** is plural, and the verb **hurt** is plural. The word that ends in *s* is the (*subject, verb*). <div align="right">1894</div>
laid, (have) laid 2162	In this and the following frames, underline the correct forms of **lie** and **lay:** (*Lay, Lie*) **your books aside and** (*lay, lie*) **down to rest for a while.** <div align="right">2163</div>
b 2431	Underline the correct words: **When the pressure is** (*good, well*)**, the sprinkler works** (*good, well*)**.** <div align="right">2432</div>
his 2700	**If a woman wants to have a family and earn a college degree, _____ can do so.** <div align="right">2701</div>
facts: 2969	**Practically all the accommodations hotels, motels, and tourist homes were jammed with vacationists.** <div align="right">2970</div>

is barking 5	a. **The argument was useless.** b. **A useless argument.** Which group of words is a sentence because it gives us a sense of completeness—*a* or *b?* _____ 6
(a) adjective (b) adverb 275	(*a*) *At feeding time,* **a large crowd always gathers** (*b*) *around the lions' cage.* (a) _____ *phrase;* (b) _____ *phrase* 276
friend 545	**I have a friend** <u>*who*</u> <u>*raises*</u> *tropical fish.* In the above sentence the relative pronoun *who* is the subject of the verb _____. 546
I read the list of winners, hoping to see my name. 815	Continue to follow the directions for the previous frame: *I read the list of winners.* **I hoped to see my name.** _____ _____ 816
Resign 1085	Underline the word or phrase which is emphasized by a change from its normal position: **Of all the cakes I have ever eaten, this was the most delicious.** 1086
sideline, wiping 1355	Lesson **37** When Does a Sentence End? [Frames 1357–1387]

No 1625	a. *Writing* **is faster than** *printing*. b. *Writing* **is faster than** *to print*. c. *To write* **is faster than** *to print*. Which is the one sentence in which the construction is not parallel? _____ 1626
subject 1894	SINGULAR: **My shoe hurts.** PLURAL: **My shoes hurt.** In either the singular or plural sentence, is there a final *s* on both the subject and the verb? (*Yes, No*). 1895
Lay, lie 2163	PRESENT PAST PAST PARTICIPLE **lie** (to rest) **lay** **(have) lain** **lay** (to put) **laid** **(have) laid** I (*laid, lay*) **awake, trying to recall where I had** (*lain, laid*) **my receipt.** 2164
good, well 2432	Underline the correct words: **You can't study** (*good, well*) **unless the light is** (*good, well*). 2433
she 2701	**Ask anybody where the Eiffel Tower is and _____ can tell you.** 2702
accommodations— homes— 2970	**The lighter seeds are scattered by the wind the heavier ones are distributed by squirrels.** 2971

a. **Helping his friend.**
b. **With the help of his friend.**
c. **Alonzo helped his friend.**

a

Which group of words is a sentence because it gives us a sense of completeness—*a*, *b*, or *c*? _____

6

7

(a) adverb
(b) adverb

276

Some words can be used as either <u>prepositions</u> or <u>adverbs</u>. These words, such as *before, behind, after, past, through, down,* and *around,* generally refer to direction. To decide how such a word is used, look for an *object.* If you find an object, the word in question is a (*preposition, adverb*).

277

---

raises

546

Let's take another look at the adjective clause signals.

RELATIVE PRONOUNS: **who (whose, whom), which, that**

> **The student . . .** *essay wins* **receives a scholarship.**

Which relative pronoun would be appropriate in this sentence? _____

547

Reading the list
of winners, I
hoped to see
my name.

816

Be sure to change the italicized sentence—not the main statement—to a participial phrase. If you lose your subject in so doing, put it back at the start of the main statement.
> *Fred stood at the window.* **He saw the lightning strike.**

_____

_____

817

Of all the
cakes I have
ever eaten,

1086

a. **The Turners had little ready money although they owned a lot of land.**
b. **Although they owned a lot of land, the Turners had little ready money.**

If you had written many sentences with the subject first, which sentence would break the monotony? _____

1087

Many sentence fragments come about in this way. You start out, for example, by writing—

> **Charles Sifford plays golf.**

Is this a complete sentence? (*Yes, No*)

1357

a. **To read a foreign language is easier than to speak it.**
b. **Reading a foreign language is easier than speaking it.**
c. **To read a foreign language is easier than speaking it.**

Which is the one sentence in which the construction is not parallel? _____

b

1626

1627

The window opens.

When you change this sentence to the plural, the final *s* on the verb **opens** (*remains, disappears*).

No

1895

1896

PRESENT	PAST	PAST PARTICIPLE
lie (to rest)	**lay**	**(have) lain**
lay (to put)	**laid**	**(have) laid**

Underline the correct words:

Your books will (*lay, lie*) **there until you** (*lay, lie*) **them somewhere else.**

lay, laid

2164

2165

How do you decide whether to use **good** or **well** after a "sense" verb?

If the "sense" verb means an action, use **well** to describe this action.

Underline the correct word:

I felt the cloth (*good, well*) **before buying the coat.**

well, good

2433

2434

Any person making a telephone call should give _____ name at once.

he

2702

2703

The water was close to the top of the levee   and it was rapidly rising.

(Punctuate so as to make the second idea very forceful.)

wind;

2971

2972

c 7	The *naming part* of a sentence is called the **complete subject.** A **complete subject** is usually built around a noun (or pronoun) that is known as the **simple subject.** The **complete subject** is likely to be (*longer, shorter*) than the **simple subject**—or **subject,** as we usually call it. 8
preposition 277	a. **The dog trotted** *behind.* b. **The dog trotted** *behind* **the car.** In which sentence is *behind* a preposition because it is followed by an object? _____ 278
whose 547	**The woman whose car we bumped was very angry.** The adjective clause starts with the relative pronoun *whose* and ends with the word _____. 548
Standing at the window, Fred saw the lightning strike. 817	**Reverend Jesse Jackson stresses education.** *He maintains it is the key to success.* _____ _____ 818
b 1087	a. **When it was first delivered, the Gettysburg Address made little impression.** b. **The Gettysburg Address made little impression when it was first delivered.** If you had written many sentences with the subject first, which sentence would break the monotony? _____ 1088
Yes 1357	**Charles Sifford plays golf.** Because you recognize this as a complete sentence with a subject and a verb, you close it with a _____. (What punctuation mark?) 1358

c 1627	Parallel construction does not mean having a word-for-word match between the parallel word groups. So long as the basic pattern is the same, minor differences do not matter. **Is he really** *calling* the police **or just** *pretending* to call them? In spite of their difference, the italicized word groups are parallel because *calling* is matched by _____. <div align="right">1628</div>
disappears 1896	In the present tense, a verb without a final *s* may be either singular or plural (*I think, We think*), but with a final *s* (*he thinks, she thinks*), the verb is *always* singular. <div align="center">.?. **thinks.**</div> Could this verb possibly have a plural subject? (*Yes, No*) <div align="right">1897</div>
lie, lay 2165	<table><tr><td>PRESENT</td><td>PAST</td><td>PAST PARTICIPLE</td></tr><tr><td>**lie** (to rest)</td><td>**lay**</td><td>**(have) lain**</td></tr><tr><td>**lay** (to put)</td><td>**laid**</td><td>**(have) laid**</td></tr></table>Underline the correct words: **Mother** (*laid, lay*) **her glasses where she had usually** (*laid, lain*) **them.** <div align="right">2166</div>
well 2434	If the "sense" verb is used as a linking verb, as it more often is, follow it with the adjective **good** to modify the subject. <div align="center">**A warm coat** *feels* (= *is*) **good on a chilly day.**</div> The adjective **good** modifies the subject _____. <div align="right">2435</div>
his 2703	Lesson **75** Review: Pronoun Problems [Frames 2705–2736]
levee— 2972	**We had only one objection to the house its distance from school.** <div align="right">2973</div>

The old black dog wagged its shaggy tail.

The **complete subject** of this sentence consists of four words—**The old black dog.**

The **simple subject,** or **subject,** is the one word _____.

longer

8

9

---

a. **Ralph fell** *down* **the stairs.**
b. **Ralph fell** *down.*

In which sentence is *down* a preposition? _____

b

278

279

The woman whose car we bumped was very angry.
The woman   was very angry.

When we omit the adjective clause, do we have a complete sentence remaining? (*Yes, No*)

bumped

548

549

Reverend
Jesse Jackson
stresses
education,
maintaining
it is the key to
success.
818

Mrs. Kern held on to the purse-snatcher. **She shouted for help.**

(Don't lose *Mrs. Kern* in your revision.)

_____

_____

819

For the sake of variety, move the adverb clause to the beginning of the sentence and set it off with a comma:
Dad would bring me a pennant whenever he returned from a trip.

a

_____

_____

1088

1089

Then as you continue thinking, you decide to qualify your statement by adding an adverb clause.

Charles Sifford plays golf. *Whenever he has time.*

period

Because you have already closed your sentence with a period, the clause becomes a sentence _____.

1358

1359

pretending	*To face your problems squarely* **is more healthful than** *to run away from them.*
	In spite of their difference, the italicized word groups are parallel because the infinitive *To face* is matched by the infinitive _____.
1628	1629
No	We add an *s* to a verb *in the present tense* whenever we talk about any singular noun (*a car, the lunch, my friend*) or about any singular pronoun in the third person (*he, she, it, one*).
	Underline the two singular subjects that would require a verb ending in *s*:
1897	**Planes** **The road** **They** **It** 1898
laid, laid	Underline the correct words:
	My pen has (*lain, laid*) **on the desk ever since I** (*lay, laid*) **it there.**
2166	2167
coat	**The popcorn smelled so** *good* **that we couldn't resist it.**
	We use the adjective *good* because the word **smelled** is used as (*an action, a linking*) verb in this sentence.
2435	2436
	In this and the following frames, underline the correct pronoun. Do not go "by ear," but think of a reason for each choice you make.
	Between you and (*I, me*), **Mrs. Colby doesn't like the gift.**
	2705
house: *or* house—	**Our cat likes only the most expensive foods for example, liver, salmon, and tuna fish.**
2973	2974

The old black dog **wagged its shaggy tail.**

The *telling part* of a sentence is called the **complete predicate.**

dog

The **complete predicate** of this sentence consists of _____ words. (How many?)

9

10

---

a. **Ralph fell** *down* **the stairs.**
b. **Ralph fell** *down.*

In sentence *a, down* is a preposition because it is followed by the object **stairs.**

a

In sentence *b, down* is an adverb that modifies the verb

279

_____.

280

A boy who had never fished before caught the most fish.

Yes

In this sentence the adjective clause starts with the relative

pronoun _____ and ends with the word _____.

549

550

Holding on to the purse-snatcher, Mrs. Kern shouted for help.

Eliminate the **and** by changing the italicized statement to a participial phrase:

The company expected a strike **and bought a large amount of steel.**

819

820

Whenever he returned from a trip, Dad would bring me a pennant.

For the sake of variety, move the adverb clause to the beginning of the sentence and set it off with a comma:

Sandy makes new friends wherever he goes.

_____

_____

1089

1090

---

fragment

Charles Sifford plays golf *whenever he has time.*

Although the sentence could have ended after **golf,** does it end at this point? (*Yes, No*)

1359

1360

to run 1629	**Miss Ross gets acquainted with her students by** *talking to them* **and** *discovering what their interests are.* Although the italicized word groups are quite different, they are parallel because the gerund *talking* is matched by the gerund _____. 1630
The road, It 1898	a. { **A factory . . .** **The boat . . .** **She . . .** } b. { **Factories . . .** **The boats . . .** **They . . .** } Suppose that each of these items were the subject of a sentence in the present tense. With which group would you use verbs that end in *s*? _____ 1899
lain, laid 2167	**To sit** means "to take a sitting position" or "to be in place." **To set** means "to place something." You always set *something*. You *set* a pan on the stove, a glass on the table, a box on the floor. **I** *set* **the pie on the windowsill to cool.** What was *set* on the windowsill? _____ 2168

a linking
 	
2436
	Underline the correct word in each sentence:
	
	   a. **Cheap perfume doesn't smell** (*good, well*).
	   b. **A person with a cold can't smell** (*good, well*).
	
	2437

me 2705	**Unless someone actually asks for your advice, don't offer** (*him, them*) **any.** 2706
foods; *or* foods— 2974	Lesson **83** How to Use Quotation Marks [Frames 2976–3014] *page 20*

four	The complete predicate is built around the simple predicate, which we shall hereafter refer to as the **verb.** A **verb** makes— or helps to make—a statement about the subject.
	The old black dog wagged its shaggy tail.
	The **simple predicate,** or **verb,** around which the complete predicate is built is the one word _____.
10	11

	a. **The farmers stood** *around* **and chatted.**
fell	b. **The farmers stood** *around* **the courthouse.**
	In which sentence is *around* a preposition? _____
280	281

	A boy who had never fished before caught the most fish.
	A boy caught the most fish.
who . . . before	When we omit the adjective clause, do we have a complete sentence remaining? (*Yes, No*)
550	551

Expecting a strike, the company bought a large amount of steel.	Eliminate the **and** by changing the italicized statement to a participial phrase:
	We walked along the shore and *looked for a place to swim.*
	_____
	_____
820	821

Wherever he goes, Sandy makes new friends.	For the sake of variety, move the adverb clause to the beginning of the sentence and set it off with a comma:
	A host should not eat until every guest has been served.
	_____
	_____
1090	1091

No	**Charles Sifford plays golf** *whenever he has time.*
	This sentence does not end after **golf** because the adverb clause modifies the verb _____ in the main statement.
1360	1361

discovering

1630

To avoid monotony, you may omit repeated words without destroying the parallelism.

Fractions *can be changed to decimals,* **and** *decimals can be changed to fractions.*

The three words that can be omitted from the word group after **and** are _____.

1631

---

a

1899

The ability of gymnasts astonishes everyone.

The verb **astonishes** agrees with the subject, which is (*ability, gymnasts*).

1900

---

pie

2168

After you *set* something, it *sits* there until you *set* it somewhere else.

Fill in the missing words:

I _____ a chair on the porch so that Dad could _____ in the sun.

2169

---

a. good
b. well

2437

In this and the following frames, underline the correct modifier after you have decided whether the verb is used as an *action* or a *linking* verb:

Mr. Sutin felt quite (*angry, angrily*) **about the bill.**

2438

---

him

2706

(*We, Us*) **fellows can finish the job in a few hours.**

2707

A **direct quotation** repeats a person's remark directly in his own words. An **indirect quotation** reports a person's remarks indirectly in someone else's words.

    a. **Pia said, "I'll be home by ten."**
    b. **Pia said that she would be home by ten.**

The direct quotation is in sentence (*a, b*).

2976

wagged	The *subject* and the *verb* are the most important words in any sentence because they carry most of the meaning.
	Two small boys | rang our doorbell.
	The *subject* of this sentence is the noun _____.
11	The *verb* is the word _____. 12

b	a. **The bus went** *by* **without stopping.** b. **The bus went** *by* **the corner without stopping.**
	In which sentence is *by* a preposition? _____
281	282

	If a complete sentence does not remain after we omit the adjective clause, we have not selected the clause correctly.
Yes	a. **The rope (which controls the curtain broke).** b. **The rope (which controls the curtain) broke.**
	The clause is correctly selected in sentence (*a, b*).
551	552

We walked along the shore, looking for a place to swim.	*Lita worked until midnight* **and finally completed her theme.**
	_____
	_____
821	822

Until every guest has been served, a host should not eat.	In this and the following frames, emphasize the italicized words by moving them from their normal position to another position in the sentence:
	He never could understand *geometry.*
	_____
1091	1092

plays	Does the fact that a sentence could end at a certain point mean that it does end at this point? (*Yes, No*)
1361	1362

can be changed 1631	**I feared** *that he would change his mind* **or** *that he would raise the price.* The three words that can be omitted from the word group after **or** are _____. 1632
ability 1900	**The ability of gymnasts astonishes everyone.** The noun **gymnasts** is not the subject of the sentence but the object of the preposition _____. 1901
set, sit 2169	PRESENT PAST PAST PARTICIPLE **sit** **sat** **(have) sat** **set** (to place) **set** **(have) set** The verb whose three forms are all alike is _____. 2170
angry 2438	**Your voice sounds** (*differently, different*) **on the tape.** 2439
We 2707	**Students should be encouraged to think for** (*themselves, theirselves*). 2708

a
 	
2976
	The word **that** is frequently used in changing a direct to an indirect quotation.
	Rewrite the following sentence to make the quotation indirect (and use no quotation marks).
	      Mother said, "I am ready."
	      Mother said _____.
	
	2977

(subject) boys (verb) rang 12	Throughout this book, we shall underscore the subject with one line and the verb with two lines. **Two small <u>boys</u> | <u><u>rang</u></u> our doorbell.** Indicate the *subject* and *verb* in the following sentence by underscoring: **A handsome blue car | stopped in front of our house.** 13
b 282	UNIT 2: THE PROCESS OF COMPOUNDING Lesson **8** **Compound Parts and Compound Sentences** [Frames 284–324]
b 552	a. **The blood (which flows from a wound) washes away the germs.** b. **The blood (which flows from) a wound washes away the germs.** The clause is correctly selected in sentence (*a, b*). 553
Working until midnight, Lita finally completed her theme. 822	**A milk truck overturned and** *caused a traffic jam for several miles.* _____ _____ 823
Geometry he never could understand. 1092	**I have never eaten** *such food.* _____ 1093
No 1362	**We built a cottage | on a hill | overlooking a lake | which was surrounded by pine trees.** At how many points could this sentence have been ended before the final period? _____ 1363

that he would 1632	Put parentheses ( ) around the three words that can be omitted without destroying the parallelism: **Ray Tall Chief, our bookkeeper, keeps track of how much is coming in and how much is going out.** 1633
of 1901	a. **The ability of gymnasts astonishes everyone.** b. **The ability of gymnasts astonish everyone.** In which sentence is the verb correct? _____ 1902
set 2170	PRESENT PAST PAST PARTICIPLE **sit** **sat** **(have) sat** **set** (to place) **set** **(have) set** Fill in the missing words: **Don't** _____ **the package where someone might** _____ **on it.** 2171
different 2439	**We looked through every drawer very** (*thorough, thoroughly*). 2440
themselves 2708	**Let's you and** (*me, I*) **try out for track.** 2709
(that) she was ready. 2977	Use quotation marks ("quotes" for short) to enclose only a *direct* quotation—one that repeats a person's exact words. a. **Dad said** **You can use the car, Jim.** b. **Dad said** **that Jim could use the car.** Which sentence requires quotes because it is a direct quotation? _____ 2978

car stopped

13

A handsome blue car | stopped in front of our house.

The subject **car** and the verb **stopped** carry more of the meaning of this sentence than any other two words we could possibly choose. (*True, False*)

14

Mr. Kwan | owns a garage.

This sentence—like all complete sentences—can be divided into two major parts: the *complete subject* and the *complete*

_____.

284

---

a

553

The clause signal **where** can start either an adverb clause or an adjective clause.

If the clause modifies a verb, it is considered an adverb clause.

If the clause modifies a noun or pronoun, it is considered an

_____ clause.

554

A milk truck overturned, causing a traffic jam for several miles.

823

Several planes circled the airport **and waited their turn to land.**

_____

_____

824

Such food I have never eaten.

1093

I never expect to be *a millionaire.*

_____

1094

---

three

1363

We built a cottage | on a hill | overlooking a lake | which was surrounded by pine trees.

This sentence could have been ended at each point marked by a vertical line. It does not end, however, until the final period because each phrase or clause modifies a word in the (*preceding, following*) phrase or clause.

1364

(how much is)

1633

Put parentheses ( ) around the two words that can be omitted without destroying the parallelism:

I showed Jimmie how to set the camera and how to take pictures.

1634

---

a

1902

   a. **The abilities of a gymnast astonishes everyone.**
   b. **The abilities of a gymnast astonish everyone.**

In which sentence is the verb correct? _____

1903

---

set, sit

2171

Underline the correct words:

Tommy (*set, sat*) down where Mrs. Gibb had (*set, sat*) the biggest piece of cake.

2172

---

thoroughly

2440

Barbara feels (*bad, badly*) about losing her library card.

(Is this an action of Barbara's hands?)

2441

---

me

2709

I don't like mine as well as (*yours, your's*).

2710

---

a

2978

Always capitalize the first word of a direct quotation because it is the beginning of someone's sentence.

   a. **Dad said, "you can use the car, Jim."**
   b. **Dad said, "You can use the car, Jim."**

Which sentence is correct? _____

2979

Verbs have a special characteristic that helps us to identify them. Verbs are the only words that can show by a change in their spelling whether they mean *present* or *past* time; for example, **cook—cooked, see—saw, speak—spoke.**

What is the *past* form of the verb **jump?** _____

15

Mr. Kwan and his <u>son</u> | <u>own</u> a garage.

The part of this sentence that now has two parts is the complete (*subject, predicate*).

285

---

a. **I eat at the store** *where I work.*
b. **I eat** *where I work.*

In one sentence the clause is an adverb clause because it modifies a verb; in the other, it is an adjective clause because it modifies a noun.

The adjective clause is in sentence (*a, b*).

555

Circling the airport, several planes waited their turn to land.

824

A present participle always ends with the letters _____.

825

(Are you moving only the italicized word or words for emphasis?)

He would *go* **in spite of everyone's advice.**

_____

_____

1095

A sentence is something like a train. A train might have only five cars. However, we cannot point to the fifth car and say, "There's the end of the train" until we look to make sure no more cars are coming.

Similarly, a sentence ends only when the (*first, last*) *grammatically connected* idea has been expressed.

1365

(how to)	Put parentheses ( ) around the two words that can be omitted without destroying the parallelism:
	A tree can stand a strong wind because it is flexible and because it has deep roots.
1634	1635

	a. **Flowers** *decorate* **each table.**
	b. **A vase of flowers** *decorates* **each table.**
b	Why are the verbs different? Their subjects are different.
	In *a*, the plural noun **Flowers** is the subject.
	In *b*, **flowers** has become the object of the preposition **of,** and the subject is now the singular noun _____.
1903	1904

sat, set	Underline the correct words:
	Why would anyone want to (*sit, set*) **where George** (*set, sat*)?
2172	2173

bad	**Rayna looked** (*beautiful, beautifully*) **in her new spring outfit.**
2441	2442

yours	**Ray Charles showed** (*we, us*) **fans his collection of gold records.**
2710	2711

b	Underline the correct word:
	Eleanor said to Sandy, ''(*that, That*)** is your third piece of pie.''**
2979	2980

jumped 15	PRESENT: **I never eat oysters.** PAST: **I never ate oysters.** In the changing of this sentence from *present* to *past* time, the only word that changed was the verb _____. 16
subject 285	**Mr. Kwan | owns and operates a garage.** The part of this sentence that now has two parts is the complete (*subject, predicate*). 286
a 555	**I eat at the store** *where I work.* The clause *where I work* is an adjective clause because it modifies the noun _____. 556
ing 825	A participle is considered a verbal because it has the characteristics of both a verb and an _____. 826
Go he would, in spite of everyone's advice. 1095	**Fran's** *original and imaginative* **paintings won the interest of a famous artist.** _____ _____ 1096
last 1365	If you close a sentence with a period before you have included a *grammatically connected* word group, you produce a sentence _____. 1366

(because it)	In this and the following frames, rewrite the word group in parentheses, making it parallel with the italicized phrase:
	An old book **is not necessarily better than** _____
	_____. (one that is new)
1635	1636

	A vase of flowers . . . each table.
vase	Since the plural noun **flowers** comes right before the verb, it will try to grab the verb, which belongs to the singular subject **vase.** If you are not on your guard, this can easily happen.
	A vase of flowers (*decorates, decorate*) **each table.**
1904	1905

sit, sat	Underline the correct words:
	The box was still (*sitting, setting*) **where I had** (*set, sat*) **it.**
2173	2174

beautiful	**You can hear very** (*good, well*) **in the balcony.**
2442	2443

us	**I repeated the directions until I was sure that he understood** (*it, them*).
2711	2712

	Pam said, "You can use the car, Jim."
That	What punctuation mark separates the direct quotation from the words that introduce it? _____
2980	2981

eat 16	PRESENT: **Some of the boys ride to school.** PAST: **Some of the boys rode to school.** Because **ride** is the only word that changed, we can be sure that it is a _____. 17
predicate 286	*Compound* means "having more than one part." When a structural part of a sentence consists of two or more parts, that part is said to be **compound.** **Mr. Kwan and his <u>son</u> | <u>own</u> and <u>operate</u> a garage.** Both parts of this sentence are _____. 287
store 556	a. **We camped** *where there were few trees.* b. **We camped on a field** *where there were few trees.* The adjective clause is in sentence (*a, b*). 557
adjective 826	A participial phrase can come either before or after the noun it modifies. (*True, False*) 827
Fran's paintings, original and imaginative, won ... *or* Original and imaginative, Fran's ... 1096	You can give a word or word group its greatest emphasis by leaving it in its normal position. (*True, False*) 1097
fragment 1366	Remember, too, that the length of a word group has nothing to do with its being a sentence or not. Two words may form a sentence provided they are a subject and verb and make sense by themselves. a. **Neighbors objected.** b. **The neighbors.** Which is a complete sentence? _____ 1367

a new one.

1636

The doctor advised Uncle John *to get a pole* **and** _____
_____. (that he should go fishing)

1637

---

decorates

1905

The operation of this machine requires much skill.

The singular verb **requires** agrees with the singular subject of this sentence, which is (*operation, machine*).

1906

---

sitting, set

2174

To rise means "to go up" or "to get up."
To raise means "to make something rise" or "to lift something."

We always raise *something*—a cover, a window, or a cloud of dust. As a result of our action, the cover, the window, or the cloud of dust (*raises, rises*).

2175

---

well

2443

I didn't sleep (*good, well*) **because of the noise.**

2444

---

them

2712

(*Those, Them*) **are the finest cattle in the state.**

2713

---

a comma

2981

Pam said, "You can use the car, Jim."

Both the comma and the period come (*before, after*) the quotation marks with which they are used.

2982

verb
 	
17
	A small number of verbs have the same form for both present and past time; for example, *hit, cut, let, put, hurt, cost.*
	
	    a. **We** *hit* **the ball back and forth.**
	    b. **We** *bat* **the ball back and forth.**
	
	In which sentence could the verb mean either present or past time? _____ 18

compound 287	**Mr. Kwan and his son │ own and operate a garage.** Although both the subject and the predicate of this sentence are compound, the sentence can still be divided into two major parts. These two major parts are the *complete subject* and the *complete* _____. 288

b
 	
557
	Although the clause signal **when** generally starts adverb clauses, it can also start an adjective clause.
	
	    a. **My friend telephoned** *when I was very busy.*
	    b. **My friend telephoned on a day** *when I was very busy.*
	
	The clause that is used as an adjective clause because it modifies a noun is in sentence (*a, b*). 558

True 827	Lesson **22** Subordination by Past Participles [Frames 829–868]
False 1097	Putting an adverb or an adverbial word group ahead of the subject should not be done too often because it is the exception rather than the rule. (*True, False*) 1098
a 1367	**The neighbors** These two words do not form a sentence because there is no _____ to make a statement about the subject **neighbors.** 1368

(to) go fishing. 1637	**Peggy had the habit** *of turning on the radio* **and** _____ _____. (to forget to turn it off) 1638
operation 1906	(Remember always to keep your eye on the subject when choosing your verb.) 　　**The operation of this machine requires much skill.** If we changed **this machine** to **these machines,** would you need to change the verb? (*Yes, No*) 1907
rises 2175	PRESENT　　　　　PAST　　　PAST PARTICIPLE **rise** (to get up)　　**rose**　　　**(have) risen** **raise** (to lift)　　　**raised**　　**(have) raised** Fill in the correct words: **Be sure to** _____ **when I** _____ **my hand.** 2176
well 2444	**Taste the soup** (*well, good*) **before you add more salt.** 2445
Those 2713	**Are you going to ride with** (*they, them*) **or** (*we, us*)? 2714
before 2982	Now let's turn our sentence around: 　　**"You can use the car, Jim," said Pam.** A comma still separates the quotation from the rest of the sentence. Does this comma still come before the quotes? (*Yes, No*) 2983

a	Underscore the subject with one line and the verb with two lines: **Players from both teams scrambled over the field.**
18	19

predicate 288	Any sentence that can be divided into two parts—a subject and a predicate—is a simple sentence. It doesn't matter if either part or both parts are compound. **Mr. Kwan and his <u>son</u> | <u>own</u> and <u>operate</u> a garage.** Although this sentence has a compound subject and a compound predicate, is it still considered a simple sentence? (*Yes, No*) 289

b 558	**A man that looked like a reporter asked me several questions.** The adjective clause starts with the word _____ and ends with the word _____. 559

	the *cracking* **ice** **a** *falling* **rock** **a** *steaming* **potato** All the italicized words are used like adjectives because they modify _____. (What class of words?) 829

True 1098	Lesson **29** Some Useful Adverb Clause Devices [Frames 1100–1138]

verb (*or* predicate) 1368	**The neighbors,** *who were annoyed by Joanne's practicing her trombone at all hours of the day and night,* Now the subject **neighbors** is followed by a long adjective clause that modifies it. As yet, does the subject **neighbors** have a verb to tell what the annoyed neighbors *did?* (*Yes, No*) 1369

(of) forgetting to turn it off. 1638	**Ruth's friends and relatives like her** *because she is generous* **and** _____. (her unselfishness) (*Note:* Do not repeat words unnecessarily.) 1639
No 1907	**The opportunity for advancement seems very good.** If we changed **opportunity** to **opportunities,** would you need to change the verb? (*Yes, No*) 1908
rise, raise 2176	PRESENT PAST PAST PARTICIPLE **rise** (to go up) **rose** **(have) risen** **raise** (to lift) **raised** **(have) raised** Underline the correct word: **Food prices had** (*risen, rose*) **because of the severe drought.** 2177
well 2445	**This engine won't run** (*good, well*) **on ordinary gasoline.** 2446
them, us 2714	(*Ours, Our's*) **steers more easily than** (*theirs, their's*). 2715
Yes 2983	**Pam said, "You can use the car, Jim."** **"You can use the car, Jim," said Pam.** When a comma and quotes or a period and quotes come together, always put the comma or period first. Punctuate this sentence completely: **This is going to be hard to explain sighed Jerry** 2984

Players <u>scrambled</u>

19

<u>A huge, spreading maple</u> <u>stands</u> in front of the church.

Underscore the subject with one line and the verb with two lines:

A huge, spreading maple stands in front of the church.

20

Yes

289

The <u>wind</u> | <u><u>was blowing</u></u>.
The <u>water</u> | <u><u>was rough</u></u>.

Each of these sentences can be divided into a subject and a predicate.

Therefore each of these sentences is a (*simple, compound*) sentence.

290

---

that . . . reporter

559

A man that looked like a reporter asked me several questions.

Write the sentence that remains after you remove the clause.

_____

_____

560

---

nouns

829

the *cracking* **ice**   **a** *falling* **rock**   **a** *steaming* **potato**

The italicized words, which resemble both adjectives and verbs, are participles.

They are *present* participles because they end in _____.

830

You are familiar with adverb clauses that begin with **if** and answer the question, "On what condition?"

If I had taken more time, **I could have done better.**

The verb in the clause consists of the two words _____

_____.

1100

No

1369

The neighbors, *who were annoyed by Joanne's practicing her trombone at all hours of the day and night,*

In spite of its eighteen words, this word group is still *not* a sentence but only a subject modified by a clause.

It cannot become a sentence until we supply a verb to make a statement about the subject _____.

1370

unselfish.	*Watching the game on television* **was almost as good as** _____. (if you were there)
1639	1640

	Don't let the object of a preposition steal your verb. It's the subject that counts.
Yes	a. **The purpose of these laws ...**
	b. **The purposes of this law ...**
	Which subject would require a singular verb—*a* or *b*? _____
1908	1909

risen	Underline the correct word:
	As the water flows into the lock, the ship (*raises, rises*).
2177	2178

well	Lesson **68** Review: Adjective and Adverb Problems
	[Frames 2448–2466]
2446	

Ours, theirs	**People should try to see** (*theirselves, themselves*) **as others see them.**
2715	2716

"This is going to be hard to explain," sighed Jerry.	a. **"I have a dream", said Martin Luther King, Jr.**
	b. **"I have a dream," said Martin Luther King, Jr.**
	Which sentence is correct? _____
2984	2985

maple stands
<u>maple</u> <u><u>stands</u></u>

20

Underscore the subject with one line and the verb with two lines:

A large white cat with yellow patches emerged from the bushes.

21

---

simple

290

Now let's combine our two simple sentences into one sentence by using the conjunction **and.**

The <u>wind</u> <u><u>was blowing</u></u>, and the <u>water</u> <u><u>was</u></u> rough.

Can we split this sentence into two parts so that we will have just a subject on one side and just a predicate on the other? (*Yes, No*)

291

A man asked me several questions.

560

The world owes its scientific progress to men and women who are driven by an insatiable curiosity.

The adjective clause starts with the word _____

and ends with the word _____.

561

---

ing

830

---

a. **the** *cracking* **ice**   **a** *falling* **rock**   **a** *steaming* **potato**
b. **the** *cracked* **ice**   **a** *fallen* **rock**   **a** *steamed* **potato**

The italicized words after letter *b* are also used as adjectives.

Were they also formed from verbs? (*Yes, No*)

831

---

had taken

1100

The "if" idea can also be expressed without using the clause signal **if** at all.

<u>Had</u> <u><u>I taken</u></u> more time, **I could have done better.**

We recognize this as a clause only because of its unusual word order. The subject *I*, instead of coming first, comes between the two parts of the _____.

1101

---

neighbors

1370

The neighbors, *who were annoyed by Joanne's practicing her trombone at all hours of the day and night,* **complained.**

Now we have a completed sentence because we have added

the verb _____, which makes a statement

about the subject **neighbors.**

1371

---

being there.

1640

Frank had the choice *of making up his back payments* **or** _____. (he would lose the car)

1641

---

a

1909

One of you *(is, are)* **always teasing the other.**

Suppose that the prepositional phrase **of you** were omitted. Which verb would you choose to agree with the subject **One?**

_____

1910

---

rises

2178

Underline the correct words:

This *(raised, rose)* **a problem that never had** *(arose, arisen)* **before.**

2179

In this and the following frames, underline the correct modifier or, in some cases, the word appropriate for formal usage:

You will *(sure, surely)* **sleep** *(soundly, sound)* **after so much strenuous exercise.**

2448

---

themselves

2716

(He, Him) **and** *(I, me)* **were the only ones who knew.**

2717

---

b

2985

For variety, we sometimes split a quoted sentence and put the *he said,* or a similar expression, between its two parts.

"A blowout at high speed," *he said,* **"may prove fatal."**

We must use two sets of quotes in order to exclude the words _____ from the quotation.

2986

---

cat emerged 21	Continue to follow the directions for the previous frame: **An expensive silver pin disappeared from the counter.** 22
No 291	**The wind was blowing, *and* the water was rough.** When we divide this sentence at the conjunction, we have a complete sentence—not just a subject or a predicate—on each side of the conjunction. This is not a simple sentence because we cannot divide it into two parts: a *subject* and a _____ 292
who . . . curiosity 561	**The statistics which the speaker quoted were out-of-date.** The adjective clause starts with the word _____ and ends with the word _____. 562
Yes 831	a. **the** *cracking* **ice** a *falling* **rock** a *steaming* **potato** b. **the** *cracked* **ice** a *fallen* **rock** a *steamed* **potato** The italicized words after *b* are also participles because they were formed from verbs and are used as adjectives. However, they are not *present* participles because they do not end in _____. 832
verb 1101	a. *I had taken more time* b. *Had I taken more time* Do both word groups contain exactly the same words? (*Yes, No*) 1102
complained 1371	Could a word group consist of fifty or sixty words and still not be a sentence? (*Yes, No*) 1372

(of) losing the car.	**Our biggest problem is** *to plan programs* **and** _____ _____. (keeping up the members' interest)
1641	1642

is	a. **One of you is always teasing the other.** b. **One of you are always teasing the other.** In which sentence is the verb correct? _____
1910	1911

raised, arisen	Underline the correct words: **Although prices** (*rose, raised*), **my salary didn't** (*raise, rise*).
2179	2180

surely, soundly	**He can't do the work** (*satisfactory, satisfactorily*) **in such a short time.**
2448	2449

He, I	**The amount of the bill surprised Dad more than** (*I, me*).
2717	2718

he said	**"A blowout at high speed,"** *he said,* **"may prove fatal."** If we omit the words *he said* from the above sentence, we have (*one sentence, two sentences*) remaining.
2986	2987

pin disappeared 22	**The pond across the road seldom freezes before December.** 23

predicate
 	
 292
	A sentence made by joining two (or more) simple sentences with the conjunction **and, but,** or **or** is called a **compound sentence.**
	    a. **The wind was blowing, and the water was rough.**
	    b. **Mr. Kwan and his son own and operate a garage.**
	 Which can be split into two separate sentences? _____
	 293

which . . . quoted 562	**This soap is for people whose skin is sensitive to ordinary soap.** The adjective clause starts with the word _____ and ends with the word _____. 563
ing 832	a. **the** *cracking* **ice** **a** *falling* **rock** **a** *steaming* **potato** b. **the** *cracked* **ice** **a** *fallen* **rock** **a** *steamed* **potato** The participles after *b* are **past participles.** The participles that do not end in -*ing* are the (*present, past*) participles. 833
Yes 1102	a. *I had taken more time* b. *Had I taken more time* Which word group by its unusual word order tells you that it is not a sentence but a clause? _____ 1103
Yes 1372	Each of the following news items consists of several word groups. Where necessary, insert a period and a capital letter to show where one sentence ends and the next begins. **Roy dropped his penny into the slot and picked up the card which was supposed to tell his fortune his friends laughed because the card was blank.** 1373

(to) keep up the members' interest.	**The Riveras were** *the first to arrive* **and** _____
	_____. (they left last)
1642	1643

	Here is another rule of subject-verb agreement:
	A verb should agree in number with its subject, not with a subject complement that may follow it.
a	a. **My favorite fruit is apples.**
	b. **Apples are my favorite fruit.**
	Which sentence contains a plural subject? _____
1911	1912

	Two forms of **lie-lay, sit-set,** or **rise-raise** (of which only the first letters are printed) are needed in each sentence. Complete each word, remembering not to use any form of **lay, set,** or **raise** unless the sentence tells to *what* the action is done.
rose, rise	
	L_____ down and I'll l_____ a cold cloth on your forehead.
2180	2181

satisfactorily	**Don's excuse seemed very** (*reasonable, reasonably*) **to his employer.**
2449	2450

me	**Dad was more surprised about the bill than** (*I, me*).
2718	2719

	"A blowout at high speed," *he said,* **"may prove fatal."**
one sentence	Because the second part of the quotation is a continuation of the same sentence that was interrupted by *he said*, it begins with a (*small, capital*) letter.
2987	2988

pond freezes	**My only key to the house fell through a crack in the steps.**
23	24

a	One of these sentences is a compound sentence; the other is a simple sentence with a compound subject and predicate.
	a. **The wind was blowing, and the water was rough.**
	b. **Mr. Kwan and his son own and operate a garage.**
	Which sentence is compound because it can be split into two
293	separate sentences? _____ 294

whose . . . soap	**The car which won the first automobile race traveled at five miles per hour.**
	The adjective clause starts with the word _____
	and ends with the word _____.
563	564

past	Most past participles end in *-ed* (entertain*ed*), *-d* (tol*d*), *-en* (brok*en*), *-n* (tor*n*), and *-t* (ben*t*).
	The past participle of a verb is the form you would use after *have;* for example, *have* **opened,** *have* **broken,** *have* **torn.**
	The past participle of **see** is _____.
833	834

b	a. *If I had taken* more time, **I could have done better.**
	b. *Had I taken* more time, **I could have done better.**
	The word order of the clause in sentence *b*—just like the
	clause signal _____ in sentence *a*—tells us that the word
1103	group is an adverb clause. 1104

fortune. His	Continue to follow the directions for the previous frame. Be careful not to produce any sentence fragments.
	To attract a deer a hunter attached a pair of antlers to his head mistaking him for a deer another hunter shot him he was not injured seriously.
1373	1374

the last to leave.	**Carlota Espinoza showed her artistry** *by looking at a subject* **and** _____
	_____. (she would draw it accurately)
1643	1644

b	**Tires . . . my biggest expense.**
	The missing verb should agree in number with the subject (*Tires, expense*).
1912	1913

Lie, lay	Continue to follow the directions for the previous frame:
	Christie I_____ **her beach towel on the sand and I**_____ **down for a nap.**
2181	2182

reasonable	**You can** (*sure, surely*) **get a job** (*easily, easy*) **right before Christmas.**
2450	2451

I	(*It's, Its*) **all** (*your's, yours*) **for the asking.**
2719	2720

small	Underline the correct word:
	"Everything here," complained Mrs. Rizzo, **"(*seems, Seems*) to be out of order."**
2988	2989

A big green milk truck

This group of words is only a subject. There is no predicate to tell what the truck did or what happened to it.

A big green milk truck   a. **ahead of our car**
                                  b. **stopped suddenly**

Which group of words is a predicate—*a* or *b*? _____   25

key fell

24

---

a. **The fall and winter are cold.**
b. **The winters are cold, and the summers are hot.**

Which is a simple sentence with a compound subject? _____

a

294   295

Lesson **15**   Variations of the Adjective Clause

[Frames 566–594]

which . . . race

564

Remember that the past participle of a verb is the same form you would use after *have*.

The past participle of **teach** is _____.

seen

834   835

---

a. *If I had taken more time,* **I could have done better.**
b. *Had I taken more time,* **I could have done better.**

The adverb clause in sentence *b* is not better or worse than the adverb clause in sentence *a*. It enables you, however, to add greater (*clearness, variety*) to your sentences.

If

1104   1105

Mr. McGeorge put up a scarecrow   to keep the robins away   from his strawberry patch   later he saw a robin perching right on the scarecrow's head.

head. Mistaking . . . him. He

1374   1375

(by) drawing it accurately. 1644	*Being a good listener* **is just as important as** _____ _____ . (to talk well) 1645
Tires 1913	a. **Tires . . . my biggest expense.** b. **My biggest expense . . . tires.** In which sentence would you use the singular verb **was—** *a* or *b?* ____ 1914
laid, lay 2182	**Judy's coat has I**_____ **on that chair ever since she** **I**_____ **it there.** 2183
surely, easily 2451	**The fan will run more** (*quiet, quietly*) **if you oil it** (*good, well*). 2452
It's, yours 2720	**Two women, Irene and** (*she, her*), **did most of the artwork.** 2721
seems 2989	**"Everything here,"** complained Mrs. Rizzo, **"seems to be out of order."** We set off **complained Mrs. Rizzo** with commas because it interrupts the quoted sentence. Both commas, as well as the period, come (*before, after*) the quotes. 2990

b

25

Do not mistake words or phrases that merely describe the subject for a predicate. A predicate must have a verb to help make a statement about the subject.

A large crowd a. **of curious and noisy youngsters**
b. **surrounded the TV truck**

Which group of words is a predicate—*a* or *b*? _____

26

---

a

295

a. **The fall and winter are cold.**
b. **The winters are cold, and the summers are hot.**

Which is a compound sentence? _____

296

RELATIVE PRONOUNS: **who (whose, whom), which, that**

These are the relative pronouns that serve as clause signals for _____ clauses.

566

---

taught

835

The past participle of **wear** is _____.

836

---

variety

1105

If you should hear of a job, **let me know.**

Eliminate the *If* in this clause by putting the subject between the two parts of the verb *should hear.*

_____, **let me know.**

1106

---

patch. Later

1375

A father advised his young son   who was interested in collecting moths   to go to the library   and get a book on moths   the boy came back with a book   entitled *A Handbook for Young Mothers.*

1376

being a
good talker.

1645

Our purpose should be *to discover the truth* rather than

_____.

(proving ourselves right)

1646

---

b

1914

Careless drivers are our main traffic problem.

Now let's turn this sentence around and supply the correct verb:

Our main traffic problem _____ careless drivers.

1915

---

lain, laid

2183

Why would anyone I_____ a glass where Allen has I_____ it?

2184

---

quietly, well

2452

The company is usually quite (*prompt, promptly*) in giving service.

2453

---

she

2721

I like to play chess because it makes (*you, me*) think.

2722

---

before

2990

Punctuate this sentence:

The only thing we have to fear   said President Franklin D. Roosevelt   is fear itself

2991

b	
26	

In this and the following frames, write *S* if the word group is just a subject; *P* if it is just a predicate; *SP* if it has both a subject and predicate that form a complete sentence. (Capitals and periods are omitted so as not to reveal the answer.)

most large European cities _____

27

---

b

Only one of these sentences is a compound sentence because it can be split into two parts—each with its own subject and predicate.
a. **I paid my check and waited for my change.**
b. **I paid my check, and the waiter brought me my change.**

Which is the compound sentence? _____

296

297

---

adjective

We sometimes use a preposition before the relative pronoun; for example, **with which, for which, to whom.** In such cases the preposition belongs to the adjective clause.

The pen *with which he wrote* **was scratchy.**

The first word of the adjective clause is (*with, which*).

566

567

---

worn

Past participles—like present participles—also form useful phrases that modify nouns and pronouns.

The woman, *annoyed by the smoke,* **changed her seat.**

The past participial phrase in this sentence modifies the noun _____.

836

837

Should you hear
of a job,

If I were in your place, **I should do the same thing.**

The verb in the adverb clause is _____.

1106

1107

---

moths. The
(boy)

Annoyed by crows   a New Brunswick farmer set a box trap for them   going to his trap the next day   he saw an unusual sight   a silver fox   and a litter of five little ones.

1376

1377

(to) prove ourselves right. 1646	The teacher can't tell whether an error is caused *by igno-rance* **or** _____. (whether you were careless) 1647
is 1915	**The main attraction of the town is the fine shops.** Now let's turn this sentence around and supply the correct verb: **The fine shops _____ the main attraction of the town.** 1916
lay, laid 2184	**Mother I_____ awake, wondering where she had I_____ her diamond ring.** 2185
prompt 2453	**If you can think** (*clearly, clear*), **you should be able to write** (*good, well*). 2454
me 2722	**Let's you and** (*I, me*) **circulate a petition.** 2723
"The only . . . fear," said President . . . Roosevelt, "is fear itself." 2991	Punctuate this sentence: **Whenever I play said Louis Armstrong I give it all I've got** 2992

S

27

S, P, or SP?

complained about the very slow service _____

28

---

b

297

Pelé's teammates shook his hand and patted him on the back.

There are a subject and a verb *before* the conjunction **and.** Are there also a subject and a verb *after* the conjunction **and?** (*Yes, No*)

298

---

with

567

The pen with (which he wrote) was scratchy.
The pen (with which he wrote) was scratchy.

Read each sentence, omitting the words in parentheses. If the remaining words are a sentence, the clause was correctly selected.

The preposition **with** (*is, is not*) part of the clause.

568

---

woman

837

A past participial phrase can often be shifted about.

Annoyed by the smoke, **the woman changed her seat.**
The woman, *annoyed by the smoke,* **changed her seat.**
The woman changed her seat, *annoyed by the smoke.*

Can a past participial phrase be some distance away from the noun it modifies? (*Yes, No*)

838

---

were

1107

a. *If I were in your place, . . .*
b. *Were I in your place, . . .*

The verb in clause *a* consists of one word—*were.*

To eliminate the *If* in clause *a*, put the verb (*before, after*)

the subject *I.*

1108

---

them. Going

1377

Motorists near Albany   suddenly turned up their car windows   and shifted into reverse gear   when they saw   three hundred skunks parading across the state highway.

1378

Lesson 46 Avoiding *Is When* and *Is Where* Constructions

[Frames 1649–1680]

---

are

1916

In this and the following frames, underline the verb that agrees in number with its subject. Don't be fooled by the object of a preposition that might come between the subject and the verb or by a subject complement that might follow the verb.

The decision of the judges (*is, are*) final.

1917

---

lay, laid

2185

Aunt Lou s_____ the biggest piece of pie at the place where Ronnie would s_____.

2186

---

clearly, well

2454

The legislature was (*kind of, rather*) indifferent to the passage of this bill.

2455

---

me

2723

In this and the following frames, underline the pronoun that is appropriate for careful speech and formal writing:

(*Who, Whom*) **will the American people elect to the Presidency next November?**

2724

"Whenever I
play," said
Louis Armstrong,
"I give it all
I've got."

Another way to obtain variety is to put the *he said* (or whatever expression you use) between two separate sentences.

"I can't believe it," *said Tom.* **"You must be joking."**

If we omit the words *said Tom* from the above sentence, we have (*one sentence, two sentences*) remaining.

2993

page 56

P	*S, P,* or *SP?* the music stopped _____
28	**29**

No	Pelé's teammates shook his hand and patted him on the back. Is this a compound sentence? (*Yes, No*)
298	**299**

is	The man for whom Matthew Henson worked urged him to get an education. The first word of the adjective clause is (*whom, for*).
568	**569**

Yes	**Hayes threw himself down,** *exhausted from the race.* The participial phrase is separated by several words from the word it modifies, the noun _____.
838	**839**

before	a. *If I were in your place,* **I should do the same thing.** b. *Were I in your place,* **I should do the same thing.** The unusual word order of the clause in sentence *b* serves the same purpose as the clause signal _____ in sentence *a* in telling us that the word group is an adverb clause.
1108	**1109**

This is all one sentence.	A farmer examined his cow's foot to see why she had been limping for the past five weeks in her hoof he found his wife's diamond ring which had disappeared exactly five weeks ago.
1378	**1379**

It is not reasonable to define something as a *time* or *place* when it clearly is *not* a time or a place.

WRONG: **A tragedy** *is when* **a play has an unhappy ending.**
WRONG: **A tragedy** *is where* **a play has an unhappy ending.**

Is a **tragedy** either a *time* or a *place?* (*Yes, No*)

1649

---

is

His only source of income (*was, were*) **odd jobs.**

1917

1918

---

set, sit

Our guest s_____ down before we had even s_____ the table.

2186

2187

---

rather

The jury was (*somewhat, sort of*) **surprised that the judge's sentence was not more** (*severe, severely*).

2455

2456

Whom

It should have been (*they, them*) **who were penalized.**

2724

2725

---

two sentences

"I can't believe it," *said Tom.* **"You must be joking."**

To show that the second part of the quotation is a new sentence, we put a period after *Tom* and follow it with a (*small, capital*) letter.

2993

2994

S, *P,* or *SP?*

supplies electric power to several states _____

30

Pelé's teammates shook his hand and patted him on the back.

Although this is not a compound sentence, one of its parts is compound.

This sentence has a compound (*subject, predicate*).

300

The man for whom Matthew Henson worked urged him to get an education.

The adjective clause begins with the preposition **for** and ends

with the word _____.

570

PRESENT PARTICIPLE: *Neglecting his friends,* **Carl read the newspaper.**

PAST PARTICIPLE: *Neglected by his friends,* **Carl read the newspaper.**

The phrase with the (*present, past*) participle represents Carl as *doing something.*

840

In this and the following frames, eliminate the *if* in each italicized adverb clause by changing the word order of the clause:

I should have written Alva *if I had known her address.*

I should have written Alva _____

_____.

1110

Alvin Phalen   a Canadian trapper   caught a wolf by its tail   he dragged it over the snow   and killed it with one of the skis   which he was wearing.

1380

No
 	
1649
	To define a **tragedy** as a *time* or a *place* seems as far off the track as to define an elephant as a kind of vegetable.
	
	   a. **A tragedy** *is when* **a play has an unhappy ending.**
	   b. **A tragedy** *is where* **a play has an unhappy ending.**
	   c. **A tragedy is a** *play* **with an unhappy ending.**
	
	Which definition makes the best sense? _____
	
	                           1650

was 1918	**Conditions in this hospital** (*require, requires*) **investigation.** 1919
sat, set 2187	**I s**_____ **my chair under a tree to avoid s**_____ **in the hot sun.** 2188
somewhat, severe 2456	**Mrs. Rosen treats the kindergarteners** (*lovely, in a lovely manner*). 2457
they 2725	**I cannot see how anybody in** (*their, his*) **right mind can believe such nonsense.** 2726

capital
 	
2994
	Punctuation and capitals are omitted from the following sentences to avoid revealing the answers.
	
	   a. **If Seaver pitches** *said Foster* **we will surely win**
	   b. **Seaver is pitching** *said Foster* **we will surely win**
	In which line does *said Foster* stand between two separate sentences? _____
	
	                           2995

S, P, or SP?

my dad has a good sense of humor _____

31

---

predicate

300

The most common conjunctions that connect the two parts of a compound sentence are **and, but,** and **or.**

a. **The movie bored the adults but pleased the children.**
b. **The movie bored the adults, but the children liked it.**

In which sentence does the conjunction **but** connect the two parts of a compound sentence? _____

301

---

worked

570

The bottle *in* which the lotion comes costs more than the lotion.

Is the preposition *in* part of the adjective clause? (*Yes, No*)

571

---

present

840

PRESENT PARTICIPLE: *Neglecting his friends,* **Carl read the newspaper.**

PAST PARTICIPLE: *Neglected by his friends,* **Carl read the newspaper.**

The phrase with the (*present, past*) participle represents Carl as *having had something done to* him.

841

---

had I known
her address.

1110

If Stover were willing to run, **he would win hands down.**

_____, **he would win hands down.**

1111

---

tail. He

1380

Because his truck wouldn't start   on a cold day   a man built a fire under the engine   a barrel of oil exploded   blowing the roof off his garage   and burning his house down   a friend was also injured.

1381

c 1650	The temptation to use *is when* or *is where* arises whenever you are asked to explain a technical term used in school studies, science, business, sports, fashions, and so on. The first step in defining something is to ask yourself what general type of thing it is. <div align="center">**A tariff is a** (*game, tax, fine*)...</div> <div align="right">1651</div>
require 1919	**One of your sleeves** (*look, looks*) **shorter than the other.** <div align="right">1920</div>
set, sitting 2188	**Although our costs have r_____ considerably, we have not r_____ our prices.** <div align="right">2189</div>
in a lovely manner 2457	**The vase of pink and white peonies looked** (*nice, nicely*) **on the desk.** <div align="right">2458</div>
his 2726	**The Martins always insist on** (*our, us*) **staying for dinner.** <div align="right">2727</div>
b 2995	Note the difference in the punctuation and capitalization in these sentences: a. **"If Seaver pitches," said Foster, "we will surely win."** b. **"Seaver is pitching," said Foster. "We will surely win."** Quotation *b* is handled differently from quotation *a* because it consists of (*one sentence, two sentences*). <div align="right">2996</div>

S, P, or *SP?*

a bottle of red ink _____

32

---

b

301

a. **The movie bored the adults but pleased the children.**
b. **The movie bored the adults, but the children liked it.**

In which sentence is a comma used before the conjunction **but?** _____

302

Yes

571

The bottle in which the lotion comes costs more than the lotion.

The adjective clause begins with the preposition **in** and ends with the word _____.

572

---

past

841

To show that something *has been done to* a person or a thing, we use a (*present, past*) participle.

842

Were Stover willing to run,

1111

I'll let you know *if I should change my mind.*

I'll let you know _____

_____.

1112

---

engine. A (barrel)
down. A (friend)

1381

A police officer gave a man a traffic ticket   for walking slowly   in front of an automobile   and forcing the driver to jam on his brakes   the man was Eddie Tolan   the former champion runner.

1382

A tariff is a *tax* . . .

tax

After you give the general classification, add a word, phrase, or clause to differentiate the thing you are defining from other things of the same class.

A tariff is a tax charged on (*income, imports*).

1651

1652

---

looks

One important cause of traffic congestion (*is, are*) **the huge office buildings.**

1920

1921

---

risen, raised

Gloria r_____ the cover to see if the dough had r_____.

2189

2190

---

nice

Should we choose the adverb *badly* to describe the action of the team's hands, or the adjective *bad* to describe the team's emotions?

The team felt (*badly, bad*) **about the poor attendance at the game.**

2458

2459

---

our

Just suppose that it was (*we, us*) **who were starving.**

2727

2728

---

two sentences

"Seaver is pitching," said Foster. "We will surely win."

"We will surely win" is a separate sentence.

Before starting our new sentence with a capital, we must close the first sentence by putting a _____ after **Foster.**

2996

2997

S, P, or SP?

the linoleum on our kitchen floor _____

33

---

b

302

a. **I can call for you or meet you at school.**
b. **I can call for you, or we can meet at school.**

In which sentence does the conjunction **or** connect the two

parts of a compound sentence? _____

303

---

comes

572

**The bottle in which the lotion comes costs more than the
lotion.**

The bottle   **costs more than the lotion.**

When we omit the adjective clause, do we have a complete
sentence remaining? (*Yes, No*)

573

---

past

842

To emphasize that the action of a participle has been
entirely completed before another action, use *having* before
the past participle (*having finished, having seen*).

a. *Glancing through the paper,* **I laid it aside.**
b. *Having glanced through the paper,* **I laid it aside.**

Which sentence is correct? _____

843

---

should I change
my mind.

1112

If it were not for the mosquitoes, **camping would be fun.**

_____ ,

camping would be fun.

1113

---

brakes.
The (man)

1382

Disturbed by yowling cats   **a woman in Maine fired her
husband's revolver**   **into the dark**   **to frighten them away
she found a dead wildcat the next morning**   **and collected
fifteen dollars**   **the state bounty for a wildcat.**

1383

imports 1652	a. **A tariff is when a tax is charged on imports.** b. **A tariff is where a tax is charged on imports.** c. **A tariff is a tax charged on imports.** Sentence *c* is correct because a **tariff** is not defined as a *when* or a *where*, but as a _____. 1653
is 1921	Movies (*was, were*) **her main topic of conversation.** 1922
raised, risen 2190	Just as they r_____ to leave, Carmen r_____ another problem. 2191
bad 2459	**Because it was April Fool's Day, Dick tasted the candy** (*suspicious, suspiciously*). 2460
we 2728	To (*who, whom*) **did Washington turn for advice?** 2729
period 2997	a. **"I love conducting," said Sarah Caldwell. "It's my life."** b. **"I love conducting," said Sarah Caldwell, "it's my life."** Which quotation is correct? _____ 2998

S

some parts of the world get mail only once or twice a year

_____

33   34

---

a. I can call for you or meet you at school.
b. I can call for you, or we can meet at school.

b

In which sentence is a comma used before the conjunction

or? _____

303   304

---

a. The things (at which the audience laughed) were very silly.
b. The things at (which the audience laughed) were very silly.

Yes

In which sentence is the clause correctly identified? _____

573   574

---

a. *Having finished his homework,* Fred went to bed.
b. *Finishing his homework,* Fred went to bed.

b

Which sentence is correct? _____

843   844

We should have started earlier *if we had known the distance.*

Were it not for
the mosquitoes,

We should have started earlier _____

_____ .

1113   1114

Benjamin Morris of Kansas City couldn't sleep   because the
scratching of a branch against his house disturbed him   after
sawing off the limb   he found himself back in bed   but
this time in a hospital   he had sat on the wrong end of the
limb   while he sawed.

away. She

1383   1384

tax 1653	a. **Astronomy is the science of the heavenly bodies.** b. **Astronomy is when you study the heavenly bodies.** Sentence *a* is correct because **astronomy** is not defined as a *when,* but as a _____. 1654
were 1922	**Kellie's years of experience** (*qualify, qualifies*) **her for the job.** 1923
rose, raised 2191	Lesson **61** Keeping Your Tenses Consistent [Frames 2193–2230]
suspiciously 2460	**Burning leaves smell very** (*pleasant, pleasantly*) **in the autumn.** 2461
whom 2729	**Nobody likes to feel that** (*he is, they are*) **being pushed around.** 2730
a 2998	Supply all necessary punctuation. (*Note:* Since **Cats** starts a new sentence, watch your punctuation after **Sally.**) **You are wrong said Sally Cats do show affection** 2999

SP

34

S, P, or *SP?*

moves through the water by a kind of jet propulsion _____

35

---

b

304

We put a comma before the conjunction **and, but,** or **or** when it connects the two parts of a compound (*sentence, predicate*).

305

---

a

574

---

a. **We were eager to try the dishes which have made this inn famous.**
b. **We were eager to try the dishes for which this inn is famous.**

In which sentence does a preposition precede the relative pronoun which signals the clause? _____

575

---

a

844

It is very simple to change a sentence to a past participial phrase when its verb consists of two words—some form of *be* followed by a past participle; for example, *is* **built,** *was* **invited,** *were* **surprised.**

It was taken from a plane.

Does the above sentence contain such a verb? (*Yes, No*)

845

---

had we known
the distance.

1114

The adverb **once** can sometimes be used as an adverb clause signal in place of *if, when, after,* or *as soon as.*

a. **If** *you break the seal,* **you can't return the film.**
b. **Once** *you break the seal,* **you can't return the film.**

In which sentence does the condition expressed by the clause seem more emphatic and final? _____

1115

---

him. After . . .
hospital. He

1384

As he saw a man   running from his delivery truck   with a crate of eggs   a milkman hurled a bottle of milk   at the thief   and knocked him unconscious   the milkman identified himself to the police as Art Wells   star pitcher for the Bowman Dairy baseball team.

1385

science

1654

Astronomy is the science of the heavenly bodies.

In defining **astronomy,** first we classify it as a **science.** Then to distinguish it from many other sciences, we add the modifying phrase _____.

1655

---

qualify

1923

This article claims that high wages (*is, are*) **the best way of preventing a business depression.**

1924

Tense means *time.* The tense of a verb shows the time of its action—present, past, or future.

        a. I *feel* **good today.**
        b. I *felt* **good yesterday.**

The verb is in the past tense in sentence _____.

2193

---

pleasant

2461

The scheme sounded rather (*dishonest, dishonestly*) **to me.**

2462

---

he is

2730

Pasadena and (*we, ourselves*) **are tied for first place.**

2731

"You are wrong," said Sally. "Cats do show affection."

2999

Supply all necessary punctuation:

This snapshot isn't good   said Dick   There wasn't enough sun

3000

P

35

S, P, or *SP?*

the kindly old doctor in this small Iowa town _____

36

---

sentence

305

The man fumbled in his pocket and pulled out a letter.

Should a comma be inserted after the word **pocket?** (*Yes, No*)

306

---

b

575

The conditions . . . *which we played* **were difficult.**

The adjective clause in this sentence requires a preposition.

Underline the preposition that would make the best sense:

by   under   at   with

576

Yes

845

(It was) taken from a plane.

To change the above sentence to a past participial phrase, start your phrase with the "ready-made" past participle

_____, dropping all the words that precede it.

846

---

b

1115

Underline the clause signal that makes the clause more emphatic:

(*Once, If*) *you feed a stray cat,* **you can't get rid of it.**

1116

---

unconscious.
The (milkman)

1385

To celebrate the opening of his theater   the owner decided to give a television set   to the person holding the lucky ticket   when the number was called   seventy-two people flocked to the box office   each having the lucky number the printer had made a slight mistake.

1386

of the heavenly bodies 1655	a. **A polygon is where a figure has more than four sides.** b. **A polygon is a figure having more than four sides.** Which definition is correct? _____ 1656
are 1924	**One in every eight persons in the United States** (*own, owns*) **a dog.** 1925
b 2193	a. I *feel* **good today.** b. I *felt* **good yesterday.** c. I *shall feel* **better tomorrow.** The verb is in the future tense in sentence _____ 2194
dishonest 2462	**Many people felt** (*badly, bad*) **about the results of the election.** 2463
we 2731	**The first ones to arrive were Olga and** (*her, she*). 2732
"This . . . good," said Dick. "There wasn't enough sun." 3000	Use only one set of quotes ("—") to cover any number of sentences provided that the quotation is not interrupted. Supposing that each line represents a separate sentence, supply the necessary quotation marks: **The announcer said,** _____ . _____ . _____ . 3001

S

a giant explosion with the force of a billion atom bombs sometimes occurs on the sun _____

36   37

No

The man fumbled in his pocket and ↓ **pulled out a letter.**

Suppose that we added the pronoun **he** at the point indicated by the arrow. Would it then be correct to insert a comma after **pocket?** (*Yes, No*)

306   307

---

under

The conditions under which we played were difficult.

The adjective clause begins with the preposition **under** and ends with the word _____.

576   577

---

taken

This is a picture of our town. (*It was*) *taken from a plane.*
This is a picture of our town *taken from a plane.*

The participial phrase modifies the noun _____.

846   847

Once

Make this sentence more emphatic by using a "once" clause:

After my tests are over, **I shall have more time.**

_____, **I shall have more time.**

1116   1117

**ticket. When . . .
number. The
(printer)**

A sparrow picked up a lighted cigarette butt   and carried the butt to its nest   on the Henrys' house   a two-story frame structure   which caught on fire   the nest was a total loss   although firefighters put out the blaze   before much damage was done to the house.

1386   1387

b

a. **Amnesia is when one loses his memory.**
b. **Amnesia is loss of memory.**

Which definition is correct? _____

1656

1657

---

owns

(Think this one over carefully before you select your verb.)

A few drops of oil (*do, does*) **the trick.**

1925

1926

---

c

a. **I** *feel* **good today.**
b. **I** *felt* **good yesterday.**
c. **I** *shall feel* **better tomorrow.**

In which sentence is a change in time shown by a change in the spelling of the verb? _____

2194

2195

---

bad

A cold shower feels (*good, well*) **on a hot day.**

2463

2464

---

she

We are unable to take a step without (*them, their*) **complaining of the noise.**

2732

2733

The announcer
said, "_____.
_____. _____."

Supply the necessary quotation marks. (Note that a colon is generally used to introduce a long or formal quotation.)

As Professor Brown remarked: A people that is ignorant of its history is like an individual without a memory. It can learn nothing from its past experience. It will make the identical mistakes again and again.

3001

3002

SP	S, P, or SP?
	several families in our neighborhood _____
37	38

Yes	The three conjunctions commonly used to connect the two parts of a compound sentence are **and, but,** and **or.**
	In a compound sentence, we generally put a comma before
307	the _____ **and, but,** or **or.** 308

	Although relative pronouns are usually a signal that an adjective clause is starting, the relative pronoun is some-times omitted.
played	**Most of the things** (*that*) *we fear* **never happen.**
	Can the clause signal be omitted in the above sentence?
577	(*Yes, No*) 578

	The roads were covered with ice.
picture	What is the two-word verb in this sentence? _____
	_____.
847	848

	Subordinate the italicized statement by changing it to a "once" clause:
Once my tests are over,	*You sign the contract,* **and you can't change your mind.**
	_____, **you**
1117	**can't change your mind.** 1118

fire. The (nest)	Lesson **38** Pronouns as a Cause of Run-on Sentences
	[Frames 1389–1430]
1387	

Of course, when we are really speaking about *time* or *place*, it is permissible to use *is when* or *is where*.

b

    a. **Saturday** *is when* **the contest closes.**
    b. **A yearling** *is when* **an animal is one year old.**

In which sentence is the use of *is when* permissible? _____

1657

1658

---

do

The construction of houses, churches, and schools (*continue, continues*) **at a high rate.**

1926

1927

---

b

    a. **I** *feel* **good today.**
    b. **I** *felt* **good yesterday.**
    c. **I** *shall feel* **better tomorrow.**

In which sentence is a change in time shown by the addition of a helping verb? _____

2195

2196

---

good

These scissors don't cut as (*well, good*) **as they once did.**

2464

2465

---

their

(*Who, Whom*) **can a child trust more than his own parents?**

(*Note:* The subject of the verb **can trust** is the noun **child.**)

2733

2734

---

remarked: "A
people
. . . again."

Whenever the speaker changes, begin a new paragraph and use another set of quotes.

It's a burglar   said Ron.   **It's a dog**   said Ann.   **It's your imagination**   said Dad.

How many paragraphs and sets of quotes would this material require? _____

3002

3003

S

38

| The *predicate* of a sentence makes a statement about the

_____.

39

---

conjunction

308

The man fumbled in his pocket and pulled out a letter.
The movie bored the adults but pleased the children.
I can call for you or meet you at school.

Not one of these sentences is a compound sentence.

Each one is a sentence with a compound (*subject, predicate*).

309

Yes

578

We can learn to recognize these "no signal" clauses if we watch for a *subject-verb* combination right after a noun.

Most of the things *we fear* **never happen.**

Here we have a *subject-verb* combination right after the

noun _____.

579

---

were covered

848

The roads *were covered* **with ice.**

Is one of the words in the two-word verb a past participle?
(*Yes, No*)

849

Once you sign
the contract,

1118

Subordinate the italicized statement by changing it to a "once" clause:

A false idea gets into circulation, **and it is difficult to up-root it.**

_____

_____, **it is difficult to uproot it.**

1119

Running one sentence into another without a period (or other end mark) and a capital letter to separate them produces a **run-on** sentence. A run-on sentence is the opposite error of a sentence fragment.

A fragment is less than a sentence; a run-on sentence is

_____ than a sentence.

1389

a

1658

a. **A pinch hitter** *is where* **one player bats for another.**
b. **The city hall** *is where* **you register to vote.**

In which sentence is the use of *is where* permissible? _____

1659

---

continues

1927

Lesson **54** Recognizing Singular and Plural Subjects

[Frames 1929–1969]

---

c

2196

Do not shift from one tense to another unless there is an actual shift in the time of the action.

Phil *accepted* **the job and then** *changes* **his mind.**

Are both italicized verbs in the same tense? (*Yes, No*)

2197

---

well

2465

Our new radio doesn't sound as (*well, good*) **as the old one.**

(*Note:* The test for this Unit is combined with the test for Unit 11.)

2466

Whom

2734

Everybody held (*his, their*) **breath as the car skidded into the intersection.**

2735

---

three

3003

In this and the following frames, circle the letter of the sentence that is correctly punctuated and capitalized:

a. **The doctor said, "That I needed more sleep."**
b. **The doctor said, "You need more sleep, Clyde."**

3004

page 78

subject 39	Every word in a sentence belongs to either the *complete subject* or the *complete* _____. 40
predicate 309	**The man fumbled in his pocket and pulled out a letter.** **The movie bored the adults but pleased the children.** **I can call for you or meet you at school.** Does any one of these sentences have a comma before the conjunction **and, but,** or **or?** (*Yes, No*) 310
things 579	**Most of the things we fear never happen.** The subject of the adjective clause is _____, and the verb is _____. 580
Yes 849	(*The roads were*) *covered with ice.* **They were treacherous.** We can change the italicized sentence to a participial phrase by starting the phrase with the past participle _____. 850

Once a false idea gets into circulation,
 	
1119
	Another more unusual type of adverb clause begins with **now that.** These words, similar in meaning to **because,** are useful in sentences stating *cause and effect.*
	    a. **Because** *you are eighteen,* **you can vote.**
	    b. **Now that** *you are eighteen,* **you can vote.**
	Which sentence suggests that the cause is recent? _____
	
	1120

more 1389	The writer of a run-on sentence doesn't know where a sentence ends. He is like an absent-minded person who reaches the end of a dock and keeps right on walking. WRONG: **The lights were dimmed the concert began.** Here one sentence runs into the next. The first sentence should end with the word 1390

b

1659

Be on guard against the *is when* and *is where* mistake whenever you are asked to point out the climax, turning point, surprise, or most interesting incident in a book or story.

a. **The turning point was where Rita decided to become a nun.**
b. **The turning point was Rita's decision to become a nun.**

Which sentence is correct? _____

1660

The following words are singular because they refer to only one person or thing at a time. They require singular verbs.

each	either	neither	any one
each one	either one	neither one	every one

Underline the correct verb:

Each (*is, are*) right.

1929

No

2197

a. **Phil** *accepted* **the job and then** *changes* **his mind.**
b. **Phil** *accepted* **the job and then** *changed* **his mind.**

Which sentence is correct because both verbs are in the same tense? _____

2198

---

good

2466

UNIT 11: SOLVING YOUR PRONOUN PROBLEMS

Lesson **69** The Nominative and the Objective Case

[Frames 2468–2501]

---

his

2735

Paul and (*myself, I*) wrote all the invitations.

2736

---

b

3004

a. **Will Rogers, the cowboy philosopher, once said, "So live that you wouldn't be afraid to sell the family parrot to the village gossip."**
b. **Will Rogers, the cowboy philosopher, once said, "so live that you wouldn't be afraid to sell the family parrot to the village gossip."**

3005

predicate 40	The heart of the *complete subject* is the *subject*. The heart of the *complete predicate* is the *simple predicate*, commonly called the _____. 41
No 310	We do not ordinarily use a comma before the conjunction that connects the two parts of a compound (*predicate, sentence*). 311
(subject) we (verb) fear 580	A good test for a "no signal" adjective clause is to see whether we can insert a relative pronoun before it. **Sue described the kind of boat she expects to build.** Can we insert *which* or *that* before the word **she?** (*Yes, No*) 581
covered 850	(*The roads were*) *covered with ice.* **They were treacherous.** <div align="right">*Covered with ice,* **they were treacherous.**</div>In changing the italicized sentence to a participial phrase, we lost the subject _____. 851
b 1120	a. *Because Dale has a job,* **he takes more interest in his appearance.** b. *Now that Dale has a job,* **he takes more interest in his appearance.** Which sentence suggests that Dale's job is something recent? _____ 1121
dimmed 1390	In most run-on sentences, we find a comma between the two run-together sentences. a. **After the lights were dimmed, the concert began.** b. **The lights were dimmed, the concert began.** Which is a run-on sentence? _____ 1391

Since words such as *climax, turning point, surprise,* and *incident* are nouns, they are best explained by other nouns or gerunds (verbal nouns ending in *-ing*).

a. **The climax** *was when* **Velvet won the National Derby.**
b. **The climax was Velvet's** *victory* **in the National Derby.**

In which sentence is **climax** explained by a noun? _____

b

1660

1661

The words **each, either,** and **neither** can be used as either pronouns or adjectives.

a. *Each* **is right.** *Either* **is right.** *Neither* **is right.**
b. *Each* **one is right.** *Either* **answer is right.** *Neither* **answer is right.**

The italicized words are used as adjectives in group (*a, b*).

is

1929

1930

It is perfectly correct to shift tense when we really mean to indicate a change in the time of the action.

I *admire* (*present*) **the courage that Sue** *showed* (*past*).

Because you *admire* at the present time the courage that Sue *showed* at a past time, the shift in tenses is (*correct, incorrect*).

b

2198

2199

---

a. *Children* **love** *dogs.*   b. *Dogs* **love** *children.*

In sentence *a, Children* is the subject and *dogs* is the direct object.

In sentence *b, Dogs* is the subject and _____ is the direct object.

2468

UNIT 12: SKILL WITH GRAPHICS

Lesson **76** Commas in Compound Sentences

[Frames 2738–2766]

I

2736

---

a. "We should have won this game," sighed Coach Higgins.
b. "We should have won this game", sighed Coach Higgins.

a

3005

3006

verb 41	When we change a sentence from *present* to *past* or from *past* to *present,* the only word that would ordinarily change is the _____. 42
predicate 311	a. **We can't give everybody everything he wants and reduce taxes at the same time.** b. **The strike was finally settled and the men went back to work.** Which sentence requires a comma before the conjunction because it is a compound sentence? _____ 312
Yes 581	**Sue described the kind of boat she expects to build.** The adjective clause begins with the word _____ and ends with the word _____. 582
roads 851	(*The roads were*) *covered with ice.* **They were treacherous.** <div align="center">the roads</div><div align="center">*Covered with ice,* ~~they~~ **were treacherous.**</div>To let the reader know what the sentence is about, we must substitute **the roads** for the pronoun _____ in the main statement. 852
b 1121	In this and the following frames, subordinate the italicized statement by changing it to a "now that" clause: *Christmas is over,* **and life can return to normal.** _____, **life** **can return to normal.** 1122
b 1391	**The lights were dimmed, and the concert began.** This is *not* a run-on sentence. It is a correct compound sentence formed by combining two simple sentences with the conjunction _____. 1392

b

1661

---

a. **The climax was Velvet's** *winning* **of the National Derby.**
b. **The climax** *was when* **Velvet won the National Derby.**

In which sentence is **climax** explained by a gerund (a verbal noun ending in *-ing*)? _____

1662

---

b

1930

---

a. **Each is right.**
b. **Each one is right.**

The subject of sentence *a* is the pronoun **Each.**

The subject of sentence *b* is the pronoun _____.

1931

---

correct

2199

Mrs. Clark *moved* (*past*) **to Omaha, where she now** *manages* (*present*) **a large drugstore.**

Because Mrs. Clark *moved* to Omaha in the past but *manages* the drugstore at the present time, the shift in tenses is (*correct, incorrect*).

2200

---

children

2468

Children **love** *dogs.* (*Dogs* **love** *children.*)

When we turn this sentence around, do we change the form or spelling of the nouns *children* and *dogs*? (*Yes, No*)

2469

The word **graphics** is one of many English words derived from the Greek word *graphein,* meaning *to write.* We have, for example, *telegraph* (distance writing), *phonograph* (sound writing), and *graphite* (the "lead" in pencils).

The word **graphics,** therefore, applies to (*speaking, writing*).

2738

---

a

3006

---

a. **"Nothing great,"** wrote Emerson, **"Was ever achieved without enthusiasm."**
b. **"Nothing great,"** wrote Emerson, **"was ever achieved without enthusiasm."**

3007

Lesson 2 A Closer Look at Subjects and Verbs

[Frames 44–82]

---

a. **A worker must stop for rest but a machine can work continuously.**

b. **I looked into the microscope but saw only a confusing blur.**

Which sentence requires a comma before the conjunction because it is a compound sentence? _____

b

312

313.

People are known by the company they keep.

We could insert the clause signal *which* or *that* before the word

_____.

she . . . build

582

583

If you lose a noun in making a participial phrase, put this noun back at the *beginning* of your main statement.

The book was autographed by Nin. **It brought a high price.**

Fill in the blank space:

Autographed by Nin, _____ **brought a high price.**

they

852

Summer is here, **and people are planning their vacations.**

_____, **people are planning their vacations.**

Now that
Christmas
is over,

1122

1123

There is another correct way of combining two simple sentences into a compound sentence.

The lights were dimmed; the concert began.

Instead of using the conjunction *and* to combine two simple sentences, we may use a _____.

and

1392

1393

a 1662	a. **The climax was where the tea was dumped into Boston Harbor.** b. **The climax was the dumping of the tea into Boston Harbor.** Which sentence is correct? _____ 1663
one 1931	each either neither any one each one either one neither one every one Watch your verb closely when an "of" phrase follows any of these words. A plural verb often tries to slip itself in. **Each one of the answers is right.** The subject of this sentence is (*one, answers*). 1932
correct 2200	a. **The story is about a man who** *achieved* **great wealth but** *loses* **his happiness.** b. **The story is about a man who** *achieved* **great wealth but** *lost* **his happiness.** Which sentence is correct? _____ 2201
No 2469	*I* **recognized** *him.* (*He* **recognized** *me.*) When we turn this sentence around, do we use the same forms of the pronouns *I* and *him*? (*Yes, No*) 2470
writing 2738	In the field of language, *graphics* means the devices that are used only in writing, not in speech. When we speak, is it possible to make an error in punctuation, capitalization, or spelling? (*Yes, No*) 2739
b 3007	a. **"We've had no rain," said the farmer. "Crops are drying up."** b. **"We've had no rain," said the farmer, "crops are drying up."** 3008

One or more helping verbs (sometimes called *auxiliary verbs*) are often used with the main verb to express our meaning more exactly.

The rope will break.

The helping verb used with **break** to make its meaning more exact is _____.

44

---

a

a. **I just returned from my vacation, and found your letter waiting for me.**
b. **Good judgment comes from experience, and experience comes from bad judgment.**

From which sentence should the comma be removed because it is not a compound sentence? _____

313

314

---

they

People are known by the company they keep.

The "no signal" clause in this sentence consists of two words:

_____ _____ .

583

584

---

the book

Put a comma after any participial phrase that comes at the beginning of a sentence.

a. *Located near a factory* **the store does a big business.**
b. **We visited an old church** *built before the American Revolution.*

Which sentence requires a comma? _____

853

854

Now that
summer
is here,

We have spent all our money, **and we might as well go home.**

_____

_____, **we might as well go home.**

1123

1124

---

semicolon

WRONG: **The lights were dimmed, the concert began.**

This sentence is wrong because there is neither a conjunction nor a semicolon to connect the two sentences.

Does a comma by itself have the power to connect two simple sentences? (*Yes, No*)

1393

1394

b 1663	The coincidence *was when* the brothers met in the Paris airport. Correct the above sentence by writing a gerund in the blank space: The coincidence was the _____ of the brothers in the Paris airport. 1664
one 1932	Each one of the answers . . . right. We pay no attention to the plural noun **answers** when we select the missing verb. The noun **answers** is not the subject of the sentence but the object of the preposition _____. 1933
b 2201	a. **Smith then invested in an oil well in which he lost all his savings.** b. **Smith then invested in an oil well in which he loses all his savings.** Which sentence is correct? _____ 2202
No 2470	NOUNS: *Children* **love** *dogs.* (*Dogs* **love** *children.*) PRONOUNS: *I* **recognized** *him.* (*He* **recognized** *me.*) The words that change in form when their use in the sentence changes are (*nouns, pronouns*). 2471
No 2739	a. **Omission of a capital** b. **Wrong form of verb** Which would be an error in graphics because it could occur only in writing? _____ 2740
a 3008	a. **My Uncle Dan remarked, "I much prefer living in a small town." "Everyone knows everyone else." "People have more time to be courteous and friendly."** b. **My Uncle Dan remarked, "I much prefer living in a small town. Everyone knows everyone else. People have more time to be courteous and friendly."** 3009

The rope will break.
The rope might break.

The meaning of the first sentence changes when we change

the helping verb from **will** to _____.

will

44

45

Ambassador Young remained calm and cool and he didn't raise his voice.

This sentence contains two **and**'s.

A comma should be placed before the (*first, second*) **and**.

a

314

315

The drawer was full of things nobody would ever want.

We could insert the clause signal *which* or *that* before the

word _____.

they keep

584

585

Put a comma before a participial phrase at the end of a sentence only if it modifies the subject at the beginning of the sentence.

   a. **We stayed at a delightful inn** *operated by the state.*
   b. **The audience grew restless** *bored by the long speech.*

Which sentence requires a comma? _____

a

854

855

Mrs. Bilby has explained the problem, **and it seems very simple.**

_____

_____, **it seems very simple.**

Now that we
have spent all
our money,

1124

1125

When we incorrectly combine two simple sentences by means of a comma, we produce a _____ sentence, which is considered just as serious an error as a fragment.

No

1394

1395

meeting

1664

A simple way to avoid the *is when* or *is where* error is to use such a verb as *occurred*, *happened*, or *took place*, thus supplying an action verb that your "when" clause can modify.

a. **The climax occurred when the submarine was grounded.**
b. **The climax was when the submarine was grounded.**

Which sentence is correct? _____

1665

---

of

1933

Either one of these recipes (*make, makes*) **a good cake.**

We select the verb _____ to agree with the subject _____.

1934

---

a

2202

When you tell a story, it is very easy to make the mistake of shifting back and forth between the past and the present tense. If you start to tell a story in the past tense, you should continue to use the _____ tense consistently throughout the entire story.

2203

---

pronouns

2471

The change in form of pronouns to show their relationship to other words in the sentence is called **case.**

he   his   him

All three pronouns can be used to refer to the same person.

Their difference in form is due to their difference in _____.

2472

---

a

2740

In this first lesson on graphics, we review the use of the comma in compound sentences.

A compound sentence consists of two (or more) main clauses joined by the conjunction **and, but,** or **or.**

In a compound sentence there are a subject and a predicate both before and after the _____.

2741

---

b

3009

In the remaining frames, punctuate each sentence and supply capitals where necessary. Remember that commas and periods always come *before*, not *after*, quotation marks.

A sign along the highway said   remember, telephone poles hit people only in self-defense.

3010

might

45

Mary <u>can rescue</u> the child.
Mary <u>should rescue</u> the child.

The meaning of the first sentence changes when we change

the helping verb from **can** to _____.

46

---

second

315

Food became cheap and plentiful and the automobile came into common use.

A comma should be placed before the (*first, second*) **and.**

316

---

nobody

585

The drawer was full of things nobody would ever want.

The "no signal" adjective clause begins with the word

_____ and ends with the word _____.

586

---

b

855

Combine each pair of sentences by changing the italicized sentence to a past participial phrase. Insert a comma wherever needed.

The trainer entered the cage. *He was armed only with a whip.* _____

_____

856

Now that Mrs. Bilby has explained the problem,

1125

We have moved to the city, **and we miss our farm very much.**

_____,

we miss our farm very much.

1126

---

run-on

1395

Let us look into a common cause of the sentence collisions that we call run-on sentences.

The <u>motor</u> <u>was</u> wet. The <u>motor</u> <u>refused</u> to start.

Here we have two separate sentences, each with its own

_____ and verb.

1396

The turning point *was when* **Josephine Baker met Bessie Smith.**

This sentence can be corrected by substituting the verb

_____ for the verb **was.**

a

1665

1666

(verb) makes
(subject) one

Supply the correct verb in sentence *b,* paying no attention to the object of the preposition.

    a. **Neither fits me.**
    b. **Neither of the coats** _____ **me.**

1934

1935

---

past (*or* same)

The following student's summary of "The Necklace," a famous story by the French author Guy de Maupassant, is written mainly—but not entirely—in the past tense. Cross out each verb in the present tense and write the past form of the verb above it. If the sentence contains no error in tense, write *Correct.*   (*Turn to the next frame.*)

2203

2204

---

case

       a. *I* **recognized** *him.*   b. *He* **recognized** *me.*

The pronoun *I* in sentence *a* and the pronoun *me* in sentence *b* mean the same person.

Are the pronouns *I* and *me* in the same case? (*Yes, No*)

2472

2473

---

conjunction

In the following diagrams, a single line represents the subject and a double line the predicate.

a. _____ ========, **and** _____ ========.
b. _____ ======== **and** _____.

Which diagram represents a compound sentence? _____

2741

2742

---

said,
"Remember . . .
self-defense."

Education is much more than studying books   **began the speaker.**

3010

3011

a. **Mary** <u>**settled**</u> **the argument.**
b. **Mary** <u>**could have settled**</u> **the argument.**

should

In sentence *a*, the main verb is used by itself.

In sentence *b*, two helping verbs have been added to change

its meaning—_____ and _____.

46

47

---

second

This paint doesn't show brush or roller marks and it dries quickly.

A comma should be placed before (*or, and*).

316

317

---

nobody . . . want

Now let's review some of the things we have learned about adjective clauses in this and the previous lesson.
a. An adjective clause is one that does the work of a single adjective.
b. An adjective clause is one that begins with an adjective.
Which definition of an adjective clause is correct? _____

586

587

The trainer entered the cage, armed only with a whip.

Continue to follow the directions for the previous frame:

Little Women *was written by Louisa May Alcott in 1868.* **It soon became a favorite story.**

_____

_____

856

857

Now that we have moved to the city,

Another unusual type of adverb clause can sometimes be used very effectively in place of an "although" clause.

Cheap as it is, **the car is no bargain.**

This adverb clause is unusual because instead of beginning with a clause signal, it begins with (*a verb, an adjective*).

1126

1127

---

subject

It
The motor was wet. ~~The motor~~ **refused to start.**

Since we are still talking about the motor, we do not need to repeat the noun **motor** in the second sentence.

We therefore put the pronoun _____ in place of the noun **motor** as the subject of the second sentence.

1396

1397

Any one of the following verbs: occurred, took place, came (about)

1666

The climax *was when* **Banquo's ghost appeared at the banquet.**

Fill in the blank so as to avoid the *was when* construction:

The climax _____ **when Banquo's ghost appeared at the banquet.**

1667

---

fits

1935

Supply the correct verb in sentence *b,* paying no attention to the object of the preposition.

  a. **Every one needs washing.**
  b. **Every one of the windows** _____ **washing.**

1936

2204

Continue to follow the directions for the previous frame:

  Mathilde was a pretty French girl who was married to a poor but pleasant clerk in the government service.

2205

No

2473

       I **recognized** *him. He* **recognized** *me.*

The pronoun *him* in sentence *a* and the pronoun *He* in sentence *b* mean the same person.

Are the pronouns *him* and *He* in the same case? (*Yes, No*)

2474

---

a

2742

---

  a. **Lupe gets high grades and plans to attend college.**
  b. **Lupe gets high grades, and her teachers urge her to attend college.**

Which sentence is compound because there are a subject and a predicate both before and after the conjunction? _____

2743

"Education . . . books," began the speaker.

3011

I find that most people know what a story is   **said Flannery O'Connor**   **until they sit down to write one**

3012

could, have
 	
47
	Learn to recognize these important helping verbs:
	
	HELPING VERBS: **shall, will** **may, can**
	                    could, would, should **must, might**
	
	        Vera _____ **study.**
	
	Could each of these helping verbs be used with the main verb **study?** (*Yes, No*) 48

and 317	**Mr. Sims had accumulated much money and property but he wasn't happy or contented.** A comma should be placed before (*and, but, or*). 318
a 587	An adjective clause, like an adjective, modifies a _____ or a pronoun. 588
Written by Louisa May Alcott in 1868, *Little Women* soon became a favorite story. 857	**Tatum intercepted the pass.** *It was intended for Warfield.* _____ _____ 858

an adjective
 	
1127
	a. *although it is cheap*
	        b. *cheap as it is*
	
	In which clause is the subject complement *cheap* not in its normal position? _____
	
	                  1128

It
 	
1397
	a. **The motor refused to start.**
	        b. **It refused to start.**
	
	Both *a* and *b* are complete sentences.
	
	If you were writing only one sentence in isolation, which sentence would you write? _____
	
	                  1398

Any one of the following verbs: occurred, took place, came (about) 1667	**The climax** *was when* **Banquo's ghost appeared at the banquet.** Fill in the blank so as to avoid the *was when* construction: **The climax was the _____ of Banquo's ghost at the banquet.** 1668
needs 1936	Singular subjects joined by **and** are plural and require a plural verb. Underline the correct verb: **The air** *and* **the water** (*was, were*) **perfect for swimming.** 1937
Correct 2205	**Because of his small income, her husband is not able to give her the life of luxury and romance for which she had always yearned.** 2206
No 2474	A pronoun is in the **nominative case** when it fits *before* an action verb as its subject—*he* laughed; *she* fell; *we* won; *they* lost. Underline the nominative pronoun: *They* **blamed** *us.* 2475
b 2743	Use a comma generally before the conjunction **and, but,** or **or** in a compound sentence. The comma gives each part greater distinctness and makes the sentence easier to read. Insert the necessary comma: **We had only five minutes to play and every second counted.** 2744
"I find that most people know what a story is," said Flannery O'Connor, "until they sit down to write one." 3012	**The coffee wasn't too strong commented Uncle Pete the people were just too weak.** 3013

Yes
 	
48
	The three verbs below may serve as either *main verbs* or *helping verbs*.
	
	    be (is, am, are—was, were, been)
	    have (has, had)
	    do (does, did)
	
	Which verb has the largest number of forms? _____
	                                           49

but 318	A sentence that can be separated into two parts—a subject and a predicate—is a (*simple, compound*) sentence. 319
noun 588	An adjective clause always comes (*before, after*) the word it modifies. 589
Tatum intercepted the pass intended for Warfield. 858	*The candidate was questioned about his policies.* **He gave only vague answers.** _____ _____ 859

b
 	
1128
	a. *cheap as it is*
	        b. *although it is cheap*
	
	In which clause does the adjective *cheap* occupy a more prominent position? _____
	  1129

a
 	
1398
	a. **The motor refused to start.**
	    b. **It refused to start.**
	
	If the sentence were to follow another sentence that had already mentioned the **motor,** which sentence would you write? _____
	  1399

appearance *or* appearing 1668	**The turning point** *is when* **Coach Perry takes charge of the team.** Eliminate the *is when* construction: _____ when **Coach Perry takes charge of the team.** 1669
were 1937	Underline the correct verb. (Keep in mind that a verb that ends in *s* is always singular.) **Her face** *and* **her way of talking** (*remind, reminds*) **me of you.** 1938
was <s>is</s> 2206	**One day he joyously brings home an invitation to a fancy ball.** 2207
They 2475	. . . invited Rosa. Underline three pronouns that are in the nominative case because they could serve as the subject in the sentence above: **I him she we them her** 2476
play, and 2744	Insert the necessary comma: **His eyes were closed but he wasn't sleeping.** 2745
"The . . . strong," commented Uncle Pete. "The . . . weak." 3013	**Miss Morris said, Never offer too many excuses. Too many excuses make people suspicious. People are more likely to believe a single excuse.** 3014

be

49

a. **The <u>weather</u> <u>is</u> bad.**
b. **The <u>weather</u> <u>is</u> improving.**

In one sentence **is** serves as the main verb; in the other, as a helping verb.

Does **is** serve as a helping verb in sentence *a* or *b*? _____ 50

---

simple

319

A compound sentence can be formed by combining two simple sentences with a _____.

320

---

after

589

If a clause can be shifted from one position to another in a sentence, it is an (*adjective, adverb*) clause.

590

Questioned about his policies, the candidate gave only vague answers.
859

The bandit was surrounded by police. **He gave himself up.**

_____

_____

860

---

a

1129

a. *Although it is cheap,* **the car is no bargain.**
b. *Cheap as it is,* **the car is no bargain.**

In which sentence does the clause give more emphasis to the *cheapness* of the price? _____

1130

---

b

1399

The motor was wet. It refused to start.

It refused to start is a complete sentence because the reader knows from the previous sentence that the word **It** means _____.

1400

The turning point occurs (takes place, comes, comes about) 1669	**The turning point** *is where* **Coach Perry takes charge of the team.** Eliminate the *is where* construction: **The turning point is Coach Perry's** _____ **charge of the team.** 1670
remind 1938	When the two singular subjects joined by **and** mean the same person or thing, a singular verb is proper. a. **The owner** *and* **manager is Mr. Harris.** b. **The owner** *and* **the manager is pleased with each other.** In which sentence is the singular verb **is** correct? _____ 1939
brought ~~brings~~ 2207	**His wife, however, was not happy because she lacks suitable clothes for such an affair.** 2208
I, she, we 2476	A pronoun is in the **objective case** when it fits *after* an action verb as its direct object—pushed *me;* stopped *him;* asked *her;* beat *us;* called *them.* Underline the objective pronoun: *They* **blamed** *us.* 2477
closed, but 2745	Insert the necessary comma: **The clothes must be slightly damp or the wrinkles will not iron out.** 2746
Miss Morris said, "Never . . . a single excuse." 3014	Lesson **84** When Quotations Are Questions [Frames 3016–3049]

b

50

a. **I have brought my camera along.**
b. **I have my camera with me.**

Is **have** used as a helping verb in sentence *a* or *b?* _____

51

---

conjunction

320

The three most common conjunctions are *and,* _____,
and *or.*

321

---

adverb

590

The adjective clause signals **who (whose, whom), which,** and
that are called *relative (adjectives, pronouns).*

591

Surrounded by
police, the
bandit gave
himself up.

860

Eliminate the **and** by changing the italicized statement to a
past participial phrase. Insert a comma wherever needed.
The car was forced off the road **and went into a ditch.**

_____

_____

861

---

b

1130

a. *Large as the house is,* **we find it too small for our family.**
b. *Although the house is large,* **we find it too small for our
family.**

In which sentence does the clause give more emphasis to
the *largeness* of the house? _____

1131

---

motor

1400

You need have no hesitation in starting a new sentence with
the pronoun **It.** Don't let this pronoun trick you into making
a run-on sentence error.

a. **The motor was wet, it wouldn't start.**
b. **The motor was wet. It wouldn't start.**

Which is correct? _____

1401

taking 1670	In this and the following frames, fill in the blank space so as to eliminate the *is when* or *is where* construction: **A pinch hitter is where one player bats for another.** **A pinch hitter** _____ **who bats for another.** <div align="right">1671</div>

a
 	
1939
	If the two singular subjects joined by **and** are thought of as a single unit, use a singular verb.
	
	    a. **Tea** *and* **coffee is served with every meal.**
	    b. **Bread** *and* **butter is served with every meal.**
	
	In which sentence is the singular verb **is** correct? _____
	
	<div align="right">1940</div>

lacked <s>lacks</s> 2208	**Although her husband gave up buying a gun in order to finance a new dress, she was still unhappy because she had no jewels to wear.** <div align="right">2209</div>
us 2477	**Rosa invited . . .** Underline three pronouns that are in the objective case because they could serve as the direct object in the sentence above: **I** **him** **we** **she** **them** **her** <div align="right">2478</div>
damp, or 2746	<u>The pilot</u> <u>received a storm warning</u>, and *she* <u>moved up to a higher altitude</u>. If you omitted the italicized pronoun *she* from this compound sentence, would you still retain the comma? (*Yes, No*) <div align="right">2747</div>
	When a quotation asks a question, you first decide whether you are repeating the actual words of the question or merely reporting in your own words what was asked. When you repeat the actual words of the question, your quotation is (*direct, indirect*). <div align="right">3016</div>

a

51

a. **We did the dishes.**
b. **Yes, we did wash the dishes.**

Is **did** used as a helping verb in sentence *a* or *b*? _____

52

---

but

321

Should a comma be placed before the conjunction that connects the two parts of a compound predicate? (*Yes, No*)

322

---

pronouns

591

When we omit an adjective clause from a sentence, a grammatically (*complete, incomplete*) sentence remains.

592

Forced off the
road, the car
went into a
ditch.

861

Follow the directions given in the previous frame:

A crowd gathered around the excavation, and *they were* *fascinated by the steam shovel.*

_____

_____

862

---

a

1131

Sometimes this type of clause begins with an adverb shifted from its usual position at the end of the sentence.

a. *Although we came early,* **we got poor seats.**
b. *Early as we came,* **we got poor seats.**

In which sentence does the clause give more emphasis to

the adverb *early?* _____

1132

---

b

1401

Sentences may begin with other pronouns, too.

He will watch the baby.

Since you would know from some previous sentence whom the pronoun **He** stands for, this is a (*fragment, sentence*).

1402

is a player 1671	Arson is when someone commits the crime of willfully setting fire to property. Arson _____ of willfully setting fire to property. 1672

b
 	
1940
	A phrase introduced by **with, along with, together with,** or **as well as** often follows the subject. Do not mistake the noun in such a phrase for part of the subject.
	
	    a. **Mr. Davis and his son are in Alaska.**
	    b. **Mr. Davis, with his son, are in Alaska.**
	
	In which sentence is the plural verb **are** correct? _____
	
	1941

Correct 2209	She solves her problem by borrowing a diamond necklace from a friend in better circumstances. 2210
him, them, her 2478	a. **I** **he** **she** **we** **they** b. **me** **him** **her** **us** **them** Which group consists of objective pronouns? _____ 2479
No 2747	Coach Blair moved some of his boys around and ∧ put several new players into the game. If you added *he* at the point indicated, would you insert a comma after the word **around**? (*Yes, No*) 2748
direct 3016	a. **Leroy asked, "Where's my ticket?"** b. **Leroy asked where his ticket was.** In which sentence is the question a direct quotation? _____ 3017

b

52

a. **I have studied my lesson.**
b. **I should have studied my lesson.**
c. **I should have been studying my lesson.**

In which sentence does the verb have the largest number of helping verbs? _____

53

No

322

In a compound sentence, there are a subject and verb both before and after the conjunction. (*True, False*)

323

---

complete

592

Is a relative pronoun such as **who, which,** or **that** always the first word in an adjective clause? (*Yes, No*)

593

A crowd
gathered around
the excavation,
fascinated by the
steam shovel.
862

The article was written hastily **and contained many inaccuracies.**

_____

_____

863

---

b

1132

In this and the following frames, make each "although" clause more emphatic by beginning it with an adjective or an adverb, always followed by the word *as.*

Although I replied courteously, **Don took offense.**

_____, **Don took offense.**

1133

---

sentence

1402

a. **Jorge is staying home today. He will watch the baby.**
b. **Jorge is staying home today, he will watch the baby.**

Which is correct? _____

1403

is the crime

1672

Osmosis is where plants absorb moisture from the soil.

Osmosis is the process by which _____

_____.

1673

---

a

1941

By shifting the prepositional phrase to the end of this sentence, we see that the noun **son** is not part of the subject.

> **Mr. Davis,** *with his son,* **is in Alaska.**
> **Mr. Davis is in Alaska** *with his son.*

This sentence has only one subject, which is _____.

1942

---

solved
~~solves~~

2210

After making a great hit at the ball because of her clothes and her beauty, she found, when she arrives home, that the necklace is gone.

2211

---

b

2479

You **saw** *it.* (*It* **saw** *you.*)

Do the pronouns *You* and *it* change in form when we turn this sentence around? (*Yes, No*)

2480

Yes

2748

---

a. **Our dog often runs away, but it always comes back.**
b. **Our dog often runs away, but always comes back.**

From which sentence should the comma be dropped? _____

2749

---

a

3017

Leroy asked *where his ticket was.*

Are the italicized words the actual words of the original question? (*Yes, No*)

3018

The driver should have been watching the road.

The three helping verbs in this frame are _____,

_____, and _____.

c

53

54

True

In a compound sentence, the comma should be placed (*before, after*) the conjunction.

323

324

We called a doctor **whom** a neighbor had recommended.

We called a doctor a neighbor had recommended.

No

Does an adjective clause always contain a relative pronoun? (*Yes, No*)

593

594

Written hastily, the article contained many inaccuracies.

Mrs. Li owns a sports car, and *it was imported from Italy.*

_____

_____

863

864

Courteously as I replied,

I had to finish my theme, *although it was late.*

I had to finish my theme, _____.

1133

1134

Suppose that you had just written this sentence:

Carew hit a single.

Then you wished to explain what followed. Circle the letter indicating the way in which you would continue your thought:

a

a. **Carew hit a single, this won the game.**

b. **Carew hit a single. This won the game.**

1403

1404

plants absorb
moisture from
the soil.

1673

The climax is when Tina reveals family secrets on a children's television program.

The climax _____ when Tina reveals family secrets on a children's television program.

1674

Mr. Davis

1942

a. The camera, together with the case, sell for $39.
b. The camera and the case sell for $39.

In which sentence is the plural verb **sell** incorrect? _____

1943

---

arrived
~~arrives~~
was
~~is~~

2211

By going hopelessly into debt, they buy another necklace to replace the one they had lost.

2212

No

2480

You **saw** *it. It* **saw** *you.*

Do *you* and *it*—like the other pronouns—have different forms for the nominative and objective case? (*Yes, No*)

2481

---

b

2749

a. **New words may become part of our language or they may soon disappear.**
b. **New words may become part of our language or may soon disappear.**

In which sentence should a comma be inserted after the word **language?** _____

2750

No

3018

When you do not repeat the actual words of the question but report it in your own words, your quotation is (*direct, indirect*).

3019

should,
have,
been

54

The *complete* verb in any sentence includes the main verb plus whatever helping verbs it may have.

The driver should have been watching the road.

The *complete* verb in this sentence consists of _____ words. (How many?)

55

---

before

324

Lesson **9** **The Proper Use of the Compound Sentence**

[Frames 326–359]

No

594

Lesson **16** **Choosing Your Relatives**

[Frames 596–636]

Mrs. Li owns a
sports car
imported from
Italy.

864

Small boats were warned by the Coast Guard **and headed for shore.**

_____

_____

865

---

late as it was.

1134

Although we tried hard, **we couldn't make a touchdown.**

_____, **we couldn't make a touchdown.**

1135

---

b

1404

a. **Many advertisements do not state the total price, they merely state the monthly payments.**
b. **Many advertisements do not state the total price. They merely state the monthly payments.**

Which is correct? _____

1405

occurs (takes place, comes, comes about) 1674	To baste is when you sew with long, loose, temporary stitches. To baste is _____ with long, loose, temporary stitches. (*Note:* Don't forget the principle of parallel construction.) 1675
a 1943	Underline the correct verb: A tennis court, as well as a swimming pool, (*is, are*) available to guests. 1944
bought ~~buy~~ 2212	For ten years they lived in attics and scrimped and struggled to pay off their enormous debt. 2213
No 2481	Use the nominative case of a pronoun when it is used as the subject of a verb. Underline the correct pronoun: You and (*I, me*) can study together. (*Note:* The use of the nominative case after forms of the verb **be** will be studied in the following lesson.) 2482
a 2750	A compound sentence without a comma might sometimes be misread. We found it too expensive to stay at hotels and motels were hard to find. We can prevent the misreading of this compound sentence by inserting a comma after _____. 2751
indirect 3019	Leroy asked *where his ticket was.* Since the italicized words are not the actual words of a question, do we need to use either a question mark or quotes? (*Yes, No*) 3020

four 55	We shall now, for a moment, need to turn our attention to **adverbs,** which most commonly modify verbs. **This <u>has happened</u> frequently.** Because **frequently** modifies the verb **has happened,** it is an _____. 56
	A compound sentence is very easy to make. We merely need to combine two simple sentences by using one of these conjunctions: *and,* _____, or _____. 326
	Here again are the **relative pronouns** that are used as clause signals to start adjective clauses. RELATIVE PRONOUNS: **who (whose, whom), which, that** Are these the same clause signals that start adverb clauses? (*Yes, No*) 596
Warned by the Coast Guard, small boats headed for shore. 865	a. **hearing, intending, thinking, falling** b. **filled, sold, spoken, worn, spent, followed** Which group of words could be used as past participles? _____ 866
Hard as we tried, 1135	In the remaining frames, subordinate each italicized statement by changing it to an adverb clause beginning with an adjective or an adverb. *Webb is able,* **but he is not able enough for this job.** _____, **he is not able enough for this job.** 1136
b 1405	a. **Jerry was smiling in a peculiar way. He had apparently been up to some mischief.** b. **Jerry was smiling in a peculiar way, he had apparently been up to some mischief.** Which is correct? _____ 1406

to sew 1675	The turning point was where Columbus went to Queen Isabella for help. The turning point _____ Columbus went to Queen Isabella for help. 1676

is
 	
1944
	Singular subjects joined by **or** or **nor** are singular and require a singular verb.
	
	     a. **A doctor** *and* **a nurse ...**
	     b. **A doctor** *or* **a nurse ...**
	
	Which subject is singular because it means only one person
	—*a* or *b?* _____
	
	1945

Correct 2213	**In the meantime, she loses her beauty and becomes so plain and worn that no one could have recognized her for the beautiful girl she once had been.** 2214
I 2482	Use the objective case of a pronoun when it is used as the object of a verb or a preposition. Underline the correct pronouns: **Several friends save** (*them, they*) **for** (*me, I*). 2483
hotels 2751	Commas are generally omitted in short compound sentences. The reader can find his way without their help. a. **British humor depends on understatement** *but* **American humor is based largely on exaggeration.** b. **I knocked** *but* **no one answered.** Which compound sentence does not require a comma? _____ 2752

No
 	
3020
	(*Note:* Punctuation is omitted from the following sentences to avoid revealing the answer.)
	
	     a. **The child asked whether our dog bites**
	     b. **The child asked Does your dog bite**
	
	Which sentence contains an indirect question, which requires neither a question mark nor quotes? _____
	
	3021

adverb 56	a. **This has happened frequently.** b. **This has frequently happened.** In which sentence does the adverb **frequently** break into or interrupt the verb? _____ 57
but, or 326	Because compound sentences are so easy to make, we must avoid overusing them. Use a compound sentence to combine only *similar* or *related* ideas that are of equal importance. **Natachee studies Spanish, and our school has a gym.** Should these two ideas have been combined? (*Yes, No*) 327
No 596	Use **who, whose,** and **whom** to refer only to *people.* Underline the correct relative pronoun: **The clerk** (*who, which*) **took my order made a mistake in the bill.** 597
b 865	A phrase built on either a present or a past participle is used as an _____ to modify a noun or pronoun. 867
Able as Webb is, 1136	*Mr. Gross was angry,* **but he didn't show his temper.** _____, **he didn't show his temper.** 1137
a 1406	A sentence may begin with a pronoun such as *it, he, she,* or *they* even though the noun that the pronoun stands for is in another sentence. (*True, False*) 1407

occurred (took place, came, came about) when	A straw vote is when an unofficial vote is taken to find out public opinion.
	A straw vote _____ taken to find out public opinion.
1676	1677
b	Underline the correct verb:
	A doctor or a nurse (*is, are*) **always on hand.**
1945	1946
lost ~~loses~~ became ~~becomes~~	**One day she happens to meet the friend who had lent her the unlucky necklace that had brought them so much misfortune.**
2214	2215
them, me	Pronoun errors occur most often when pronouns are used in pairs or when a noun and a pronoun are coupled together.
	a. *He* **refereed the game.**
	b. **Frank and** (*he, him*) **refereed the game.**
	In sentence *b*, which pronoun is correct? _____
2483	2484
b	A short compound sentence does not need to be broken into shorter units for the convenience of the reader.
	a. **Several parents complained about overcrowding in the schools** *and* **the mayor agreed to take immediate action.**
	b. **They rode** *and* **we walked.**
	In which sentence would you use a comma before *and?* _____
2752	2753
a	Now let's look at a question that is quoted directly:
	Leroy asked, "Where's my ticket?"
	To show that the quotation is a question, we put the question mark (*inside, outside*) the quotes.
3021	3022

b	a. **This engine will immediately start in the coldest weather.** b. **This engine will start immediately in the coldest weather.** In which sentence does an adverb come between the main verb and its helper? _____
57	58

No	a. **Natachee studies Spanish, and our school has a gym.** b. **Natachee studies Spanish, and Carol studies French.** Which compound sentence is better because the ideas are similar? _____
327	328

who	Use **which** to refer only to *things* and *animals*. Underline the correct relative pronoun: **The store (***who, which***) sells these games is making a fortune.**
597	598

adjective	a. **Frank was raised on a farm.** b. **He knew the problems of the farmer.** Which sentence could be changed to a past participial phrase? _____
867	868

Angry as Mr. Gross was,	*The material cost of war is great,* **but the human cost is infinitely greater.** _____, **the human cost is infinitely greater.**
1137	1138

True	There are several methods of correcting a run-on sentence. WRONG: **I approached the squirrel, it ran away.** RIGHT: **I approached the squirrel. It ran away.** 1. Separate the run-together sentences by using a period and a _____ letter.
1407	1408

is an unofficial vote 1677	The surprise is where the father demands that the kidnappers pay him to take back his rowdy son. The surprise is the father's _____ that the kidnappers pay him to take back his rowdy son. 1678
is 1946	Father *and* Elsie do the dishes. Suppose that you changed *and* to *or*. Would you need also to change the plural verb **do** to the singular verb **does**? (*Yes, No*) 1947
happened <s>happens</s> 2215	Now that they had finally got out of debt, she decides to tell her friend how she had lost the borrowed necklace and had supplied a substitute for which she had paid such a great price. 2216
he 2484	You would never say, "*Him* pushed the car" or "*Me* pushed the car"; so don't make the same mistake by saying, "*Him* and *me* pushed the car." Underline the correct pronouns: (*He, Him*) **and** (*I, me*) **counted the votes.** 2485
a 2753	Do not mistake a sentence with a compound predicate for a compound sentence. Flo Kennedy <u>was pleased</u> *and* <u>praised the program.</u> The above sentence is not compound because there is no (*subject, predicate*) after the conjunction *and*. 2754
inside 3022	a. Roberta asked, "Is this poison ivy"? b. Roberta asked, "Is this poison ivy?" In which sentence is the question mark properly placed to show that the question, not the entire sentence, is a quotation? _____ 3023

One should immediately try artificial respiration.

a

What adverb comes between the main verb and its helper?

_____

58   59

---

b

a. **The road was muddy, and we bought eggs at a farm.**
b. **The road was muddy, and we got stuck several times.**

Which compound sentence is better because the ideas are

related? _____

328   329

---

which

Use **which** to refer to *things* and *animals*.

It was the Rosses' dog (*which, who*) **tore up our flower bed.**

598   599

---

a

Lesson **23** Making Use of Gerunds

[Frames 870–907]

868

Great as
the material
cost of war is,

Lesson **30** Two Useful Adjective Clause Devices

[Frames 1140–1166]

1138

---

capital

WRONG: **I approached the squirrel, it ran away.**
RIGHT: **I approached the squirrel, and it ran away.**

2. Correct the run-on sentence by adding the conjunction

_____.

1408   1409

demand (demanding)	A boondoggler is where a person is hired to do a needless job.
	A boondoggler _____ hired to do a needless job.
1678	1679

	a. Father and Elsie do the dishes.
Yes	b. Father or Elsie do the dishes.
	In which sentence is the plural verb **do** incorrect? _____
1947	1948

	"Oh, my poor Mathilde!" her friend gasps with amazement.
decided decides	"Why, that necklace I lent you was only paste!"
	(*End of story*)
2216	2217

	When you use pronouns in pairs or when you couple a pronoun with a noun, use the same case that you would use if the pronouns were used singly.
He, I	**These flowers are from** *Pete*. **These flowers are from** *me*.
	Underline the correct pronoun:
2485	**These flowers are from** *Pete* **and** (*I, me*).
	2486

	Do not ordinarily use a comma before the conjunction that connects the two parts of a compound predicate.
subject	a. **Gary left his salad, but ate his dessert.**
	b. **Gary left his salad, but he ate his dessert.**
	From which sentence should the comma be omitted? _____
2754	2755

	Now we shall put the same question at the beginning of the sentence:
b	**"Is this poison ivy?" asked Roberta.**
	When the quotation is a question, is a comma used between the question and the rest of the sentence? (*Yes, No*)
3023	3024

There is something else besides adverbs that can separate a main verb from its helper.

STATEMENT: **Judy can drive.**
QUESTION: **Can Judy drive?**

The verb **can drive** is interrupted in the (*statement, question*).

immediately

59

_____

60

Our tree is small. It gives very little shade.

b

Because there is a relationship between the size of a tree and the amount of shade, these sentences would make a (*good, poor*) compound sentence.

329

330

Use **that** to refer to anything—*people, things,* or *animals.*

Underline the correct relative pronoun:

which

Marian wrote a theme about the teacher (*which, that*) **had helped her most.**

599

600

Present and past participles, as we have seen, are forms of verbs that serve as adjectives. Now we look at verbs that have crossed over into noun territory.

Tennis **is good exercise.**

Tennis is an ordinary noun. It is the subject of the verb

_____.

870

A special type of adjective clause is useful when you wish to state a fact about only a *part* or a *number* of a larger group.

Gloria has three sisters, *one of whom is a nurse.*

The adjective clause states a fact about (*all, one*) of the sisters.

1140

WRONG: **I approached the squirrel, it ran away.**
RIGHT: **I approached the squirrel; it ran away.**

and

3. The third way to correct a run-on sentence is to insert a

1409

_____ .

1410

is a person

1679

The climax of the story was when Jeff announced that he would not study law.

The climax of the story was _____
_____ that he would not study law.

1680

---

b

1948

Oil, lotion, *or* cold cream relieves sunburn.

Suppose that you changed *or* to *and*. Would you need to change the singular verb **relieves** to the plural verb **relieve**? (*Yes, No*)

1949

---

gasped
~~gasps~~

2217

Use the present tense to state facts that are permanently true—for example, the facts of science, mathematics, geography, etc.

    a. **There** *are* **eight quarts in a peck.**
    b. **There** *are* **eight people in the car.**

Which sentence states a permanent truth? _____

2218

---

me

2486

You can't blame the *Kirks* for objecting.
You can't blame *them* for objecting.

Underline the correct pronoun:

You can't blame the *Kirks* or (*them, they*) for objecting.

2487

---

a

2755

a. **Shall we buy a new car or shall we repair the old one?**
b. **Shall we buy a new car or repair the old one?**

Which sentence requires a comma? _____

2756

No

3024

"Is this poison ivy?" asked Roberta.

The question mark is placed at the end of the (*question, sentence*).

3025

question

60

STATEMENT: <u>Dad</u> <u>will want</u> the car tonight.
QUESTION: <u>Will</u> <u>Dad</u> want the car tonight?

The verb **will want** is interrupted in the (*statement, question*).

_____

61

---

good

330

Our tree is small. We bought it at a nursery.

Although both these sentences are about a tree, they have little relationship to each other. Therefore, they would make a (*good, poor*) compound sentence.

331

---

that

600

The main point to remember is never to use **which** to refer to *people*.

Underline the correct relative pronoun:

citizens (*who, which*)

601

---

is

870

Tennis **is good exercise.**
Walking **is good exercise.**

Both *Tennis* and *Walking* are nouns used as subjects of the verb **is.**

Which one of these two italicized nouns was formed from a verb? _____

871

---

one

1140

Along the coast are many small islands, *some of which are uninhabited.*

The clause states a fact about (*some, all*) of the islands.

1141

---

semicolon

1410

There is sometimes a fourth way to correct a run-on sentence. The best solution may be to subordinate one of the sentences.

WRONG: **I approached the squirrel, it ran away.**
RIGHT: *As I approached the squirrel,* **it ran away.**

4. Change one of the sentences to a phrase or clause. In this case, we used a _____.

1411

Lesson 47   Do Your Pronouns Have Antecedents?

Yes

1949

Underline the correct verb:

A thick hedge or a high wall (*give, gives*) **a feeling of privacy.**

1950

---

a

2218

a. **There** *are* **eight quarts in a peck.**
b. **There** *were* **eight quarts in a peck.**

In which sentence is the tense of the verb wrong? _____

2219

---

them

2487

The *Smiths* **will call for you.**
We **will call for you.**

Underline the correct pronoun:

The *Smiths* **or** (*us, we*) **will call for you.**

2488

---

a

2756

In this and the following frames, insert any necessary commas. If no comma is required, write *None*.

Kim's arm was around the collie's neck and the dog was licking her face affectionately.

2757

---

question

3025

When the question comes first, be sure to put the question mark at the end of the question, not at the end of the sentence.

a. **"What are we having for dinner?" questioned Don.**
b. **"What are we having for dinner," questioned Don?**

The question mark is properly placed in sentence (*a, b*).

3026

question 61	**Will Dad want the car tonight?** The main verb **want** is separated from its helper **will** by the subject _____. 62
poor 331	a. **Our tree is small, and it gives very little shade.** b. **Our tree is small, and we bought it at a nursery.** Which compound sentence is better? _____ 332
who 601	Underline the correct relative pronoun: **the horse** (_who, which_) 602
Walking 871	_Walking_ **is good exercise.** The noun _Walking_ was formed by adding _____ to the verb _walk_. 872
some 1141	These adjective clauses begin with such words as **one of whom, several of whom, two of which, most of which.** **The room has three windows,** _one of which is always locked._ The word in the clause that specifies the number to which the statement applies is the (_first, last_) word. 1142
clause 1411	WRONG: **I approached the squirrel, it ran away.** RIGHT: _On my approaching the squirrel,_ **it ran away.** Here we used a (_phrase, clause_). 1412

Pronouns are generally used in place of nouns to avoid repeating the nouns.

Marian Anderson said she practiced her singing daily.

The two pronouns in this sentence are _____ and

_____.

1682

---

gives

1950

Neither Gary's mother *nor* his father was at home.
(Neither his mother *was* at home nor his father *was* at home.)

Because we are thinking of Gary's parents one at a time, we use a (*singular, plural*) verb.

1951

---

b

2219

When a fact permanently true follows an expression in the past tense such as "I didn't know that . . ." or "I forgot that . . . ," you might feel a strong pull to state this fact in the past, instead of the present, tense.

I forgot that there *were* eight quarts in a peck.

Is the verb *were* in the proper tense? (*Yes, No*)

2220

---

we

2488

The reporter snapped a picture of *her*.
The reporter snapped a picture of *me*.

Underline the correct pronouns:

The reporter snapped a picture of (*her, she*) and (*I, me*).

2489

---

neck, and

2757

The waves pound the rocks and gradually break them up into sand.

2758

---

a

3026

Here is another type of problem:

"Don't feed the animals."

Is this quotation a question? (*Yes, No*)

3027

Most of the questions we ask begin with a *helping verb.*

a. **Will this pen write?**   c. **Who borrowed my book?**
b. **Is the water boiling?**   d. **Does Tom like spinach?**

Dad

Which is the only one of the above questions that does not begin with a helping verb? _____

62   **63**

The two parts of a compound sentence should be *equal in importance.*

The Ortegas have a dog, and it is brown.

a

The fact that the dog is brown is much less important than the fact that the Ortegas have a dog.

Is this a good compound sentence? (*Yes, No*)

332   **333**

---

which

Underline the correct relative pronoun:

any doctor (*which, that*)

602   **603**

A noun that is formed by adding *-ing* to a verb is called a **gerund** (pronounced *jare-und*). We can turn any verb into a gerund by adding *-ing* to it (sometimes making minor changes in the spelling).

ing

The gerund form of the verb *cook* is _____.

872   **873**

The number of the group that these clauses single out may vary from **none of whom** to **all of whom.**

Fill in the missing words to show that *none* of the coins are rare. (*None* may take either a singular or plural verb.)

first

I have many old coins, _____ *are*
rare.

1142   **1143**

---

a. **I approached the squirrel; it ran away.**
b. **On my approaching the squirrel, it ran away.**
c. **I approached the squirrel. It ran away.**
d. **I approached the squirrel, it ran away.**
e. **As I approached the squirrel, it ran away.**

phrase

Which is a run-on sentence? _____

1412   **1413**

she, her 1682	**Marian Anderson said** *she* **practiced** *her* **singing daily.** The pronouns **she** and **her** refer to the noun _____. 1683
singular 1951	Underline the correct verb: **Neither Jack nor his sister** (*drive, drives*) **the car.** 1952
No 2220	**I** *forgot* **that there** *were* **eight quarts in a peck.** It is the verb *forgot* in the past tense that influenced the writer of this sentence to use the past tense *were* to express the permanent truth, instead of the present tense _____. 2221

her, me
 	
2489
	The *Whittens* **and** *we* **were the first to arrive.**
	
	This sentence is correct because if we used each subject separately, we would say:
	
	    The *Whittens* **were the first to arrive.**
	    (*Us, We*) **were the first to arrive.**
	
	2490

None 2758	**An intriguing book title may get your attention but it takes a strong plot and interesting characters to hold it.** 2759
No 3027	**Did you hear the keeper say, "Don't feed the animals"?** The question is (*quotation, entire sentence*). 3028

c
 	
63
	A helping verb at the beginning of a sentence is the signal that a question is coming.
	
	    a. **Will this pen write?**
	    b. **Does Tom like spinach?**
	
	In each of these questions, we find the subject between the two parts of the _____.
	
	                                                    64

No
 	
333
	a. **The Ortegas have a brown dog.**
	    b. **The Ortegas have a dog, and it is brown.**
	
	Sentence *a* is a *simple* sentence; sentence *b* is a *compound* sentence. The sentence which is better because it doesn't give too much importance to the color of the dog is the (*simple, compound*) sentence.
	
	                                                    334

that
 	
603
	Underline the correct relative pronoun:
	
	                    the school (*which, who*)
	
	                                                    604

cooking 873	The gerund form of the verb *lie* is _____. 874
none of which 1143	Fill in the missing words to show that *all* the coins are rare: **I have many old coins,** _____ *are rare.* 1144

d
 	
1413
	Before you correct a run-on sentence, consider the possibility of subordination.
	
	WRONG: **Illinois has a quarterback, nobody can stop him.**
	
	    a. **Illinois has a quarterback, and nobody can stop him.**
	    b. **Illinois has a quarterback whom nobody can stop.**
	
	Which sentence is a better repair—*a* or *b?* _____
	
	                                                1414

Marian Anderson 1683	**Marian Anderson said *she* practiced *her* singing daily.** The noun to which a pronoun refers is called its **antecedent.** It is the antecedent that gives a pronoun definite meaning. The antecedent of the pronouns *she* and *her* is the noun ——————. 1684
drives 1952	If one of the subjects joined by **or** or **nor** is singular and the other plural, the verb should agree with the closer word. **Neither the words nor the music . . . very original.** The noun **words** is plural, and the noun **music** is singular. The missing verb should agree with (*words, music*) and should be (*is, are*). 1953
are 2221	**I forgot that there were eight quarts in a peck.** Although this sentence is acceptable in colloquial (conversational) English, it does not meet the more rigid standards of formal speech or writing, which require that a fact that is permanently true should be stated in the (*present, past*) tense. 2222
We 2490	**There will be plenty of room for *you* and *me*.** This sentence is correct because if we used each pronoun separately, we would say: **There will be plenty of room for *you*.** **There will be plenty of room for (*me, I*).** 2491
attention, but 2759	**Most of us think of taxes as a necessary evil and we seldom think of what we get in return for them.** 2760
entire sentence 3028	**Did you hear the keeper say, "Don't feed the animals"?** Since the entire sentence and not the quotation is a question, we put the question mark (*inside, outside*) the quotes. 3029

verb	**Does this key fit?** The verb in this sentence consists of the two words _____ _____.
64	65

simple	**We have an old apple tree, and it is in our back yard.** The important fact is that we have an apple tree. Whether it is located in the back yard or the front yard is a mere detail. The two ideas are (*equal, unequal*) in importance.
334	335

which	Underline the correct relative pronoun: **a bumblebee** (*who, which*)
604	605

lying	We often wish to talk about actions. We can't talk about *walked, stole,* or *studied,* but we can talk about *walking, stealing,* or _____.
874	875

all of which	Fill in the missing words to show that *a few* of the coins are rare: **I have many old coins,** _____ *are rare.*
1144	1145

b	One of the following sentences is a run-on sentence. Correct this sentence by supplying a period and a capital. Write only the word before and after the period.
	
	    a. **I don't believe this rumor, it can't be true.**
	    b. **If the fan is oiled, it will run more quietly.**

1414	_____ 1415

Marian Anderson	**The break was so small that I could hardly see** *it*.
	The antecedent of the pronoun *it* is the noun _____.
1684	1685

music	**Neither the words nor the music** *seems* **very original.**
is	If we reversed the order of **words** and **music,** would we need to change the verb *seems*? (*Yes, No*)
1953	1954

present	In this and the following frames, the first verb in each sentence is in the past tense. Underline the second verb which is in the proper tense. Remember that standard usage requires that a fact permanently true should be expressed in the present tense.
	The article *stated* **that potatoes** (*are, were*) **fattening.**
2222	2223

me	In this and the following frames, underline the correct pronouns. In each case, choose the form of the pronoun that you would use if the pronoun were used by itself.
	The remark made Roxanne and (*me, I*) **angry.**
2491	2492

evil, and	**Nations rise and nations fall.**
2760	2761

outside	a. **Would any good American want to admit to a child, "I didn't vote because the weather was bad"?**
	b. **Would any good American want to admit to a child, "I didn't vote because the weather was bad?"**
	The question mark is properly placed in sentence (*a, b*).
3029	3030

Does fit	**Must the tire be changed?** The verb in this sentence consists of the three words _____ _____ _____.
65	66

	a. **We have an old apple tree in our back yard.** b. **We have an old apple tree, and it is in our back yard.** Sentence *a* is *simple;* sentence *b* is *compound.*
unequal	The sentence which is better because it doesn't give too much importance to the location of the tree is the (*simple, compound*) sentence.
335	336

which	Underline the correct relative pronoun: **the nurse** (*who, which*)
605	606

studying	To talk about actions, we must give them names. We give actions names by adding *-ing* to verbs, thus changing the verbs into nouns which we call by the special name of _____.
875	876

a few of which	In using this type of clause, be careful to use **whom,** and not **which,** to refer to people. **The Adamos have three sons,** *two of* (*which, whom*) *are now attending college.*
1145	1146

rumor. It	Continue to follow the directions for the previous frame: a. **Whenever we buy a used car, we have a mechanic check it thoroughly.** b. **The Smiths didn't come, we waited until 9 o'clock.**
1415	1416

break 1685	**Bananas are harvested while** *they* **are still green.** The antecedent of the pronoun *they* is _____. 1686
Yes 1954	a. **A few flowers or a plant is a good gift.** b. **A plant or a few flowers is a good gift.** Which sentence is correct? _____ 1955
are 2223	**The teacher** *reminded* **us that "all right"** (*was, is*) **two separate words.** 2224
me 2492	**Roger and** (*her, she*) **disturbed everyone with their talking.** 2493
None 2761	**The customer upset everything on the counter but finally bought nothing.** 2762
a 3030	a. "_____?" "_____!" b. "_____"? "_____"! In diagrams *a*, the question mark and exclamation point are inside the final quotes; in diagrams *b*, outside the quotes. Which diagrams show that the entire sentence, not the quotation, is a question or an exclamation? _____ 3031

Must be
changed

66

Sometimes, for emphasis, we put the verb ahead of its subject.

    a. **The <u>rain</u> <u>came</u> down.**
    b. **Down <u>came</u> the rain.**

In which sentence does the verb precede the subject? _____

67

---

simple

336

a. **She bought an old lamp at a rummage sale, and it was brass.**
b. **She bought an old lamp at a rummage sale, and it turned out to be a valuable antique.**

Which compound sentence is better because the two ideas are more nearly equal in importance? _____

337

---

who

606

How do we choose between **who** and **whom?** Which form we use depends on its use *within* the clause itself.
Use **who** when the pronoun is the subject of the verb.
Use **whom** when it is the object of a verb or preposition.

    Any player *<u>who</u> <u>can</u> <u>beat</u> Evert* **must be very good.**

The pronoun *who* is the subject of the verb _____.

607

---

gerunds

876

A gerund is a noun that is formed from a _____.

877

---

whom

1146

Customs officials, *many of (whom, which) speak English,* **examine your luggage.**

1147

---

come. We

1416

a. **This song is not original, it was adapted from a popular piece.**
b. **Although Cambridge was a small town, it produced several of our most famous authors.**

1417

Bananas

1686

Bananas are harvested while *they* are still green.

The noun **Bananas** is the _____ of the pronoun *they*.

1687

a

1955

The teacher or the students (*select, selects*) the topic.

The singular subject **teacher** requires a singular verb, but the plural subject **students** requires a plural verb.

Because the plural subject **students** is closer to the verb, we choose the plural verb _____.

1956

is

2224

The family *moved* to Hollywood, where Verna (*gets, got*) a job as an extra.

2225

she

2493

Neither the Mannings nor (*us, we*) would sell our land.

2494

None

2762

It took Columbus seventy days to cross the Atlantic but a modern jet makes the trip in less than six hours.

2763

b

3031

First decide whether just the quotation or the entire sentence is a question. Then complete the punctuation at the end of this sentence:

When you get the wrong number, do you say, "I'm sorry

3032

You are more likely to select the right subject if you look for the verb first.

Out jumped the rabbit.

After you find the verb **jumped,** ask yourself, "*Who* or *what* **jumped?**" The answer will always tell you the subject.

The subject of this sentence is _____.

b

67   68

---

a. **The house was attractive. The neighborhood appealed to us.**
b. **The house was attractive. Rents are high in our city.**

Which pair of sentences would make a better compound sentence because their ideas are similar? _____

b

337   338

The relative pronoun that starts an adjective clause is not always the subject.

Any player *whom Ross can beat* **must be very poor.**

The subject of the verb *can beat* is not the pronoun *whom,*

but the noun _____.

can beat

607   608

Do you remember that we also formed present participles by adding *-ing* to verbs?

Could the word *swinging* be either a present participle or a gerund? (*Yes, No*)

verb

877   878

In this and the following frames, subordinate the italicized statement by changing it to an adjective clause built on the "one of which" or "some of whom" pattern:

We have three clocks, *and none of them keeps good time.*

We have three clocks, _____ *keeps good time.*

whom

1147   1148

---

a. **If you will sometimes agree with other people, they will be more likely to agree with you.**
b. **Whales do not actually spout water, they merely blow out their moist breath.**

original. It

_____

1417   1418

antecedent 1687	The pronouns *I* and *you* require no antecedents because there can be no doubt about to whom they refer. *I* always means the speaker and *you* the person(s) spoken to. If someone should say to you, "I know him" or "You know him," the only pronoun about which there can be any doubt is the pronoun (*I, you, him*). 1688
select 1956	Though a sentence with a singular and a plural subject joined by **or** or **nor** is correct when the verb agrees with the closer word, careful writers try to avoid such sentences. a. **The teacher or the students select the topic.** b. **The teacher selects the topic, or the students do.** A careful writer would prefer sentence (*a, b*). 1957
got 2225	**Copernicus** *believed* **that the earth** (*revolves, revolved*) **around the sun.** 2226
we 2494	**I understand that Rick told** (*them, they*) **and** (*us, we*) **entirely different stories.** 2495
Atlantic, but 2763	**Are we solving this problem or merely postponing it?** 2764
. . . sorry"? 3032	When *both* the sentence and the quotation are questions, we use only one question mark, not two. This question mark goes inside the quotation. **Did the referee ask, "Are you ready?"** Complete the punctuation at the end of this sentence: **Will Elena ask, "Have you seen Ralph** 3033

rabbit 68	**This story the class really enjoyed.** First find the verb—**enjoyed.** Then ask yourself, "*Who or what* **enjoyed?**" The subject of this sentence is _____. 69
a 338	a. **Brad apologized to Cathy. She was with her sister.** b. **Brad apologized to Cathy. She accepted his apology.** Which pair of sentences would make a better compound sentence because their ideas are related? _____ 339
Ross 608	**Any player** *whom Ross can beat* **must be very poor.** Look at the arrow in the above sentence. The relative pronoun *whom* stands for the noun _____. 609
Yes 878	To decide whether an *-ing* word is a present participle or a gerund, we must see how it is used in the sentence. If the *-ing* word is used as an adjective, it is a _____ _____. 879
none of which 1148	**Rita baby-sits with two children,** *and one of them is very mischievous.* **Rita baby-sits with two children,** _____ *is very mischievous.* 1149
water. They 1418	In this and the following frames, correct each run-on sentence by adding a conjunction (*and, but, or*), with a comma at the end of the first statement. Write only the word before and after the conjunction. **It wasn't what he said, it was the way he said it.** _____ 1419

him

1688

Pronouns require antecedents whenever there can be any doubt about *whom* or *what* they refer to.

    a. **As soon as the boys got paid, they spent** *it.*
    b. **As soon as the boys got their pay, they spent** *it.*

In which sentence does the pronoun *it* have an antecedent?
_____

1689

---

b

1957

---

a. **The kitchen wasn't large enough, and neither were the bedrooms.**
b. **Neither the kitchen nor the bedrooms were large enough.**

Although each subject has its proper verb, a careful writer would prefer sentence (*a, b*).

1958

---

revolves

2226

Ethel Waters *met* **an editor who** (*urged, urges*) **her to write her life story.**

2227

---

them, us

2495

We have decided that Ken and (*I, me*) **will play against Iris and** (*him, he*).

2496

None

2764

The producers must give the program more variety or it will not survive.

2765

Ralph?''

3033

Exclamation points are handled in exactly the same way as question marks.

        "Which tooth hurts?" asked the dentist.
        "It's another home run!" shouted Lisa.

Is a comma used in addition to either a question mark or an exclamation point in these sentences? (*Yes, No*)

3034

class 69	In this and the following frames, underscore the verb with two lines; then underscore the subject with one line: **To this old inn came a strange visitor.** 70
b 339	a. **Cars were a luxury in those days, and they did not have self-starters.** b. **Cars were a luxury in those days, and few people could afford them.** Which is a better compound sentence? _____ 340
player 609	Keeping in mind that the pronoun *whom* stands for the noun *player,* let us straighten out the clause. (player)　　　　　　　　　　(player) *whom $\underline{Ross}$ $\underline{\underline{can\ beat}}$ = $\underline{Ross}$ $\underline{\underline{can\ beat}}$ whom* In this clause, the subject of the verb *can beat* is *Ross,* and its direct object is the relative pronoun _____. 610
present participle 879	If the *-ing* word is used as a noun, it is a _____. 880
one of whom 1149	**The air is full of bacteria,** *but most of them are harmless.* **The air is full of bacteria,** _____ *are harmless.* 1150
said, but it 1419	**There will be a thorough inquiry, the truth will come out.** _____ 1420

b

1689

a. **Collecting stamps is an interesting hobby if one can afford to buy** *them.*
b. **Stamp collecting is an interesting hobby if one can afford to buy** *them.*

In which sentence does the pronoun *them* have an antecedent? _____

1690

---

a

1958

A few flowers or a plant is a good gift.

Although this sentence is correct, rewrite it so that each of the two subjects will have its own verb that agrees with it in number.

_____

_____

1959

---

urged

2227

Dorothea Dix's work *proved* **that the nurse** (*was, is*) **an indispensible aid in any war.**

2228

I, him

2496

Unfortunately, neither (*him, he*) **nor Connie remembered to feed the dog.**

2497

---

variety, or

2765

Andy eats like a horse but gains no weight.

2766

No

3034

a. **"Just look at that sunset!" exclaimed Mother.**
b. **"Just look at that sunset," exclaimed Mother!**

The exclamation point is properly placed in sentence (*a, b*).

3035

came <u>visitor</u>	Underline the verb and its subject: **Away sped the blue car.**
70	71

| b | a. **My birthday was approaching, and I was beginning to think about gifts.**
b. **My birthday was approaching, and I had always wanted to go deer hunting.**

Which is a better compound sentence? _____ |
| 340 | 341 |

| whom | Here is a quick way to decide whether the clause signal is a subject or an object: When you see no other word before the verb that could possibly serve as its subject, then the relative pronoun is its subject, and **who** is correct.

who escaped   *who were absent*   *who bought* our car
The only word that could be the subject here is _____. |
| 610 | 611 |

| gerund | a. *Swinging* **makes me dizzy.**
b. **She went through the** *swinging* **door.**

In which sentence is *swinging* a present participle because it is used as an adjective to modify a noun? _____ |
| 880 | 881 |

| most of which | **The college has eight hundred students,** *and many of them come from foreign countries.*

The college has eight hundred students, _____

_____ *come from foreign countries.* |
| 1150 | 1151 |

| inquiry, and the | **You had better take your time, you might make many mistakes.**

_____ |
| 1420 | 1421 |

a 1690	a. **It is advisable to have farming experience before buying** *one.* b. **It is advisable to have experience on a farm before buying** *one.* In which sentence does the pronoun *one* have an antecedent? _____ 1691
A few flowers are a good gift, and so is a plant. (*or* a similar sentence) 1959	If you were to add the words printed in parentheses at the point marked by the caret (ʌ), would you need to change the italicized verb? If a change would be necessary, write only the form of the verb that would be required. If the verb would remain the same, write *Correct.* **Neither** ʌ *has* **a fur collar. (of my coats)** _____ 1960
is 2228	**The bus driver** *informed* **us that Philadelphia** (*is, was*) **very close to New York.** 2229
he 2497	**The "Devil's Ride" made Kathy and** (*she, her*) **sick.** 2498
None 2766	Lesson **77** Commas After Introductory Expressions [Frames 2768–2801]
a 3035	a. **Mr. Lutz exclaimed, "What a silly thing to buy!"** b. **Mr. Lutz exclaimed, "What a silly thing to buy"!** The exclamation point is properly placed in sentence (*a, b*). 3036

ˌsped car 71	Underline the verb and its subject: **Here stands the monument to Frederick Douglass.** 72

a 341	**You can always add salt to your food, but you cannot remove it once it is in.** The first part of this sentence concerns adding salt to food; the second part concerns removing it. This compound sentence, therefore, is (*good, poor*). 342
who 611	If, on the other hand, the verb already has a subject, then the relative pronoun must be its object, and **whom** is correct. *whom I admire* *whom we invited* *whom the dog bit* The verbs in the above clauses already have subjects; therefore *whom* must be the (*subject, object*) in each clause. 612
b 881	a. *Swinging* **makes me dizzy.** b. **She went through the** *swinging* **door.** In which sentence is *swinging* a gerund because it is used as a noun to name an action? _____ 882
many of whom 1151	**The school has twelve rooms,** *and three of them are not used.* **The school has twelve rooms,** _____ *are not used.* 1152
time, or you 1421	**The election was close at hand, everyone was discussing politics.** _____ 1422

b 1691	Jo became a *scientist* because *science* interested her. Vi became a *musician* because *music* interested her. Jan became a *lawyer* because _____ interested her. <div align="right">1692</div>
Correct 1960	∧ These buses *go* to the stadium. (Either of) _____ <div align="right">1961</div>
is 2229	The author *went* back to Italy, where she (*visits, visited*) her birthplace. <div align="right">2230</div>
her 2498	The Chandlers and (*they, them*) attend the same church. <div align="right">2499</div>
	For variety or emphasis, we often begin a sentence with an adverbial modifier—a word, a phrase, or a clause. <div align="center">a. Our team has been winning recently. b. Recently our team has been winning.</div> Which sentence begins with an introductory adverb? _____ <div align="right">2768</div>
a 3036	In this and the following frames, circle the letter of the sentence that is properly punctuated and capitalized: a. Our neighbor asked, "If he could borrow our lawnmower?" b. Our neighbor asked, "May I borrow your lawnmower?" <div align="right">3037</div>

stands
monument

72

Underline the verb and its subject. Don't overlook the help-ing verb.

Never has our team played any better.

73

---

good

342

Arthur drove most of the way, and we had two flat tires.

This compound sentence is (*good, poor*).

343

---

object

612

whom I admire   whom we invited   whom the dog bit

When the relative pronoun that stands for a person is the direct object of the verb within the clause, we use the object form (*who, whom*).

613

---

a

882

Although gerunds serve as nouns, they still bear some re-semblance to verbs. Like verbs, gerunds may take direct objects or subject complements, as no ordinary noun can do.

Observing ants **is fascinating.**

Because the noun *ants* receives the action of the gerund *observing*, it is its (*direct object, subject complement*).

883

---

three of which

1152

Ralph brought his parents, *and I had met neither of them before.*

Ralph brought his parents, _____

I had met before.

1153

---

hand, and
everyone

1422

In this and the following frames, correct the run-on sentence by inserting a semicolon. Write only the word before and after the semicolon.

It isn't the car that kills, it's the driver behind the wheel.

_____   1423

law	**Jan wants to be a lawyer because *it* interests her.**
	The person who made this sentence had *law* in mind when he used the pronoun *it*.
	As the sentence turned out, is the noun *law* present to serve as the antecedent for the pronoun *it*? (*Yes, No*)
1692	1693

goes	**Unseasonable weather ∧ *forces* us to cut our prices. (and a heavy stock)**
	_____
1961	1962

visited	Lesson **62** Using the Present Perfect Tense
	[Frames 2232–2261]
2230	

they	**Gloria, not (*me, I*), thought up this slogan.**
2499	2500

b	To decide whether to use a comma after an introductory adverb such as *Recently* or *Finally* requires judgment. Using a comma sets the adverb apart and gives it more emphasis.
	a. *Finally,* **Ted arrived with the refreshments.**
	b. *Finally* **Ted arrived with the refreshments.**
	In which sentence is *Finally* given more emphasis? _____
2768	2769

b	a. "How does the story end?" asked Miss Nolan.
	b. "How does the story end," asked Miss Nolan?
3037	3038

<u>has</u> <u>team</u> <u>played</u>	Underline the verb and its subject:
	Neither did Pam receive an invitation.
73	74
poor	**We cannot prevent tornadoes, but we can minimize their destructiveness.**
	This compound sentence is (*good, poor*).
343	344
whom	**Mr. Dolby is a person . . . <u>worries</u> about nothing.**
	Since the clause has no other subject, the relative pronoun would have to be the subject.
	We would therefore choose the subject form (*who, whom*).
613	614
direct object	***Being selfish* is a good way to lose friends.**
	(Do you recall that *be*, with all its forms, is a linking verb?)
	Because the adjective *selfish* completes the meaning of the gerund *Being*, it is its (*direct object, subject complement*).
883	884
neither of whom	In a similar type of adjective clause, a noun precedes the words **of which;** for example, **the price of which, the result of which, the purpose of which.**
	There are many words *the meanings of which have changed.*
	What noun precedes *of which*? _____
1153	1154
kills; it's	**Male mosquitoes do not bite people, they live on the juice of plants.**
	_____
1423	1424

WRONG: Jan wants to be a lawyer because *it* interests her.
RIGHT: Jan wants to be a lawyer because *law* interests her.

This sentence was corrected by (*changing the pronoun to a noun, supplying an antecedent*).

1694

The sprayer ∧ *sells* for two dollars. (with the chemical)

_____

1963

A tense formed by combining a past participle with a form of **have** is called a **perfect tense.**

a. **decided**   b. **have decided**

Which verb is an example of a perfect tense? _____

2232

This is something for you and (*me, I*) to think about

2501

The pause at the comma gives the meaning of the introductory adverb more time to "sink in."

a. *Fortunately,* **the water was shallow.**
b. *Fortunately* **the water was shallow.**

The adverb *Fortunately* gets more attention in sentence *a* because it is set off with a _____.

2770

---

a. "Just what I wanted!" exclaimed Ellen as she opened the box.
b. "Just what I wanted!", exclaimed Ellen as she opened the box.

3039

did Pam receive
<u>did</u> <u>Pam</u> receive

74

Underline the verb and its subject:

Must each member participate in the discussion?

75

---

good

The car had no lights, and the accident occurred on our corner.

This compound sentence is (*good, poor*).

344

345

---

who

Mr. Dolby is a person . . . *nothing* <u>*worries*</u>.

Since the clause already has the subject *nothing*, the relative pronoun would have to be the object.

We would therefore choose the object form (*who, whom*).

614

615

---

subject
complement

The phrases formed by gerunds with their related words are called **gerund phrases.** These phrases can be used in any way that nouns are used.

Reading this book **changed her entire life.**

In this sentence the gerund phrase *Reading this book* is

used as the _____ of the verb **changed.**

884

885

---

meanings

Mr. Kerr bought several stocks *the value of which is very doubtful.*

What noun precedes *of which?* _____

1154

1155

---

people; they

It is not enough merely to feel appreciation, one should also express it.

_____

1424

1425

changing the pronoun to a noun	WRONG: **Jan wants to be a lawyer because** *it* **interests her.** RIGHT: **Jan wants to study** *law* **because** *it* **interests her.** This sentence was corrected by (*changing the pronoun to a noun, supplying an antecedent*).
1694	1695
Correct	∧ **These questions** *are* **answered in this chapter. (Every one of)** ————
1963	1964
b	Just as we have three simple tenses—the present, past, and future—we also have three corresponding perfect tenses—the present perfect, the past perfect, and the _____ perfect.
2232	2233
me	Lesson **70** Informal and Formal Pronoun Usage [Frames 2503–2546]
2501	

comma	An introductory phrase gets more attention, too, when it is set off with a comma.
	    a. *For a child* **he was remarkably strong.**
	    b. *For a child,* **he was remarkably strong.**
	Which sentence gives more emphasis to the prepositional phrase? ____

2770	2771
a	a. **Lucinda screamed, "Look out for that child"!** b. **Lucinda screamed, "Look out for that child!"**
3039	3040

| Must member |
| participate |

75

Underline the verb and its subject:

Where does Mother keep the tools?

76

---

poor

345

Use a compound sentence when you want your reader to think of two ideas in connection with each other.

    a. **The engine runs smoothly. It uses too much gas.**
    b. **The engine runs smoothly, but it uses too much gas.**

Which arrangement brings the two ideas into closer relationship—*a* or *b?* _____

346

---

whom

615

Underline the correct relative pronoun after deciding whether it is used as the subject or the object of the verb:

People (*who, whom*) <u>are</u> *honest themselves* **usually trust others.**

616

---

subject

885

Your mistake was *enclosing money in a letter.*

The gerund phrase completes the meaning of the linking verb **was** and explains the subject **mistake.** The gerund phrase is therefore a (*direct object, subject complement*).

886

---

value

1155

Ordinarily, the relative pronoun **whose** provides a smoother sentence than **of which** and requires fewer words.

    a. **I read a novel** *the ending of which is disappointing.*
    b. **I read a novel** *whose ending is disappointing.*

Sentence *b* is _____ words shorter than sentence *a*. (How many?)

1156

---

appreciation; one

1425

One of the following sentences is a run-on sentence. In the other, the error was avoided by subordination.

a. **After the children left, the cozy home seemed empty and cheerless.**
b. **The children left, the cozy home seemed empty and cheerless.**

Which sentence is correct?

1426

When a pronoun lacks an antecedent, we can correct the sentence in either of two ways: (1) Eliminate the pronoun; (2) supply an _____ to give the pronoun meaning.

1696

The janitor ∧ *helps* the younger children cross the street. (or an older pupil)

_____

1965

Whether a verb is in the present perfect, past perfect, or future perfect tense depends on whether the participle is combined with a present, past, or future form of **have.**

Underline the two present forms of **have:**

has   had   have   will have

2234

Now we consider a rule that holds more rigidly for writing than it does for speaking:

Use the nominative case for a pronoun that follows any form of the verb **be** (*is, am, are—was, were, been*).

Underline the correct pronoun:

It must be (*they, them*) **who called.**

2503

In desperation **the mayor threatened to resign.**

To give more emphasis to the introductory phrase, would you put a comma after *desperation*? (*Yes, No*)

2772

---

a. **I get tired of being asked, "Is it hot enough for you"?**
b. **I get tired of being asked, "Is it hot enough for you?"**

3041

<table>
<tr><td>

does
<u>Mother</u>
<u>keep</u>

76

</td><td>

Underline the verb (three words) and its subject:

Can this dress be washed in soap and water?

77

</td></tr>
<tr><td>

b

346

</td><td>

    a. **You must shut the gate, or the dog will get out.**
    b. **You must shut the gate. The dog will get out.**

Which arrangement brings out the relationship between the

two ideas more clearly? _____

347

</td></tr>
<tr><td>

who

616

</td><td>

Underline the correct relative pronoun:

The speaker (*who, whom*) **he introduced was embarrassed
by so much praise.**

617

</td></tr>
<tr><td>

subject
complement

886

</td><td>

    a. **We paid thirty dollars for** *repairs.*
    b. **We paid thirty dollars for** *repairing the motor.*

In which sentence is a gerund phrase the object of the

preposition **for?** _____

887

</td></tr>
<tr><td>

two

1156

</td><td>

The relative pronoun **whose,** unlike **who** and **whom,** can be
used for things as well as for persons.

a. **I ordered a French soup** *the name of which I can't
    pronounce.*
b. **I ordered a French soup** *whose name I can't pronounce.*

Are both sentences correct? (*Yes, No*)

1157

</td></tr>
<tr><td>

a

1426

</td><td>

a. **We hiked through a dense woods, the sunlight hardly
    penetrated the thick foliage.**
b. **We hiked through a dense woods, where the sunlight
    hardly penetrated the thick foliage.**

Which sentence is correct? _____

1427

</td></tr>
</table>

page 153

a

1697

We often move a word group used as a subject to the end of the sentence and use an introductory *It* to fill the gap. (Such a subject, by the way, is called a *delayed subject.*)

    a. *To walk* **would be fun.**   b. *It* **would be fun** *to walk.*

In sentence *b,* the subject *to walk* has been moved to the end, and the gap is filled by the word _____.

1698

---

satisfies

1966

A pedigreed cocker spaniel ∧ *goes* **to the winner. (, as well as a year's supply of dog food,)**

_____

1967

---

a

2235

Using a future form of **have** (*shall have* or *will have*) with a participle gives us the **future perfect** tense.

a. **have decided**   b. **shall have decided**   c. **had decided**

Which verb is in the future perfect tense? _____

2236

Yes

2504

The *chairman* **was** *he.* (*He* **was the** *chairman.*)

This sentence can be turned around because any pronoun that follows a form of **be** means the same person or thing as the subject.

In the above sentence, the pronoun *he* means the same person as the subject _____.

2505

---

a

2773

After short introductory phrases that state *time* or *place* (*In June, On Monday, At Buffalo*), commas are usually omitted.

a. **On Friday, the Student Council meets.**
b. **On the last Friday of each month, the Student Council meets.**

The comma might well be omitted in sentence (*a, b*). 2774

---

a

3042

In the remaining frames, punctuate each sentence and supply capitals where necessary. Each sentence requires, among other things, a question mark or an exclamation point.

Are these flowers from your own garden   **asked Mrs. Chavez**

3043

does
Mother
keep

76

Underline the verb (three words) and its subject:

Can this dress be washed in soap and water?

77

---

b

346

a. **You must shut the gate, or the dog will get out.**
b. **You must shut the gate. The dog will get out.**

Which arrangement brings out the relationship between the

two ideas more clearly? _____

347

---

who

616

Underline the correct relative pronoun:

The speaker (*who, whom*) **he introduced was embarrassed by so much praise.**

617

---

subject
complement

886

a. **We paid thirty dollars for** *repairs.*
b. **We paid thirty dollars for** *repairing the motor.*

In which sentence is a gerund phrase the object of the

preposition **for?** _____

887

---

two

1156

The relative pronoun **whose,** unlike **who** and **whom,** can be used for things as well as for persons.

a. **I ordered a French soup** *the name of which I can't pronounce.*
b. **I ordered a French soup** *whose name I can't pronounce.*

Are both sentences correct? (*Yes, No*)

1157

---

a

1426

a. **We hiked through a dense woods, the sunlight hardly penetrated the thick foliage.**
b. **We hiked through a dense woods, where the sunlight hardly penetrated the thick foliage.**

Which sentence is correct? _____

1427

antecedent 1696	*It* is sometimes used not as a pronoun, but as an introductory word to get a sentence started—especially in remarks about *time* or the *weather*. This usage is perfectly correct. a. *It* **was ten o'clock, and** *it* **was starting to rain.** b. **I guess I'm not musical because I've never enjoyed** *it*. In which sentence is *it* correctly used? _____ 1697
Correct 1965	**A few cookies** ∧ *satisfy* **my hunger after school. (or a sandwich)** _____ 1966
has, have 2234	Using a present form of **have** (*have* or *has*) with a participle gives us the **present perfect** tense. Using the past form of **have** (*had*) with a participle gives us the **past perfect** tense. a. **have decided** b. **had decided** Which verb is in the present perfect tense? _____ 2235
they 2503	Why is it that after every other verb in the English language we use an objective pronoun but that after any form of the verb **be** we use a nominative pronoun? **The** *chairman* **was** *he*. (*He* **was the** *chairman*.) Can this sentence be turned around without changing the meaning? (*Yes, No*) 2504
Yes 2772	A comma is more frequently used after a long introductory phrase than after a short one. a. **After several weeks of hard and persistent practice the team perfected this play.** b. **For weeks the team practiced this play.** In which sentence would you use a comma? _____ 2773
b 3041	a. **Can't you just hear Aunt Inés saying, "I told you so"?** b. **Can't you just hear Aunt Inés saying, "I told you so?"** 3042

<u>Can dress</u> <u>be washed</u>	Can a verb consist of more than one word? (*Yes, No*)
77	78

a	a. **I liked the dog. It was a collie.** b. **I liked the dog. The dog liked me.** Which pair of sentences would you connect with *and* to bring the two ideas into closer relationship? _____
347	348

whom	Underline the correct relative pronoun: **Lucille Clifton is the poet** (*who, whom*) **I selected for my report.**
617	618

b	In this and the following frames, underline each gerund phrase and indicate its use by writing one of the following abbreviations in the parentheses: $S = Subject$ $SC = Subject\ Complement$ $DO = Direct\ Object$ $OP = Object\ of\ Preposition$ **The sign forbids** *fishing from this dock.* ( )
887	888

Yes	Even though **whose** may be used for things, there are times when you might prefer the **of which** construction. Change the **whose** to the **of which** construction (*see frame 1154*): **She makes chili** *whose preparation takes an entire day.* **She makes chili** _____ _____ *takes an entire day.*
1157	1158

b	a. **The restaurant being crowded, we decided not to wait.** b. **The restaurant was crowded, we decided not to wait.** Which sentence is correct? _____
1427	1428

a 1697	We often move a word group used as a subject to the end of the sentence and use an introductory *It* to fill the gap. (Such a subject, by the way, is called a *delayed subject*.) a. *To walk* **would be fun.** b. *It* **would be fun** *to walk*. In sentence *b*, the subject *to walk* has been moved to the end, and the gap is filled by the word _____. 1698
satisfies 1966	**A pedigreed cocker spaniel** ∧ *goes* **to the winner. (, as well as a year's supply of dog food,)** _____ 1967
a 2235	Using a future form of **have** (*shall have* or *will have*) with a participle gives us the **future perfect** tense. a. **have decided** b. **shall have decided** c. **had decided** Which verb is in the future perfect tense? _____ 2236
Yes 2504	**The** *chairman* **was** *he*. (*He* **was the** *chairman*.) This sentence can be turned around because any pronoun that follows a form of **be** means the same person or thing as the subject. In the above sentence, the pronoun *he* means the same person as the subject _____. 2505
a 2773	After short introductory phrases that state *time* or *place* (*In June, On Monday, At Buffalo*), commas are usually omitted. a. **On Friday, the Student Council meets.** b. **On the last Friday of each month, the Student Council meets.** The comma might well be omitted in sentence (*a, b*). 2774
a 3042	In the remaining frames, punctuate each sentence and supply capitals where necessary. Each sentence requires, among other things, a question mark or an exclamation point. **Are these flowers from your own garden asked Mrs. Chavez** 3043

78

Yes

a. **shall, could, should, can, must, might**
b. **soon, never, now, always, not, surely**

Which group of words consists of helping verbs? _____

79

348

b

I liked the dog, and the dog liked me.

Because both parts of the sentence concern the relationship between the person and the dog, this is a (*good, poor*) compound sentence.

349

618

whom

When the relative pronoun is the object of a preposition, use the object form **whom**; for example, **to whom, for whom, from whom.**

Underline the correct relative pronoun:

Most of the candidates *for* (*who, whom*) *I voted* **were elected.**

619

888

fishing from this dock (DO)

S = Subject *SC = Subject Complement*
DO = Direct Object *OP = Object of Preposition*

His violation was *driving through a red light.* **(   )**

889

1158

the preparation of which

Change the **whose** to the **of which** construction:

The minister told a story *whose point most people missed.*

The minister told a story _____

most people missed.

1159

1428

a

a. **Having no one to play with, the child turned to books for companionship.**
b. **The child had no one to play with, she turned to books for companionship.**

Which sentence is correct? _____

1429

Move the italicized subject to the end of the sentence and put the introductory word *It* in its place:

To take chances **is foolish.**

_____

1699

Correct

1967

ʌ **The boys** *are* **very willing to help. (Each of)**

_____

1968

---

b

2236

a. **Barbra Streisand** *sang* **for an hour.**
b. **Barbra Streisand** *has sung* **for an hour.**

In which sentence is the verb in the present perfect tense?

_____

2237

---

chairman

2505

The *chairman* **was** *he.*

Since *he* could just as well be the subject of this sentence, we put it in the same case as if it were the subject of the sentence—that is, in the (*nominative, objective*) case.

2506

---

a

2774

Use a comma after an adverb clause that comes at the beginning of a sentence, ahead of the main clause.

a. **You will change your mind** *when you hear all the facts.*
b. *When you hear all the facts* **you will change your mind.**

Which sentence requires a comma because the adverb clause comes first? _____

2775

"Are . . . garden?" asked Mrs. Chavez.

3043

The agent asked   is the lady of the house at home

3044

a	A main verb is sometimes separated from its helper by other words. (*True, False*)
79	80

good	a. **I was born in Utah. Our family soon moved to Oregon.** b. **I was born in Utah. This state has magnificent scenery.** Which pair of sentences could better be combined into a compound sentence? ____
349	350

whom	**Most of the candidates** *for whom I voted* **were elected.** We use the object form *whom* because the relative pronoun is the object of the preposition _____.
619	620

driving through a red light (SC)	(Beginning with this frame, gerund phrases are not italicized.) $S = Subject \qquad SC = Subject\ Complement$ $DO = Direct\ Object \qquad OP = Object\ of\ Preposition$ **Saving the precious topsoil is one of the aims of conservation. ( )**
889	890

the point of which	Change the **whose** to the **of which** construction: **The doctor recommended a cough medicine** *whose name I can't recall.* **The doctor recommended a cough medicine** _____ _____ *I can't recall.*
1159	1160

a	a. **Ruth looked admiringly at Bob, she was impressed with his quick thinking.** b. **Ruth looked admiringly at Bob, impressed with his quick thinking.** Which sentence is correct? ____
1429	1430

It is foolish to take chances.	Move the italicized subject to the end of the sentence and put the introductory word *It* in its place:
	That he forgot his own birthday **seems strange.**
1699	_____
	_____ 1700

is	**The superb acting** ∧ *makes* **this an outstanding movie. (and the fine directing)**
1968	_____ 1969

b	Use the present perfect tense for an action that began in the past but that continues, or whose effect continues, into the present.
	a. **Pat** *lived* **in Chicago for ten years.**
	b. **Pat** *has lived* **in Chicago for ten years.**
2237	In which sentence is Pat still living in Chicago? _____ 2238

nominative	WRONG: **The** *chairman* **was** *him.*
	If we used the objective pronoun *him* after the verb **was,** could we turn this sentence around without changing the pronoun? (*Yes, No*)
2506	2507

b	**Shorthand is difficult** *unless you are a good speller.*
	Unless you are a good speller, **shorthand is difficult.**
	Only one of the above sentences contains a comma.
	The comma is used when the adverb clause comes (*first,*
2775	*last*). 2776

The agent asked, "Is . . . home?"	**Stop shouted the bandleader**
3044	3045

True	The subject always comes ahead of the verb in every sentence. (*True, False*)
80	81

---

a	**I was born in Utah, but our family soon moved to Oregon.** This is a good compound sentence because both parts concern (*location, growth*).
350	351

---

for	Underline the correct relative pronoun: **My grandfather was a man to** (*whom, who*) **everyone came for advice.**
620	621

Saving the precious topsoil (S)	$S = Subject$ $SC = Subject\ Complement$ $DO = Direct\ Object$ $OP = Object\ of\ Preposition$ **The clerk made an error in adding the figures. (** **)**
890	891

---

the name of which	In this and the following frames, subordinate each italicized statement to an **of which** construction, preceded by a noun ("the cause of which," "the price of which"): **Our school had an assembly,** *and the purpose was to improve sportsmanship.* **Our school had an assembly** _____
1160	_____ *was to improve sportsmanship.* 1161

---

b	Lesson **39** Adverbs as a Cause of Run-on Sentences [Frames 1432–1465]
1430	*page 161*

It seems strange
that he forgot
his own birthday.

1700

Although such expressions as **"It says"** are commonly
used, they are rather roundabout and clumsy.

It says **in the Bible that all men are brothers.**

Is there any noun in this sentence that tells you *who* or *what*
the mysterious *It* is? (*Yes, No*)

1701

---

make

1969

Lesson **55** An Agreement Problem in
Adjective Clauses

---

b

2238

If a past action or its effect continues into the present time,
use the (*present perfect, present*) tense.

2239

No

2507

Underline the correct pronoun—the one that you could use
if you turned the sentence around:

The culprits were (*they, them*).

2508

---

first

2776

a. **Most voters have made up their minds before the campaign starts.**
b. **Before the campaign starts most voters have made up
their minds.**

Which sentence requires a comma? _____

2777

"Stop!"
shouted the
bandleader.

3045

**Will all these new inventions   asked the speaker   make
people any happier**

3046

False 81	You are less likely to make a mistake in selecting the subject and the verb if you select the _____ first. 82
location 351	Use the conjunction **and** merely to add one idea to another. Use the conjunction **but** to point out a contrast or contradiction between the two ideas. **I didn't want a reward, . . . Mr. Lopez made me take it.** Would **and** or **but** make better sense in this sentence? _____ 352
whom 621	a. **Everyone values a friend . . . is dependable.** b. **Everyone values a friend upon . . . he can depend.** In which sentence would **whom** be correct? _____ 622
adding the figures (OP) 891	$S = Subject$ $SC = Subject\ Complement$ $DO = Direct\ Object$ $OP = Object\ of\ Preposition$ **Being a road hog increases the likelihood of automobile accidents. (** **)** 892
the purpose of which 1161	**My tropical fish contracted a disease,** *and the cause of it is not known.* **My tropical fish contracted a disease** _____ _____ *is not known.* 1162

	There is a special group of *adverbs* that we use to lead the reader smoothly from one sentence to the next:
	
	    then **besides** **furthermore** **otherwise**
	    therefore **however** **consequently** **nevertheless**
	
	Would you be likely to start a new piece of writing with one of these adverbs as your very first word? *(Yes, No)*
	                                      1432

No

1701

---

a. **It says in the Bible that all men are brothers.**
b. **The Bible says that all men are brothers.**

Which sentence is more direct and to the point? _____

1702

---

present perfect

2239

In an adjective clause, a verb should agree with its subject—often the relative pronoun **who, which,** or **that.**

Whether these pronouns are singular or plural depends on whether their antecedents are singular or plural.

I like a dog *that is friendly.*

The antecedent of the pronoun *that* is the noun _____.

1971

Mr. Carter *spoke* **for an hour.**

This could mean that Mr. Carter spoke yesterday, last year, or ten years ago. The action belongs entirely to the past. To show that Mr. Carter is still speaking, we must replace *spoke* with the present perfect verb _____ *spoken.*

2240

---

they

2508

Underline the correct pronoun:

The only other girl in the class was (*her, she*).

2509

---

b

2777

---

a. **As the number of cars increases, many highways become inadequate.**
b. **Many highways become inadequate, as the number of cars increases.**

From which sentence should the comma be omitted? _____

2778

"Will . . .
inventions,"
. . . speaker,
"make . . . happier?"

3046

In punctuating this sentence, place the exclamation point just as you would place a question mark if the quotation were a question.

The people behind him were shouting   sit down

3047

---

verb

82

Lesson 3 Two Sentence Patterns Built on Action Verbs

[Frames 84–128]

---

but

352

Use the conjunction **or** to express a choice between two ideas.

a. **I steered for the shore, . . . the wind kept turning the boat.**
b. **The course is getting harder, . . . I am getting lazier.**

In which sentence would **or** make good sense? _____   353

---

b

622

When a phrase such as **I think, I suppose, we hope** follows the relative pronoun, choose the same form of the pronoun you would choose if the phrase were not there.

It is John *who* I think *should apologize.*

Disregarding the phrase *I think,* we choose *who* because it is the subject of the verb _____ _____.

623

Being a road
hog (S)

892

Railroads are still one of the cheapest means of hauling heavy loads. (   )

893

---

the cause
of which

1162

Our television set has a knob, *and I have never discovered its purpose.*

Our television set has a knob _____

_____ *I have never discovered.*

1163

No

1432

then	besides	furthermore	otherwise
therefore	however	consequently	nevertheless

These words usually refer to something previously said. Besides pointing back to something previously said, do these adverbs lead on to the next idea? (*Yes, No*)

1433

page 165

b

1702

---

a. **The sign said that hunting was not allowed.**
b. **It said on the sign that hunting was not allowed.**

Which sentence is more direct and to the point? _____

1703

---

dog

1971

I like a dog *that is friendly.*

Because the pronoun *that* stands for the singular noun **dog,**

it requires the singular verb _____.

1972

---

has (spoken)

2240

---

a. **Lynn** *built* **a fire.**
b. **Lynn** *has built* **a fire.**

One sentence means that the fire is past history. The other means that, although the fire was built in the past, the effect of the action continues into the present moment.

Which sentence means that the fire is still burning? _____

2241

---

she

2509

Why is this rule so frequently disregarded in informal English? It is because after every verb except **be,** we are accustomed to hearing and seeing the *objective* form of pronouns.

Tom knows *me.*   **The police stopped** *him.*   **Colby beat** *us.*

The verb in each of the above sentences is followed by (*a nominative, an objective*) pronoun.

2510

---

b

2778

If an introductory adverb clause is shifted to the end of a sentence, a comma is usually (*necessary, unnecessary*).

2779

---

shouting, ''Sit down!''

3047

It was Cain who asked   am I my brother's keeper

3048

Nearly every simple sentence that we make falls into one of three basic patterns. Two of these patterns involve *action verbs*.

Underline the one verb which indicates an *action:*

was	pushed	seemed

84

---

b

353

Our school is small, . . . we have good teams.

Which conjunction would bring out the meaning more clearly—**and** or **but?** _____

354

---

should apologize

623

I think	I suppose	we hope	we guess

When a clause like one of these follows the relative pronoun, pay no attention to it when choosing between **who** and **whom.**

Briggs is the candidate (*who, whom*) *will win.*
Briggs is the candidate (*who, whom*) I suppose *will win.*

In both sentences, the correct pronoun is (*who, whom*). 624

---

hauling heavy loads (OP)

893

The next step is removing the tire from the rim. (   )

894

---

the purpose of which

1163

The county constructed a road, *and the need for it was very great.*

The county constructed a road _____

_____ *was very great.*

1164

Yes

1433

then	besides	furthermore	otherwise
therefore	however	consequently	nevertheless

Because these special adverbs point both backward and forward, they are useful steppingstones between sentences. Which of these adverbs would fit in best below?

I enjoy movies. _____, **I seldom go.**

1434

a

1703

It shows in the diagram how to adjust the carburetor.

Rewrite the above sentence, eliminating the introductory **It.**

____

____

1704

is

1972

a. **I like a dog** *that is friendly.*
b. **I like dogs** *that are friendly.*

In which sentence does the relative pronoun *that* have a plural antecedent? _____

1973

b

2241

The present perfect tense always ties up the action in some way with the present. If the action is not still continuing, it at least has some effect upon a present situation.

Underline the correct verb:

If Dad (*took, has taken*) **the car, we shall have to walk.**

2242

an objective

2510

People find it difficult to make a single exception to the general pattern of our language and often say, "It was *us*" or "It was *them*"—just as they say, "It followed *us*" or "It followed *them.*"

Underline the pronouns that are *formally* correct:

It was (*we, us*). **It was** (*they, them*).

2511

unnecessary

2779

An adverb clause that comes at the end of a sentence does not usually require a comma. However, when the end clause begins with **for** (meaning **because**), a comma is needed to prevent misreading.

She had to wait *for* **the doctor was out.**

Without a comma, might this sentence be puzzling? (*Yes, No*)

2780

asked, "Am . . . keeper?"

3048

Wasn't it P. T. Barnum who said there's a sucker born every minute

3049

pushed

84

Some action verbs indicate actions of the *body;* others indicate actions of the *mind.*

    a. **worked, drove, washed, wrote, lifted**
    b. **thought, hoped, believed, decided, understood**

Which group of verbs indicates actions of the mind—*a* or *b?*

_____

85

---

but

354

Hockey originated in Canada, . . . many of the best players are Canadians.

Which conjunction would bring out the meaning more clearly—**and** or **but?** _____

355

---

who

624

There are some customers . . . *you can never please.*

Because *you* is the subject of the verb *can please* in the adjective clause, the missing relative pronoun would be its direct object.

We would therefore choose the relative pronoun (*who, whom*).

625

---

removing the
tire from the
rim (SC)

894

Norman dreaded going to the dentist. (   )

895

---

the need
for which

1164

We studied a poem by Alice Walker, *and its meaning was very difficult.*

We studied a poem by Alice Walker _____

_____ *was very difficult.*

1165

However,
(*or* Nevertheless,)

1434

---

then	besides	furthermore	otherwise
therefore	however	consequently	nevertheless

These adverbs modify the entire word group to which they are attached rather than a single word.

    I enjoy movies. *However,* **I seldom go.**

The adverb *However* modifies (*go, I seldom go*).

1435

The diagram
shows how to
adjust the
carburetor.

1704

In this movie it shows how flour is manufactured.

Rewrite the above sentence, eliminating the introductory **It**.

_____

_____

1705

---

b

1973

I like dogs *that are friendly.*

Because the pronoun *that* stands for the plural noun **dogs**,
it requires the plural verb _____.

1974

---

has taken

2242

---

a. **Mrs. Perkins** *was* **our mayor for twelve years.**
b. **Mrs. Perkins** *has been* **our mayor for twelve years.**

Which sentence would mean that Mrs. Perkins is still
your mayor? _____

2243

---

we, they

2511

The use of objective pronouns after **be** has been gaining
ground in informal usage. "It's *me*" is now generally accepted as correct speech. "It's *us*" is trailing close behind.

Although "It's *me*" violates the formal rule, it is acceptable
in free-and-easy conversation. (*True, False*)

2512

Yes

2780

---

a. **I did not apply for the job was in another town.**
b. **I did not apply because the job was in another town.**

In which sentence is a comma needed to prevent misreading? _____

2781

---

said, "There's ...
minute"?

3049

Lesson **85** Pinning Down the Apostrophe

[Frames 3051–3093]

b

85

Action verbs can sometimes make complete statements about their subjects without the need of any other words.

    a. **Harvey stumbled.**
    b. **Harvey sharpened** . . .

Does the action verb make a complete statement about its subject in *a* or *b?* ____

86

---

and

355

Machinery is supposed to make life easier, . . . people seem to be busier than ever.

Which conjunction would bring out the meaning more clearly—**and** or **but?** _____

356

---

whom

625

There are some customers *whom you can never please.*

Now insert the phrase *I suppose* after the clause signal *whom.*

Underline the correct relative pronoun:

There are some customers (*who, whom*) I suppose *you can never please.*

626

---

going to the
dentist (DO)

895

We can sometimes improve a weak compound sentence by changing one of its statements to a gerund phrase used as the object of a preposition.

Nan watched the men work, **and she learned about motors.**
By *watching the men work,* **she learned about motors.**

We change the verb *watch* to the gerund _____.

896

---

the meaning
of which

1165

We camped at the foot of Silver Mountain, *and its top is snow-capped.*

We camped at the foot of Silver Mountain _____

_____ *is snow-capped.*

1166

I seldom go

1435

then	besides	furthermore	otherwise
therefore	however	consequently	nevertheless

Because these special adverbs are useful in leading smoothly from one idea to the next, they are called **conjunctive adverbs.** They are, however, adverbs. Do adverbs have the power of conjunctions to form compound sentences? (*Yes, No*)

1436

This movie
shows how flour
is manufactured.

1705

We often use the pronoun *you* to mean people in general.
It is best to avoid this usage when it leads to absurdity.

You should remove all lipstick for a photograph.

This sentence becomes absurd when it is addressed to
(*a girl, your father*).

1706

---

are

1974

Duke Ellington wrote the piece *which was played.*

If you changed the noun **piece** to **pieces**, would you
also need to change the verb that follows it? (*Yes, No*)

1975

---

b

2243

---

a. **From that day on, I always** *feared* **the water.**
b. **From that day on, I always** *have feared* **the water.**

Which sentence is correct because the fear continues to

exist at the present time? _____

2244

True

2512

Many people who accept "It's *me*" and perhaps "It's *us*"
draw the line at "It's *him*," "It's *her*," and "It's *them*."

You are less likely to be criticized for saying "It's *me*" than
for saying "It's *them*." (*True, False*)

2513

---

a

2781

Use a comma before **for** whenever you can put **because** in
its place.

a. **They sold us two** *for* **the price of one.**
b. **We didn't stop** *for* **the light had turned green.**

Which sentence requires a comma before *for?* _____

2782

**Fred Sims misplaces and loses keys and other things and
then blames his brothers.**

How many words in this sentence end with **s?** _____

3051

a

86

a. **Our guest** <u>brought</u>
b. **Our guest** <u>arrived</u>

Does the action verb make a complete statement about its subject in *a* or *b?* _____

87

---

but

356

It is not a good idea to begin a sentence with a conjunction. Let the conjunction stand between the two parts of the sentence where it can do its job of connecting.

a. **It was a hot day. And all the windows were open.**
b. **It was a hot day, and all the windows were open.**

The conjunction **and** is properly used in (*a, b*).

357

---

whom

626

Underline the correct relative pronoun in this and the following frames. (Pay no attention to the added phrase **I believe**.)

It is the parents (*who, whom*) **I believe are responsible.**

627

---

watching

896

Nan watched the men work, **and she learned about motors.**
By *watching the men work,* **she learned about motors.**

After changing the verb *watch* to the gerund *watching*, we put an appropriate preposition before it—in this case, the preposition _____.

897

---

the top
of which

1166

Lesson **31** Noun Clause Devices

[Frames 1168–1196]

No

1436

Many run-on sentences result from mistaking conjunctive adverbs for conjunctions. It is easy to prove that these words are not conjunctions.

The line broke, *and* **the fish got away.**

Can the conjunction *and* be shifted to any other position in this sentence? (*Yes, No*)

1437

your father 1706	You should remove all lipstick for a photograph. One should remove all lipstick for a photograph. Girls should remove all lipstick for a photograph. Because **You** does not apply to the person spoken to, we can substitute the pronoun _____ or the noun _____. 1707
Yes 1975	a. **Banks will not hire people** *who gamble.* b. **Banks will not hire a person** *who gambles.* In which sentence would you consider *who* a plural pronoun? _____ 1976
b 2244	a. **Archie** *has lost* **his voice.** b. **Archie** *lost* **his voice.** Which sentence would you use to indicate that Archie's voice is still gone? _____ 2245
True 2513	Is there general agreement about the informal usage of all pronouns after forms of the verb **be?** (*Yes, No*) 2514
b 2782	When an introductory adverb clause is short, you may omit the comma, as you do in short compound sentences. a. **When I saw the price, I changed my mind.** b. **When I saw that the price was unreasonably high, I changed my mind.** From which sentence might the comma be omitted? _____ 2783
eight 3051	**Fred Sims misplaces and loses keys and other things and then blames his brothers.** Every word in this sentence is correctly spelled. Is there an apostrophe before any one of the eight final **s's?** (*Yes, No*) 3052

The action verb that makes a complete statement about its subject gives us our first sentence pattern:

PATTERN I: *Subject—Action Verb*

a. **Our guest brought . . .**
b. **Our guest arrived.**

Which word group represents **Pattern I?** _____

b

87

88

---

a. **I dropped the light bulb, but it didn't break.**
b. **I dropped the light bulb. But it didn't break.**

The conjunction **but** is properly used in (*a, b*).

b

357

358

Most of the women (*who, whom*) **take our business course get excellent jobs.**

who

627

628

Nan watched the men work, **and she learned about motors.**

Nan

By *watching the men work,* ~~she~~ **learned about motors.**

Since we lost the subject *Nan,* we put it back at the beginning of the main statement in place of the pronoun _____.

By

897

898

A noun clause is one that is used as a _____.

1168

WRONG: **The line broke,** *therefore* **the fish got away.**
WRONG: **The line broke, the fish** *therefore* **got away.**

Can the adverb *therefore* be shifted from its position between the two statements? (*Yes, No*)

No

1437

1438

(pronoun) One (noun) Girls 1707	**Mother, you can't play professional football without getting a few scratches.** Substitute another word for **you:** **Mother, _____ can't play professional football without getting a few scratches.** 1708
a 1976	Ordinarily we have no trouble in making the subject and verb of an adjective clause agree. When the relative pronoun stands for a singular noun, we use a singular verb. When the relative pronoun stands for a plural noun, we use a _____ verb. 1977
a 2245	Underline the correct verb: **When I was a small child, I** (*disliked, have disliked*) **spinach.** 2246
No 2514	What are we to do while we wait for time to settle this problem of pronoun usage? One solution might be to use whatever pronoun seems natural and comfortable to us in our everyday speech (as many people do). If you adopted this policy, would you be entirely free from criticism? (*Yes, No*) 2515
a 2783	Use a comma wherever it is needed to prevent misreading—regardless of the length of the introductory phrase or clause. Insert a comma to prevent misreading of this sentence. (Try pausing after each word until you find the point where the pause makes sense.) **If you can get some information about campus life.** 2784
No 3052	Should you put an apostrophe before the final **s** in every word that ends in **s?** (*Yes, No*) 3053

b	Any sentence is **Pattern I** if the action verb *by itself* makes a complete statement about its subject—no matter how many other words and phrases may be present. a. **Our guest arrived.** b. **Our guest from Ohio arrived by plane this morning.** Both *a* and *b* are **Pattern I** sentences. (*True, False*)
88	89

a	a. **You must follow the recipe precisely. Or the fudge will be a failure.** b. **You must follow the recipe precisely, or the fudge will be a failure.** The conjunction **or** is properly used in (*a, b*).
358	359

who	**Most of the women** (*who, whom*) **we train get excellent jobs.**
628	629

she	**He sent a check, and** *he didn't sign his name.* **He sent a check** _____ *signing his name.* After you've changed the verb *sign* to the gerund *signing,* what preposition would make good sense in the blank space? _____
898	899

noun	Many noun clauses begin with the clause signal **that.** *That I had saved the receipt* **was fortunate.** The noun clause is the _____ of the verb **was.**
1168	1169

Yes	WRONG: **The line broke,** *therefore* **the fish got away.** WRONG: **The line broke, the fish** *therefore* **got away.** If *therefore* had the power of the conjunction *and* to bind these two sentences together, could it be shifted from its position between the two statements? (*Yes, No*)
1438	1439

one, a person, a player (*or a similar word*) 1708	In this and the following frames, if the italicized pronoun needs an antecedent, cross out the pronoun and write in the parentheses the word or words it is supposed to mean. Where the pronoun is correctly used, write *Correct*. **I seldom cook because I don't enjoy** *it*. (_____) 1709
plural 1977	However, in sentences that contain expressions like "one of those fellows who . . . ," people are sometimes confused as to which of two words the relative pronoun stands for. **Roy was one of those fellows** *who . . . always in debt.* If *who* stands for **one,** we would say *who is;* if *who* stands for **fellows,** we would say *who* _____. 1978
disliked 2246	Underline the correct verb: **Ever since I was a small child, I** (*disliked, have disliked*) **spinach.** 2247
No 2515	Another solution might be to use the nominative case on "dress-up" occasions or when we are with people who observe the traditional rule. a. **It must have been** *them.* b. **It must have been** *they.* Which sentence would be preferred by people who strictly follow the traditional rules of English? _____ 2516
can, get 2784	Insert a comma to prevent misreading: **To help the government started an extensive relief program.** 2785
No 3053	An apostrophe is not an ornament for decorating a final **s.** One of its main uses is to show ownership. To own something means to possess it. We say, therefore, that a word that shows ownership is in the **possessive case.** Underline two nouns that are in the possessive case: **Another boy's name was in Paul's book.** 3054

Our guest from Ohio arrived by plane this morning.

True

This is a **Pattern I** sentence because **Our guest arrived** is (*complete, incomplete*) in its meaning.

89

90

---

b

359

---

whom

It was the principal (*who, whom*) issued the order.

629

630

Eliminate the **and** by changing each italicized statement to a gerund phrase used as the object of a preposition.

(Prepositions: *by, for, of, on, in, before, after, without*)

Jerry has an annoying habit, and *it is slamming doors.*

without

_____

_____

899

900

Using a "that" noun clause at the beginning of a sentence sounds rather stiff and formal for ordinary conversation.

subject

  a. *That I had saved the receipt* **was fortunate.**
  b. **It was fortunate** *that I had saved the receipt.*

Which sentence sounds more informal? _____

1169

1170

WRONG: **The line broke,** *therefore* **the fish got away.**

No

The above sentence is a run-on sentence because there is no (*adverb, conjunction*) to hold the two statements together.

1439

1440

cooking	Continue to follow the directions for the previous frame:
	Typing would make your paper look neater if you can borrow
	one. (_____)
1709	1710

	Roy was one of those fellows *who . . . always in debt.*
are	Does *who* stand for **one** or **fellows?** Let's reason it out: Roy is just one of many fellows. What kind of fellows? Fellows *who are* always in debt. Since *who* refers to the plural noun **fellows,** we use the plural verb (*is, are*) in our problem sentence.
1978	1979

have disliked	Underline the correct verb:
	We don't want to move because we (*lived, have lived*) **in our present house for many years.**
2247	2248

	Or you can play safe by putting your sentence in a way that avoids the problem altogether (and offends no one).
b	a. **It was** *we* **who made the suggestion.**
	b. **We were the** *ones* **who made the suggestion.**
	Which sentence sidesteps the problem of whether to use the nominative or the objective case after a form of **be?** _____
2516	2517

help, the	Insert a comma to prevent misreading:
	With John Sonia formed a business partnership.
2785	2786

	To form the possessive case of a singular noun, add an apostrophe *s* (**'s**) without making any change in the spelling.
	a boy's haircut **the boss's desk**
boy's, Paul's	**a lady's dress** **Miss Jones's room**
	Look at the word that precedes each apostrophe.
3054	Each of these words is (*singular, plural*).
	3055

a. **The coaches agreed with each other.**
b. **The coaches compared the two teams.**

complete

Read just the *subject* and *verb* in each sentence, omitting the words that follow them.

Which sentence is **Pattern I** because the verb by itself can make a statement about its subject that is *complete* in meaning? _____

90   91

In a compound sentence, the conjunction **and, but,** or **or** stands between two word groups, each with a subject and a predicate.

Hank swung at the ball, but he missed it by a foot.

What is the subject of the part of the sentence that follows the conjunction **but?** _____

361

---

who

The major under (*who, whom*) **he served was a strict disciplinarian.**

630   631

Jerry has an annoying habit of slamming doors.

(Prepositions: *by, for, of, on, in, before, after, without*)

We used the old lumber **and saved a lot of money.**

_____

_____

900   901

---

b

That I had saved the receipt **was fortunate.**
. . . was fortunate *that I had saved the receipt.*

Moving the noun clause to the end of the sentence leaves a gap that must be filled before the verb _____.

1170   1171

---

conjunction

a. **The line broke,** *therefore* **the fish got away.**
b. **The line broke, and** *therefore* **the fish got away.**

Which sentence is correct because a conjunction connects the two statements? _____

1440   1441

a typewriter (a machine) 1710	The straight and narrow path would not be so narrow if more people traveled *it*. (_____) 1711
are 1979	Underline the correct verb: **Roy was one of those fellows** *who (is, are) always in debt.* 1980
have lived 2248	Underline the correct verb: **Before entering law school, my brother** (*spent, has spent*) **three years in the Navy.** 2249
b 2517	a. **It was Irene who answered the phone.** b. **It was she who answered the phone.** c. **She was the one who answered the phone.** The two sentences that are so worded as to avoid the problem of case after the verb **be** are _____ and _____. 2518
John, Sonia 2786	This and the following frames review the main points of this lesson. *In England* **motor traffic keeps to the left-hand side of the road.** Would inserting a comma after the italicized phrase make this phrase more emphatic? (*Yes, No*) 2787
singular 3055	To form the possessive case of a plural noun that ends in **s** (as most plural nouns do), add only an apostrophe. the boys' voices the players' uniforms the ladies' coats the Joneses' cottage Look at the word that precedes each apostrophe. Each of these words is (*singular, plural*). 3056

a	a. **The coaches agreed** b. **The coaches compared** Which group of words requires the addition of other words to complete its meaning? _____
91	92

he	**Hank <u>swung at the ball</u>, but (he) <u>missed it by a foot</u>.** Would this sentence still make good sense if we omitted the subject **he** that follows the conjunction? (*Yes, No*)
361	362

whom	**All the young people** (*who, whom*) **the company hires must have high school diplomas.**
631	632

By using the old lumber, we saved a lot of money.	(Prepositions: *by, for, of, on, in, before, after, without*) **The customer left the store, and** *he didn't wait for his change.* _____ _____
901	902

was	*It* **was fortunate** *that I had saved the receipt.* We fill the gap left as a result of moving the noun clause with the *introductory* word _____.
1171	1172

b	**then** **besides** **furthermore** **otherwise** **therefore** **however** **consequently** **nevertheless** If you mistake these conjunctive adverbs for conjunctions, you are likely to write many run-on sentences. **Al shut off the alarm,** *then* **he went back to sleep.** This sentence is a (*run-on, correct*) sentence.
1441	1442

Correct 1711	If you park there, *they* (_____) will tow away your car. 1712
are 1980	On the other hand, our meaning might be different so that the pronoun refers to the singular word **one,** and not to the plural noun that follows it. **Fred was the** *only one* **of those fellows** *who was hired.* Several fellows applied for the job, but only _____ was hired. 1981
spent 2249	Now we shall consider a problem that sometimes arises when we use infinitives. Infinitives, too, have a present perfect form in which they are combined with the verb **have.** a. **to write** b. **to have written** Which infinitive is in the present perfect tense? _____ 2250
a, c 2518	In all formal speech or writing, remember to use a nominative pronoun after any form of the verb **be** (*is, am, are—was, were, been*). a. **I** **he** **she** **we** **they** b. **me** **him** **her** **us** **them** The pronouns to be used after forms of **be** are in group (*a, b*). 2519
Yes 2787	*Recently* **complaints about rising taxes have been increasing.** Inserting a comma after *Recently* would give this adverb (*more, less*) emphasis. 2788
plural 3056	a. **boy's** **lady's** **teacher's** **player's** b. **boys'** **ladies'** **teachers'** **players'** The plural possessive pronouns are those that end with an (*apostrophe, apostrophe s*). 3057

The coaches compared . . . (What?)

b

What did the coaches compare—the fans, the stadiums, or the teams? We don't know.

Until we answer this question, the meaning of the sentence is (*complete, incomplete*).

92

93

Yes

Hank swung at the ball but missed it by a foot.

This is no longer a compound sentence because, after the conjunction **but,** we now have only a (*subject, predicate*).

362

363

---

whom

This water color was painted by a girl (*who, whom*) **I think has unusual talent.** (Pay no attention to the explanatory words **I think.**)

632

633

The customer
left the store
without waiting
for his change.

(Prepositions: *by, for, of, on, in, before, after, without*)

I consulted a number of people **and decided to become a chemist.**

_____

_____

902

903

It

That anyone should believe this story **seems absurd.**
It **seems absurd** *that anyone should believe this story.*

After moving the noun clause to the end of the sentence, we put the *introductory* word *It* in the (*subject, object*) position, which has become vacant.

1172

1173

---

run-on

A true conjunction would have to stand between the two word groups that it holds together.

WRONG: **Al shut off the alarm,** *then* **he went back to sleep.**
WRONG: **Al shut off the alarm, he** *then* **went back to sleep.**

We know that *then* is not a conjunction because it (*can, cannot*) be shifted to another position.

1442

1443

the police (*or whoever it might be*) 1712	**Although Mr. Neville was very wealthy, he made poor use of** *it.* (_____) 1713
one 1981	**Fred was the** *only one* **of those fellows** *who was hired.* If we said ". . . **fellows** *who were hired,*" we should be stating something that isn't true. Because only *one* of the fellows was hired, the pronoun *who* stands for the noun (*one, fellows*). 1982
b 2250	Verbs such as **hope, plan, expect,** and **intend** all look ahead to some future action or event. Can you hope, plan, expect, or intend to do something in time that is already past? (*Yes, No*) 2251
a 2519	In this and the following frames, underline the *two* pronouns —nominative or objective—that would be correct in each sentence. Where pronouns follow any form of the verb **be,** select only nominative pronouns, according to the standard of formal usage. **If I were** (*he, her, them, she, him*), **I should accept the offer.** 2520
more 2788	**Plants grew on our earth** *long before people appeared on the scene.* If you shifted the italicized clause to the beginning of the sentence, would you insert a comma after the word *scene?* (*Yes, No*) 2789
apostrophe 3057	a. **the boy's room** b. **the boys' room** Which means the room of *one* boy because the word that precedes the apostrophe is the singular noun **boy?** _____ 3058

The coaches compared the two teams.

incomplete	Now we know what the coaches compared, and the meaning of our sentence is complete.
	Which word follows the verb **compared** to complete the meaning of the sentence? _____
93	94

Hank swung at the ball but missed it by a foot.

predicate	This sentence has two predicates.
	Each predicate makes a statement about the same subject,
363	_____. 364

---

who	**The magician called up a boy** (*who, whom*) **I suppose he had planted in the audience.**
633	634

After consulting a number of people, I decided to become a chemist.	Continue to follow the directions for the previous frames:
	Leslie has a handy gadget, and *it slices vegetables.*
	_____
	_____
903	904

---

subject	*That the weather affects people's moods* **has been proved.**
	Supply the missing words, using the introductory word *It:*
	_____ *that the weather*
	affects people's moods.
1173	1174

---

	a. **Al shut off the alarm. Then he went back to sleep.**
	b. **Al shut off the alarm; then he went back to sleep.**
can	c. **Al shut off the alarm, then he went back to sleep.**
	Which is a run-on sentence? _____
1443	1444

his wealth (his money) 1713	Here is a remark about the weather: *It (_____) is always cool in the evening.* 1714
one 1982	Underline the correct verb: **Fred was the** *only one* **of those fellows** *who* *(was, were)* **hired.** 1983
No 2251	After verbs that point to the future, such as **hope, plan, expect,** and **intend,** use a present infinitive (*to go, to see*), not a present perfect infinitive (*to have gone, to have seen*). Underline the correct infinitive: **I intended** (*to write, to have written*) **you about my operation.** 2252
he, she 2520	**Judy drove Phil and** (*I, us, she, they, her*) **to the game.** *Note:* When a pronoun is coupled with a noun—or another pronoun—remember the device of using each pronoun singly: **Judy drove Phil to the game.** **Judy drove __?__ to the game.** 2521
Yes 2789	*On Tuesday* **the new semester begins.** *In Europe* **gasoline is more expensive.** Is a comma necessary after a short introductory phrase that states *time* or *place*? (*Yes, No*) 2790
a 3058	a. **the boy's room** b. **the boys' room** Which means the room of *more than one* boy because the word that precedes the apostrophe is the plural noun **boys?** ———— 3059

teams

94

A word that follows a verb and completes the meaning of a sentence is known as a **complement,** which is the grammar name for a *completer.*

A complement, or completer, is sometimes needed after a

verb to _____ the meaning of a sentence.

95

Hank

364

a. **Hank swung at the ball, but he missed it by a foot.**
b. **Hank swung at the ball but missed it by a foot.**

Sentence *a* is a compound sentence because the conjunction **but** connects two sentences.

Sentence *b* is a simple sentence with a compound predicate

because the conjunction **but** connects two _____.

365

---

whom

634

In free-and-easy conversation, **who** has largely driven out **whom.** In formal speech and writing, however, **whom** should be used for all objects.

a. INFORMAL: **I just met a woman . . . you know.**
b. FORMAL: **Our director is a woman . . . citizens respect.**

The pronoun **who** would be considered an error in (*a, b*).

635

Leslie has a handy gadget for slicing vegetables.

904

Sue got out of the car **and turned her ankle.**
(It happened as Sue was getting out.)

_____

_____

905

It has been proved

1174

Make the following sentence more informal by moving the noun clause to the end:

That Norma won both prizes **seems unfair.**

_____

_____

1175

---

c

1444

His parents needed his help, or *otherwise* **Ken would have gone to college.**

If you omitted the conjunction **or,** the above sentence would then be a (*compound, run-on*) sentence.

1445

Correct	**We found a delightful souvenir shop where** *they* (_____) **spoke English and Zuñi.**
1714	1715

was	To make a statement about the *only one* among a larger number, always use a singular verb in the adjective clause. Otherwise, your clause will apply to the entire group.
	We bought the *only one* **of the TV sets** *that was on sale.*
1983	How many TV sets were on sale? (*Only one, More than one*) 1984

to write	Underline the correct infinitive:
	I had hoped (*to have baked, to bake*) **a cake for your birthday.**
2252	2253

us, her	**Bob and** (*me, him, her, I, he*) **secured most of the advertisements.**
2521	2522

No	*Whenever you are in doubt about manners,* **do what seems reasonable to you.**
	If you shifted the italicized clause to the end of the sentence, would this sentence still require a comma? (*Yes, No*)
2790	2791

b	There are a small number of plural nouns that do not end in **s,** as nearly all plural nouns do.
	a. **boy** **doctor** **student** **engineer**
	b. **men** **women** **children** **people**
	In neither group do the nouns end in **s.**
3059	Which group consists of plural nouns? _____ 3060

The police blocked the road.

complete

Because the noun **road** is needed to complete the meaning of this sentence, it is a _____.

95

96

---

predicates
(*or* verbs)

A careful writer streamlines his writing by eliminating all useless words. Words that add nothing to the meaning, clearness, or interest of a sentence should be dropped.

    a. **Hank swung at the ball, but he missed it by a foot.**
    b. **Hank swung at the ball but missed it by a foot.**

Which sentence says the same thing in fewer words? _____

365

366

---

b

    a. **It is the original thinker . . . the world needs today.**
    b. **Is Dick the boy . . . you invited?**

In which sentence would *who* be acceptable as informal usage? _____

635

636

In (on, *etc.*)
getting out of
the car, Sue
turned her
ankle.
905

Paul parked the car on a hill, and *he didn't pull the brake.*

_____

_____

906

It seems unfair
that Norma won
both prizes.

Make the following sentence more informal by moving the noun clause to the end:

That snakes have the power to hypnotize **is a false idea.**

_____

_____

1175

1176

---

run-on

WRONG: **His parents needed his help,** *otherwise* **Ken would
have gone to college.**

You can repair this run-on sentence either by inserting a period after the word *help* and then using a capital letter or by inserting a _____. (What punctuation mark?)

1445

1446

the clerks, the owners (*or whoever it might have been*) 1715	**Our friends fished all morning but didn't catch a single** *one.* (_____) 1716
Only one 1984	Now we shall change the meaning by making the verb in the adjective clause plural: **We bought** *one* **of the TV sets** *that were on sale.* How many TV sets were on sale? (*One, More than one*) 1985
to bake 2253	Underline the correct infinitive: **I meant** (*to pay, to have paid*) **this bill on time.** 2254
I, he 2522	Be on the alert for pronouns that follow forms of the verb **be** (*is, am, was—are, were, been*). **How can you be sure that it was** (*we, us, me, they, her*)? 2523
No 2791	**We had to cut our speed** *because* **the road suddenly became very rough.** If you changed *because* to *for,* would you insert a comma after the word **speed?** (*Yes, No*) 2792
b 3060	Of the nouns having irregular plurals that do not end in **s,** the most frequently used are— **men women children people** These plural nouns look like singular nouns. We make them possessive in the same way that we make singular nouns possessive: by adding an (*apostrophe, apostrophe s*). 3061

complement
or
completer

96

The kind of complement that *receives the action* of the verb or *shows the result* of this action is called a **direct object**.

The teacher will correct the tests.

Which word is a direct object because it *receives the action* of the verb **will correct?** _____

97

---

b

366

Bobby frightened the bird, and it flew up into a tree.

What is the subject of the part of the sentence which follows the conjunction **and?** _____

367

---

b

636

Lesson **17** Subordination by Adjective Clauses

[Frames 638–676]

Paul parked the car on a hill without pulling the brake.

906

Beth had not yet completed her commercial course, **and she was offered a good job.** (Try *before.*)

_____

_____

907

It is a false idea that snakes have the power to hypnotize.

1176

Combine each pair of sentences into a single sentence by changing the italicized sentence to a noun clause. Begin your sentence with *It* and put the noun clause at the end.

I took along a flashlight. **This was very lucky.**

_____

_____

1177

---

semicolon

1446

It was his own fault. *Nevertheless,* **I felt sorry for him.**
It was his own fault; *nevertheless,* **I felt sorry for him.**

Are both arrangements correct? (*Yes, No*)

1447

fish 1716	*It* (_____) **is very strange that Briggs refused the promotion.** 1717
More than one 1985	When you use the words *the only one,* always use a singular verb in the adjective clause. Otherwise the clause will apply to the entire group, which you don't want it to do. Underline the correct word: **This is** *the only one* **of our clocks which** (*keeps, keep*) **accurate time.** 1986

to pay
 	
2254
	On the other hand, you can be happy or unhappy about an action that has already been completed.
	
	    a. **I intended** *to have seen* **this game.**
	    b. **I am happy** *to have seen* **this game.**
	
	In which sentence does the present perfect infinitive make good sense because it refers to a completed action? _____
	
	2255

we, they 2523	**My brother divided his stamp collection between Cliff and** (*she, me, him, he, I*). 2524
Yes 2792	**When I read** *long and tiresome descriptions of nature,* **I get drowsy.** If you omitted the italicized words, would it be all right to omit the comma? (*Yes, No*) 2793

apostrophe s
 	
3061
	To form the possessive of the few plural nouns that do not end in **s,** add **'s**—just as you do with any singular noun.
	
	    the men's lounge **the children's program**
	    women's fashions **the people's choice**
	
	We know that each of these possessive nouns is plural because the word that precedes each apostrophe is (*singular, plural*).
	
	3062

tests	**The cashier made a slight mistake.**
	Which word is a direct object because it *shows the result* of the action of the verb **made?** _____
97	98

it	**Bobby frightened the bird, and (it) flew up into a tree.**
	Would this sentence still make good sense if we omitted the subject **it,** which follows the conjunction? (*Yes, No*)
367	368

	The adjective clause is useful in combining sentences when one sentence states an explanatory fact about a noun or pronoun in the previous sentence.
	Our yearbook comes out in June. *It sells for one dollar.*
	The italicized sentence states an explanatory fact about the noun _____ in the first sentence.
	638

Before completing her commercial course, Beth was offered a good job.	Lesson **24** Making Use of Infinitives
	[Frames 909–943]
907	

It was very lucky that I took along a flashlight.	Continue to follow the directions for the previous frame:
	Emily Dickinson rarely went out. **This seemed strange to the neighbors.**
	_____
	_____
1177	1178

Yes	a. **If you don't care about your appearance,** *then* **nobody else will.**
	b. **The salesman neglected his appearance,** *then* **he began to lose business.**
	Which sentence is a run-on sentence? _____
1447	1448

Correct	**In British traffic** *they* **(_____) keep to the left.**
1717	1718

keeps	Suppose that you have *several* library books that *are* overdue. *The Yearling* is just one of them. Underline the verb which shows that *The Yearling* is among these overdue books. *The Yearling* **is one of my library books that** (*is, are*) **overdue.**
1986	1987

b	a. **Roberta was disappointed** *to have sold* **so few tickets.** b. **Roberta hoped** *to have sold* **many more tickets than she did.** In which sentence is the perfect infinitive correctly used because it refers to a completed action? _____
2255	2256

me, him	**Marge and** (*me, I, her, him, we*) **were in charge of the decorations.**
2524	2525

Yes	**While we tour we eat lightly.** Is a comma necessary after the word **tour?** (*Yes, No*)
2793	2794

plural	a. **all singular nouns** b. **the few plural nouns not ending in s** c. **plural nouns ending in s** To form the possessive case, add an **'s** to all nouns except those in group _____.
3062	3063

page 197

mistake 98	a. **The company manufactures trucks.** b. **The company repairs trucks.** In one sentence, the **trucks** already exist and receive the action of the verb; in the other, the **trucks** are the result of the action. The direct object *receives the action* in sentence (*a, b*). _____ <div style="text-align:right">99</div>
No 368	**Bobby frightened the bird, and (it) flew up into a tree.** Our word-saving device does not work here because each predicate makes a statement about (*a different, the same*) subject. <div style="text-align:right">369</div>
yearbook 638	**Our yearbook comes out in June.** *It sells for one dollar.* Which word in the italicized sentence means the same thing as the noun **yearbook** in the first sentence? _____ <div style="text-align:right">639</div>
	Infinitives are the forms of verbs most commonly listed in the dictionary. If you should look up the words *grew* and *broken,* the dictionary would refer you to the words *grow* and _____. <div style="text-align:right">909</div>
It seemed strange to the neighbors that Emily Dickinson rarely went out. 1178	*Children pick up a foreign language very fast.* **This is a well-known fact.** _____ _____ <div style="text-align:right">1179</div>
b 1448	a. **All our bills were paid,** *consequently* **we had little to worry about.** b. **Because all our bills were paid, we** *consequently* **had little to worry about.** Which sentence is a run-on sentence? _____ <div style="text-align:right">1449</div>

cars, automobiles, drivers, people (*or similar* *words*) 1718	Telly Savalas is bald, but his brother is well supplied with *it*. (_____) 1719
are 1987	Now, on the other hand, suppose that you have several library books but that *only one* of them *is* overdue. Underline the correct verb: *The Yearling* is the *only one* of my library books that (*is, are*) overdue. 1988
a 2256	Underline the correct infinitive: We are happy (*to be, to have been*) of service to you in the recent sale of your home. 2257
I, we 2525	The evidence indicates that it was (*he, them, her, they, me*) who divulged this secret information. 2526
No 2794	If Jim doesn't tell the truth will never be known. Is a comma necessary in this sentence? (*Yes, No*) 2795
c 3063	A simple way to apply these rules is to look at the word you have written and ask yourself, "Who is the owner?" Then put the apostrophe right after the word that answers this question. this boys jacket (Who is the owner? boy) Now go back and put the apostrophe after boy. 3064

b

99

The sentence that contains a direct object gives us our second sentence pattern.

PATTERN II: *Subject—Action Verb → Direct Object*

A sentence in Pattern II has three basic parts.

The third basic part is the _____ object.

100

---

a different

369

Hank swung at the ball, but (he) missed it by a foot.

We can change this compound sentence to a sentence with a *compound predicate* because both predicates make statements about the same person, _____.

370

It

639

which
Our yearbook comes out in June. ~~It~~ *sells for one dollar.*

To change the italicized sentence to an adjective clause, we put the relative pronoun _____ in place of *It.*

640

---

break

909

An **infinitive** is the basic form of a verb from which all other forms are derived. The infinitive is usually combined with the preposition *to;* for example, *to walk, to drive, to sleep.*

The infinitive from which the verbs *flew, flying,* and *flown* are derived is _____.

910

It is a well-known fact that children pick up a foreign language very fast.

1179

A noun clause is often used as an appositive after the words **the fact.**

The fact *that the door was open* **made me suspicious.**

The clause *that the door was open* is an appositive because it explains the noun _____.

1180

---

a

1449

a. **We printed our own programs,** *thus* **saving considerable expense.**
b. **We printed our own programs,** *thus* **we saved considerable expense.**

Which sentence is a run-on sentence? _____

1450

page 199

Lesson **48** Making Pronoun Reference Clear

is

1988

There are many factors that cause war. Greed is one of them.

Underline the correct verb:

Greed is one of the many factors that (*cause, causes*) **war.**

1989

to have been

2257

Underline the correct infinitive:

Jim had hoped (*to receive, to have received*) **a college recommendation.**

2258

he, they

2526

The car missed Donna and (*him, we, he, me, she*) **by only a hair's breadth.**

2527

Yes

2795

In this and the following frames, insert any necessary commas. If no comma is required, write *None.*

In the writings of Maxine Hong Kingston a past time is brought to life.

2796

this boy's
jacket

3064

these boys grades   (Who is the owner?   **boys**)

Now go back and put the apostrophe after **boys.**

3065

PATTERN II: The speaker showed a movie of his travels.

Notice that the action begins with the subject and ends with the direct object. The direct object of an action verb is the goal of its action.

Which word is the *direct object* in the example above?

_____

direct	
100	101

Bobby frightened the bird, and (it) flew up into a tree.

We *cannot* change this compound sentence to a sentence with a *compound predicate* because the first predicate makes a statement about **Bobby,** and the second predicate makes a statement about _____.

Hank	
370	371

---

which

Our yearbook comes out in June. ~~It~~ *sells for one dollar.*

The clause *which sells for one dollar* should be inserted in the sentence right after the noun (*yearbook, June*), which it modifies.

which	
640	641

An infinitive—like a gerund—is often used to name an action. It is often interchangeable with a gerund.

GERUND: *Walking* **is good exercise.**
INFINITIVE: *To walk* **is good exercise.**

Both the gerund and the infinitive are used as nouns. Each is the _____ of the verb **is.**

to fly	
910	911

The "the fact that . . ." construction sometimes proves useful in tightening up a loose compound sentence.

I ate the stew, **but that doesn't mean that I liked it.**

Supply the "the fact that" construction:

_____ *I ate the stew* **doesn't mean that I liked it.**

fact	
1180	1181

If the second word group begins with a conjunctive adverb, supply a period and a capital. If it begins with a conjunction, merely add a comma. Write only the word before and after your punctuation mark.

The play was dull   besides, the acting was mediocre.

_____

b	
1450	1451

The meaning of a pronoun usually depends upon its antecedent, the word to which it refers. This referring to another word is known as the **reference** of a pronoun.

When a pronoun has no antecedent to give it meaning, we say the pronoun lacks _____.

1721

---

cause

1989

Your friend has had many pictures taken, but you think that only one of them looks at all like him.

Underline the correct verb:

This is the only one of the pictures that (*look, looks*) **at all like you.**

1990

---

to receive

2258

Underline the correct infinitive:

Alison intended (*to apply, to have applied*) **for this job.**

2259

---

him, me

2527

It was (*us, they, him, me, she*) **who objected to the new policy.**

2528

Kingston, a

2796

If dogs and cats have such a remarkable sense of direction why do so many get lost only a block or two away from their homes?

2797

---

these boys'
grades

3065

man's	children's	women's	child's	woman's	men's
1	2	3	4	5	6

These mixed-up singular and plural possessive nouns all end in **'s.** However, we can tell which are which by looking at the word that precedes the apostrophe and names the owner(s).

The numbers of the plural possessive nouns are _____ _____ _____.

3066

movie 101	Don't mistake another word that may follow an action verb for a direct object. To be a **direct object,** a word must either receive the action of the verb or show the result of this _____. 102
it *or* bird 371	We can change a compound sentence to a sentence with a compound predicate only when both predicates make statements about the _____ subject. 372
yearbook 641	a. **Our yearbook,** *which sells for one dollar,* **comes out in June.** b. **Our yearbook comes out in June,** *which sells for one dollar.* In which sentence is the adjective clause properly placed? —— 642
subject 911	Fill the blank with the infinitive form of *traveling:* GERUND: *Traveling* **broadens the mind.** INFINITIVE: _____ **broadens the mind.** 912
The fact that 1181	In this and the following frames, improve each compound sentence by changing the italicized statement to the "the fact that" construction: *Fred's mom is a dentist,* **and that influenced him to study dentistry.** _____ _____ 1182
dull. Besides, 1451	Continue to follow the directions for the previous frame: **We play one game for several weeks then we tire of it and take up another.** _____ 1452

reference 1721	When we say that a pronoun lacks reference, we mean that there is no word that serves as its _____. 1722
looks 1990	Another situation that invites trouble is the sentence in which we use an expression like "one of the best games that..." or "one of the worst floods that...." We solve this problem in the same way: If the relative pronoun refers to **one,** we choose a singular verb; if it refers to a plural noun, we choose a _____ verb. 1991
to apply 2259	Underline the correct infinitive: **Our town seems** (*to change, to have changed*) **a lot during the past five years.** 2260
they, she 2528	**The entire incident was no surprise to the Sampsons or** (*us, we, them, I, they*). 2529
direction, why 2797	**When he tries he succeeds.** 2798
2, 3, 6 3066	In this and the following frames, ask yourself, "Who is the owner?" or "Who are the owners?" Underline the part of the possessive noun that answers this question and insert an apostrophe at this point; for example, **one man's car, both men's cars.** **these girls voices** 3067

a. **Mr. Price returned** *recently*.
b. **Mr. Price returned the** *money*.

action

Does the word *recently* or *money* receive the action of the

verb **returned?** _____

102

103

The students went to England by boat. They returned by plane.

same

In combining these two sentences, which word would you

omit? _____

372

373

---

a. **Our yearbook comes out in June, and it sells for one dollar.**
b. **Our yearbook, which comes out in June, sells for one dollar.**

a

One sentence is *compound;* the other is *complex.*

The sentence that is complex because it contains a subordinate clause is (*a, b*).

642

643

Fill the blank with the infinitive form of *swimming:*

To travel

GERUND: **Her favorite sport is** *swimming.*

INFINITIVE: **Her favorite sport is** _____ .

912

913

The fact that
Fred's mom is a
dentist influenced
him to study
dentistry.

Smith knew Madden. **That doesn't make him a party to the crime.**

_____

_____

1182

1183

---

weeks. Then

It had rained all night   and consequently the field was muddy.

_____

1452

1453

antecedent 1722	In the previous lesson we repaired sentences in which the pronouns had no antecedents to make their meaning clear. a. **Odetta sang and everyone enjoyed** *it*. b. **Odetta sang a song, and everyone enjoyed** *it*. Which sentence is faulty because the pronoun *it* lacks reference? _____ 1723
plural 1991	**The wheel was one of the greatest inventions** *that* **. . . ever made.** The antecedent of *that* is **inventions,** not **one,** for we surely do not mean to say that only *one* great invention was ever made. Since the relative pronoun *that* stands for **inventions,** it requires a (*singular, plural*) verb. 1992
to have changed 2260	Underline the correct infinitive: **I meant** (*to mail, to have mailed*) **this card on my way home from school.** 2261
us, them 2529	**It could not have been** (*us, them, we, I, him*) **who broke the window.** 2530
None 2798	**To unite the Colonies needed to forget their local interests and rivalries.** 2799
girls' 3067	Be sure to underline the part of the possessive noun that identifies the owner or owners before inserting the apostrophe at this point: **my doctors opinion** 3068

money

103

104

a. **Mr. Price returned** *recently*.
b. **Mr. Price returned the** *money*.

Which sentence contains a direct object? _____

They

373

374

a. **The coach went to the blackboard, and he drew a diagram of the play.**
b. **The curtain went up, and the show began.**

Which compound sentence can be changed to a sentence with a compound predicate because both predicates make statements about the same subject? _____

---

b

643

644

a. **Our yearbook comes out in June, and it sells for one dollar.**
b. **Our yearbook, which comes out in June, sells for one dollar.**

The two facts are brought into closer relationship by the (*compound, complex*) sentence.

---

to swim

913

914

Like participles and gerunds, infinitives can take direct objects and subject complements, as no ordinary noun can do.

To waste food **is sinful.**

Because the noun *food* receives the action of the infinitive *To waste,* it is its (*direct object, subject complement*).

The fact that Smith knew Madden doesn't make him a party to the crime.

1183

1184

The lights were on, **and that made me think that the Lins were at home.**

_____

_____

---

night, and

1453

1454

People once considered the night air poisonous   therefore they kept their windows tightly closed.

_____

a

1723

Sentences are even more confusing when it is not clear to which of two words a pronoun refers. Suppose that while staying at a summer cottage, you received the following message.

Take the motor off the boat and sell *it*.

Could *it* refer to either the **motor** or the **boat**? (*Yes, No*)

1724

---

plural

1992

Underline the correct verb:

The wheel was one of the greatest inventions that (*was, were*) **ever made.**

1993

---

to mail

2261

Lesson **63** Using the Past Perfect and the Future Perfect Tenses

[Frames 2263–2298]

---

we, I

2530

In this and the following frames, the italicized pronouns are correct. If a person should find them awkward to say, how could he change the wording to eliminate the pronoun after the form of the verb **be**?

"May I speak to Pedro?"   "This is *he* speaking."
"May I speak to Pedro?"   "This is _____ speaking."

2531

---

unite, the

2799

The messenger kept feeling his pocket for the papers were very valuable.

2800

---

doctor's

3068

the childrens department

3069

b	a. **The rain stopped the** game.
	b. **The rain stopped** suddenly.
	Which sentence contains a direct object? _____
104	105

a	**The coach went to the blackboard, and he drew a diagram of the play.**
	The coach went to the blackboard and drew a diagram of the play.
	When we change a compound sentence to a sentence with a compound predicate, we (*keep, drop*) the comma.
374	375

complex	**Our yearbook comes out in June, and it sells for one dollar.**
	By using a compound sentence we give (*equal, unequal*) emphasis to the two facts that the conjunction **and** connects.
644	645

direct object	*To be healthy* **is a great advantage.**
	The adjective *healthy* completes the meaning of the infinitive *To be.*
	The adjective *healthy*, therefore, is the (*direct object, subject complement*) of the infinitive.
914	915

The fact that the lights were on made me think that the Lins were at home.	We shall now learn to avoid a common error that is sometimes made when using noun clauses.
	I knew *that the cement would harden.*
	This sentence contains a _____ clause.
1184	1185

poisonous. Therefore	**The plane took off an hour late or otherwise we should have missed it.**
	_____
1454	1455

	Take the motor off the boat and sell _it_.
Yes	Because this sentence has two possible meanings, we say that it is **ambiguous,** which means "having more than one possible meaning."
	The word that makes this sentence ambiguous is the pronoun
1724	_____. <div align="right">1725</div>
	Suppose that someone made a list of the most unusual stories that _were_ ever written. It is likely that Stevenson's "The Bottle Imp" would be one of these.
were	Underline the correct word:
	Stevenson's "The Bottle Imp" is one of the most unusual
1993	**stories that** (_was, were_) **ever written.** <div align="right">1994</div>
	The past perfect tense is formed by combining **had** (the past tense of **have**) with the past participle of a verb (_seen, walked, taken_).
	<div align="center">a. **had decided** b. **has decided**</div>
	Which verb is in the past perfect tense? _____
	<div align="right">2263</div>
Pedro	**It might have been _we_ who were hurt.**
	We might have been the _____.
2531	<div align="right">2532</div>
pocket, for	**I know that Juan can keep a secret because he has never told me anything confidential about anyone else.**
2800	<div align="right">2801</div>
children's	<div align="center">**both parents consent**</div>
3069	<div align="right">3070</div>

a 105	*Pattern I* is built around a two-part framework: a *subject* and an *action verb*. *Pattern II* is built around a three-part framework: a *subject*, an *action verb*, and a _____ _____. 106
drop 375	a. **We won our first game, but we lost the second.** b. **We won our first game but lost the second.** No comma is used before a conjunction that connects the two parts of a compound (*sentence, predicate*). 376
equal 645	You have learned that to *subordinate* a fact or an idea means to put it into a word group that is (*more, less*) than a sentence. 646
subject complement 915	Since an infinitive is a mixture of both a verb and a noun, it may be modified by an adverb. **Test pilots like** *to live dangerously.* The adverb *dangerously* modifies the infinitive _____. 916
noun 1185	**I knew** *that the cement would harden* *if I didn't hurry.* Besides a noun clause, this sentence now has a second clause, which is an (*adverb, adjective*) clause. 1186
late, or 1455	Continue to follow the directions for the previous frame, with only one change: Use a semicolon where you have previously been using a period and a capital. Both are equally correct. **I had paid my bill** **however, I could not find my receipt.** _____ 1456

Take the motor off the boat and sell *it*.

This sentence is ambiguous because there are *two* nouns before the pronoun *it* that could serve as its antecedent.

These nouns are _____ and _____.

it

1725

1726

Many large catfish were caught in Mud Lake. Dad caught one of these many large fish.

Underline the correct verb:

Dad caught one of the largest catfish that (*was, were*) **ever caught in Mud Lake.**

were

1994

1995

Ellen *bought* **a flute but later** *returned* **it.**

There are two verbs in this sentence.

Does the order of the verbs represent the order in which the actions occurred? (*Yes, No*)

a

2263

2264

I'm sure that it was *she* **in the front seat.**

I'm sure that _____.

ones who were
hurt.

2532

2533

None

Lesson **78** Commas to Separate Items in a Series

[Frames 2803–2839]

2801

Be careful with this one! Who are the owners of the property?

some peoples property

parents'

3070

3071

direct object

106

a. **All good citizens vote on Election Day.**
b. **All good citizens cast their vote on Election Day.**

Which sentence is **Pattern II** because the verb is followed by a direct object? _____

107

---

predicate

376

a. **We heard a voice, but we couldn't recognize it.**
b. **We heard a voice, but couldn't recognize it.**

In which sentence should the comma before the conjunction be dropped because it is not a compound sentence? _____

377

---

less

646

a. **It sells for one dollar.**
b. **which sells for one dollar**

Both word groups state a fact about *price*.

The word group that *subordinates* the fact about *price* is the (*clause, sentence*).

647

---

to live

916

The phrases formed by infinitives with their related words are called **infinitive phrases.** These phrases can be used in most of the ways that nouns are used.

> *To teach a dog tricks* **requires endless patience.**

The infinitive phrase is used as the _____ of the verb **requires.**

917

---

adverb

1186

a. **I knew** *that the cement would harden   if I didn't hurry.*
b. **I knew** *that   if I didn't hurry   the cement would harden.*

In which sentence is the adverb clause inserted between parts of the noun clause? _____

1187

---

bill; however,

1456

I wrote down my answer   and then I changed my mind.

_____

1457

a. **Take the** *motor* **off the** *boat* **and sell** *it.*
b. **Sell the** *motor* **after you take** *it* **off the** *boat.*

motor, boat

Which sentence is clear because there is only *one* noun before the pronoun *it* that could serve as its antecedent?

1726

———

1727

In this and the following frames, think over each sentence to decide whether the adjective clause applies to **only one** or to the plural noun that follows it. Then underline the verb that expresses the intended meaning.

were

Mr. Slocum is one of those speakers who never (*seem, seems*) **to come to the point.**

1995

1996

---

a. **Ellen** *bought* **a flute but later** *returned* **it.**
b. **Ellen** *returned* **the flute that she** *had bought.*

Yes

In which sentence is the last action mentioned first and the first action mentioned last? _____

2264

2265

WHO AND *WHOM* AS INTERROGATIVE PRONOUNS

Who is nominative; **whom** is objective.

she was
(the one) in
the front seat.

Who **was the inventor of wireless telegraphy?**

The nominative pronoun *Who* is correct because it is the subject of the verb _____.

2533

2534

A series is a number of similar things that follow one after another. We speak of a series of games, accidents, or coincidences. In a sentence, a series is *three or more* words, phrases, or clauses all used in the same way.

There was sand *on the floor,* *in our beds,* **and** *in our food.*
This sentence contains a series of (*words, phrases, clauses*).

2803

---

people's

the boys locker room

3071

3072

a. **Each student keeps a list of every misspelled word.**
b. **The wheezing motor finally stopped completely.**

Which sentence is **Pattern II** because the verb is followed by a direct object? _____

108

---

a. **A large tree had fallen and was blocking traffic.**
b. **A large tree had fallen and traffic was slowed down.**

In which sentence should a comma be inserted before the conjunction? _____

378

---

a. **Our yearbook,** *which sells for one dollar,* **comes out in June.**
b. **Our yearbook comes out in June, and it sells for one dollar.**

In which sentence is the *price* of the yearbook subordinated?

_____

648

Shirley Bluewind's plan is *to save money for law school.*

The infinitive phrase completes the meaning of the linking verb **is** and identifies the subject **plan.**

The infinitive phrase, therefore, is a (*direct object, subject complement*).

918

We often interrupt a noun clause after the clause signal *that* to insert an adverb phrase or clause.

Put parentheses around the adverb clause that now interrupts the noun clause:

I knew *that if I didn't hurry the cement would harden.*

1188

The two essays were judged equally good   therefore the prize was divided between us.

1458

the motor
Take the motor off the boat and sell ~~it~~.

b

Another very simple way to clear up the meaning of this sentence is to eliminate the pronoun *it* by repeating the noun _____.

1727

1728

---

seem

Hawley's is the only one of the gas stations that (*stay, stays*) **open all night.**

1996

1997

---

b

a. **Ellen** *bought* **a flute but later** *returned* **it.**
b. **Ellen** *returned* **the flute that she** *had bought*.

In which sentence do you find a verb in the past perfect tense? ____

2265

2266

---

was

Whom **did the Yankees defeat for the pennant?**
(The Yankees did defeat *whom* **for the pennant?)**

The objective pronoun *Whom* is correct because it is the direct object of the verb _____ _____.

2534

2535

---

phrases

It takes at least _____ items to form a series. (How many?)

2803

2804

---

boys'

SINGULAR: **lady**   PLURAL: **ladies**

When you write a possessive noun, be sure that you have the correct spelling of the owner(s) before the apostrophe.

a. **a ladie's coat**   b. **a lady's coat**

Which is correct because the word before the apostrophe is correctly spelled? ____

3072

3073

The pitcher threw Reggie a fast curve.

After the verb **threw,** we have two nouns—**Reggie** and **curve.**

a

To decide which is the **direct object,** ask yourself, "What did the pitcher throw?"

The direct object is the noun _____.

108

109

The teacher liked the movie. She urged her classes to see it.

b

If you were to combine these two sentences, it would be better to use a compound (*sentence, predicate*).

378

379

To subordinate a fact or an idea is like taking an article from the front of a showcase and putting it in the back, where it is less conspicuous.

a

A fact or an idea gets less emphasis when we put it in a (*sentence, clause*).

648

649

---

subject
complement

A good citizen does not refuse *to be a witness.*

The infinitive phrase is used as a (*direct object, subject complement*).

918

919

When we interrupt a noun clause in this way, we must guard against a common error.

WRONG: **I knew** *that (if I didn't hurry) that the cement would harden.*

(if I didn't hurry)

The sentence above is incorrect because the clause signal _____ is repeated.

1188

1189

---

good; therefore

The doctor was exhausted   but nevertheless she kept on working.

_____

1458

1459

motor

1728

After Mother left Eve at camp, *she* **felt lonesome.**

This sentence is ambiguous because *she* might refer to either _____ or _____.

1729

---

stays

1997

The Netherlands was one of the many neutral countries that (*was, were*) **invaded by the Nazis.**

1998

---

b

2266

Use the past perfect tense of a verb for an earlier action that is mentioned after a later action.

Suppose that John *picked* an apple and then *ate* it.

You would put the verb *picked* in the past perfect tense if you mentioned it (*first, last*).

2267

---

did defeat

2535

To *whom* **will the President entrust this responsibility?**

The objective form *whom* is correct because it is the object of the preposition _____.

2536

---

three

2804

a. **Many friends and relatives were invited.**
b. **Many friends, relatives, and neighbors were invited.**

Which sentence contains a series of nouns? _____

2805

---

b

3073

SINGULAR: **baby**   PLURAL: **babies**

a. **the babies' mothers**   b. **the babys' mothers**

Which is correct because the word before the apostrophe is correctly spelled? _____

3074

curve 109	**The pitcher threw Reggie a fast curve.** What does the noun **Reggie** do? It shows *to whom* the pitcher threw the **curve**. We call such a noun (or pronoun) an **indirect object**. **Curve** is the *direct object;* **Reggie** is the _____ *object.*　　110
predicate 379	**The teacher liked the movie and urged her classes to see it.** Should a comma be inserted before the conjunction **and?** (*Yes, No*) 380
clause 649	**Our yearbook,** *which comes out in June,* **sells for one dollar.** This complex sentence states two facts: one about *price* and another about *time of issue*. This sentence gives greater emphasis to the fact about (*price, time of issue*).　　650
direct object 919	In addition to being used as nouns, infinitives are also used as modifiers—both as adjectives and as adverbs. 　**I want a chance** *to work.*　　**I want a chance** *to play.* 　**I want a chance** *to rest.*　　**I want a chance** *to travel.* Each sentence means a different kind of **chance** because the _____ is different in each sentence.　　920
that 1189	It is easy to forget that you have already written the word *that* and repeat it when you continue the clause. a. **I decided that after I graduated I would go to college.** b. **I decided that after I graduated that I would go to college.** Which sentence is correct? _____　　1190
exhausted, but 1459	**The job provided me with spending money　furthermore, it built up my self-confidence.** _____ 1460

Mother, Eve 1729	You can often get rid of ambiguity by shifting the "false" antecedent to a position *after* the pronoun, where it can't confuse the reader. **Mother felt lonesome after** *she* **left Eve at camp.** Now we know that *she* means **Mother** and not **Eve** because the noun _____ has been put after the pronoun *she*. <div align="right">1730</div>
were 1998	**His boss was one of those employers who** (*don't, doesn't*) **welcome suggestions from their employees.** <div align="right">1999</div>
last 2267	**John** *ate* **the apple that he** *had picked.* Are the actions mentioned in the order in which they occurred? (*Yes, No*) <div align="right">2268</div>
To 2536	a. . . . **was Bess Myerson's Consul General?** b. . . . **did Bess Myerson appoint as her Consul General?** In which sentence would **Whom** be correct because it is the direct object of the verb? _____ <div align="right">2537</div>
b 2805	Use commas *between* the items in a series but not before or after the series (unless a comma is required for another reason). Punctuate the following sentence: **Many of the world's greatest books paintings and inventions were produced by people past sixty.** <div align="right">2806</div>
a 3074	Here is another problem that concerns apostrophes: WRONG: **the dentist who pulled my tooth's office** This sentence is wrong because the apostrophe is not in the right word. The owner of the office is not **tooth** but _____. <div align="right">3075</div>

The pitcher threw Reggie a fast curve.

indirect

The indirect object **Reggie** comes (*before, after*) the direct object **curve**. _____

110

111

No

We have good traffic laws. They are strictly enforced.

If you were to combine these two sentences, you would need to use a compound (*sentence, predicate*).

380

381

---

a. **Our yearbook,** *which comes out in June,* **sells for one dollar.**
b. **Our yearbook,** *which sells for one dollar,* **comes out in June.**

price

One sentence emphasizes the *price;* the other, the *time of issue.* Which emphasizes the *time of issue?* _____

650

651

I want a chance *to work.*   **I want a chance** *to play.*
I want a chance *to rest.*   **I want a chance** *to travel.*

infinitive

Each infinitive in the above sentences modifies the noun

_____.

920

921

---

a. **We knew that if we appeared too eager that the price would be raised.**
b. **We knew that if we appeared too eager the price would be raised.**

a

Which sentence is correct? _____

1190

1191

Copy each pair of sentences, inserting the word in parentheses between them. Show by your punctuation whether they form one sentence or two.

money;
furthermore,

The trip takes all day. The scenery is interesting. (*but*)

_____

1460

_____

1461

Lola backed the car out of the garage and cleaned _it_.

Eve

This sentence is ambiguous because we don't know whether _it_ refers to the **car** or to the _____.

1730

1731

---

don't

Are you one of those newspaper readers who (_read, reads_) **only the headlines?**

1999

2000

No

Use the past perfect tense when the first action is mentioned (_first, last_).

2268

2269

---

b

In ordinary conversation, the nominative form **who** is generally used even though it may be the object of a verb or a preposition.

INFORMAL: _Who_ **did you see at church today?**

This violates the rule for formal usage because _Who_ is the direct object of the verb _____ _____.

2537

2538

---

books,
paintings,

Make a count to see how, in a series, the number of commas compares with the number of items:

_____, _____, **and** _____
_____, _____, _____, **and** _____

The number of commas is always one (_more, less_) than the number of items in a series.

2806

2807

---

dentist

The apostrophe belongs in the word that shows the owner, not in a word that is part of a modifying phrase or clause.

WRONG: **The dentist who pulled my tooth's office**

Now switch the **'s** to the noun **dentist,** and read the sentence with this change.

Does moving the **'s** to **dentist** solve the problem? (_Yes, No_)

3075

3076

before 111	a. **The pitcher threw Reggie a fast curve.** b. **The pitcher threw him a fast curve.** In which sentence is the indirect object not a noun but a pronoun? _____ 112
sentence 381	**We have good traffic laws and they are strictly enforced.** Should a comma be inserted before the conjunction **and**? (*Yes, No*) 382
b 651	The type of sentence we use depends on the emphasis we wish to give various facts or ideas. If we wish to give two facts equal emphasis, we would use a (*compound, complex*) sentence. 652
chance 921	**I want a chance** *to work.* **I want a chance** *to play.* **I want a chance** *to rest.* **I want a chance** *to travel.* Because each infinitive modifies the noun **chance**, it is used as an _____. 922
b 1191	a. **I am sure that if we don't buy the car someone else will.** b. **I am sure that if we don't buy the car that someone else will.** Which sentence is correct? _____ 1192
The trip takes all day, but the scenery is interesting. 1461	**The trip takes all day. The scenery is interesting.** (*however*) _____ _____ 1462

We can always reconstruct a faulty sentence to make the reference of a pronoun perfectly clear.

garage

Lola cleaned the car after backing *it* out of the garage.
Lola cleaned the garage after backing out the car.

Does either sentence leave any doubt as to what was cleaned? (*Yes, No*)

1731
1732

---

read

This was one of the worst floods that (*has, have*) ever occurred in the South.

2000
2001

---

last

a. **Howard . . . off the alarm and went back to sleep.**
b. **Howard went back to sleep after he . . . off the alarm.**

In which sentence should the past perfect verb **had shut** be used? _____

2269
2270

---

did see

The widespread use of **who** instead of **whom** is due to the fact that it comes in the subject position at the head of the sentence, and position is an important factor in our language.

Whom **did Rosie Casals beat in a tennis match?**

Can a word occupy the subject position and still not be the subject of the sentence? (*Yes, No*)

2538
2539

---

less

In a series of *three* items, we would use *two* commas.

In a series of *four* items, we would use _____ commas.

2807
2808

No

WRONG: **the dentist who pulled my tooth's office**

To avoid this error, it is necessary to show the ownership of the office by using an **of** phrase.

RIGHT: **the office of the dentist who pulled my tooth**

Instead of using an **'s** to show ownership, we use the prepositional phrase _____.

3076
3077

An indirect object can show **to what,** as well as **to whom,** something was done.

These shoes give your feet more support.

The noun **support** is the _____ *object.*

The noun **feet** is the _____ *object.*

b

112   113

The crowded bus stopped. It took on still more people.

If you were to combine these two sentences, it would be better to use a compound (*sentence, predicate*).

Yes

382   383

If we wish to subordinate one idea to another, we would use a (*compound, complex*) sentence.

compound

652   653

I learned a new way *to play checkers.*

The infinitive phrase *to play checkers* modifies the noun

_____.

adjective

922   923

Copy each sentence, inserting the word group in parentheses after the clause signal **that.** Do not repeat *that* when you continue the interrupted clause.

I was afraid that I would not be ready. (*when my turn came*)

a

_____

_____

1192   1193

The dogs growled at each other. They began to fight. (*then*)

day. However,
or
day; however,

_____

_____

1462   1463

a. **Stan was out of practice when Jack beat** *him.*
b. **Stan beat Jack when** *he* **was out of practice.**
c. **Jack was out of practice when Stan beat** *him.*

In which sentence is the reference of the italicized pronoun confusing because we can't tell to whom the pronoun refers?

No

1732

———

1733

---

have

This is just one more of those stupid prejudices that (*is, are*) passed on from one generation to another.

2001

2002

---

b

a. **The police captured the prisoner who . . . .**
b. **The prisoner . . . but the police captured him.**

In which sentence should the past perfect verb **had escaped** be used? _____

2270

2271

Yes

In formal writing or speaking, use **whom** if the interrogative pronoun is the object of a verb or a preposition.

a. *Who* **did Jimmy take to the prom?**
b. *Who* **will the new party select for its first candidate?**

Your use of *Who* instead of *Whom* would be more subject to criticism in sentence _____.

2539

2540

---

three

a. **We export, food, cotton, and machinery to many countries.**
b. **We export food, cotton, and machinery to many countries.**
c. **We export food, cotton, and machinery, to many countries.**

Which sentence is correctly punctuated? _____

2808

2809

---

of the dentist

a. **the wife of the man in the other car**
b. **the man in the other car's wife**

Which is correct? _____

3077

3078

(support) direct (feet) indirect 113	Besides showing *to whom* (or *to what*) something was done, an **indirect object** can also show *for whom* (or *for what*) something was done. **Cindy Yazzie sang us a song.** *For whom* did Cindy Yazzie sing? For _____. <div align="right">114</div>
predicate 383	In this and the following frames, combine each pair of sentences, using a compound predicate whenever possible. Indicate your answer by writing the conjunction and the two words surrounding it. Insert any necessary comma. **Garvey made a two-base hit. The ball game was over.** _____ <div align="right">384</div>
complex 653	Now let's look more closely into the process of subordinating an idea by changing it to an adjective clause. **Tony read some notices.** *Few students heard them.* The italicized sentence provides information about the noun _____ in the first sentence. <div align="right">654</div>
way 923	**I learned a new way** *to play checkers.* Because the infinitive phrase modifies the noun **way**, it is used as an _____. <div align="right">924</div>
I was afraid that when my turn came I would not be ready. 1193	Continue to follow the directions for the previous frame: **Many believe that they could write a song hit.** (*if they took the time*) _____ _____ <div align="right">1194</div>
other. Then *or* other; then 1463	**The college is small. Its school spirit is excellent.** (*nevertheless*) _____ _____ <div align="right">1464</div>

In this and the following frames, one of each pair of sentences is clear. The other is ambiguous because the pronoun has two possible antecedents. Circle the letter of the correct sentence.

a. **When our bus reached the station, it was almost empty.**
b. **Our bus was almost empty when it reached the station.**

Milner was the only one of our players who (*was, were*) **selected for the all-state team.**

After you decide which action came first, underline the preferred verb:

The witness made this statement but later (*denied, had denied*) **it.**

In this and the following frames, underline the pronoun that is proper for formal usage:

(*Who, Whom*) **will be in favor of this new tax?**

Punctuate the following sentence:

Immediate pursuit quick arrest and certain conviction reduce crime.

Rewrite the following sentence correctly, using a prepositional phrase, instead of a possessive noun, to show the owner of the name:

The girl in the front seat's name is Linda.

_____

_____

Cindy Yazzie sang us a song.

us

The direct object is _____.

The indirect object is _____.

114

115

It is important that you read the directions in the previous frame once again. Then be sure to select a conjunction that expresses the meaning most clearly.

hit, and the

Supply a comma *only* when you form a compound sentence.

Paul wanted a date. He was too timid to ask.

384

_____

385

---

notices

Tony read some notices. *Few students heard them.*

Which word in the italicized sentence means the same thing as **notices** in the first sentence? _____

654

655

I learned a new way *to play checkers.*

We have seen that the infinitive *to play,* like an ordinary adjective, modifies the noun **way.**

adjective

The fact that the infinitive *to play* can at the same time take the direct object *checkers* shows that an infinitive can also do

924

the job of a _____.

925

Many believe that if they took the time they could write a song hit.

The study shows that school grades drop sharply. (*when students get their own cars*)

_____

1194

_____

1195

---

small.
Nevertheless,
or
small;
nevertheless,
1464

The college is small. Its school spirit is excellent. (*but*)

_____

_____

1465

b 1734	Continue to circle the letter of the correct sentence: a. **As soon as Larry gets a kennel, he is going to keep the dog in it.** b. **Larry is going to keep the dog in a kennel as soon as he gets one.** 1735
was 2003	Lesson **56** A Few Remaining Problems [Frames 2005–2044]
denied 2272	Underline the preferred verb: **The witness later denied the statement that he** (*made, had made*). 2273
Who 2541	**By** (*who, whom*) **will this new tax be favored?** 2542
pursuit, arrest, 2810	Punctuate the following sentence: **The bellhop stopped me asked me my name and handed me a telegram.** 2811
The name of the girl in the front seat is Linda. 3079	Rewrite the following sentence correctly: **The family next door's dog tears up our lawn.** _____ _____ 3080

(direct object)
song
(indirect object)
us

115

Cindy Yazzie sang us a song.

As it always does when it is present, the indirect object comes (*before, after*) the direct object.

116

---

date but was

385

It was getting late. The children were growing restless.

_____

386

---

them

655

---

which

Tony read some notices. *Few students heard* ~~them~~.

To change the italicized sentence to an adjective clause, we put the relative pronoun _____ in place of *them*.

656

---

verb

925

---

a. **I learned a new way** *to play checkers.*
b. **I learned a new way of** *playing checkers.*

One sentence contains a gerund phrase; the other an infinitive phrase.

Which sentence contains an infinitive phrase? _____

926

The study shows that when students get their own cars school grades drop sharply.

1195

Employers find that production increases. (*when rest periods are allowed*)

_____

_____

1196

---

small, but its

1465

Lesson **40** Review: The Sentence Unit

[Frames 1467–1486]

a

1735

---

a. **The Red Sox will play the Yankees. They have a great team.**
b. **The Red Sox will play the Yankees, who have a great team.**

1736

To make sentences more forceful, we often start them with the words **There is, There are,** or **Here is, Here are.**

      a. **A <u>spot</u> <u>is</u> on your coat.**
      b. **There <u>is</u> a <u>spot</u> on your coat.**

In which sentence is the usual order of the subject and verb turned around? _____

2005

---

had made

2273

Underline the preferred verb:

I read the article and (*made, had made*) **a summary of it.**

2274

---

whom

2542

(*Who, Whom*) **will the President appoint to this new post?**

2543

---

me, name,

2811

Three or more short and closely related sentences may be written in series as a single sentence without being considered a run-on sentence error.

Punctuate the following sentence:

The toast burned the coffee boiled over and Bobby spilled his orange juice.

2812

The dog of the
family next
door tears up
our lawn.

3080

Be sure to recognize possessive nouns when the thing that is owned is understood but not expressed.

      Your voice sounds just like Mary's (voice).

We put an apostrophe in the word **Mary's** because the noun

_____ is understood.

3081

before 116	**The club bought the church a new organ.** The indirect object is the noun _____. 117
late, and the 386	(Are you sure that you recall all points in the directions given in frames 384 and 385?) **Most Americans want their children to attend college. They will make great sacrifices to send them.** _____ 387
which 656	*which* **Tony read some notices.** *Few students heard* ~~them.~~ **Tony read some notices,** *which few students heard.* Since a relative pronoun usually starts an adjective clause, we move **which** to the front of the clause, before the word _____. 657
a 926	**Lyle ran** *to catch the bus.* The infinitive phrase *to catch the bus* explains **why** about the verb _____. 927
Employers find that when rest periods are allowed production increases. 1196	Lesson **32** **Three Effective Sentence Devices** [Frames 1198–1229]
	In this and the following frames, one of each pair of items is a sentence; the other is a fragment. Circle the letter of the complete sentence. a. **A good citizen helps with the work of his community.** b. **A good citizen who helps with the work of his community.** 1467

b

1736

a. **If you find any worms in the cabbages, destroy them.**
b. **Destroy any worms that you find in the cabbages.**

1737

---

b

2005

In sentences that begin with **There is, There are,** or **Here is, Here are,** the verb precedes the subject.

There is a spot on your coat.

We use the singular verb **is** because its subject _____ is singular.

2006

---

made

2274

Underline the preferred verb:

I remembered what the coach (*said, had said*) **about forward passes.**

2275

Whom

2543

(*Who, Whom*) **was the patriot who said, "Give me liberty or give me death"?**

2544

---

burned, over,

2812

a. **I looked at the dog, the dog looked at me, and we immediately became friends.**
b. **I looked at the dog, the dog looked at me.**

Which is a correct series of sentences and not a run-on sentence? _____

2813

---

voice

3081

Supply the missing apostrophe:

A porpoise's brain is as large as a persons.

3082

church 117	An **indirect object** shows *to whom* or *what* or _____ *whom* or *what* something is done. 118
college and will 387	**You must be completely satisfied. We will return your money.** _____ 388
few 657	**Tony read some notices,** *which few students heard.* The adjective clause is in its proper position right after the word _____, which it modifies. 658
ran 927	**Lyle ran** *to catch the bus.* Because the infinitive phrase modifies the verb **ran,** it is used as an _____. 928
	1. The "no sooner . . . than" device: a. **When we sat down to eat, company arrived.** b. *No sooner* **had we sat down to eat** *than* **company arrived.** Which sentence shows more effectively that one event followed the other almost immediately? _____ 1198
a 1467	Circle the letter of the complete sentence: a. **Posted in the most conspicuous place on the bulletin board.** b. **The notice was posted on the bulletin board.** 1468

b

1737

a. **Father said to Bobby, "Your hands are always dirty."**
b. **Father told Bobby that his hands were always dirty.**

1738

---

spot

There are spots on your coat.

We use the plural verb **are** because its subject _____ is plural.

2006

2007

---

had said

Even though the actions are mentioned in the order of their occurrence, we sometimes use the past perfect tense to emphasize that the first action was completed before the second action began.

    After we _had washed_ **the car, it** _rained_ **very hard.**

Was the washing completed when it began to rain? (*Yes, No*)

2275

2276

Who

(*Who, Whom*) **does the law hold responsible in such cases?**

2544

2545

---

a

If there is a comma *before* a series, it is not used because of the series but for another reason.

When I arrived home from school, Louis, Ron, and Carlos were waiting for me.

The comma after the word **school** is correct because it follows (*an introductory, a main*) clause.

2813

2814

---

person's

In this and the following frames, supply the necessary apostrophes. Remember that possessive pronouns are never written with apostrophes—*yours, hers, its, ours, theirs*. If no apostrophes are required, write *None*.

Eleanors theme was more original than either Pats or hers.

3082

3083

118

for

An **indirect object**—if one is present—always comes *before* the **direct object,** and the word *to* or *for* is understood but never used.

> a. **I offered** *Frank* **my ticket.**
> b. **I offered my ticket to** *Frank.*

Is *Frank* an indirect object in sentence *a* or *b*? _____

119

---

satisfied, or we

388

My sister can play several instruments. Her favorite is the violin.

_____

389

---

notices

658

Several of Don's friends play college football. *He went to high school with them.*

The pronoun *them* is the object of the preposition *with.*

Underline the clause signal you would put in place of *them* in changing the italicized sentence to an adjective clause:

which   whose   whom   who

659

---

adverb

928

We can sometimes combine two sentences by changing one sentence to an infinitive phrase.

Larry gave a cough. (*This was*) *to prove that he was sick.*
Larry gave a cough *to prove that he was sick.*

To change the italicized sentence to an infinitive phrase, we drop the words before the _____.

929

---

b

1198

No sooner **had we sat down to eat** *than* **company arrived.**

The words *no sooner* must be followed later in the sentence by the word _____.

1199

---

b

1468

Continue to circle the letter of the complete sentence:

a. **Which was Mr. Egan's way of getting us to read a book.**
b. **This was Mr. Egan's way of getting us to read a book.**

1469

a

1738

a. **At the time of Clem's birth, his father was a bandleader.**
b. **Clem's father was a bandleader at the time of his birth.**

1739

---

spots

2007

There is no stamp on this letter.

If you changed the noun **stamp** to **stamps,** you would need to change the verb **is** to _____.

2008

Yes

2276

PAST: I *finished* **my work when Jim arrived.**
PAST PERFECT: I *had finished* **my work when Jim arrived.**

Do both sentences have the same meaning? (*Yes, No*)

2277

Whom

2545

To (*who, whom*) **can small nations appeal for protection?**

2546

---

an introductory

2814

If there is a comma *after* a series, it is not used because of the series but for another reason.

For better schools, better roads, and clean government, cast your vote for Mrs. Henshaw.

The comma after **government** is used because it follows an introductory (*phrase, clause*) which includes a series.

2815

Eleanor's, Pat's

3083

Both suspects fingerprints were in the police departments files.

(*Note:* The fingerprints belong to two **suspects;** the files belong to one police **department.** Place your apostrophes to show this.)

3084

a	An indirect object tells *to whom* or *for whom* by its position alone—by coming *before* the direct object. A noun or pronoun used with *to* or *for* is never an indirect object.
	a. **Jan found a better job for her** *friend.*
	b. **Jan found her** *friend* **a better job.**
119	Is *friend* an indirect object in sentence *a* or *b*? _____ 120

instruments, but her	**Shall I write a new theme? Shall I revise the old one?**
	_____
	(*Note:* Because these sentences are questions, this problem is slightly different. Besides omitting the second subject, you will also need to omit the helping verb **shall.**)
389	390

whom	**Several of Don's friends play college football.** *He went to*
	whom
	high school with ~~them.~~
	We choose *whom* rather than *who* because it is the object of the preposition _____.
659	660

infinitive	Change the italicized sentence to an infinitive phrase:
	Wendy touched the flowers. *She wanted to see if they were real.*
	_____
	_____
929	930

than	a. **When I last saw Ben, he was looking for a job.**
	b. **When the picnic table was set, it began to rain.**
	Which of the above sentences could best be put into the "no sooner . . . than" arrangement because the two events occurred at about the same time? _____
1199	1200

b	a. **Virginia Woolf was a fine writer.**
	b. **Virginia Woolf, one of the finest writers of English literature.**
1469	1470

a 1739	a. **Whenever Dad discusses politics with Mr. Hart, he gets very excited.** b. **Dad gets very excited whenever he discusses politics with Mr. Hart.** 1740
are 2008	In sentences that begin with **There is, There are,** or **Here is, Here are,** don't choose your verb until you look ahead to see whether a singular or a plural subject is coming. **There . . . several ways of making frosting.** Before we supply **is** or **are** in this sentence, we must look ahead to the subject _____. 2009
No 2277	a. I *finished* **my work when Jim arrived.** b. I *had finished* **my work when Jim arrived.** In which sentence was your work already completed at the time of Jim's arrival? _____ 2278
whom 2546	Lesson **71** **A Number of Pronoun Problems** [Frames 2548–2586]
phrase 2815	Although it's not wrong to omit the comma between the last two items of a series, many writers prefer to use this comma —especially in formal writing. a. **Gas, electricity, and water are included in the rent.** b. **Gas, electricity and water are included in the rent.** Are both sentences punctuated correctly? (*Yes, No*) 2816
suspects' department's 3084	**The girls study hall is right next to the boys.** 3085

a. **This machine will save much time.**
b. **This machine will save the company much time.**

The noun **time** is the direct object in both sentences. Which sentence also contains an indirect object? _____

121

Sometimes we want the balanced effect of a compound sentence even though a compound predicate would express our meaning in fewer words.

a. **Fashions come and fashions go.**
b. **Fashions come and go.**

Which sentence gives a more balanced effect? _____

391

Several of Don's friends play college football. *He went to*
                                    whom
high school with ~~them.~~

After we move *with whom* to the front of the clause, we should insert it in the sentence after the word (*friends, football*), which it modifies.

661

Wendy touched
the flowers to
see if they
were real.

930

Change the italicized sentence to an infinitive phrase:

Vic's dad set the clock ahead. *This was to prevent Vic from being late.*

_____

_____

931

---

a. **When the picnic table was set, it began to rain.**
b. *No sooner* **was the picnic table set** *than* **it began to rain.**

Which sentence is more novel and forceful? _____

1201

---

a. **We consider spinach good for our health.**
b. **Because we consider spinach good for our health.**

1471

b 1740	Sentences that report someone's remark often leave the reader guessing as to which person the pronoun *he* or *she* means. **The doctor told Dad that** *he* **needed a vacation.** This sentence is ambiguous because *he* could mean either the _____ or _____. 1741
ways 2009	Underline the correct verb: **There** (*is, are*) **several ways of making frosting.** 2010
b 2278	a. **We** *had* **just** *finished* **scrubbing the floor when Larry came in with his muddy shoes.** b. **We just** *finished* **scrubbing the floor when Larry came in with his muddy shoes.** Which sentence emphasizes the fact that the first action had been completed when the second action occurred? _____ 2279
	PRONOUNS IN COMPARISONS When we use the word **than** or **as** to make a comparison, we generally shorten our sentence by omitting one or more unnecessary words. **The Smiths have a larger house than we (have).** The omitted word in this sentence is _____. 2548
Yes 2816	Do not omit the comma between the last two items of a series if there is any chance of misunderstanding. **We served** *coffee, salad, cheese* **and** *egg* **sandwiches.** Can you be sure whether one or two kinds of sandwiches were served? (*Yes, No*) 2817
girls' boys' 3085	**His mother buys and sells all kinds of stamps and coins.** 3086

Father made the boys some sandwiches.

b

The direct object is _____.

The indirect object is _____.

121

122

---

a. **He couldn't eat and couldn't sleep.**
b. **He couldn't eat, and he couldn't sleep.**

a

Which sentence is more effective because of the repetition

of the subject? _____

391

392

---

a. **Several of Don's friends play college football** *with whom*
   he went to high school.
b. **Several of Don's friends** *with whom he went to high*
   school **play college football.**

friends

In which sentence is the clause properly placed? _____

661

662

After changing the italicized sentence to an infinitive phrase,
insert it in the sentence next to the noun it modifies:

Vic's dad set
the clock ahead
to prevent Vic
from being late.

Johnny's ambition was typical of a child. *It was to be-*
come a firefighter. _____

_____

931

932

---

a. *No sooner* **was the picnic table set** *than* **it began to rain.**
b. **The picnic table was** *no sooner* **set** *than* **it began to rain.**

b

In which arrangement does the subject **table** come between

the two parts of the verb? _____

1201

1202

---

a. **In time to save the firefighter from being crushed by the**
   toppling wall.
b. **She shouted her warning in time to save the firefighter.**

a

1471

1472

doctor, Dad 1741	**The doctor told Dad that _he_ needed a vacation.** Usually the only way to eliminate the ambiguity in a sentence like this is to use a direct quotation. **The doctor told Dad, "You need a vacation."** This means that (_the doctor, Dad_) needs a vacation. 1742
are 2010	a. **Here . . . the key to the car.** b. **Here . . . the keys to the car.** Which sentence requires the plural verb **are?** _____ 2011
a 2279	Here is a sentence with an "if" clause that states a condition under which something could have or would have happened: **If I _had seen_ the light, I _would have stopped._** The past perfect verb is used in the part of the sentence that states the (_condition, result_). 2280
have 2548	**Mr. Metz gave Fred just as good a grade as (he gave) me.** The omitted words in this sentence are _____. 2549
No 2817	**These sports shoes are available in** _green, red, brown_ **and** _white._ If four different kinds of shoes are available, would you insert a comma after _brown?_ (_Yes, No_) 2818
None 3086	**These childrens good manners reflect their parents training at home.** (_Note:_ This is a high-error frame because **children** is one of those few plural nouns that do not end in **s.** Be sure to place the apostrophe after the part of the noun that names the owners.) 3087

(direct object) sandwiches (indirect object) boys 122	A sentence in **Pattern II** always contains an action verb and its direct object. Does it always contain an indirect object? (*Yes, No*) 123
b 392	Except where we wish to produce a special effect, we should try to save words by using a compound (*sentence, predicate*). 393
b 662	**A local firm got the order.** *Its bid was the lowest.* Underline the clause signal you would put in place of the possessive pronoun *Its* in changing the italicized sentence to an adjective clause: **who whose that which** 663
Johnny's ambition to become a firefighter was typical of a child. 932	**Jerry pounded the table once again.** *This showed that he was his own boss.* **Jerry pounded the table once again** *to show that he was his own boss.* We changed the italicized sentence to an infinitive phrase by changing the verb *showed* to the infinitive _____. 933
a 1202	In a "no sooner . . . than" sentence, we usually need a helping verb such as **was, did,** or **had** with the main verb. a. **The two boys met, and they began to argue.** b. **No sooner had the two boys met than they began to argue.** The verb **met** in sentence *a* becomes _____ in *b*. 1203
b 1472	a. **This fact surprised even our closest friends.** b. **A fact that surprised even our closest friends.** 1473

Dad 1742	**The doctor told Dad, "You need a vacation."** If it were the doctor who needed the vacation, we would change **You** to _____. 1743
b 2011	Since **There's** and **Here's** are contractions of **There is** and **Here is,** they should be used only before singular subjects. a. . . . **no battery in this flashlight.** b. . . . **no batteries in this flashlight.** In which sentence would **There's** be correct? _____ 2012
condition 2280	**If I** _had seen_ **the light, I** _would have_ **stopped.** Notice that _would have_ is used in only one part of the sentence—the part that shows what _would have_ happened if an earlier action (past perfect) _had_ occurred. Are the words _would have_ used in the "if" clause? (_Yes, No_) 2281
he gave 2549	When a pronoun follows the word **than** or **as** in a comparison, think of the missing words and you will have no trouble in deciding which case of the pronoun to use. **Don can print much better than** _I_ **(can print).** We use the nominative pronoun _I_ because it is the subject of the omitted verb _____ _____. 2550
Yes 2818	Do not use commas when all the items in a series are connected by _and, or,_ or _nor._ **The heat** _and_ **the noise** _and_ **the confusion were too much for my mother.** Does this sentence require any commas? (_Yes, No_) 2819
children's parents' 3087	**Mr. Barrys daughter knows all the players batting averages.** 3088

In this and the following frames, $S = $ *Subject*, $V = $ *Verb*, $IO = $ *Indirect Object*, $DO = $ *Direct Object*.

Fill in the missing word:

This bakery makes the best doughnuts in town.

S	V	DO
bakery	**makes**	_____

124

---

predicate

393

Lesson **11** The Semicolon as a Connector

[Frames 395–437]

---

whose

663

whose
A local firm got the order. ~~Its~~ *bid was the lowest.*

a. **A local firm** *whose bid was the lowest* **got the order.**
b. **A local firm got the order** *whose bid was the lowest.*

In which sentence is the clause properly placed? _____

664

---

to show

933

Change the italicized sentence to an infinitive phrase:

We boiled our drinking water. *This killed all the bacteria.*

_____

_____

934

---

had met

1203

a. **When I sit down to study, someone usually disturbs me.**
b. **No sooner do I sit down to study than someone usually disturbs me.**

The verb **sit** in sentence *a* becomes _____ in

sentence *b*.

1204

---

a

1473

a. **We stood at the door and waited for the store to open.**
b. **Standing at the door and waiting for the store to open.**

1474

I	**Paula told Doris that _her_ friend was waiting.**
	Complete this sentence with a direct quotation to show that _Doris's_ friend was waiting:
	Paula told Doris, "_____
	_____**."**
1743	1744

	a. . . . **some scraps for your dog.**
a	b. . . . **a bone for your dog.**
	In which sentence would **Here's** be correct? _____
2012	2013

	Be sure not to use the words _would have_ in the "if" clause.
No	a. **If I** _would have_ **seen the light, I** _would have_ **stopped.**
	b. **If I** _had seen_ **the light, I** _would have_ **stopped.**
	Which sentence is correct? _____
2281	2282

	The noise didn't bother Dad as much as (it bothered) _her_.
can print	We use the objective pronoun _her_ because it is the direct
	object of the omitted verb _____.
2550	2551

	Books about space exploration, sports, _or_ **animals interest many readers.**
No	If you inserted another _or_ before **sports,** would this sentence require any commas? (_Yes, No_)
2819	2820

Mr. Barry's	**Peoples ages are nobodys business but their own.**
players'	(Do you recall that a few irregular plural nouns do not end in **s?**)
3088	3089

Anyone can show you the way to the bridge.

Fill in the missing words:

S	V	IO	DO
Anyone	_____ _____	_____	**way.**

DO
doughnuts

124

125

We have seen that two *similar* or *related* sentences that are *equal in importance* can be combined into a compound sentence by using the _____ **and,** **but,** or **or.**

395

A local firm *whose bid was the lowest* **got the order.**

a

The adjective clause is properly placed because it comes after the noun _____, which it modifies.

664

665

Change the italicized sentence to an infinitive phrase:

Always keep receipts. *They will prove that you have paid your bills.*

We boiled our drinking water to kill all the bacteria.

_____

_____

934

935

Put this sentence into the "no sooner . . . than" arrangement. Count your sentence right whether the *no sooner* comes at the beginning of your sentence or later.

When I saw him, I recognized him.

do sit

_____

_____

1204

1205

---

a

a. **Each family taking a favorite dish to the church supper.**
b. **Each family took a favorite dish to the church supper.**

1474

1475

Paula told Doris that *her* friend was waiting.

Complete this sentence with a direct quotation to show that *Paula's* friend was waiting:

Paula told Doris, "_____

_____.**"**

1745

"Your friend is waiting."

1744

The problem of subject-verb agreement is the same when a sentence begins with **There was, There were, There has been, There have been.**

Underline the correct verb:

There (*was*, *were*) sixteen lighted candles on the cake.

2014

---

b

2013

---

a. **If it had rained another ten minutes, the game would have been called off.**
b. **If it would have rained another ten minutes, the game would have been called off.**

Which sentence is correct? _____

2283

---

b

2282

Sometimes the meaning of a sentence depends on whether we use the nominative or objective case of a pronoun.

Hank owes Roy more money than *I* (owe him).
Hank owes Roy more money than (he owes) *me*.

Do the sentence with *I* and the sentence with *me* have the same meaning? (*Yes, No*)

2552

---

bothered

2551

---

a. **Jerry couldn't decide whether to add, or subtract, or multiply the numbers.**
b. **Jerry couldn't decide whether to add or subtract or multiply the numbers.**

Which sentence is correct? _____

2821

No

2820

Sudden starts and stops wear out tires and brakes very rapidly.

3090

People's
nobody's

3089

V can show IO you 125	Franklin's experiments with electricity brought him international fame. Fill in the missing words: | S	V	IO	DO
---	---	---	---
experiments	brought	_____	_____	 126
conjunction 395	Another useful device for holding two sentences together is the semicolon (;). In many compound sentences, we can use a semicolon in place of the conjunction. **The ceiling was low,** *and* **all planes were grounded.** **The ceiling was low; all planes were grounded.** The semicolon replaces the conjunction _____. 396
firm 665	We can often strengthen a weak compound sentence by changing one of the statements to an adjective clause. **We have a neighbor, and she has her own private plane.** **We have a neighbor** *who has her own private plane.* The two facts are brought into closer relationship by the (*compound, complex*) sentence. 666
Always keep receipts to prove that you have paid your bills. 935	*Don't nag a child to practice.* **It does no good.** *To nag a child to practice* **does no good.** Here we have replaced the words *Don't nag* with the infinitive _____. 936
No sooner had I seen him than I recognized him. *or* I no sooner saw him than I recognized him. 1205	Continue to follow the directions for the previous frame. (*Note:* Be sure to follow the "no sooner" construction with "than," not "when.") **When the concert started, the lights went out.** _____ _____ 1206
b 1475	In this and the following frames, label each item according to the following key: S = *Correct Sentence;* F = *Fragment;* R-S = *Run-on Sentence* **Although cotton is still an important crop in the South.** ____ 1476

"My friend is waiting."

1745

The cashier told the clerk that *she* had made a mistake.

Rewrite this sentence with a direct quotation to show that the *clerk* had made a mistake:

_____

_____

1746

---

were

2014

Underline the correct verb:

There (*has, have*) **been too many accidents lately.**

2015

---

a

2283

Sometimes the "if" clause comes at the end of the sentence.

Underline the correct verb:

It is very likely that they would have struck oil if only they (*had drilled, would have drilled*) **twenty feet more.**

2284

No

2552

---

a. **Sue wrote Bob more often than** *I.*
b. **Sue wrote Bob more often than** *me.*

Each of the above sentences has a different meaning.

Which sentence means that Sue wrote to Bob more often

than she wrote to you? _____

2553

---

b

2821

Use a comma between two adjectives—even though they are not a series—when they modify the same noun and are not connected by a conjunction.

Sanding rust off a car is a *messy* **and** *tiresome* **job.**

If you omitted the conjunction **and,** would you insert a comma after the adjective *messy*? (*Yes, No*)

2822

None

3090

Their guests cars were blocking the Donaldsons driveway.

(*Note:* The cars belong to the **guests;** the driveway belongs to all the **Donaldsons.**)

3091

IO
him
DO
fame

126

The editor gave a better title to my article.

Fill in the missing words:

S	V	DO
editor	gave	_____

127

---

and

396

The ceiling was low; all planes were grounded.

After the semicolon, the compound sentence continues with a (*small, capital*) letter.

397

---

complex

666

In this and the following frames, convert each *compound* sentence into a *complex* sentence by changing the italicized sentence to an adjective clause:

We parked next to a fireplug, and *nobody had noticed it.*

_____

_____

667

To nag

936

Change the italicized sentence to an infinitive phrase:

Don't start eating before your host. **It is bad manners.**

_____

_____

937

The concert
had no sooner
started (No sooner
had the concert
started) than the
lights went out.

1206

We got to the corner, and the engine stopped.

_____

_____

1207

F

1476

S = Correct Sentence; F = Fragment;
R-S = Run-on Sentence

You can't run away from a problem, it has a way of trailing you. _____

1477

The cashier told the clerk (*or* said to the clerk), "You have made a mistake." 1746	Clear up the meaning of this sentence by substituting a noun for the ambiguous pronoun: **If the lids won't fit the jars, throw *them* out.** **If the lids won't fit the jars, _____** **_____.** 1747
have 2015	In interrogative sentences, too, the verb (or part of the verb) usually precedes the subject, and we must look ahead to see whether a singular or a plural subject is coming. a. **Where . . . your father? How . . . your father?** b. **Where . . . your parents? How . . . your parents?** Which sentences require the plural verb **are?** _____ 2016
had drilled 2284	Underline the correct verb: **I'm certain Frank would not have bought the car if he (*would have known, had known*) the reputation of the dealer.** 2285
b 2553	**Sue wrote Bob more often than (she wrote) *me*.** The objective pronoun *me* is the direct object of the omitted verb _____. 2554
Yes 2822	Insert the necessary comma: **There are long dreary stretches of desert in the West.** 2823
guests' Donaldsons' 3091	**Todays paper tells about these girls experience in Sundays blizzard.** (*Note:* Look for three possessive nouns.) 3092

DO title 127	**The editor gave my article a better title.** Fill in the missing words: S V IO DO editor gave _____ _____ 128
small 397	**The committee discussed the problem,** *but* **they reached no conclusions.** **The committee discussed the problem; they reached no conclusions.** The semicolon replaces the conjunction _____. 398
We parked next to a fireplug, which (that) nobody had noticed. 667	**Bill Cosby planned the puppet show, and** *he is very fond of children.* (Be sure to put the clause after the word it modifies.) _____ _____ 668

To start eating before your host is bad manners.
 	
937
	A sentence with an infinitive phrase as subject may sound stiff and formal. We can move the phrase to the end of the sentence, putting an introductory *It* in its place.
	
	    a. *To change one's mind* **is no crime.**
	    b. **It is no crime** *to change one's mind.*
	
	Which sentence sounds more informal? _____ 938

No sooner had we got to the corner than the engine stopped. 1207	**When I reached the dentist's office, my tooth stopped aching.** _____ _____ 1208
R-S 1477	*S = Correct Sentence; F = Fragment; R-S = Run-on Sentence* **We hunted for night crawlers, using our pocket flashlights.** _____ 1478

throw the lids (the jars) out 1747	Clear up the meaning of this sentence by substituting a noun for the ambiguous pronoun: **When Fred saw Bruce, *he* was in uniform.** _____ 1748
b 2016	Underline the correct verb: **How much (*is, are*) the tickets?** 2017
had known 2285	Supply the proper tense of the verb **see:** **You too would have bought the dress if you** _____ _____ **it.** 2286
wrote 2554	a. **Sue wrote Bob more often than *I*.** b. **Sue wrote Bob more often than *me*.** Which sentence means that Sue wrote Bob more often than you wrote Bob? _____ 2555
long, dreary 2823	Insert the necessary comma: **Their smiling friendly faces gave me confidence.** 2824
Today's girls' Sunday's 3092	**Ladies fashions change more frequently than mens.** 3093

---

but

398

The deadline was rapidly approaching; we worked furiously to meet it.

In this sentence, the semicolon replaces the conjunction

_____.

399

Bill Cosby, who
is very fond
of children,
planned the
puppet show.
668

Mrs. Won owned a beagle, and *she was very much attached to it.* (Try *to which.*)

_____

_____

669

---

b

938

To beat a dead horse **does no good.**

Rewrite this sentence, moving the infinitive phrase to the end of the sentence and putting an introductory *It* in its place.

_____

_____

939

No sooner had
I reached the
dentist's office
than my tooth
stopped aching.
1208

We raised the price, and our sales dropped.

_____

_____

1209

S

1478

S, F, or R-S?

Never paying the least attention to how he dressed or what people thought of him. _____

1479

Bruce (*or* Fred)

1748

Clear up the meaning of this sentence by substituting a noun for the ambiguous pronoun:

If there are any misspelled words in your themes, copy *them* **correctly.**

If there are any misspelled words in your themes, _____

_____.

1749

---

are

2017

Underline the correct verb:

(*Has, Have*) **there been any complaints about the service?**

2018

---

had seen

2286

The future perfect tense is formed by combining **will have** or **shall have** with the past participle of a verb.

    a. **will save**   b. **had saved**   c. **will have saved**

Which verb is in the future perfect tense? _____

2287

---

a

2555

Sue wrote Bob more often than *I* **(wrote Bob).**

The nominative pronoun *I* is the subject of the omitted verb _____.

2556

---

smiling, friendly

2824

Do not put a comma after the last adjective in a series of adjectives. Put commas only *between* the adjectives, just as you do in any other series.

    Irish terriers are friendly, intelligent, and obedient dogs.

Should a comma be inserted after the adjective **obedient**? (*Yes, No*)

2825

Ladies'
men's

3093

Lesson **86**   **Apostrophes for Contractions and Special Plurals**

[Frames 3095–3129]

Suppose that you wish to point out that your friend Henry is happy. You would not be likely to say—

Happy Henry
Henry happy

Is either of these pairs of words a sentence? (*Yes, No*)

130

---

and

399

I could see them; they couldn't see me.

In this sentence, the semicolon replaces the conjunction

_____.

400

Mrs. Won owned a beagle to which she was very much attached.

669

I have a friend, and *her mother is a judge.*

_____

_____

670

It does no good to beat a dead horse.

939

In this and the following frames, eliminate the **and** by changing the italicized statement to an infinitive phrase:

I have a job, and *I must finish it before dinner.*

_____

_____

940

No sooner had we raised the price than our sales dropped.

1209

2. The "not only . . . but also" device:

a. **Jimmy cooked the dinner and washed the dishes.**
b. *Not only* **did Jimmy cook the dinner,** *but* **he** *also* **washed the dishes.**

Which sentence is more forceful in emphasizing how much work Jimmy did? _____

1210

F

1479

S, F, or R-S?

The only one in our family who plays a musical instrument.

_____

1480

Rewrite each sentence so that the italicized pronoun can mean only the underlined word. Do not merely substitute nouns for pronouns. (Count any answer correct if the antecedent of the pronoun is entirely clear.)

If the <u>blouse</u> doesn't match the skirt, you can return *it*.

_____

1750

Have

2018

The nouns **kind, sort,** and **type** are singular and require singular verbs.

The other kind of cookies *is* easier to make.

We use the singular verb *is* because the subject in the above sentence is (*kind, cookies*).

2019

---

c (will have saved)

2287

Use the future perfect tense for an action that *will have been completed* at a specified future time.

By tomorrow night, this car *will have traveled* one hundred thousand miles.

What is the specified future time at which the action will have been completed? _____

2288

---

wrote

2556

Underline the correct pronoun:

Mick is jealous because Dad praises Boyd more than (*he, him*).

2557

No

2825

Insert the necessary commas:

The company needs an honest reliable and experienced salesman with a thorough understanding of cars and people.

2826

As a short cut, we frequently run two separate words together by omitting one or more letters; for example, **we've** (*we have*), **doesn't** (*does not*).

These two-in-one words are called **contractions.**

Let's is a contraction of the two words _____ _____.

3095

No

130

---

a. **Happy Henry**
b. **Henry happy**
c. **Henry is happy.**

Which one of these groups of words is a sentence? _____

131

---

but

400

The bottle should be tightly closed; the perfume will evapo-rate.

In this sentence, the semicolon replaces the conjunction

_____.

401

I have a friend
whose mother is
a judge.

670

Some friends arrived suddenly, and *we were not expecting them.* (Be sure to put the clause after the word it modifies.)

_____

_____

671

I have a job
to finish
before dinner.

940

We sent out cards, and *these reminded members of the meeting.*

_____

_____

941

---

b

1210

---

a. *Not only* **did Jimmy cook the dinner,** *but* **he** *also* **washed the dishes.**
b. **Jimmy** *not only* **cooked the dinner,** *but* **he** *also* **washed the dishes.**

In which sentence is the subject **Jimmy** put between two parts of the verb? _____

1211

F

1480

S, F, or *R-S?*
I cleaned and adjusted all the spark plugs, then I replaced them in the motor.

_____

1481

You can return the blouse (the skirt) if it doesn't match the skirt (the blouse). 1750	**Whenever Miss Ross talks to Sally,** *she* **seems embarrassed.** _____ _____ (*Note:* **She** will become *her* in your revised sentence.) 1751
kind 2019	Underline the correct verb: **The newer type of automatic machines** (*washes, wash*) **the clothes faster.** 2020
(By) tomorrow night 2288	a. **When Mother unwraps the gift, she** *will have discovered* **who sent it.** b. **After I buy gas, I** *shall have spent* **my last cent.** In which sentence is the future perfect tense correctly used because the action will have been completed at a specified future time? _____ 2289
him 2557	Underline the correct pronoun: **Since Jack always feeds the dog, it obeys him better than** (*me, I*). 2558
honest, reliable(,) 2826	Sometimes an adjective is used so commonly with a noun that we think of it as part of the noun—for example, *old man, little boy, gold watch, fresh air, wild animal.* a. **gold watch**　　　　**fur coat**　　　　**brick house** b. **expensive watch**　　**worn-out coat**　　**comfortable house** We think of the adjectives as part of the nouns after (*a, b*). 2827
Let us 3095	Put an apostrophe in place of the omitted letter or letters in a contraction. 　　a. **it** ̶i̶s = **it's**　　　　　d. **we** ̶w̶i̶l̶l̶ = **we'll** 　　b. **who** ̶i̶s = **who's**　　　e. **I** ̶h̶a̶v̶e = **I've** 　　c. **I** ̶w̶o̶u̶l̶d̶ = **I'd**　　　f. **you** ̶a̶r̶e = **you're** In which of the above contractions does the apostrophe take the place of the largest number of letters? _____　　3096

c

131

a. **Henry happy**
b. **Henry is happy.**

The adjective **happy** by itself cannot make a statement about **Henry.**

We change *a* to a sentence by adding the verb _____.

132

---

or

401

A semicolon can also take the place of **because,** which is not a regular conjunction such as **and, but,** or **or.**

a. **Doris had made up her mind; nothing could change it.**
b. **Virginia didn't vote; she couldn't make up her mind.**

In which sentence does the semicolon take the place of

because? _____

402

Some friends whom (that) we were not expecting arrived suddenly.
671

The teacher asked a question, and *nobody could answer it.*

_____

_____

672

We sent out cards to remind members of the meeting.
941

The city issued a request, and *it was to refrain from wasting water.*

_____

_____

942

---

a

1211

The food was expensive and poor.

Supply the missing words to complete the "not only . . . but also" device:

Not only _____,

but _____.

(Some variation in the wording is allowable.)

1212

R-S

1481

S, F, or R-S?

While he was looking for his lost nickel, Harvey found a quarter. _____

1482

Sally seems
embarrassed
whenever Miss
Ross talks
to her.

1751

When Fred saw Bruce, *he* **was in uniform.**

(*Note: He* will become *him* in your revised sentence.)

1752

---

washes

2020

Because the nouns **kind, sort,** and **type** are singular, use the singular adjectives **this** and **that** (not the plural adjectives **these** and **those**) to point them out.

    a. **This kind of berries is better for shipping.**
    b. **These kind of berries are better for shipping.**

Which sentence is correct—*a* or *b?* _____

2021

---

b

2289

Underline the correct verb:

By next week, I (*shall save, shall have saved*) **enough money for a vacation.**

2290

---

me

2558

PRONOUNS AS APPOSITIVES

Pronouns are frequently used as appositives; that is, they are set after nouns to explain more precisely to whom the nouns refer.

Underline the pronoun used as an appositive:

    Both players, Greg and he, were penalized.

2559

---

a

2827

Do not use a comma between two adjectives when you think of the second adjective as part of the noun it modifies.

      The tiger is a ferocious *wild animal.*

We do not use a comma between the adjectives *ferocious* and *wild* because we think of the adjective *wild* as part of the noun _____.

2828

---

c *or* I'd

3096

The adverb **not,** shortened to **n't,** is part of many contractions.

isn't	**don't**	**hasn't**	**couldn't**
aren't	**doesn't**	**wasn't**	**shouldn't**

The apostrophe always comes between the **n** and the **t** because it takes the place of the missing letter _____.

3097

Henry happy
Henry is happy.

The verb **is** helps to turn the adjective **happy** into a statement about the subject _____.

is

132

133

---

a. **The child fell asleep; she was tired out from playing.**
b. **We listened very carefully; we could hear nothing.**

In which sentence does the semicolon take the place of *because?* _____

b

402

403

The teacher asked a question that (which) nobody could answer.

672

Someone made a rude remark, and *there was no excuse for it.* (Try *for which.*)

_____

_____

673

The city issued a request to refrain from wasting water.

942

We are planning a pageant, and *it will dramatize the history of our town.*

_____

_____

943

(Not only) was the food expensive, (but) it was also poor.

1212

The food was expensive and poor.

This sentence can be changed to the "not only . . . but also" arrangement in still another way. Supply the missing words:

The food _____

but _____ **poor.**

1213

S

1482

S, F, or R-S?

The dodo, a large, clumsy bird that was unable to fly. _____

1483

Bruce was in uniform when Fred saw him. 1752	**My aunt heard <u>Vikki Carr</u> sing when *she* was a child.** _____ _____ 1753
a 2021	Underline the correct words: (*This, These*) **sort** (*is, are*) **much harder to grow.** 2022
shall have saved 2290	In this and the following frames, underline the verb whose tense expresses the time relationship in the sentence more accurately: **Lincoln felt that his speech at Gettysburg** (*had been, was*) **a failure.** 2291
he 2559	When you use a pair of pronouns (or a noun and a pronoun) as appositives after a noun, use the same pronouns that you would use if you omitted the noun they explain. Underline the correct pronoun: ~~Two girls,~~ **Diane and** (*she, her*)**, made all the posters.** 2560
animal 2828	a. **All of us respected this dignified old man.** b. **All of us respected this dignified elderly man.** In which sentence would you insert a comma after the adjective **dignified?** _____ 2829
o 3097	a. **is'nt** **does'nt** **was'nt** **should'nt** b. **isn't** **doesn't** **wasn't** **shouldn't** The apostrophes are correctly placed in group (*a, b*). 3098

Henry

133

---

a. **Henry washed the car.**
b. **Henry is happy.**

Which sentence does *not* contain an *action* verb? _____

134

---

a

403

---

a. **Few people attended the game because of the bad weather.**
b. **Paula didn't worry because she was well-prepared for the test.**

In which sentence could a semicolon take the place of **because?** _____

404

Someone made
a rude remark
for which there
was no excuse.

673

My sister works for Dr. Mack, and *his office is downtown.*

_____

_____

674

We are planning
a pageant to
dramatize the
history of
our town.

943

Lesson **25** Subordination by Appositives

[Frames 945–984]

(The food)
was not only
expensive (but)
also poor.

1213

---

a. **The food was** *not only* **expensive** *but also* **poor.**
b. **The food was** *not only* **expensive** *but* **poor.**

Both sentences are correct.

In which sentence do we omit the word *also* from our device?

_____

1214

F

1483

S, F, or *R-S?*

We had been eating sweets, therefore we had no appetite for dinner. _____

1484

When Vikki Carr
was a child,
my aunt heard
her sing.

1753

If you use high-grade oil in your <u>motor</u>, *it* **will last longer.**

_____

_____

1754

This, is

2022

Underline the correct words:

   (*That, Those*) **type** (*seems, seem*) **sturdier to me.**

2023

---

had been

2291

The fire inspector eventually found the short circuit that (*had caused, caused*) **the fire.**

2292

---

she

2560

Underline the correct pronoun:

All the posters were made by ~~two girls,~~ **Diane and** (*she, her*)**.**

2561

---

b

2829

In this and the following frames, insert the necessary commas. If no commas are required, write *None*.

The child's shiny hair large eyes and wide smile make her an artist's dream.

2830

---

b

3098

Insert the needed apostrophes:

   It wouldnt burn because it wasnt dry enough.

3099

Henry is happy.

The verb **is** does not show action—like *washed* or *fixed*. What does it do?

The verb **is** ties up or *links* the adjective **happy** with the subject _____, which it *describes*.

135

We can combine two simple sentences into a compound sentence by using either a conjunction or a _____.

405

---

a. **The woman** *who owns the lot* **lives across the street.**
b. **The woman** *who lives across the street* **owns the lot.**

Which of the above sentences emphasizes where the woman lives—*a* or *b?* _____

675

Joseph Priestley discovered oxygen.

Because most people might not know who **Joseph Priestley** was, it would be well to add an explanation.

Joseph Priestley, *an English minister,* **discovered oxygen.**

The noun *minister* explains the noun _____

_____.

945

Put each sentence into the "not only . . . but also" arrangement, omitting the *also* if you wish. Count your answer right so long as the words *not only* and *but* are present.

Linda is a good student and a good athlete.

_____

_____

1215

S, F, or *R-S?*

Many settlers headed back to the East, discouraged by all the hardships of pioneer life. _____

1485

Your motor will last longer if you use high-grade oil in it. 1754	<u>Mom</u> doesn't like Diane to practice when *she* is tired. _____ _____ 1755

That, seems
 	
2023
	A noun that means a group or collection of persons or animals is called a **collective noun.**
	
	    a. **member, child, student, chairman, goat**
	    b. **team, family, class, audience, flock**
	
	Which group of words consists of collective nouns? ____
	
	2024

had caused 2292	**Mr. Dawson wrote an angry letter and then** (*tore, had torn*) **it up.** 2293
her 2561	Underline the correct pronouns: **The article mentioned only two players,** (*he, him*) **and** (*I, me*). 2562
hair, eyes(,) 2830	**Bob and Leslie came to the test without paper or pens or pencils.** 2831
wouldn't wasn't 3099	When you write contractions, don't change any letters in the original words. (The contractions *won't* for *will not* and *can't* for *cannot* are the exceptions.) Merely substitute an apostrophe for the letter or letters you omit. The contraction for **does not** is (*doesn't, dosen't*). 3100

Henry	**Henry was the chairman.** In this sentence, the verb **was** ties up or *links* the noun _____ with the subject **Henry**, which it *identifies.*
135	136

semicolon	When might we use a semicolon in preference to a conjunction? If there are too many *and*'s in a sentence, we may get rid of one by substituting a semicolon. **The patient asked for steak and potatoes, and the doctors and nurses were astonished.** How many **and**'s are there in this sentence? _____
405	406

a	**Ron's mother,** *who bandaged my arm,* **is a doctor.** Rewrite this sentence so as to emphasize the fact that Ron's mother *bandaged my arm* and to subordinate the fact that she is a *doctor.* _____ _____
675	676

Joseph Priestley	A noun or pronoun—often with modifiers—that is set after another noun or pronoun to explain it is called an **appositive.** **Joseph Priestley,** *an English minister,* **discovered oxygen.** The appositive is the noun _____.
945	946

Linda is not only a good student but (also) a good athlete. *or* **Not only is Linda . . . but (also) . . .**	Continue to follow the directions for the previous frame: **The article misspelled my name and gave a wrong age.** _____ _____
1215	1216

S	One of the following items is *not* correct: a. **Some drugs quicken the heartbeat, others slow it down.** b. **Some drugs quicken the heartbeat; others slow it down.** c. **Some drugs quicken the heartbeat, and others slow it down.** The run-on sentence is _____.
1485	1486

When Mom is tired, she doesn't like Diane to practice. 1755	**Vern couldn't notify Earl because** *he* **has no telephone.** _____ _____ (*Note:* Use an adjective clause beginning with *who*.) 1756

b
 	
2024
	A collective noun takes a singular verb when the group acts together *as a single unit;* a plural verb when the members of the group act *individually.*
	
	  a. **The class** *is* **now in the library.**
	  b. **The class** *are* **giving their talks on famous inventors.**
	
	We think of the class *as a single unit* in sentence (*a, b*).
	
	2025

tore 2293	**Fortunately, Mr. Dawson tore up the angry letter that he** (*wrote, had written*). 2294
him, me 2562	To decide between **we** and **us** in expressions like ''*we* (or *us*) fellows'' or ''*we* (or *us*) girls,'' omit the appositive *fellows* or *girls,* and you will see instantly which pronoun is right. Underline the correct pronoun: (*We, Us*) ~~boys~~ **can get our own lunch.** 2563
None 2831	**Tom Black Bull sat down on the sofa opened a book and began reading.** 2832
doesn't 3100	The contraction for **are not** is (*aren't, arn't*). 3101

chairman

136

Henry is happy.

Henry was the chairman.

A verb like **is** or **was** is called a **linking verb** because it *links* a noun, pronoun, or adjective that follows it with the

_____ of the sentence.   137

---

three

406

The patient asked for steak and potatoes, and the doctors and nurses were astonished.

To get rid of one of the three **and**'s, we can substitute a

semicolon for the **and** which follows the word _____.

407

Ron's mother, who is a doctor, bandaged my arm.

676

---

minister

946

Anna won the first prize, *a trip to Washington.*

The noun *trip* explains the noun _____.

947

The article not only misspelled my name but (also) gave a wrong age.

1216

Insulation saves fuel and keeps a house more comfortable.

_____

_____

1217

---

a

1486

Vern couldn't notify Earl, who has no telephone. 1756	**Mr. Brock said to <u>Dad</u> that _he_ needed more insurance.** _____ _____ 1757
a 2025	a. **The class _is_ now in the library.** b. **The class _are_ giving their talks on famous inventors.** We think of the members of the class as acting _individually_ in sentence (_a, b_). 2026
had written 2294	**Loren would probably have driven more carefully if Peggy** (_would have, had_) **suggested it.** 2295
We 2563	Underline the correct pronoun: **The man asked** (_we, us_) **fellows to push his car.** 2564
sofa, book(,) 2832	**It was a gray cold cheerless morning in February.** 2833
aren't 3101	The contraction for **were not** is (_weren't, were'nt_). 3102

subject 137	**Be** is by far the most common *linking verb*. Be sure that you can recognize its various forms. FORMS OF *BE*: **is, am, are—was, were, been** The crops . . . good. Which two forms of *be* could be used to link **good** with **crops** in the above sentence? _____, _____ 138
potatoes 407	**The weather was hot and sticky, and the boys and girls were listless.** To get rid of one of the three **and**'s, we can substitute a semicolon for the **and** which follows the word _____. 408

	And is a good word to use when you wish merely to *add* one idea to another equal idea.
	
	  a. **I recognized Jo, and she recognized me.**
	  b. **I recognized Jo, and I hadn't seen her for years.**
	
	In which sentence is **and** more appropriate—*a* or *b*? _____
	
	678

prize 947	**Anna won the first prize,** *a trip to Washington.* The appositive is the noun _____. 948
Insulation not only saves fuel but (also) keeps a house more comfortable. 1217	**Franklin was a great statesman and a distinguished scientist.** _____ _____ 1218

	The meaning of a sentence often depends on where we place adverbs such as *only, just, merely, almost, nearly,* and *even.*
	
	  a. **Steve** *only* **glanced at the advertisements.**
	  b. **Steve glanced** *only* **at the advertisements.**
	
	Which sentence means that Steve did not read the advertisements thoroughly? _____
	
	1488

Mr. Brock said to Dad, "You need more insurance."

1757

---

b

Underline the correct verb in each sentence:

a. **The class** (*is, are*) **now in the library.**
b. **The class** (*is, are*) **giving their talks on famous inventors.**

2026

2027

---

had

If we (*had urged, would have urged*) **him a little more, Rafael would have sung for us.**

2295

2296

---

us

Underline the correct pronouns:

The lifeguard had warned (*we, us*) **boys, but** (*we, us*) **boys wouldn't listen.**

2564

2565

---

gray, cold,

Grange went dodging and twisting and bucking through the Buckeye tackles.

2833

2834

---

weren't

Write in the contractions for the italicized words:

It *does not* (_____) **taste good when it is** *not*

(_____) **ripe.**

3102

3103

I . . . the first speaker.

Which two forms of *be* could be used to link **speaker** with **I**

in the above sentence? _____, _____

(any two)
are, were,
have been,
had been

138

139

---

sticky

408

The gold and the silver finally gave out, and many miners settled down and became farmers.

To get rid of one of the three **and**'s, we can substitute a

semicolon for the **and** which follows the word _____.

409

---

a

678

a. **I recognized Jo,** *and* **I hadn't seen her for years.**
b. **I recognized Jo** *although* **I hadn't seen her for years.**

Which word brings the two facts into closer relationship—

and or *although*? _____

679

---

trip

948

Both parties, the Republicans and the Democrats, favored the bill.

This sentence contains _____ appositives. (How many?)

949

Franklin was
not only a great
statesman but
(also) a
distinguished
scientist.

1218

Joan Baez wrote the words and composed the music.

_____

_____

1219

---

a

1488

a. **Steve** *only* **glanced at the advertisements.**
b. **Steve glanced** *only* **at the advertisements.**

Which sentence means that Steve paid no attention to the

news articles or editorials? _____

1489

When the same form of a word fits in two places in a sentence, we may avoid repetition by using it only once and taking it for granted in the other position.

You *have* **four and I** *have* **three.**

May we omit the second *have*? (*Yes, No*)

1759

---

a. is
b. are

2027

Underline the correct verb in each sentence:

a. **The team** (*has, have*) **not yet worn their new uniforms.**
b. **The team** (*has, have*) **won every game this season.**

2028

---

had urged

2296

By the time my sister Dorothy is ready for college, she (*will save, will have saved*) **a thousand dollars.**

2297

---

us, we

2565

a. **... girls can meet at my house.**
b. **All of ... girls can meet at my house.**

In which sentence would the objective pronoun **us** be correct? _____

2566

None

2834

Heavy drapes rugs and overstuffed furniture are giving way to simpler streamlined furnishings.

(*Note:* This sentence requires two commas with a third comma optional.)

2835

---

doesn't, isn't

3103

Write in the contractions for the italicized words:

Edward *did not* (_____) **come because he** *was not* (_____) **invited.**

3104

(any two)
am, was,
had been

139

We have seen that some *action verbs* make complete statements about their subjects and that others do not.

   a. **The engine started.**
   b. **The engine uses . . .**

In which sentence does the action verb make a complete statement? _____

140

---

out

409

If you have a good ear for the sound of sentences, you have noticed that a semicolon produces a quicker, brisker rhythm than a conjunction.

   a. **You need your school, and your school needs you.**
   b. **You need your school; your school needs you.**

Which sentence is more brisk and forceful? _____

410

---

although

679

   a. **His mother wasn't home. Luis started the dinner.**
   b. **Luis started the dinner. His mother finished it.**

Which pair of sentences would it be better to combine by **and** to form a compound sentence—*a* or *b?* _____

680

---

two

949

Both parties, the Republicans and the Democrats, favored the bill.

The two appositives are the words _____

and _____.

950

Joan Baez not only
wrote the words
but (also)
composed the
music.
1219

3. The "the more . . . the more" or "the more . . . the less" device:

      The more **you eat,** *the more* **you want.**

Does this sentence have any connecting word between the two word groups? (*Yes, No*)

1220

---

b

1489

   a. **Eng's Shop** *just* **repairs radios.**
   b. **Eng's Shop repairs** *just* **radios.**

Which sentence means that the shop repairs radios but not other appliances? _____

1490

Yes

1759

---

a. **You** *have* **four and I . . . three.**
b. **You** *have* **four and he . . . three.**

In which sentence would the verb *have* not fit in the blank space? _____

1760

---

a. have
b. has

2028

It is sometimes difficult to decide whether a group is acting as a single unit or as individuals. Whatever you decide, be sure to keep your pronoun consistent with the verb.

a. **The class was** (*singular*) **ready for their** (*plural*) **test.**
b. **The class was** (*singular*) **ready for its** (*singular*) **test.**

The pronoun is consistent with the verb in sentence (*a, b*).

2029

---

will have saved

2297

After I sell two more tickets, I (*shall sell, shall have sold*) **my quota for the game.**

2298

---

b

2566

A very common error is the expression "Let's you and I . . . ," which should be "Let's you and *me*. . . ."

Let's is a contraction of *Let us*. Since *us* is the object of the verb *Let,* the pronouns that explain whom we mean by the objective pronoun *us* should also be in the (*nominative, objective*) case.

2567

---

drapes, rugs(,)
simpler,

2835

After we planted the corn potatoes and cabbages we had little room for anything else.

2836

---

didn't, wasn't

3104

Write in the contractions for the italicized words:

Let us (_____) **see if** *they will* (_____) **help us.**

3105

a	However, a linking verb cannot by itself make a complete statement about its subject. Since the purpose of a *link* is to connect two things, a *linking verb* must be followed by a complement that it can link with the _____ of the sentence.
140	141

b	a. **You can sell your home; you can't sell rent receipts.** b. **You can sell your home, but you can't sell rent receipts.** Which sentence is more brisk and forceful? _____
410	411

b	**Luis started the dinner, and his mother finished it.** This is a good compound sentence because the **and** connects two *similar* ideas of (*equal, unequal*) importance.
680	681

Republicans Democrats	An appositive generally comes (*before, after*) the noun or pronoun it explains.
950	951

No	This sentence device is useful to show that as one thing increases or decreases, something else increases or decreases. *The more* **you eat,** *the more* **you want.** As your eating increases, your wanting (*increases, decreases*).
1220	1221

b	a. **Eng's Shop** *just* **repairs radios.** b. **Eng's Shop repairs** *just* **radios.** Which sentence means that the shop repairs radios but does not sell them? _____
1490	1491

WRONG: **You** *have* **four and he three.**

1760 — b

This sentence is wrong because with **You** we use *have*, but with **he** we need (*have*, *has*).

1761

2029 — b

Underline the correct words:

The audience (*was*, *were*) **rattling their programs.**

(Does the audience as a single unit rattle a single program?)

2030

---

shall have sold

2298

Lesson 64 Using Active Verbs for Directness

[Frames 2300–2334]

---

objective

2567

For the same reason that we say "Let *me*," we should also say, "Let's you and (*I*, *me*)."

2568

---

corn, potatoes(,)
cabbages,

2836

Mr. Stein has an anecdote to prove or disprove almost any political economic or educational theory.

(*Note:* This sentence requires one comma with a second comma optional.)

2837

Let's, they'll

3105

Do not confuse contractions with possessive pronouns which are pronounced the same.

CONTRACTIONS: **it's   you're   they're   who's**
POSSESSIVE PRONOUNS: **its   your   their   whose**

To show ownership you would choose one of the above words (*with*, *without*) an apostrophe.

3106

The paint was . . . (What?)

Was the paint wet, dry, or sticky?

subject

Until we add a word that the linking verb **was** can connect with the subject, the meaning of the sentence is (*complete, incomplete*).

141

142

---

a

a. **Clyde sat right in front of me, and we soon became close friends.**
b. **The brakes failed, and the car crashed into the truck.**

In which sentence is the action more exciting? _____

411

412

His mother wasn't home. Luis started the dinner.

Here the first sentence explains *why* about the second sentence.

equal

Which word would bring out this relationship more clearly—*and* (before **Luis**) or *because* (before **His**)? _____

681

682

The soprano, Camilla Williams, sang at the White House.
Camilla Williams, the soprano, sang at the White House.

after

Is the appositive the same in both sentences? (*Yes, No*)

951

952

The more **one learns,** *the less* **positive one becomes.**

increases

This means that as one's learning increases, one's positiveness (*increases, decreases*).

1221

1222

Wherever misunderstanding might occur, place the adverb *only, just, merely, almost, nearly,* or *even* as near as possible to the word it modifies and generally before it.

a

We __(a)__ wash __(b)__ the towels.

To mean that you wash the towels, but not the sheets or pillowcases, put the word *only* in space (*a, b*).

1491

1492

has	a. **You** *have* **four and he three.**
	b. **You** *have* **four and I three.**
	Which sentence is correct? _____
1761	1762

were	Weights, measurements, periods of time, and amounts of money generally take singular verbs because they are thought of as single quantities rather than separate units. **Fifty feet of hose** *is* **enough. Ten dollars** *seems* **a fair price.** Although the subjects of these sentences are plural in form, they take (*singular, plural*) verbs.
2030	2031

	a. **The catcher dropped the ball.**
	b. **The ball was dropped by the catcher.**
	In one sentence, the subject of the verb performs an action; in the other, the subject is acted upon.
	The subject performs an action in sentence (*a, b*).
2300	

me	Underline the correct pronoun:
	Let's you and (*me, I*) **exchange letters.**
2568	2569

political, economic(,)	**A neat little girl with curly red hair was bouncing a big rubber ball on the sidewalk.**
2837	2838

without	a. **it's** **you're** **they're** **who's**
	b. **its** **your** **their** **whose**
	From which group would you choose your word if you could put two words in its place? _____
3106	3107

The paint was *sticky.*

incomplete

We have now completed our sentence by adding the complement *sticky.*

The complement *sticky* describes the subject _____.

142

143

---

a. **Clyde sat right in front of me, and we soon became close friends.**
b. **The brakes failed, and the car crashed into the truck.**

b

Which sentence, because of its more exciting action, would benefit more from the brisk effect of a semicolon? _____

412

413

---

a. **His mother wasn't home,** *and* **Luis started the dinner.**
b. *Because* **his mother wasn't home, Luis started the dinner.**

because

Which sentence is better because it makes clear the relationship between the two facts—*a* or *b?* _____

682

683

The modifiers of an appositive may consist of words, phrases, and clauses.

Alfred Nobel, *the inventor of dynamite,* **established the Nobel prizes.**

No

The appositive *inventor* is modified by a (*phrase, clause*).

952

953

---

a. *The more* **one learns,** *the less* **positive one becomes.**
b. **As one learns more, one becomes less positive.**

decreases

Which sentence makes the relationship between the two facts more striking? _____

1222

1223

We __(a)__ wash __(b)__ the towels.

b

To mean that you wash the towels but do not iron them, put the word *only* in space (*a, b*).

1492

1493

b

1762

a. **Sue** *goes* **to high school, and he . . . to college.**
b. **Sue** *goes* **to high school, and I . . . to college.**

In which sentence do we not need to repeat the verb *goes*

because the same form would fit in the blank space? _____

1763

---

singular

2031

a. **Five minutes is enough time for my announcement.**
b. **Four yards of material are enough for a dress.**

In which sentence is the verb correct? _____

2032

---

a

2300

A verb is said to be **active** when its subject performs an action.

a. **The catcher** *dropped* **the ball.**
b. **The ball** *was dropped* **by the catcher.**

In which sentence is the verb *active* because its subject performs an action? _____

2301

---

me

2569

POSSESSIVE PRONOUNS BEFORE GERUNDS

A gerund, as you have learned, is a special kind of noun that is formed by adding *-ing* to a verb.

I enjoy all *sports,* **but I like** *skiing* **best.**

Which of the two italicized words is a gerund? _____

2570

None

2838

Because it was the day before Thanksgiving planes trains and buses were filled to capacity.

2839

---

a

3107

a. **. . . lunch is ready.**
b. **. . . making a mistake.**

The contraction **You're** would be correct in sentence (*a, b*).

3108

paint
 	
143
	Now instead of using an adjective to complete our sentence, we shall use a noun as our complement.
	
	    Angela was . . . (What?)
	    Angela was **the driver.**
	
	The complement **driver** completes the meaning of the sentence and identifies the subject _____. 144

b 413	a. **The strike was called, and five thousand workers laid down their tools.** b. **The game was very slow, and many fans left the stadium.** In which sentence would the use of a semicolon reinforce the excitement of the action? _____ 414

b
 	
683
	And is objectionable only when it steals the job of words such as **who, which, as, when, because,** and **although,** which show exactly *how* two ideas are related to each other.
	
	    a. **The water boils** *and* **the kettle whistles.**
	    b. *As soon as* **the water boils, the kettle whistles.**
	
	Which of the above sentences gives more specific information—*a* or *b*? _____ 684

phrase 953	**Alfred Nobel,** *the chemist who invented dynamite,* **established the Nobel prizes.** The appositive *chemist* is modified by a (*phrase, clause*). 954
a 1223	In this and the following frames, put each sentence into "the more . . . the more" or "the more . . . the less" arrangement: **As he earns more, he spends more.** _____ _____ 1224
a 1493	**Vi can __(a)__ play __(b)__ any instrument.** To mean that Vi can play many instruments, put *almost* in space (*a, b*). 1494

a 1763	WRONG: **Sue** *goes* **to high school, and I to college.** This sentence is wrong because with **Sue** we use *goes,* but with **I** we need _____. 1764
a 2032	**One dollar seems too much to pay for this cake.** If you changed **One dollar** to **Three dollars,** would you need to change the verb **seems?** (*Yes, No*) 2033
a 2301	a. **The catcher** *dropped* **the ball.** b. **The ball** *was dropped* **by the catcher.** In which sentence is the subject of the verb acted upon? _____ 2302
skiing 2570	a. **I was surprised at** *his* **behavior.** b. **I was surprised at** *his* **offering a tip.** In which sentence is the possessive pronoun *his* followed by a gerund? _____ 2571
Thanksgiving, planes, trains(,) 2839	Lesson **79** **Commas for Interrupting Expressions** [Frames 2841–2876]
b 3108	a. **I wonder if . . . ready.** b. **Which is . . . house?** The contraction **they're** would be correct in sentence (*a, b*). 3109

Angela

144

A complement that follows a linking verb and describes or identifies the subject is sometimes called a *predicate nominative, predicate adjective,* or *subject complement.* In this text, we shall use the term **subject complement.** It is called a **subject complement** because it *describes* or *identifies* the

_____.

145

---

a

414

Don't use a comma without a conjunction to connect sentences. Only a semicolon has the power to hold two sentences together without the help of **and, but,** or **or.**

a. **Bea shook the branches, the apples came tumbling down.**
b. **Bea shook the branches; the apples came tumbling down.**

Which sentence is correctly punctuated? _____

415

---

b

684

You will greatly improve your writing if you use **and** only when you are sure that no *more specific* relationship exists.

a. *After* **Juan visited the club, he decided to join.**
b. **Juan visited the club,** *and* **he decided to join.**

The relationship between the two facts is clearer in (*a, b*).

685

---

clause

954

An appositive with its modifiers forms an **appositive phrase.**

Pete, *their youngest son,* **has just started college.**
Pete   **has just started college.**

When we omit the appositive phrase, does a complete sentence remain? (*Yes, No*)

955

The more he
earns, the more
he spends.

1224

Sometimes a comparative form (*-er*) of an adjective or an adverb is used in these arrangements.

When you drive faster, you see less.

_____

_____

1225

---

b

1494

Vi can __(a)__ play __(b)__ any instrument.

To mean that Vi really can't quite play any one instrument, put *almost* in space (*a, b*).

1495

I never have *eaten* **and never will** *eat* **an oyster.**

go

Does the same form of the verb *eat* follow both **have** and **will?** (*Yes, No*)

1764

1765

No

In this and the following frames, underline the correct verb. Remember that a verb ending in *s* in the present tense is always singular.

There (*is, are*) **about twenty-four electric light bulbs in the average car of today.**

2033

2034

---

b

A verb is said to be **passive** when its subject is acted upon.

    a. **The catcher** *dropped* **the ball.**
    b. **The ball** *was dropped* **by the catcher.**

In which sentence is the verb *passive* because its subject is acted upon? _____

2302

2303

---

b

    a. **I was surprised at** *his* **behavior.**
    b. **I was surprised at** *his* **offering a tip.**

In which sentence might you sometimes hear the objective pronoun *him* used instead of the possessive pronoun *his?*

2571

_____

2572

We often interrupt a sentence to insert an expression that is aside from our main thought. In speech, we keep such expressions in the background by dropping our voice and pausing before and after; in writing, we use commas.

Punctuate the interrupting expression:

    The stories *on the whole* **are lacking in originality.**

2841

---

a

    a. **I think . . . boiling.**
    b. **I like . . . design.**

The contraction **it's** would be correct in sentence (*a, b*).

3109

3110

The **subject complement** brings us to our third sentence pattern:

PATTERN III: *Subject—Linking Verb ← Subject Complement*

    a. **A forest ranger guards our forests.**
    b. **A forest ranger's life is rather lonely.**

Which sentence is an example of **Pattern III?** _____

subject

145

146

---

    a. **The weather was raw, and the field was muddy.**
    b. **The weather was raw, the field was muddy.**

In which sentence is the comma correctly used? _____

b

415

416

By using fewer **and's** and more clause signals such as **which, whose, since, whenever,** and **although,** you will show the relationship between your ideas (*more, less*) clearly.

a

685

686

An appositive is useful for avoiding an "I-forgot-to-tell-you" type of sentence that explains something you have just named in the previous sentence.

    Mrs. Cross is the editor. *She is a friend of my teacher's.*

The second sentence explains _____ in the first sentence.

Yes

955

956

If a car is heavier, it rides more smoothly.

_____

_____

(Some variation in the wording is allowable.)

The faster you drive, the less you see.

1225

1226

Sue __(a)__ earned __(b)__ ten dollars.

To mean that Sue came close to earning this money but that she didn't get the job, put *nearly* in space (*a, b*).

a

1495

1496

No

1765

WRONG: **I never have and never will** *eat* **an oyster.**

This sentence is wrong because with **will** we use *eat,* but with **have** we need _____.

1766

---

are

2034

(*Here's, Here are*) **the list of contributors.**

2035

---

b

2303

a. **The catcher** *dropped* **the ball.**
b. **The ball** *was dropped* **by the catcher.**

In sentence *a,* the performer of the action is shown by the subject.

In sentence *b,* the performer of the action is shown by the prepositional phrase _____.

2304

---

b

2572

a. **I was surprised at** *his* **behavior.**
b. **I was surprised at** *his* **offering a tip.**

Since you would never use the objective pronoun *him* before the noun **behavior,** it would likewise seem reasonable not to use *him* before the gerund _____.

2573

, on the whole,

2841

There are several types of interrupting expressions. Any of them can be omitted without damaging the meaning or completeness of your sentence.

Underline and put commas around three words that form an interrupting expression:

The refreshments by the way were excellent.

2842

---

a

3110

a. . . . **ringing the doorbell?**
b. . . . **ticket is this?**

The pronoun **Whose** would be correct in sentence (*a, b*).

3111

Some cameras are very expensive.

b

The subject complement that follows the linking verb in this sentence is _____.

146

147

---

a

a. **The weather was raw, the field was muddy.**
b. **The weather was raw; the field was muddy.**

Which sentence is correctly punctuated? _____

416

417

---

more

a. **This part controls the shutter,** *and* **it is very delicate.**
b. **This part,** *which* **controls the shutter, is very delicate.**

Which sentence is tighter because it brings the two facts into closer relationship—*a* or *b?* _____

686

687

Mrs. Cross

Mrs. Cross is the editor. *She is a friend of my teacher's.*
Mrs. Cross, *a friend of my teacher's,* **is the editor.**

We changed the italicized sentence to an appositive and put it next to the noun _____, which it explains.

956

957

The heavier a car is, the more smoothly it rides.

As you get older, you have more responsibilities.

_____

_____

1226

1227

---

a

Sue __(a)__ earned __(b)__ ten dollars.

To mean that Sue earned slightly less than ten dollars, put *nearly* in space (*a, b*).

1496

1497

eaten 1766	a. **I never have** *eaten* **and never will** *eat* **an oyster.** b. **I never have and never will** *eat* **an oyster.** Which sentence is correct—*a* or *b*? _____ 1767
Here's 2035	**License statistics show that there** (*is, are*) **more fishers than hunters in the United States.** 2036
by the catcher 2304	a. **The band** *played* **a march.** b. **A march** *was played* **by the band.** Which sentence contains an active verb? _____ 2305
offering 2573	INFORMAL: **I was surprised at** *him* **offering a tip.** Although an objective pronoun before a gerund is frequently heard in conversation, a possessive pronoun is more appropriate for careful writing and speaking. Underline the preferred pronoun: **The likelihood of** (*them, their*) **winning the game is slight.** 2574
by the way, 2842	PARENTHETICAL EXPRESSIONS Turn to the following frame, in which you will find some common interrupters known as **parenthetical expressions.** We often add these words and phrases to sentences to make their meaning clearer or more emphatic or to tie them up with the preceding sentences.　　(*Turn to the next frame.*) 2843
b 3111	In this and the following frames, underline the correct word in each pair. Be sure to choose the contraction whenever you can substitute two words: (*It's, Its*) **trying to escape from** (*it's, its*) **cage.** 3112

FORMS OF *BE*: is, am, are—was, were, been

expensive

147

Although a form of **be** can be used by itself as a linking verb, it is often used as a *helper* with the main verb.

    a. **The leaves are green.**   b. **The leaves are falling.**

In which sentence is **are** used as a helper? _____

148

---

b

417

If you omit the conjunction from a compound sentence, put a (*comma, semicolon*) in its place.

418

---

b

687

Eliminate the **and** in each sentence by changing the italicized idea to either an adverb or adjective clause, as the meaning requires. Write the full sentence.

    Grandmother has many friends, and *they visit her often.*

_____

_____

688

Mrs. Cross

957

a. **Mrs. Cross is the editor.** *She is a friend of my teacher's.*
b. **Mrs. Cross,** *a friend of my teacher's,* **is the editor.**

Which arrangement is better because it puts the explanation of **Mrs. Cross** where it belongs—directly after the noun it explains? _____

958

The older
you get,
the more
responsibilities
you have.
1227

You go out farther, and the water gets deeper.

_____

_____

1228

---

b

1497

The man paid the bill with a *worthless* **check.**
The man paid the bill with a check *that was worthless.*

The adjective *worthless* comes before the noun **check,** which it modifies.

The adjective clause *that was worthless* comes (*before, after*) the noun **check,** which it modifies.

1498

a

We always have *paid* **and always will** *pay* **our bills on time.**

Can we omit the verb *paid*? (*Yes, No*)

1767

1768

---

are

How much (*are, is*) **those pads of paper?**

2036

2037

ACTIVE: **The band** *played* **a march.**

↓

PASSIVE: **A march** *was played* **by the band.**

a

What happens to the direct object **march** when we change the verb from active to passive?

It becomes the _____ of the passive verb *was played*.

2305

2306

Underline the preferred pronoun:

their

Political experts now see many reasons for (*his, him*) **winning the election.**

2574

2575

---

however	of course	for example	after all
therefore	by the way	nevertheless	if possible

    a. **The cake was a failure** *after all* **our efforts.**
    b. **Freddy** *after all* **is only ten years old.**

In which sentence should *after all* be set off with commas because it is an interrupter? _____

2843

2844

It's, its

(*It's, Its*) **lightness is** (*it's, its*) **greatest advantage.**

3112

3113

b 148	a. **The leaves <u>are</u> green.** b. **The leaves <u>are falling</u>.** Which sentence contains a subject complement? _____ 149
semicolon 418	There are a number of adverbs that are sometimes mistaken for conjunctions. ADVERBS: **however otherwise nevertheless** **therefore consequently furthermore** Since these words are adverbs, they do not have the power of _____ to combine sentences. 419
Grandmother has many friends who visit her often. 688	Follow the directions given in the previous frame. Count your sentence right if it makes good sense even if you did not use the same clause signal given in the answer. **I got a poor seat, and** *I arrived very early.* _____ _____ 689
b 958	Watch your writing for a weak sentence explaining something you have just written. If it contains the verb **is, are, was,** or **were,** followed by a noun, change it to an appositive phrase and fit it into the previous sentence. a. **Ms. Lee urged us to win.** b. **She is our new coach.** Which sentence can be changed to an appositive? _____ 959
The farther out you go, the deeper the water gets. 1228	**Traveling has made me appreciate my own town more.** _____ _____ 1229
after 1498	Unless an adjective clause is placed directly *after* the word it modifies, your reader is likely to connect it with the wrong thing. **The pill came from this bottle** *that the baby swallowed.* The adjective clause is meant to modify **pill**, but it appears to modify the noun _____. 1499

No

1768

a. **Did you put** *a* **pear or** *a* **peach in my lunch?**
b. **Did you put** *a* **pear or** *an* **apple in my lunch?**

We use the article **a** before a consonant sound (**a** *fish*) and the article **an** before a vowel sound (**an** *eel*).

In which sentence could we omit the article *a* because the same form of the article fits in both places? _____

1769

---

are

2037

There (*hasn't, haven't*) **been any changes in the rules.**

2038

---

subject

2306

ACTIVE: **The band** *played* **a march.**

PASSIVE: **A march** *was played* **by the band.**

Follow the arrow to see what happens to the subject **band** when we change the verb from active to passive.

The subject **band** becomes the object of the preposition _____.

2307

---

his

2575

Underline the preferred pronoun:

The principal has no objection to (*us, our*) **using her name.**

2576

---

b

2844

Here are other parenthetical expressions:

| perhaps | you know | on the whole | on the other hand |
| it seems | I suppose | on the contrary | generally speaking |

a. **The coach** *I suppose* **was very pleased.**
b. *I suppose* **that the coach was very pleased.**

I suppose should be set off with commas in sentence (*a, b*).

2845

Its, its

3113

(*It's, Its*) **tongue hangs out when** (*it's, its*) **thirsty.**

3114

The fans were *cheering.*
The fans were *enthusiastic.*

One of the italicized words is part of an action verb; the other is a subject complement.

The subject complement is the word _____.

a

149

150

---

a. **The air is humid, therefore the paint dries slowly.**
b. **The air is humid, and therefore the paint dries slowly.**

Which sentence is incorrect because there is no conjunction

to connect its two parts? _____

conjunctions

419

420

Shirley Chisholm made a statement, and *most people agreed with it.* (Try *with which.*)

I got a poor
seat although
I arrived very
early.

_____

_____

689

690

---

a. **Ms. Lee urged us to win.**   b. *She is our new coach*

Why is it easy to change sentence *b* to an appositive phrase?
It is easy because sentence *b* contains the verb *is*, followed

by the noun _____, which will become the appositive to
explain **Ms. Lee** in sentence *a*.

b

959

960

The more I
travel, the more
I appreciate my
own town.

Lesson **33** The Useful Noun–Participle Phrase

[Frames 1231–1260]

1229

---

a. **The pill came from this bottle** *that the baby swallowed.*
b. **The pill** *that the baby swallowed* **came from this bottle.**

Which sentence is better because the adjective clause comes

right after the noun it modifies? _____

bottle

1499

1500

Did you put _a_ pear or _an_ apple in my lunch?

a

We cannot omit the _an_ before **apple** because with **pear** we use _a_, but with **apple** we need to use _____.

1769

1770

---

haven't

(_Those, That_) **type of scissors** (_are, is_) **made for cutting hair.**

2038

2039

---

by

A passive verb always consists of a past participle combined with one of the tense forms of the verb **be**.

Underline two passive verbs:

took   was taken   will give   will be given

2307

2308

---

our

In this and the following frames, underline the correct pronouns or, in some cases, the pronouns appropriate for formal usage.

(_We, Us_) **boys saw no good reason for** (_them, their_) **postponing the game.**

2576

2577

---

a

Insert the necessary commas:

She plays the radio for example after everyone has gone to bed.

2845

2846

Its, it's

(_You're, Your_) **circulation slows down when** (_you're, your_) **asleep.**

3114

3115

enthusiastic

150

Be is not the only linking verb. Among other verbs that can serve as linking verbs are **seem, become, appear, look, feel,** and **get** (when it means **become**).

The candidate appeared cheerful.

The linking verb in this sentence is _____.

151

---

a

420

The air is humid, and therefore the paint dries slowly.

The word **therefore** is not a conjunction and has no connecting power. For this reason, we need to use the conjunction

_____ in this sentence.

421

Shirley Chisholm
made a statement
with which
most people agreed.

690

Cars become more complicated, **and mechanics require more training.**

_____

_____

691

---

coach

960

Ms. Lee once played college tennis. (*She is*) *our new coach.*
Ms. Lee, *our new coach,* **once played college tennis.**

In changing the italicized sentence to an appositive phrase,

we dropped everything except the noun _____ and

its modifiers.

961

A **noun-participle** phrase consists of a noun followed by a present or past participle that modifies this noun.

Knees trembling, **Dick stepped up to the stage.**

In the italicized phrase, the noun *Knees* is modified by the (*present, past*) participle *trembling.*

1231

---

b

1500

We sold our car to a used-car dealer *that had a cracked cylinder head.*

This sentence is absurd because the adjective clause appears

to modify the noun **dealer** when it is really meant to modify

the noun _____.

1501

an	a. Shall I make *an* apple or apricot pie? b. Shall I make *an* apple or pumpkin pie? Which sentence is correct? _____
1770	1771
That, is	(*This, These*) **kind** (*wears, wear*) **much longer than the cheaper ones.**
2039	2040
was taken, will be given	Underline two passive verbs: **sees is seen has sent has been sent**
2308	2309
We, their	*Reminder:* In expressions like *we* (or *us*) *boys,* use the same pronoun you would use if the noun (*boys*) were omitted. **Most of** (*we, us*) **boys are just as busy as** (*him, he*).
2577	2578
, for example,	Sometimes there is so little interruption—if any—that commas would only tend to make the reading jerky. *Of course* **I'm going.** *Perhaps* **you will find it.** a. **We** *therefore* **sent a telegram.** b. **We decided** *therefore* **to send a telegram.** In which sentence would you use commas? _____
2846	2847
Your, you're	(*You're, Your*) **not in** (*you're, your*) **right seat.**
3115	3116

appeared 151	The animals . . . cold. Underline the two words that can be used as *linking verbs* in the above sentence: **feel like look avoid** 152
and 421	**The air is humid; therefore the paint dries slowly.** This sentence is correct because a semicolon has the power of a _____ to connect the two parts of a compound sentence. 422
As cars become more complicated, mechanics require more training. 691	**A friend recommended this book, and** *I value her opinion highly.* (Try *whose.*) _____ _____ 692
coach 961	**Ms. Lee once played college tennis.** (*She is*) *our new coach.* **Ms. Lee,** *our new coach,* **once played college tennis.** Then we put the appositive phrase directly after the noun _____, which it explains. 962
present 1231	*The dinner prepared,* **we waited for our guests.** In the italicized phrase, the noun *dinner* is modified by the (*present, past*) participle *prepared.* 1232
car 1501	a. **We sold our car** *that had a cracked cylinder head* **to a used-car dealer.** b. **We sold our car to a used-car dealer** *that had a cracked cylinder head.* Which sentence is better because the adjective clause comes directly after the noun it modifies? _____ 1502

a

1771

Repeat an article (*a, an, the*) or a possessive pronoun (*my, your, his,* etc.) if there is any chance of misunderstanding.

    a. **The McCanns have** *a* **black and white dog.**
    b. **The McCanns have** *a* **black and** *a* **white dog.**

Which sentence means two dogs? _____

1772

This, wears

2040

The entire Apache tribe (*was, were*) **against the sale of its property.**

2041

---

is seen,
has been sent

2309

A sentence with an active verb is shorter, stronger, and more direct than one with a passive verb.

    ACTIVE: **Paul** *found* **a dollar.**
    PASSIVE: **A dollar** *was found* **by Paul.**

The sentence that gives a clumsy, roundabout effect is the one with the (*active, passive*) verb.

2310

---

us, he

2578

Let's you and (*me, I*) **insist on** (*his, him*) **paying his own way.**

2579

---

b

2847

When the word **well, why, yes,** or **no** is used as a sentence opener, it is generally followed by a comma.

Punctuate the following sentences:

        Well maybe you're right.
        Why this is a surprise!

2848

You're, your

3116

(*You're, Your*) **eyes show that** (*you're, your*) **tired.**

3117

feel, look 152	**The animals . . . cold.** Underline the two words that can be used as *linking verbs* in the above sentence to make **cold** describe **animals**. **fear become prefer get** 153
conjunction 422	a. **It rained all day, nevertheless everyone had a good time.** b. **It rained all day, but everyone had a good time.** Which sentence is correct because its two parts are connected by a conjunction? _____ 423
A friend whose opinion I value highly recommended this book. 692	*The score was tied,* **and we had to play another game.** _____ _____ 693
Ms. Lee 962	a. **Ms. Lee once played college tennis.** *She is our new coach.* b. **Ms. Lee,** *our new coach,* **once played college tennis.** In which arrangement does the explanation of **Ms. Lee** sound less like an afterthought? _____ 963
past 1232	A noun-participle phrase has no grammatical connection with the rest of the sentence. *Knees trembling,* **Dick stepped up to the stage.** Is there any connecting word such as *when, because, who,* or *which* to connect the phrase with the main statement? (*Yes, No*) 1233
a 1502	a. **The book is very modern that we use in our literature class.** b. **The book that we use in our literature class is very modern.** Which sentence is better because the adjective clause comes directly after the noun it modifies? _____ 1503

a. **Harvey ordered** *a* **cheese and** *a* **ham sandwich.**
b. **Harvey ordered** *a* **cheese and ham sandwich.**

Which sentence means two sandwiches? _____

1773

---

was

2041

(*Note:* A verb and a pronoun used with a collective noun must be consistent with each other in number.)

The band (*was, were*) **tuning up** (*its, their*) **instruments.**

2042

---

passive

2310

a. **The pitcher** *took* **a chance and** *threw* **the ball to first base.**
b. **A chance** *was taken* **by the pitcher, and the ball** *was thrown* **to first base.**

Which sentence is better because it is more direct? _____

2311

---

me, his

2579

(*Us, We*) **girls think that the leading role suits you better than** (*her, she*).

2580

Well,
Why,

2848

Punctuate the following sentences:

Yes I agree with you.
No I didn't see Joan.

2849

Your, you're

3117

(*They're, Their*) **delicious when** (*they're, their*) **toasted.**

3118

become, get

153

You can be sure that a verb is a linking verb if you can put some form of **be** (**is, am, are—was, were, been**) in its place.

    a. **The customer** *feels* **the material.**
    b. **The weather** *feels* **muggy.**

In which sentence can you substitute **is** for **feels?** _____

154

---

b

423

a. **It rained all day, nevertheless everyone had a good time.**
b. **It rained all day; nevertheless everyone had a good time.**

Which sentence is correctly punctuated? _____

424

Because the score was tied, we had to play another game.

693

This was my first speech, **and I wasn't nervous at all.**

_____

_____

694

---

b

963

Do not confuse an appositive phrase with an adjective clause. An appositive phrase consists only of a noun (or pronoun) with its modifiers. An adjective clause always has a subject and a _____.

964

No

1233

In the participial phrases we studied earlier, the participle modified a noun or pronoun in the main statement.

    Trembling with excitement, **Bert stepped up to the stage.**

In the above sentence the present participle *Trembling* modifies the noun _____ in the main statement.

1234

---

b

1503

    a. **No joke** *that hurts our feelings* **amuses us.**
    b. **No joke amuses us** *if it hurts our feelings.*

One sentence contains an adverb clause; the other, an adjective clause.

Which sentence contains the adverb clause? _____

1504

a

1773

a. *My* cousin and best friend will go with me.
b. *My* cousin and *my* best friend will go with me.

Which sentence means two persons? _____

1774

---

were, their

2042

Five tons (*were, was*) **too big a load for the truck.**

2043

---

a

2311

a. This play was practiced by the team until it was perfect.
b. The team practiced this play until it was perfect.

Which sentence is better? _____

2312

We, her

2580

I intend to ask both our neighbors, Mr. Doyle and (*he, him*), if they object to (*me, my*) using their names for references.

2581

Yes,
No,

2849

We often use a "not" phrase to show what we do *not* mean in contrast to what we do mean. Such phrases require commas because they are strong interrupters.

The company, *not the salesman,* **is to blame.**

Punctuate the following sentence:

Graphite not oil should be used on locks.

2850

They're, they're

3118

(*They're, Their*) **bringing out** (*they're, their*) **new models in October.**

3119

a. **The customer** *feels* **the material.**
b. **The weather** *feels* **muggy.**

b

In one sentence **feels** is used as an *action* verb; in the other it is used as a *linking* verb.

In which sentence is it used as a *linking* verb? _____

154   155

---

a. **Our team was overconfident; consequently we lost.**
b. **Our team was overconfident, and consequently we lost.**
c. **Our team was overconfident, consequently we lost.**

b

Which one of these three sentences is incorrectly punctuated? _____

424   425

Although this was my first speech, I wasn't nervous at all.

My uncle had a tent, and *he had no further use for it.*

_____

_____

694   695

---

a. **Ms. Lee,** *our new coach from Denver,* **played college tennis.**
b. **Ms. Lee,** *who is our new coach from Denver,* **played college tennis.**

verb
(*or* predicate)

Which sentence contains an appositive phrase? _____

964   965

Knees trembling, **Bert stepped up to the stage.**

Bert

In the noun-participle phrase, however, the present participle *trembling* does not modify a word in the main statement. It modifies the noun _____ in the phrase itself.

1234   1235

---

a. **No joke** *that hurts our feelings* **amuses us.**
b. **No joke amuses us** *if it hurts our feelings.*

b

The clause that can be shifted to other positions in the sentence is the (*adjective, adverb*) clause.

1504   1505

b

a. We invited *our* coach and *our* math teacher to the picnic.
b. We invited *our* coach and math teacher to the picnic.

Which sentence means two persons? _____

1774

1775

---

was

Two hours (*seems, seem*) hardly enough time to see all the sights.

2043

2044

---

b

Unless you have a good reason for not doing so, always use (*an active, a passive*) verb.

2312

2313

---

him, my

I couldn't understand (*him, his*) wanting to pay for all (*us, we*) students.

2581

2582

, not oil,

Punctuate the following sentence:

It is the motion of the cloth not the red color that excites the bull.

2850

2851

They're, their

(*They're, Their*) fenders prove that (*they're, their*) poor drivers.

3119

3120

b

155

a. **The restaurant** *looked* **crowded.**
b. **The speaker** *looked* **at his watch.**

In which sentence can you substitute **was** for **looked?** _____

156

---

c

425

**however   otherwise   nevertheless
therefore   consequently   furthermore**

It is equally correct to start a new sentence with one of these adverbs. Many writers prefer to do so.

Our team was overconfident. Consequently we lost.

This sentence is (*correct, incorrect*).

426

My uncle had a
tent for which
he had no
further use. (*Or
which he had no
further use for.*)

695

You switch the tires around, **and they will wear longer.**

_____

_____

696

---

a

965

a. **We visited Monticello,** *which was the home of Thomas
Jefferson.*
b. **We visited Monticello,** *the home of Thomas Jefferson.*

Which sentence contains an appositive phrase? _____

966

Knees

1235

a. *Trembling with excitement,* **Bert stepped up to the stage.**
b. *Knees trembling,* **Bert stepped up to the stage.**

In which sentence does the participle *trembling* modify a
word in the main statement, thus connecting it grammatically with that statement? _____

1236

---

adverb

1505

a. *If it hurts our feelings,* **no joke amuses us.**
b. **No joke,** *if it hurts our feelings,* **amuses us.**
c. **No joke amuses us** *if it hurts our feelings.*

Does an adverb clause, like an adjective clause, need to
come directly after the word it modifies? (*Yes, No*)

1506

Do not omit a word required by the meaning or grammatical construction of a sentence or by customary usage.

Bob made fun . . . my suggestion.
Bob made fun . . . and ridiculed my suggestion.

What preposition is missing from both sentences? _____

1776

Lesson **57** Review: Agreement of Subject and Verb

[Frames 2046–2072]

The nomination will be accepted by Nolan.

To change this sentence to one with an active verb, you would make _____ the subject of your revised sentence.

2314

The other boys, Louis and (*he, him*), were envious because Mr. Ringler didn't pay them as much as (*I, me*).

2583

APPOSITIVES

An appositive is a noun or pronoun—often with modifiers—that follows another noun or pronoun to explain it.

Mary Lou Williams, *a composer,* spoke to the teen-agers.

Can the italicized appositive be omitted without damaging the meaning or completeness of this sentence? (*Yes, No*)

2852

Let's decide (*who's, whose*) going in (*who's, whose*) car.

3121

a. **The restaurant** *looked* **crowded.**
b. **The speaker** *looked* **at his watch.**

In one sentence, *looked* is used as an action verb; in the other, as a linking verb for which we could substitute *was*.

In which sentence is *looked* used as a linking verb and followed by a subject complement? _____

a

156 | 157

---

a. **I lost my car keys; otherwise I would have driven.**
b. **I lost my car keys, otherwise I would have driven.**
c. **I lost my car keys. Otherwise I would have driven.**

Which one of these three sentences is incorrectly punctuated? _____

correct

426 | 427

A sentence consisting of a main statement and an adverb or adjective clause is a (*compound, complex*) sentence.

If you switch the tires around, they will wear longer.

696 | 697

An appositive phrase should be set off from the rest of the sentence by two commas (or a single comma if it ends the sentence) because it is an "extra" that could be omitted.

Punctuate the following sentence:

Only one other team the New York Giants did as well.

b

966 | 967

Because a noun-participle phrase has no grammatical connection with the rest of the sentence, it is often called an **absolute** phrase, *absolute* meaning *independent*. An example of an absolute phrase is a (*participial, noun-participle*) phrase.

a

1236 | 1237

Modifiers—words, phrases, and clauses—sometimes get in one another's way and produce an awkward or absurd sentence. When this happens, you can often solve your problem by shifting the (*adverb, adjective*) clause to the beginning of the sentence.

No

1506 | 1507

of

1776

The team had no respect . . . their coach.
The team had no respect . . . or confidence in their coach.

What preposition is missing from both sentences? _____

1777

One situation causes more errors in subject-verb agreement than any other:

The color . . . changes.

No matter what plural nouns in prepositional phrases might come between the subject and the verb, the verb must remain (*singular, plural*).

2046

Nolan

2314

a. **The nomination** *will be accepted* **by Nolan.**
b. **Nolan** *will accept* **the nomination.**

The verb in sentence *b* is active because its subject **Nolan** (*acts, is acted upon*).

2315

---

he, me

2583

(*Us, We*) **girls get out of school earlier than** (*her, she*).

2584

Yes

2852

Set off an appositive and its modifiers with commas because it is not an essential part of the sentence.

Punctuate the following sentence:

Our principal an enthusiastic football fan attends every game.

2853

---

who's, whose

3121

(Be especially careful with this sentence!)

(*Who's, Whose*) **the girl** (*who's, whose*) **taking the part of the grandmother?**

3122

a 157	We have now studied two kinds of complements: *direct objects* and *subject complements*. With a little reasoning, we can avoid confusing the two. A *direct object* can follow only an *action verb*. A *subject complement* always follows a _____ verb. 158
b 427	a. **Education must include the whole person; otherwise it is not true education.** b. **Education must include the whole person. Otherwise it is not true education.** Both *a* and *b* are correct. (*True, False*) 428
complex 697	The exact relationship between two facts or ideas is more clearly brought out by a (*compound, complex*) sentence. 698
team, . . . Giants, 967	Punctuate the following sentence: **The car belongs to Virginia Wade the English tennis star.** 968
noun-participle 1237	Because a noun-participle phrase, unlike a participial phrase, is related to the rest of the sentence only by our thought, it is classified as an ab _____ phrase. 1238
adverb 1507	**Grace couldn't say good-by to her uncle who was leaving the country because she had measles.** **Because she had measles, Grace couldn't say good-by to her uncle who was leaving the country.** We get rid of the absurdity by shifting the (*adjective, adverb*) clause to the beginning of the sentence. 1508

for 1777	The teacher referred . . . a book. The book . . . which the teacher referred was not in the library. What preposition is missing from both sentences? _____ 1778
singular 2046	The color of the lights . . . The color of the sky and the water . . . The color of various fish, birds, and animals . . . The color of the leaves on most trees and shrubs . . . The singular verb **changes** would be correct in each of these sentences. (*True, False*) 2047
acts 2315	Change the following sentence to one with an active verb: **These souvenirs** *will be appreciated* **by the children.** _____ _____ 2316
We, she 2584	**Let's you and** (*me, I*) **see if Miss Haines won't let** (*we, us*) **girls organize a softball team.** 2585
, an enthusiastic football fan, 2853	Punctuate the following sentence: **The antelope the fastest animal in existence has been known to achieve a speed of sixty-two miles per hour.** 2854
Who's, who's 3122	(*Who's, Whose*) **mother is the woman** (*who's, whose*) **taking them camping?** 3123

linking 158	Usually the subject and direct object are two *different* things, and the action passes from one to the other. 1 ————————————➔ 2 **The heavy downpour flooded many basements.** The action passes from **downpour** to _____. <div align="right">159</div>
True 428	In this and the following frames, insert the proper punctuation between the two word groups. Copy the word *before* the punctuation and *after* the punctuation. If a conjunction is present, insert a comma. If a conjunction is missing, insert a semicolon. **The field was muddy it didn't stop the Rangers.** _____ <div align="right">429</div>
complex 698	In changing a compound sentence to a complex sentence, you (*drop, add*) the conjunction *and, but,* or *or.* <div align="right">699</div>
Virginia Wade, 968	Punctuate the following sentence: **The Icelanders immigrants from Norway colonized their island in the ninth century.** <div align="right">969</div>
absolute 1238	To change a sentence to a noun-participle phrase is very simple. SENTENCE: **The fuel** *was running* **low.** NOUN-PARTICIPLE PHRASE: **The fuel** *running* **low . . .** We change the verb *was running* to a present participle by dropping the helping verb _____. <div align="right">1239</div>
adverb 1508	**Grace couldn't say good-by to her uncle who was leaving the country because she had measles.** Did Grace's uncle leave the country because of her measles? This amusing sentence contains an adjective clause beginning with the word **who** and an adverb clause beginning with the word _____. <div align="right">1509</div>

to

1778

---

a. **We** *did* **many things that were fun.**
b. **We swam, fished, and many other things that were fun.**

What word is missing from sentence *b*? _____

1779

True

2047

If you were to add the words printed in parentheses at the point marked by the caret (∧), would you need to change the italicized verb? If a change would be necessary, write only the form of the verb that would be required. If the verb would remain the same, write *Correct*.

∧ **Those records** *belong* **to Maxine. (One of)** _____

2048

The children
will appreciate
these souvenirs.

2316

Although you should generally try to use active verbs, there are times when passive verbs are very useful; for example, when the doer of an action is not known.

    a. **Our dog** *was stolen* **last night.**
    b. **The game** *was won* **by the Mustangs.**

In which sentence is the doer of the action not known? _____

2317

---

me, us

2585

My two friends, Walt and (*him, he*), **were disappointed because Mr. Hill didn't give them as good parts in the play as** (*me, I*).

2586

, the fastest
animal in
existence,

2854

DIRECT ADDRESS

Direct address is a noun or other identifying words with which we sometimes interrupt a sentence to show to whom we are speaking.

    You know, *Nancy,* **that you're always welcome.**

Is the noun *Nancy* essential to the sentence? (*Yes, No*)

2855

Whose, who's

3123

APOSTROPHES FOR SPECIAL PLURALS

You have learned not to use apostrophes with ordinary plural nouns that do not show ownership.

    Several *girls'* **took** *boys'* **parts.**

The ordinary plural noun in this sentence that should not be written with an apostrophe is (*girls, boys*).

3124

basements 159	A subject complement, however, always *means the same thing* as the subject or *describes* the subject. We are dealing with *one* thing—not *two*. 1 ————→2 1 ←———— 1 a. **Mrs. Ford hired a lawyer.** b. **Mrs. Ford is a lawyer.** The noun **lawyer** is a subject complement in sentence (*a, b*). 160
muddy; it 429	Follow the directions given in the previous frame: **The wise are so uncertain the ignorant are so positive.** _____ 430
drop 699	Every compound sentence can be improved by changing it to a complex sentence. (*True, False*) 700
Icelanders, . . . Norway, 969	Punctuate the following sentence: **A fierce battle of World War II was fought on Iwo Jima a very small Pacific island.** 970
was 1239	Sometimes we need to change a one-word verb to a present participle. SENTENCE: **The fuel *ran* low.** NOUN-PARTICIPLE PHRASE: **The fuel *running* low . . .** Here we change the verb *ran* to the present participle _____. 1240
because 1509	Adverb phrases as well as adverb clauses are generally movable. Underline the adverb phrase that could be shifted to the beginning of the sentence to get rid of its absurdity: **Dad glued together the vase that Chuck had broken with remarkable skill.** 1510

did	a. **The author has lived** *among* **the Eskimos.** b. **The author has lived, as well as written about, the Eskimos.** What word is missing from sentence *b?* _____
1779	1780

belongs	**A friendly note** ∧ *doesn't* **take much time. (or a telephone call)** _____
2048	2049

a	a. **The test** *had been passed* **by the student.** b. **The kitten** *had been left* **at our door.** In which sentence is a passive verb preferable because the doer of the action is not known? _____
2317	2318

he, me	Lesson **72** Reflexive, Intensive, Demonstrative, and Possessive Pronouns [Frames 2588–2625]
2586	

No	Use commas to set off direct address because it interrupts the sentence and is not essential to its meaning. Underline and set off the direct address with commas: **Our team my friends needs your full support.**
2855	2856

girls	However, there are a few special cases where there is a good reason for using apostrophes to form ordinary plurals. a. **Your os look like as.** b. **Your o's look like a's.** Which sentence is easier to figure out? _____
3124	3125

a. **The owner of the restaurant hired a new cook.**
b. **The owner of the restaurant is the cook.**

b

In which sentence is the noun **cook** a subject complement because it means the same person as the subject? _____

160   161

---

uncertain; the

There are thirteen dogs on our block   and all of them seemed to be barking at once.

_____

430   431

False

For combining two similar or related ideas of equal importance, a (*compound, complex*) sentence is better.

700   701

Change each italicized sentence to an appositive phrase, and insert it in the first sentence right after the word it explains. Supply the necessary commas.

Iwo Jima,

Edith Hamilton is a respected scholar. *She is an expert on Greek mythology.* _____

_____

970   971

A noun-participle phrase consists of a noun plus a present participle that modifies *this noun*—not a noun in the main statement.

The fuel *running* **low . . .**

running

This is a noun-participle phrase because the present participle *running* modifies the noun _____.

1240   1241

---

a. **We almost know everyone in town.**
b. **We know almost everyone in town.**

with remarkable
skill

In which sentence is the adverb **almost** placed more sensibly?

_____

1510   1511

among

Do not omit *that* from a noun clause used as a subject complement after any form of the linking verb *be*.

RIGHT: **His excuse was that he didn't see the stop sign.**
WRONG: **His excuse was he didn't see the stop sign.**

What word is missing from the sentence that is labeled

1780

WRONG? _____

1781

Correct

The shortage of goods ∧ *makes* prices skyrocket. (and the abundance of money)

2049

_____

2050

---

b

Passive verbs are also useful when the doer of an action is obvious or unimportant.

a. **The package *will be delivered* tomorrow.**
b. **The deliveryman *will deliver* the package tomorrow.**

Which sentence is better because the doer of the action is

2318

unimportant and had better be omitted? _____

2319

REFLEXIVE AND INTENSIVE PRONOUNS

Pronouns that end with *-self* or *-selves* can be used as either *reflexive* or *intensive* pronouns. When they reflect or turn back the action of the verb to the doer of the action, they are called **reflexive** pronouns.

A reflexive pronoun always ends with *-self* or _____.

2588

---

my friends,

Punctuate the following sentence:

Let me know you lucky girl how you manage to get such high grades.

2856

2857

---

b

Use apostrophes to form the ordinary plurals of letters, numbers, signs, and words referred to as words.

There are two 3's and two 5's in our number.
The +'s should be changed to −'s.

Insert the needed apostrophes:

The temperature is usually in the 70s or 80s.

3125

3126

The owner of the restaurant is energetic.

b

Because the adjective **energetic** describes the subject **owner** and is not something apart from it, **energetic** is a (*subject complement, direct object*).

161

162

---

block, and

Much of the soil is poor   consequently the Japanese farmer depends greatly upon fertilizers.

_____

431

432

---

compound

As you develop greater writing skill and see the relationship between your ideas more clearly, you tend to use (*more, fewer*) compound sentences.

701

702

Edith Hamilton, an expert on Greek mythology, is a respected scholar.

Farewell to Manzanar **was written by Jeanne Wakatsuki Houston.** *She is an American writer.*

_____

_____

971

972

---

fuel

a. *Running low,* **the fuel was insufficient to carry the plane to its destination.**
b. *The fuel running low,* **the pilot made an emergency landing.**

Which sentence contains a noun-participle phrase? _____

1241

1242

---

b

a. **With trembling knees, Bill walked into the office where the principal was sitting.**
b. **Bill walked into the office where the principal was sitting with trembling knees.**

In which sentence are the modifiers placed more sensibly?

1511

——

1512

In this and the following frames, if the omission is incorrect, add the necessary word. If the omission is allowable, write *Correct*.

I *was* on one side and my two friends _____ on the other.

1782

---

make

2050

His father ∧ *plays* **the piano. (, as well as his mother,)**

_____

2051

---

a

2319

Use a passive verb when you wish to avoid naming the person who made a mistake or did something wrong.

   a. **My boss *threw* out this important letter.**
   b. **This important letter *was thrown* out by mistake.**
Which sentence would you use to avoid embarrassing your boss? _____

2320

-selves

2588

   a. **Frank blamed *me* for his failure.**
   b. **Frank blamed *himself* for his failure.**

Which sentence contains a reflexive pronoun that turns the action back to the doer of the action? _____

2589

, you lucky girl,

2857

Punctuate the following sentence:

   I wonder Fred if you have heard about Nancy Lopez.

2858

70's, 80's

3126

Insert the needed apostrophes:

Bookkeeping **is the only English word having three double letters in a row—two os, two ks, and two es.**

3127

a. **Otters are animals.**
b. **Otters are** *playful* **animals.**

In both sentences, the noun **animals** is a subject complement that identifies the subject **Otters.** In sentence *b*, we added the adjective *playful* to describe the noun **animals.**

In sentence *b*, the subject complement is (*playful, animals*).

---

subject complement

162

163

---

poor; consequently

Mrs. Merrill may be old   however, she is not old-fashioned.

_____

432

433

---

fewer

Lesson **19** **Recognizing Noun Clauses**

[Frames 704–743]

702

Farewell to Manzanar was written by Jeanne Wakatsuki Houston, an American writer.

972

A great patriot founded the American Red Cross. *She was Clara Barton.*

_____

_____

973

---

b

The fuel running low, **the pilot made an emergency landing.**

This is a noun-participle phrase because the participle *running* modifies the noun *fuel,* which is (*inside, outside*) the phrase.

1242

1243

---

a

a. **They moved the chairs on which they were sitting closer to the fire.**
b. **They moved the chairs closer to the fire on which they were sitting.**

Which sentence is better? _____

1512

1513

were	I *was* on one side and my friend _____ on the other.
1782	1783

Correct	∧ These stories *deal* with sports. (Every one of) _____
2051	2052

b	a. **The room** *had* **not** *been cleaned* **after the party.** b. **Virginia** *had* **not** *cleaned* **the room after the party.** Which sentence is more tactful because it would not embarrass Virginia? _____
2320	2321

b	When pronouns that end with -*self* or -*selves* are used after a noun or another pronoun to emphasize or intensify it, they are called **intensive** pronouns. a. **The manager** *himself* **waited on me.** b. **The manager blamed** *himself* **for the mistake.** Is *himself* used as an intensive pronoun in *a* or *b*? _____
2589	2590

, Fred,	### DATES AND ADDRESSES The date in the following sentence consists of three parts: **On** *Sunday, July 9, 1961,* **the new church was dedicated.** After the first part of the date, is there a comma both before and after each additional part? (*Yes, No*)
2858	2859

o's, k's, e's	Apostrophes make reading easier when we write the plurals of words referred to as words. a. **Tony has spelled all his toos wrong.** b. **Tony has spelled all his too's wrong.** Which sentence is easier to read? _____
3127	3128

animals

163

Do not mistake an adjective that describes the subject complement for the subject complement of the sentence.

Otters are *playful* **animals.**

The subject complement in this sentence is (*the noun* **animals,** *the adjective* **playful**).

164

---

old; however

433

Fruit trees must be sprayed at the right time   or the fruit will be wormy.

_____

434

We have now completed our study of adverb and adjective clauses. We turn next to the third (and last) type of clause—the **noun clause.**

As its name suggests, a noun clause is a clause that is used

as a _____.

704

A great patriot, Clara Barton, founded the American Red Cross.

973

John's mother gave him his first lessons in reporting. *She was the editor of a country paper.*

_____

_____

974

---

inside

1243

Now let's change a sentence to a noun-participle phrase that contains a past participle:

SENTENCE: **Her test** *was completed.*
NOUN-PARTICIPLE PHRASE: **Her test** *completed . . .*

We change the verb *was completed* to the past participle *completed* by dropping the helping verb _____.

1244

---

a

1513

a. **The letter carrier has to walk all day without sitting down to rest in the slushy snow.**
b. **The letter carrier has to walk all day in the slushy snow without sitting down to rest.**

Which sentence is better? _____

1514

Correct	**Alva never has** _____ **and never will** *join* **a sorority.**
1783	1784

deals	**The vacuum cleaner** ∧ *sells* **for $69. (and all its attachments)** _____
2052	2053

a	When you have a good reason for not mentioning the doer of an action or when you wish to focus attention on the person(s) or thing(s) acted upon, use (*an active, a passive*) verb.
2321	2322

a	a. **The manager** *himself* **waited on me.** b. **He** *himself* **waited on me.** In which sentence does the intensive pronoun emphasize another pronoun? _____
2590	2591

Yes	The address in the following sentence consists of three parts: **The Atlas Company of** *240 Oak Street, Dayton, Ohio 45417,* **will send you a catalogue.** After the first part of the address, is there a comma both before and after each additional part? (*Yes, No*)
2859	2860

b	Insert the needed apostrophes: **Too many ands and sos make writing sound childish.**
3128	3129

the noun *animals* 164	$S = Subject, LV = Linking\ Verb, SC = Subject\ Complement$ **This shallow lake often gets extremely rough.** Fill in the missing words: S LV SC lake _____ _____ 165
time, or 434	**Fruit trees must be sprayed at the right time otherwise the fruit will be wormy.** _____ 435
noun 704	We have seen that adverb and adjective clauses offer almost endless possibilities for showing the various kinds of rel_____ that exist among our ideas. 705
John's mother, the editor of a country paper, gave him his first lessons in reporting. 974	**Thursday is named after Thor.** *He is the god of thunder in Norse mythology.* 975
was 1244	**Her test** *completed . . .* This is a noun-participle phrase because the past participle *completed* modifies the noun _____ within the phrase. 1245
b 1514	a. **The car was taken for investigation to the factory where it had been made after the crash.** b. **After the crash, the car was taken for investigation to the factory where it had been made.** Which sentence is better? _____ 1515

joined	I must find *a* book or _____ article about politics.
1784	1785
sell	The vacuum cleaner ∧ *sells* for $69. (, with all its attach-ments,) _____
2053	2054
a passive	In this and the following frames, make each sentence more direct by changing the verb from passive to active. To do so, make the object of the preposition **by** the subject of your revised sentence. **Nothing** *had been said* **by the teacher about a test.** _____ _____
2322	2323
b	Be sure that you know the correct forms of the various reflexive and intensive pronouns: SINGULAR: **myself** **himself** **itself** **yourself** **herself** **oneself** PLURAL: **ourselves, yourselves, themselves.** Is there such a word as **hisself?** (*Yes, No*)
2591	2592
Yes	After writing the first part of a date or an address, put a comma both before and after each additional part. Punctuate the following sentence: **On Monday August 7 we left Phoenix Arizona and headed for El Paso Texas.**
2860	2861
and's, so's	Lesson **87** Controlling Your Capitals [Frames 3131–3162]
3129	

LV gets SC rough 165	$S = Subject, LV = Linking\ Verb, SC = Subject\ Complement$ **Hera was the powerful queen of the old Greek gods.** Fill in the missing words: S LV SC **Hera** _____ _____ 166
time; otherwise 435	**Before reading** *Jaws* **I never thought about sharks** **after reading** *Jaws* **I worried about sharks every summer.** _____ 436
relationship 705	Noun clauses do not begin to have the usefulness of the other clauses for sentence improvement. We use noun clauses so naturally that we study them mainly to complete our picture of the three kinds of clauses that we find in (*compound, complex*) sentences. 706
Thursday is named after Thor, the god of thunder in Norse mythology. 975	Eliminate the **and** by changing the italicized sentence to an appositive phrase and inserting it in the first sentence right after the word it explains. **Bermuda consists of 360 small islands, and** *it is a British* *colony.* _____ _____ 976
test 1245	a. *Her test completed,* **Carol turned in her paper.** b. *Completing her test,* **Carol turned in her paper.** Which sentence contains a noun-participle phrase? _____ 1246
b 1515	In this and the following frames, rewrite each sentence to improve the placement of the modifiers: **The branch suddenly broke that she was climbing on.** _____ _____ 1516

an 1785	Dr. Shorr is looking for *a* typist and _____ receptionist. (Two persons) 1786
Correct 2054	Greene's is ∧ one of the groceries that *deliver*. (the only) ——————————— 2055
The teacher had said nothing about a test. 2323	Continue to follow the directions for the previous frame: **All your worries** *will be forgotten* **by you at this comedy.** ——————————— ——————————— 2324
No 2592	Underline the correct intensive pronoun: **Charlie Pride gave me this album** (*himself, hisself*). 2593
Monday, August 7, Phoenix, Arizona, El Paso, 2861	Punctuate the following sentence: **In Hants County England Jane Austen was born on December 16 1775.** 2862
	The eleven rules for capitals presented in this and the next lesson are all based upon one general principle: Use a capital letter for a proper noun—a name that fits only *one particular* person, group of people, place, or thing. Use a small letter for a common noun—a name that fits *any one* of its kind. *(Turn to the next frame.)* 3131

LV was SC queen 166	$S = Subject, LV = Linking\ Verb, SC = Subject\ Complement$ **An officer should feel responsible for those in his unit.** Fill in the missing words: S LV SC _____ **should feel** _____ 167
sharks; after 436	**Athletics keep a person physically fit and furthermore they develop a sense of teamwork.** _____ 437
complex 706	Since noun clauses are used exactly as nouns, let us review the various ways in which nouns are used. **His** *remark* **puzzled us.** The noun *remark* is the *subject* of the verb _____. 707
Bermuda, a British colony, consists of 360 small islands. 976	Continue to follow the directions for the previous frame: **My friend made cream puffs, and** *they are my favorite dessert.* _____ _____ 977
a 1246	*Her test completed,* **Carol turned in her paper.** This is a noun-participle phrase because the past participle *completed* modifies the noun *test,* which is (*inside, outside*) the phrase. 1247
The branch that **she** was climbing on suddenly broke. 1516	Continue to follow the directions for the previous frame: **Every student passed to whom the test was given.** _____ _____ 1517

a	Supply a second verb only if the first verb does not fit in this position: **Cliff *is* seventeen and his sister _____ sixteen.**
1786	1787

delivers	**The yield of corn ∧ *has* been increased. (and wheat)** _____
2055	2056

You will forget all your worries at this comedy.	(*Note:* There is no need to move the introductory phrase from its present position.) **After a long voyage, Tahiti *was reached* by the mutineers.** _____ _____
2324	2325

himself	SINGULAR: **myself** **himself** **itself** **yourself** **herself** **oneself** PLURAL: **ourselves, yourselves, themselves** Is there such a word as **theirselves?** (*Yes, No*)
2593	2594

Hants County, England, December 16,	A one-part address is set off with commas only when there is no preposition such as *of, at,* or *on* to connect it with the sentence. a. **Andy Shaw *of* 778 Montclair Avenue was the winner.** b. **Andy Shaw 778 Montclair Avenue was the winner.** The one-part address requires commas in sentence (*a, b*).
2862	2863

	1. Capitalize geographical names that apply to *particular* countries, sections of countries, states, cities, oceans, rivers, lakes, etc. **Canada** **North Dakota** **Pacific Ocean** **Hudson River** Copy one italicized word that requires a capital: **He lives in a *city* not far from *cleveland*.** _____
	3132

S officer SC responsible 167	**The drunken driver is the greatest danger on our highways today.** Fill in the missing words: *S* *LV* *SC* **driver** _____ _____ 168

UNIT 3: THE COMPLEX SENTENCE TO SHOW RELATIONSHIP

Lesson **12** Recognizing Adverb Clauses

[Frames 439–480]

fit, and 437	

puzzled 707	a. **His** *remark* **puzzled us.** b. *What he said* **puzzled us.** The clause *What he said* does the same job in sentence *b* that the noun *remark* does in sentence *a*. It is therefore a _____ clause. 708

My friend made cream puffs, my favorite dessert. 977	**Kitty Hawk is in North Carolina, and** *it was the birthplace of aviation.* (*Note:* The first sustained airplane flight was made by Orville Wright at the village of Kitty Hawk in 1903.) _____ _____ 978

inside 1247	*Her eyes shining with joy,* **Judy showed me her new car.** **Judy,** *her eyes shining with joy,* **showed me her new car.** **Judy showed me her new car,** *her eyes shining with joy.* Can a noun-participle phrase be shifted from one position to another in a sentence? (*Yes, No*) 1248

Every student to whom the test was given passed. 1517	**Rita Moreno was given the part in** *West Side Story* **of Anita.** _____ _____ 1518

Correct	Our country must be strong *on* the sea and _____ the air.
1787	1788

Correct	The team *was* ∧ in the gym. (weighing themselves) _____
2056	2057

After a long voyage, the mutineers reached Tahiti.	The high cost of medical service *is pointed* out by this article. _____ _____
2325	2326

No	Underline the correct reflexive pronoun: The Lamberts have bought (*theirselves, themselves*) a boat.
2594	2595

b	The Speedy Cleaners *at* 600 Main Street give three-hour service on request. If you omitted the preposition *at,* would you set off 600 Main Street with commas? (*Yes, No*)
2863	2864

Cleveland	Copy one italicized word that requires a capital: Are there more *lakes* in *wisconsin* or in our *state?* _____
3132	3133

LV
is

SC
danger

The young children in the back seat were becoming very restless.

Fill in the missing words:

S	LV	SC
_____	_____	_____	_____

169

---

a. **The whistle blew.**
b. **When the whistle blew**

Although both word groups have a subject and a verb, only one word group makes sense by itself.

Which word group makes sense by itself? _____

439

---

noun

708

We have seen that when we omit an adverb or adjective clause, we still have a grammatically complete sentence remaining.

What he said **puzzled us.**

When we omit the noun clause in this sentence, does a complete sentence remain? (*Yes, No*)

709

Kitty Hawk, the birthplace of aviation, is in North Carolina.

978

The game drew a crowd of 1,500, and *it was the largest attendance of the year.*

_____

979

Yes

1248

a. **The audience grew restless, their patience exhausted.**
b. **Their patience exhausted, the audience grew restless.**

In which sentence does the noun-participle phrase come at

the end of the sentence? _____

1249

Rita Moreno was given the part of Anita . . . *or* In *West Side Story* Rita Moreno . . .

1518

I saw people waiting for the bus that looked frozen.

_____

1519

in	The steak *was* tough and the potatoes _____ overcooked.
1788	1789
were	∧ These doors *lead* to the basement. (Either of) _____
2057	2058
This article points out the high cost of medical service.	This event *will* always *be remembered* by our family. _____ _____
2326	2327
themselves	All the *-self* pronouns are solid words. Do not split them! a. **my self, your self, her self, our selves, them selves** b. **myself, yourself, herself, ourselves, themselves** The pronouns are printed correctly after (*a, b*).
2595	2596
Yes	In line with the modern tendency to eliminate unnecessary commas, many publications omit commas in dates when *only* the month and the year are stated. a. **In May 1961 construction of the bridge was started.** b. **On May 27 1961 construction of the bridge was started.** Which sentence can do without commas? _____
2864	2865
Wisconsin	Copy only the words to which capitals should be added: **The Mississippi river begins at lake Itasca in minnesota.**
3133	3134

The coach of the other team was looking worried.

Fill in the missing words:

S	*LV*	*SC*
_____	_____ _____	_____

170

---

a

439

  a. **The whistle blew.**
  b. **When the whistle blew**

Which word group is a sentence because it makes sense by itself? _____

440

No

709

(*What he said*) **puzzled us.**

If we omitted the noun clause, the sentence would lack a (*subject, direct object*).

710

The game drew
a crowd of 1,500,
the largest
attendance of
the year.
979

Doug Williams made the touchdown, and *he is the quarterback.*

_____

_____

980

---

a

1249

  a. **His eyelids drooping with sleepiness, Bob struggled through the last chapter.**
  b. **Bob struggled through the last chapter, his eyelids drooping with sleep.**

In which sentence does the noun-participle phrase come at the end of the sentence? _____

1250

I saw people
that looked
frozen waiting
for the bus.
1519

You should not put a glass into hot water that is cold.

_____

_____

1520

were 1789	In this and the following frames, insert any word that has been *incorrectly* omitted. If the omission of the word is allowable, write *Correct*. **My sister takes Latin and I Spanish.** 1790
leads 2058	**In many parts of the world, the opportunity for education** ∧ *does* **not exist. (and personal development)** ——————————— 2059
Our family will always remember this event. 2327	**The rushing life of big cities** *was* **never** *enjoyed* **by my father.** ——————————— ——————————— 2328
b 2596	Underline the correct reflexive pronoun: **Try to put** (*yourself, your self*) **in my place.** 2597
a 2865	In this and the following frames, insert the necessary commas. If no commas are required, write *None*. **It is doubtful however whether any good will result from the change.** 2866

River, Lake, Minnesota
 	
3134
	Capitalize **north, east, south,** and **west** when they name geographical sections of a country or of the world. Use small letters when they indicate directions on the compass.
	
	    a. **The road turns** *south.*
	    b. **The** *south* **is quite industrial.**
	
	Capitalize *south* in sentence (*a, b*).
	
	3135

S
coach
LV
was looking
SC
worried

170

---

a. **The whistle blew.**
b. **When the whistle blew**

Word group *b* is not a sentence because the word _____ has been added.

a

440

441

We raise *vegetables*.

In this sentence the noun *vegetables* is the direct object of the verb _____.

subject

710

711

An appositive generally comes (*before, after*) the noun it explains.

Doug Williams,
the quarterback,
made the
touchdown.

980

981

A noun-participle phrase is a rather mature construction used by experienced writers to combine ideas.
In this and the following frames, combine the sentences by changing each italicized sentence to a noun-participle phrase.

I stood in the icy water. *My teeth were chattering.*

I stood in the icy water, _____.

b

1250

1251

Write the numbers of the three word groups to show in which order you would combine them. Be careful to avoid giving your sentence a ridiculous meaning.

    1. the club will show a movie
    2. on how to play football
    3. in the public library

You should not
put a glass
that is cold
into hot water.

____ ____ ____

1520

1521

I *take* Spanish	**The truck was turning left and our car right.**
1790	1791
Correct	^ **The sparrows** *wake* **me every morning. (The noisy chirp-ing of)**
	_____
2059	2060
My father (has) never enjoyed the rushing life of big cities.	Change the verb from active to passive to eliminate the present subject, which is obvious, unimportant, or tactless. Start your sentence with the thing or things *acted upon* and omit the doer of the action.
	Someone *took* **the injured man to the hospital.**
	_____
2328	_____ 2329
yourself	Supply the proper reflexive pronoun:
	The Marines hid _____ **behind some large rocks.**
2597	2598
, however,	**Send me word Virginia when you are well enough to have visitors.**
2866	2867
b	a. **Our house is on the** *West* **side of the street.**
	b. **The movie industry is in the** *West.*
	The word *west* should not be capitalized in sentence (*a, b*).
3135	3136

Some action verbs can make complete statements about their subjects. Other action verbs require another word to complete the meaning of the sentence.

An action verb is (*always, sometimes*) followed by a direct object.

172

When

441

A word group that has a subject and a verb but does not make sense by itself is a **clause.**

    a. **The road was rough.**
    b. **Because the road was rough**

Which word group is a clause? _____

442

---

raise

711

    a. **We raise** *vegetables.*
    b. **We raise** *whatever we need.*

The noun clause *whatever we need* in sentence *b* is used just like the direct object _____ in sentence *a*.

712

---

after

981

Does an appositive phrase, like a clause, contain a subject and a verb? (*Yes, No*)

982

---

my teeth
chattering.

1251

Continue to follow the directions for the previous frame:

The band was playing. **The team rushed onto the field.**

_____, **the team rushed onto the field.**

1252

Either of these
is correct:
3–1–2
1–3–2

1521

Continue to follow the directions for the previous frame:

    1. **we bought an ashtray**
    2. **at the souvenir stand**
    3. **made of shells** ___ ___ ___

1522

Correct	**The branch of medicine which Dr. Gomez specializes is nerve disorders.**
1791	1792

wakes	If making the change indicated after each sentence would make it necessary to change the italicized verb, write only the form of the verb that would be required. If the verb would remain the same, write *Correct*. **Where** *is* **your ticket?** (Change **ticket** to **tickets**.)
2060	_____ 2061

The injured man was taken to the hospital.	Continue to follow the directions for the previous frame: **People** *should* **not** *keep* **bananas in a refrigerator.** _____ _____
2329	2330

themselves	Supply the proper reflexive pronoun: **We can set our stove to turn _____ off.**
2598	2599

, Virginia,	**Mr. Higgins my counselor understood how I a new student felt on my first day in high school.** (*Note:* Look for two appositives.)
2867	2868

a	2. Capitalize the names of nationalities, languages, races, religions, and the adjectives formed from these names. **American Negro Catholic Protestant** **Italian Indian Methodist Jew (Jewish)** Copy the words that require capitals: **There is an ancient catholic church in this spanish town.**
3136	_____ 3137

a. **The price of steel rose as a result of the strike.**
b. **The price rose.**

sometimes

Although sentence *a* provides more detail than sentence *b*, the verb **rose** makes a (*complete, incomplete*) statement about the subject in both sentences.

172   173

Because the road was rough

b

This word group would become a sentence if we dropped

the word _____.

442   443

We raise *whatever we need.*

vegetables

When we omit the noun clause in this sentence, does a complete sentence remain? (*Yes, No*)

712   713

No

When an appositive phrase is omitted from a sentence, does a grammatically complete sentence remain? (*Yes, No*)

982   983

The dog was shivering on the doorstep. *Its rough coat was covered with snow.*

The band
playing,

The dog was shivering on the doorstep, _____

_____.

1252   1253

Either of these
is correct:

2-1-3
1-3-2

1. **my aunt flew to Florida**
2. **after María went to college**
3. **to bask in the sunshine**   ___ ___ ___

1522   1523

medicine *in* which

or

specializes *in*

1792

Tony would not take any advice except his father.

1793

---

are

2061

Selecting the right color *is* very important. (Change **color** to **colors.**)

_____

2062

Bananas should not be kept in a refrigerator.

2330

(*Note:* The passive form of *left* is *was left;* the passive form of *had left* is *had been left.*)

Jamie *had left* **the iron on all night.**

_____

_____

2331

---

itself

2599

Supply an intensive pronoun to emphasize the subject **students:**

The students _____ **patrol the corridors.**

2600

, my counselor,

, a new student,

2868

The famous Dionne quintuplets were born on May 28 1934 in Callander Ontario.

2869

Catholic, Spanish

3137

Copy the words that require capitals:

The author described several french trading posts in the north.

_____

3138

The price of steel rose as a result of the strike.

complete

Does the verb **rose** require a complement to complete the meaning of this sentence? (*Yes, No*)

173

174

Because

Every clause is used like a single word—like an *adverb*, an *adjective*, or a *noun*.

Since no adverb, adjective, or noun makes sense by itself, it follows that no clause that is used like one of these words makes sense by itself either.

Only a (*clause, sentence*) makes sense by itself.

443

444

No

We raise (*whatever we need*).

If we omitted the noun clause, the sentence would lack a (*subject, direct object*).

713

714

Yes

An appositive phrase, because it is an "extra," should be set off from the rest of the sentence by commas. (*True, False*)

983

984

---

its rough coat covered with snow.

Refugees wandered about aimlessly. *Their homes were destroyed.*

Refugees wandered about aimlessly, ⎯⎯⎯⎯⎯

⎯⎯⎯⎯⎯.

1253

1254

2-1-3
1-3-2

1. **clean your hands**
2. **after you paint**
3. **with turpentine**   ⎯ ⎯ ⎯

1523

1524

except *from* his *or* his father's 1793	**Next year we lose our best pitcher and hitter.** (one person) 1794
Correct 2062	**This is the finest stock car that *was* ever built.** (Change **the finest stock car** to **one of the finest stock cars.**) _____ 2063
The iron had been left on all night. 2331	**They *guarantee* these batteries for one year.** _____ _____ 2332
themselves 2600	Do not use a reflexive pronoun in place of a simple pronoun like *I, he,* or *we*—especially in careful speech or in formal writing. a. *I* **went fishing.** b. **Dad and *I* went fishing.** In which sentence might you sometimes hear *myself* instead of *I?* _____ 2601
May 28, 1934, Callander, 2869	**Yes we must realize my young friends that failure is often a steppingstone to success.** 2870
French, North 3138	Copy the words that require capitals: **There are americans of both the catholic and protestant faiths.** _____ 3139

No

174

Here are two different *action verb* patterns:

Subject—Action Verb (S—V)
Subject—Action Verb → Direct Object (S—V—DO)

Several athletes from our school competed.

The pattern of this sentence is (*S—V, S—V—DO*).

175

---

sentence

444

In this lesson you will study **adverb clauses.**

As its name suggests, an adverb clause is a clause that is used as an (*adjective, adverb*).

445

---

direct object

714

An *indirect* object precedes the *direct* object and shows *to whom* (or *to what*) or *for whom* (or *for what*) something is done.

She will pay the finder a reward.

The indirect object in the above sentence is the noun

_____.

715

True

984

Lesson **26** The Process of Reduction

[Frames 986–1021]

---

their homes
destroyed.

1254

Hundreds of persons work on each car. *Each person performs one small operation.*

Hundreds of persons work on each car, _____

_____.

1255

2–1–3
1–3–2

1524

1. **many people came**
2. **to see the game**
3. **from nearby towns**

____ ____ ____

1525

Correct	**A dachshund's body is long and its legs very short.**
1794	1795
were	**The principal and the assistant principal** *attend* **every game.** (Change **and** to **or**.) _____
2063	2064
These batteries are guaranteed for one year.	**The voters** *will vote* **upon this proposal at the next election.** _____ _____
2332	2333
b	a. *I* **went fishing.** b. **Dad and** *I* **went fishing.** Since you would never use *myself* in sentence *a*, it would seem just as unreasonable to use *myself* in sentence *b*. In both sentences, *I* is used as the _____ of the verb **went.**
2601	2602
Yes, , my young friends,	**It is human failure not mechanical failure that is responsible as a matter of fact for most of the slaughter on our highways.**
2870	2871
Americans, Catholic, Protestant	3. Capitalize the entire names of organizations, companies, buildings, theaters, and institutions such as schools, clubs, churches, libraries, and hospitals. a. **Evanston high school** b. **Evanston High School** Which is correctly capitalized? _____
3139	3140

S—V

Anaïs Nin filled many diaries with her careful observations of people.

The pattern of this sentence is (S—V, S—V—DO).

175   176

---

adverb

An ordinary adverb modifies a verb by answering questions such as **When? Where?** or **How?** about its action.

Our sales increased *recently.*

The word *recently* is an adverb because it tells **when** about

the verb _____.

445   446

---

finder

a. **She will pay the finder a reward.**
b. **She will pay whoever finds the dog a reward.**

Write the four-word noun clause in sentence *b* that takes the place of the indirect object **finder** in sentence *a*.

_____

715   716

When we substitute a simpler word group for a longer and more complicated word group, we say that we *reduce* the longer word group.

To reduce a word group means to (*simplify, complicate*) it.

986

---

each person
performing one
small operation.

In this and the following frames, eliminate the **and** by changing the italicized statement to a noun-participle phrase. (Rewrite the complete sentence.)

Their money was spent, **and the children left the carnival.**

_____

_____

1255   1256

1–3–2
2–1–3
3–1–2

1. **we gave the cookies**
2. **to the children**
3. **that had stuck to the pan**   ___ ___ ___

1525   1526

legs *are* very

1795

---

attends

2064

This proposal
will be voted
upon at the
next election.

2333

---

subject

2602

, not mechanical
failure,
, as a matter
of fact,

2871

---

b

3140

Cathy's reason for breaking the date was she had a bad headache.

1796

Neither his hands nor his face *was* clean. (Reverse the positions of **hands** and **face**.)

_____

2065

Ronnie *had put* the letter in the wrong envelope.

_____

_____

2334

Do not use a reflexive pronoun unless the word it stands for appears earlier in the sentence.

Corey excused *himself* and left early.

The pronoun *himself* is correctly used because it stands for the noun _____ earlier in the sentence.

2603

The Liberty Bell cracked on July 8 1835 when it was tolled for the death of John Marshall Chief Justice of the United States.

2872

Copy and capitalize the words that require capitals:

The Rotary club made a donation to the Hillside children's hospital.

_____

3141

S—V—DO 176	a. **Our teacher will return in a few days.** b. **Our teacher will return the test papers.** Which sentence is in the *S—V—DO* pattern? _____ 177
increased 446	a. **Our sales increased** *recently.* b. **Our sales increased** *when we lowered our price.* Both the adverb clause in sentence *b* and the adverb *recently* in sentence *a* tell (*where, when, how*) about the verb **increased.** 447
whoever finds the dog 716	**She will pay** *whoever finds the dog* **a reward.** An indirect object is not an essential part of the sentence framework. If we omit the clause in the above sentence, does a complete sentence remain? (*Yes, No*) 717
simplify 986	In general, express your idea in the simplest word group you can without sacrificing clearness. A good sentence, like a good machine, has no useless parts. If you can express your idea in a prepositional phrase, don't use (*a sentence, an adjective*). 987
Their money spent, the children left the carnival. 1256	*No guides were available,* **and we had to depend on ourselves.** (Change *were* to *being.*) _____ _____ 1257
1-3-2 2-1-3 1526	Lesson **42** Recognizing Dangling Word Groups [Frames 1528–1560]

was *that* she

1796

We can learn from almost everyone whom we come in contact.

1797

---

were

2065

This kind of rice *cooks* very fast. (Change **rice** to **beans**.)

_____

2066

The letter had
been put in
the wrong
envelope.

2334

Lesson **65** Review: Using Verbs Correctly

[Frames 2336–2368]

Corey

2603

a. **The two brothers put** *themselves* **through college.**
b. **Ralph and** *himself* **paid their own way through college.**

In which sentence is the reflexive pronoun used correctly?

_____

2604

July 8, 1835,
Marshall,

2872

Well the interview by the way lasted for over an hour.

2873

Club, Children's
Hospital

3141

Such words as *company, building, theater, college, high
school, church,* and *hospital* are not capitalized unless they
are a part of a particular name.

a Baptist church

Is this the name of only one particular church at a particular
location? (*Yes, No*)

3142

b

177

a. **The principal spoke a few words.**
b. **The principal spoke briefly.**

Which sentence is in the *S—V—DO* pattern? _____

178

---

when

447

a. **Our sales increased** *recently.*
b. **Our sales increased** *when we lowered our price.*

Because the clause in sentence *b* does the same job as the adverb in sentence *a*, it is an _____

clause.

448

Yes

717

a. **This is my** *recipe* **for fudge.**
b. **This is** *how I make fudge.*

Both the noun clause *how I make fudge* in sentence *b* and the noun *recipe* in sentence *a* complete the meaning of the linking verb **is.**

Both are used as (*subject complements, direct objects*).

718

---

a sentence

987

1. Sentence
2. Clause
3. Phrase (verbal, appositive, prepositional)
4. Single word (adjective, adverb)

As we proceed through this list from 1 to 4, the sentence elements become more (*simple, complicated*).

988

No guides being available, we had to depend on ourselves.

1257

Mrs. Koss entered the store, and *her three children were trailing after her.*

_____

_____

1258

You have seen that it is a good idea, now and then, to begin a sentence with an introductory phrase or clause.

PRESENT PARTICIPIAL PHRASE: *Climbing the ladder, . . .*
ADVERB CLAUSE: *As Jan climbed the ladder, . . .*

The word group that doesn't tell **who** climbed the ladder is the (*phrase, clause*).

1528

Lesson **50** Making Logical Comparisons

[Frames 1799–1837]

Correct

2066

Gambling *was* **his downfall. (Change gambling to horses.)**

_____

2067

In this and the following frames, write the correct forms of the verbs in parentheses:

If the director had _____ (*give*) **me a chance, I would have** _____ (*speak*).

2336

---

a

2604

Underline the correct pronoun:

I hope that your parents and (*you, yourself*) **can attend my commencement.**

2605

Well,
, by the way,

2873

I wonder Phyllis if you ever see our old neighbors the Burgesses at church.

2874

No

3142

a. **a new Baptist church**   b. **Calvary Baptist church**

In which item should **church** be capitalized because it is part of the special name of a particular church? _____

3143

178

a

In addition to a *direct* object, the *S—V—DO* sentence some-times contains an *indirect* object, which explains *to whom* (or *to what*) or *for whom* (or *for what*) something is done.

   a. **Mr. Harvey sold his stamp collection recently.**
   b. **Mr. Harvey sold my sister his stamp collection.**

Which sentence contains an indirect object? _____

179

---

adverb

448

Think of an adverb clause as a "stretched-out" adverb con-sisting of a number of words and having a *subject* and a

_____.

449

---

subject
complements

718

This is (*how I make fudge*).

We cannot omit the noun clause because we should lose an essential part of the sentence framework. The part we would lose is the (*subject, direct object, subject complement*).

719

---

simple

988

The process of reducing a word group to a simpler word group is called **reduction.**

   a. Changing a sentence to an appositive phrase.
   b. Changing a single word to a clause.

Which is an example of reduction—*a* or *b?* _____

989

Mrs. Koss
entered the
store, her three
children trailing
after her.

1258

The artist came to the door, and *her hands were stained with paint.* (Insert the noun-participle phrase after **artist.**)

_____

_____

1259

---

phrase

1528

PAST PARTICIPIAL PHRASE: *Packed in straw, . . .*
ADVERB CLAUSE: *When this clock is packed in straw, . . .*

The word group that doesn't tell **what** was packed in straw is the (*phrase, clause*).

1529

Make comparisons only between things of the same class.

WRONG: **Tommy's** *vocabulary* **is like an** *adult.*

This comparison is faulty because Tommy's *vocabulary* is not like an *adult.* It is like an adult's _____.

1799

---

were

Potatoes *are* **our main crop.** (Reverse the positions of **potatoes** and **our main crop.**)

_____

2067

2068

---

given, spoken

The window was _____ *(break)* **when I** _____

(see) **it.**

2336

2337

---

you

DEMONSTRATIVE PRONOUNS

Demonstrative pronouns (or adjectives) are used to point out. There are only four demonstrative words:

this   that   these   those

Do you find the word *them* among these words? (*Yes, No*)

2605

2606

, Phyllis,
, the Burgesses,

Mr. Knox the principal pointed out that the boys after all were only children not adults.

2874

2875

---

b

a. **the Kirby oil company**
b. **a large oil company**

In which item should the words **oil company** be capitalized because they are part of the name of a particular company?

3143

_____

3144

b 179	**Mr. Harvey sold my sister his stamp collection.** The indirect object in this sentence is _____. 180
verb (*or* predicate) 449	**Our farm begins** *here.* The word *here* is an adverb because it tells **where** about the verb _____. 450
subject complement 719	**We were still ten miles from our** *destination.* The noun *destination* is the object of the preposition _____. 720
a 989	a. Changing a sentence to an appositive phrase. b. Changing a single word to a clause. Which change would be preferable in your writing? _____ 990
The artist, her hands stained with paint, came to the door. 1259	**Ten scouts stood on the stage,** *and each was holding a different flag.* (Insert the phrase after **scouts.**) _____ _____ 1260
phrase 1529	PREPOSITIONAL GERUND PHRASE: *After biting six children, . . .* ADVERB CLAUSE: *After the dog had bitten six children, . . .* The phrase doesn't tell you **who** or **what** bit the children, but the clause tells you that it was a _____. 1530

vocabulary 1799	a. **Tommy's** *vocabulary* **is like an** *adult.* b. **Tommy's** *vocabulary* **is like the** *vocabulary* **of an adult.** Which comparison is correct? _____ 1800
is 2068	**One hour hardly** *seems* **enough time for this job.** (Change **One hour** to **Two hours.**) _____ 2069
broken, saw 2337	**Bob might have** _____ (*become*) **ill from all the ice water that he** _____ (*drink*). 2338
No 2606	The word *them* is not a demonstrative pronoun. It is the (*objective, nominative*) form of the personal pronoun **they.** 2607
, the principal, , after all, , not 2875	**The Chinese Telephone Exchange 743 Washington Street San Francisco California 94103 welcomes visitors.** 2876
a 3144	4. Capitalize the names of the days of the week, months, and holidays, but *not* the names of the seasons. **Wednesday** **Christmas** spring **February** **Memorial Day** fall Copy the words that require capitals: **In the autumn we look forward to thanksgiving day.** _____ 3145

sister

180

Mr. Harvey sold my sister his stamp collection.

When an indirect object is present, it always comes (*before,* *after*) the direct object.

181

---

begins

450

a. **Our farm begins** *here.*
b. **Our farm begins** *where the road turns.*

The adverb clause in sentence *b* does the same job as the adverb *here* in sentence *a*.

Both tell (*where, when, how*) about the verb **begins.**

451

---

from

720

a. **We were still ten miles from our** *destination.*
b. **We were still ten miles from** *where we were going.*

In sentence *a,* the noun *destination* is the object of the preposition **from.**

Write the noun clause in sentence *b* that is the object of the preposition **from.** _____

721

---

a

990

When you reduce a word group, you generally improve your writing by using (*fewer, more*) words.

991

Ten scouts, each holding a different flag, stood on the stage.
1260

Lesson **34** Review: Devices for Sentence Variety

[Frames 1262–1278]

---

dog

1530

INFINITIVE PHRASE: *To get more business, . . .*
ADVERB CLAUSE: *If a company wants to get more business, . . .*

The phrase doesn't tell you **who** or **what** is to get more business, but the clause tells you that it is a _____ .

1531

a. **Tommy's** *vocabulary* **is like the** *vocabulary* **of an adult.**
b. **Tommy's** *vocabulary* **is like** *that* **of an adult.**

Each of these sentences is correct because *vocabulary* is compared with *vocabulary*.

In sentence *b*, the word that stands for *vocabulary* is the pronoun _____.

---

b

1800

1801

Correct

2069

What color *is* **its hair? (Change** **hair** **to** **eyes.)**

_____

2070

---

become, drank

2338

When Connie _____ (*come*) **into the house, her ears**
were _____ (*freeze*).

2339

---

objective

2607

Use the demonstrative pronoun (or adjective) *those,* not the personal pronoun *them,* to point out persons or things.

 a. *Them* **are good cookies. I like** *them* **cookies.**
 b. *Those* **are good cookies. I like** *those* **cookies.**

The correct sentences follow the letter (*a, b*).

2608

, 743
Washington Street,
San Francisco,
California 94103,

2876

Lesson **80** Commas for Nonrestrictive
Clauses

[Frames 2878–2911]

Thanksgiving
Day

3145

 a. **Our winter sale begins after New Year's.**
 b. **Our Winter sale begins after new year's.**

Which sentence is correctly capitalized? _____

3146

before	**The charcoal gives the meat a tangy flavor.**
	The indirect object in this sentence is _____.
181	182

	a. **Mr. Cruz spoke** *seriously.*
	b. **Mr. Cruz spoke** *as if he meant business.*
where	Both the adverb clause in sentence *b* and the adverb *seriously* in sentence *a* tell (*when, where, how*) about the verb **spoke.**
451	452

	We were still ten miles from (*where we were going*).
where we were going	We cannot omit the noun clause because the preposition **from** would then be without an _____.
721	722

	We have spent many frames on reducing sentences to subordinate word groups—to clauses and various kinds of phrases. Now we shall practice other types of reduction.
fewer	**Ann stumbled** *while she was coming down the stairs.*
	Which two words can you omit from the adverb clause without changing the meaning? _____ _____
991	992

	Each sentence lettered *a* represents one of the devices you have studied in this unit. Rewrite each sentence lettered *b*, putting it in the same arrangement as *a*.
	a. **This fact no sensible person will deny.**
	b. **The dog refused to eat these biscuits.**
	_____
	_____ 1262

	CLAUSES: *As Jan climbed the ladder, . . .*
	When this clock is packed in straw, . . .
	After the dog had bitten six children, . . .
company	*If a company wants to get more business, . . .*
	Do clauses have subjects that tell **whom** or **what** they are about? (*Yes, No*)
1531	1532

that 1801	**Tommy's** *vocabulary* **is like an** *adult's.* This comparison is also correct because the possessive noun *adult's* implies an adult's _____. <div align="right">1802</div>
are 2070	**This is the best fair that** *was* **ever held here. (Change the best fair to one of the best fairs.)** _____ <div align="right">2071</div>
came, frozen 2339	**Terry had** _____ (*grow*) **so much that you would hardly have** _____ (*know*) **him.** <div align="right">2340</div>
b 2608	Underline the correct word: **Why don't we ask** (*those, them*) **students to help us?** <div align="right">2609</div>
	Adjective clauses begin with the relative pronouns **who (whose, whom), which,** and **that.** An adjective clause, like an adjective, modifies a noun or a _____. <div align="right">2878</div>
a 3146	5. Capitalize the brand names of particular products, but *not* the types of products that they identify. **Sunkist oranges Chrysler car Protecto paint** Copy the words that require capitals: **The makers of broadway shirts recommend that you use swish detergent.** _____ <div align="right">3147</div>

meat

182

---

a. **Shirley read** *Cynthia* **her letter.**
b. **Shirley read her letter to** *Cynthia.*

In which sentence is *Cynthia* an indirect object? _____

183

---

how

452

Besides telling **when, where,** and **how** about verbs, as adverbs can do, adverb clauses can also tell **why.**

a. **We moved** *because our house was too small.*
b. **We moved** *where there were very few other houses.*

In which sentence does the adverb clause tell **why** about the verb **moved?** _____

453

---

object

722

An *appositive* is a noun or pronoun set after another noun or pronoun to explain it.

Our last hope, *rescue* **by the Marines, was soon to be realized.**

The appositive *rescue,* with its modifiers, follows and explains the noun _____.

723

---

she was

992

Ann stumbled *while (she was) coming down the stairs.*

The two words that we can omit from the adverb clause are the subject and a part of the _____.

993

These biscuits
the dog refused
to eat.

1262

---

a. **For a person of his age, such exercise seems much too strenuous.**
b. **Barbara Jordan held the interest of Congress from her first sentence.**

_____

_____

1263

Yes

1532

PHRASES: *Climbing the ladder, . . .*
Packed in straw, . . .
After biting six children, . . .
To get more business, . . .

Do phrases have subjects that tell **whom** or **what** they are about? (*Yes, No*)

1533

vocabulary 1802	a. **Tommy's vocabulary is like the vocabulary of an adult.** b. **Tommy's vocabulary is like that of an adult.** c. **Tommy's vocabulary is like an adult.** d. **Tommy's vocabulary is like an adult's.** The only incorrect comparison is in sentence _____. <div align="right">1803</div>
were 2071	**There** *was* **only one street between our house and the park.** (Change **one street** to **three streets.**) _____ <div align="right">2072</div>
grown, known 2340	**I have** _____ (*write*) **a letter to the company, complaining that the shirt has** _____ (*shrink*). <div align="right">2341</div>
those 2609	<div align="center">POSSESSIVE PRONOUNS</div>Possessive pronouns show possession without the use of apostrophes. *Your's* or *our's* is just as incorrect as *hi's*. POSSESSIVE PRONOUNS: **yours, his, hers, its, ours, theirs** <div align="center">*Yours* **is just like** *ours.*</div>Do the italicized pronouns require apostrophes? (*Yes, No*) <div align="right">2610</div>
pronoun 2878	To decide whether or not to set off an adjective clause with commas, ask yourself what purpose it serves. <div align="center">a. **all students** b. **all students** *who can typewrite*</div>The adjective clause in *b* makes the noun **students** refer to (*more, fewer*) students. <div align="right">2879</div>
Broadway, Swish 3147	<div align="center">a. **Blue Star Gasoline** b. **Blue Star gasoline**</div>Which item is correctly capitalized? _____ <div align="right">3148</div>

A linking verb can never by itself make a complete statement about its subject.

A linking verb must (*always, sometimes*) be completed by a subject complement that describes or identifies the subject of the sentence.

a

183

184

An adverb clause can also answer the question **On what condition?** or **Under what condition?** about the verb.

    a. **The engine will start** *if you push the car.*
    b. **The engine will start** *when you turn the key.*

In which sentence does the adverb clause tell **on what condition** the engine will start? _____

a

453

454

---

    a. **Our last hope,** *rescue by the Marines,* **was soon to be realized.**
    b. **Our last hope,** *that the Marines would rescue us,* **was soon to be realized.**

The noun clause in sentence *b* does the same job as the appositive _____ in sentence *a*.

hope

723

724

The word *elliptical* means "having words omitted." An adverb clause from which words have been omitted is an **elliptical clause.**

    Ann stumbled *while (she was) coming down the stairs.*

In the above sentence, using an elliptical clause eliminates _____ words. (How many?)

verb
(*or* predicate)

993

994

---

    a. **The land, dry and rocky, is useless for farming.**
    b. **The old, dingy city hall was being remodeled.**

_____

_____

From her first
sentence,
Barbara Jordan
held the interest
of Congress.

1264

Since a phrase leaves your reader in the dark, you must answer the question **Who?** or **What?** at the beginning of the main statement that follows.

    a. *Going up the ladder,* **a branch hit Jan's head.**
    b. *Going up the ladder,* **Jan hit her head on a branch.**

Which sentence answers the question **Who?** _____

No

1533

1534

c

1803

a. **Our customs are different from the customs of Mexico.**
b. **Our customs are different from Mexico.**
c. **Our customs are different from Mexico's.**
d. **Our customs are different from those of Mexico.**

The only incorrect comparison is in sentence _____.

1804

---

were

2072

Lesson **58** A Group of Similar Three-Part Verbs

[Frames 2074–2109]

---

written, shrunk

2341

You would not have _____ (*eat*) **it if you had** _____ (*see*) **it made.**

2342

No

2610

Because apostrophes are needed to make nouns possessive, it is a natural and common mistake to use them with pronouns, too.

Underline the italicized word which requires an apostrophe to show possession:

We parked *ours* **in** *Stanleys* **driveway.**

2611

---

fewer

2879

a. **people**
b. **people** *who fail to vote*

People means *all* people.

By adding the clause *who fail to vote*, we (*increase, limit*) the number of people we are talking about.

2880

---

b

3148

6. Capitalize the names of governmental bodies, agencies, departments, and offices.

Senate   **Board of Education**   **City Council**
Supreme Court   **Treasury Department**   **Department of Health**

Copy the words that require capitals:

The congress referred the matter to the state department.

3149

---

always

a. **are, were, seemed, became**
b. **ate, took, studied, listened**

Would you expect to find a subject complement after the words in group *a* or group *b?* _____

185

---

a

a. **Vern went to school** *because a test was scheduled.*
b. **Vern went to school** *although he had a bad cold.*

In which sentence does the adverb clause tell **under what condition** Vern went to school? _____

454

455

---

rescue

Our last hope, *that the Marines would rescue us,* **was soon to be realized.**

Our last hope . . . was soon to be realized.

When we omit the noun clause used as an appositive, does a complete sentence remain? (*Yes, No*)

724

725

---

two

Crackers will stay crisp *if they are kept in a tin box.*

Write the elliptical clause to which the italicized adverb clause can be reduced: _____.

994

995

The city hall, old and dingy, was being remodeled.

a. **The job would have been simple had I used the right tools.**
b. **Helen would have sung if we had urged her.**

(In revising sentence *b*, eliminate the adverb clause signal **if,** and keep the ideas in the same order.)

_____

_____

1264

1265

---

b

WRONG: *Going up the ladder,* **a branch hit Jan's head.**

Since there is no word for the italicized phrase to modify, it appears to modify the noun **branch.**

Is it the **branch** that is *going up the ladder?* (*Yes, No*)

1534

1535

Always make sure that your comparisons are logical.

b

WRONG: **Montreal is larger than** *any city* **in Canada.**

Does *any city* include the city of Montreal? (*Yes, No*)

1804

1805

The three basic forms of a verb from which all its various tenses are formed are called the **principal parts** of the verb.

PRESENT	PAST	PAST PARTICIPLE
talk	**talked**	**(have) talked**

Both the *past* and the *past participle* of this verb end with the two letters _____.

2074

---

eaten, seen

When I _____ (*run*) **to the window, the car had already** _____ (*drive*) **away.**

2342

2343

Stanley's

a. *Carols* **coat is newer than** *Virginias.*
b. *Yours* **is newer than** *hers.*

Which sentence is correct without apostrophes? _____

2611

2612

---

limit

To restrict means "to limit the number."

When we say the use of a parking lot is *restricted* to customers, we mean that its use is _____ to customers and that not everyone can park there.

2880

2881

Congress, State Department

a. **Federal Bureau of Investigation**
b. **Federal bureau of investigation**

Which item is correctly capitalized? _____

3149

3150

a 185	*Subject—Linking Verb ← Subject Complement* (*S—LV—SC*) $$1 \longrightarrow 2$$ a. **Larry lost his voice.** $$1 \longleftarrow 1$$ b. **Larry became hoarse.** Which sentence is in the *S—LV—SC* pattern? _____ <div align="right">186</div>
b 455	Learn to recognize the clause signals that tell us that an adverb clause is beginning. They are grouped according to the kind of information that the clauses supply. WHEN? **while, when, whenever, as, as soon as, before, after, since, until** Look for adverb clauses (*before, after*) these words. <div align="right">456</div>
Yes 725	A noun clause is generally an essential part of the sentence framework and cannot be omitted. The only exceptions are noun clauses used as indirect objects or as appositives. If a noun clause is used as a subject, direct object, subject complement, or object of a preposition, it (*can, cannot*) be omitted. <div align="right">726</div>
if kept in a tin box. 995	*While he was looking for a job,* **Ted had many disappointments.** Write the elliptical clause to which the italicized adverb clause can be reduced: _____. <div align="right">996</div>
Helen would have sung had we urged her. 1265	a. **Now that Eva has a driver's license, she wants to drive all the time.** b. **I have a typewriter, and my work looks neater.** _____ _____ <div align="right">1266</div>
No 1535	A phrase that has no word to modify or appears to modify the wrong word is a **dangling phrase.** It is like a plane circling in the air with no place to land. a. *Going up the ladder,* **Jan hit her head on a branch.** b. *Going up the ladder,* **a branch hit Jan's head.** Which sentence contains a dangling phrase? _____ <div align="right">1536</div>

Yes 1805	WRONG: **Montreal is larger than** *any city* **in Canada.** Since *any city* includes Montreal, this sentence states that Montreal is larger than itself. Therefore, this comparison is (*logical, illogical*). 1806
ed 2074	The past participle of a verb is the form we use in combination with any form of the helping verb **have** or **be**. PRESENT PAST PAST PARTICIPLE **talk** **talked** **(have) talked** In the case of the verb **talk,** is there any difference between the past and past participle form? (*Yes, No*) 2075
ran, driven 2343	**Sue** _____ (*give*) **the police a description of the bicycle that had been** _____ (*steal*). 2344

b
 	
2612
	No blunder is more common than confusing the possessive pronoun **its** (belonging to *it*) with the contraction **it's** (= *it is*).
	
	    RIGHT: *It's* (= *It is*) **waiting for** *its* (*possessive*) **meal.**
	
	Underline the correct words in the following sentence:
	
	    (*It's, Its*) **mother knows when** (*it's, its*) **hungry.** 2613

limited 2881	A clause that restricts or limits the number of the word it modifies is called a **restrictive clause.** A restrictive clause makes the word it modifies mean (*less, more*) than it would mean without the clause. 2882
a 3150	In this and the following frames, copy only the words in each sentence to which capitals need to be added, according to the rules presented in this lesson: **Memorial day comes in the spring, not in the fall.** 3151

a. **Larry became a . . .**
b. **Larry found a . . .**

Which sentence would be completed by a subject complement? _____

187

There are only two clause signals which can start adverb
clauses that answer the question **Where?**

WHERE? **where, wherever**

      We hid the candy *where no one could find it.*

The adverb clause modifies the word (*hid, candy*).

457

A noun clause is a clause that is used in any way that a
_____ can be used.

727

An adverb clause can often be reduced to a present participial phrase.

      When I saw the child, **I put on the brakes.**
      Seeing the child, **I put on the brakes.**

This reduction eliminates _____ words. (How many?)

997

Now that I have
a typewriter,
my work looks
neater.

1266

a. **Once a forest fire starts, it is hard to control.**
b. **After you play a card, you can't take it back.**

_____

_____

1267

Going up the ladder, **Jan hit her head on a branch.**

Now the phrase no longer dangles because the question

Who? is answered by the noun _____.

1537

illogical 1806	a. **Montreal is larger than** *any* **city in Canada.** b. **Montreal is larger than** *any other* **city in Canada.** Which comparison is correct? _____ 1807
No 2075	English verbs fall into two general classes: **regular** and **irregular** verbs. Verbs are classified as regular when both their past and past participle forms end with *-ed*. PRESENT PAST PAST PARTICIPLE **talk** **talked** **(have) talked** The verb **talk** is (*regular, irregular*). 2076
gave, stolen 2344	**The bell was** _____ (*ring*) **just after Walter had** _____ (*begin*) **his talk.** 2345
Its, it's 2613	Do not write the word **it's** unless you can put the words _____ _____ in its place. 2614
less 2882	**Students** *who do failing work* **may not participate in sports.** This sentence does not make a statement about *all* students. It makes a statement only about those *who* _____ _____. 2883
Day 3151	**The hurricane veered west on monday night and struck several states along the atlantic ocean.** (Does **west** indicate a direction, or does it name a geographical section of the country? See frame 3135, page 340.) 3152

In one sentence, *are getting* is an action verb followed by a direct object; in the other, it is a linking verb followed by a subject complement.

a

    a. **The boys** *are getting* **their own lunch.**
    b. **The boys** *are getting* **hungry.**

The verb *are getting* is a linking verb in sentence _____.

187

188

Only two clause signals can start adverb clauses that answer the question **How?**

HOW? **as if, as though**

hid

    a. **Mrs. Kay frowned** *as we told her our plan.*
    b. **Mrs. Kay frowned** *as if she were doubtful.*

The clause in sentence (*a, b*) tells **how** Mrs. Kay frowned.

457

458

The words **that, whether, what, how,** and **why** are often used as clause signals to start noun clauses.

noun

    That anyone should believe this rumor **is absurd.**

The noun clause begins with the word _____ and

ends with the word _____.

727

728

Fill in the present participial phrase to which the adverb clause can be reduced:

two

Because I wanted experience, **I fixed the radio myself.**

_____, **I fixed the**

radio myself.

997

998

Once you play
a card, you can't
take it back.

    a. **Good as the play was, many did not appreciate it.**
    b. **The book was long, but it held my interest.**

_____

_____

1267

1268

Jan

    Packed in straw, **you can ship this clock anywhere.**

Is the introductory phrase followed closely by a word that tells **what** is *packed in straw?* (*Yes, No*)

1537

1538

b 1807	WRONG: **Montreal is the largest of** *any other city* **in Canada.** The words *any other city* mean only *one* city. Can Montreal be the largest of *one* city? (*Yes, No*) 1808
regular 2076	Of the thousands of verbs in our language, fewer than 150 are irregular. A verb is classified as irregular when its past and past participle forms do not end with *-ed*. **work** **worked** **(have) worked** **drive** **drove** **(have) driven** The irregular verb is (*work, drive*). 2077

rung, begun
 	
2345
	Look at these memory rhymes once again:
	
	    "Yes-ter-day **"In pain**
	      In bed he lay." **he has lain."**
	
	In this and the following frames, underline the correct verbs:
	
	The dog (*lay, laid*) **down under the chair where Noreen was** (*sitting, setting*).
	
	2346

it is 2614	Underline the correct words: (*It's, Its*) **not in** (*it's, its*) **usual place.** 2615
do failing work 2883	**Students** *who do failing work* **may not participate in sports.** Because the clause *who do failing work* restricts or limits the number of students we are talking about, it is a re_____ clause. 2884
Monday, Atlantic Ocean 3152	(Be sure to capitalize an entire name, not just a part of it.) **The Studio theater on Madison avenue features english, italian, and other foreign films.** 3153

The boys are getting hungry.

The word **hungry** is a (*direct object, subject complement*).

b

188

189

Several clause signals can start adverb clauses that answer the question **Why?**

WHY? **because, since, as, so that**

    a. **I couldn't concentrate** *because of the noise.*
    b. **I couldn't concentrate** *because the room was noisy.*

In which sentence does *because* start a clause? ____

b

458

459

That anyone should believe this rumor **is absurd.**

The noun clause in the above sentence is used as the

_____ of the verb **is.**

That . . . rumor

728

729

An adverb clause that starts with the clause signal **so that** can often be reduced to an infinitive phrase.

    I set the alarm *so that it would wake me at six.*
    I set the alarm *to wake me at six.*

This reduction eliminates _____ words. (How many?)

Wanting
experience,

998

999

---

a. **A lady asked me to baby-sit with her two children, neither of whom I had ever seen before.**
b. **Ann applied to two colleges, and both of them accepted her.**

_____

_____

Long as the
book (it) was,
it (the book) held
my interest.

1268

1269

Packed in straw, **you can ship this clock anywhere.**

The italicized phrase is a (*dangling, correct*) phrase.

No

1538

1539

No

1808

WRONG: **Montreal is the largest of all the *other* cities in Canada.**

The words *all the other cities* exclude Montreal.

Since Montreal is not among *all the other cities,* can it be the largest among them? (*Yes, No*)

1809

---

drive

There is great variety among irregular verbs because they came into English from other languages and their forms have changed over the centuries without following any set pattern.

| **drive** | **drove** | **(have) driven** |
| **do** | **did** | **(have) done** |

Are the forms of these two irregular verbs similar? (*Yes, No*)

2077

2078

---

lay, sitting

When the curtain (*raised, rose*), **a body was** (*lying, laying*) **on the floor of the living room.**

2346

2347

It's, its

In this and the following frames, underline the correct pronouns or, in some cases, the pronouns appropriate for formal usage:

At a buffet dinner, the guests serve (*themselves, theirselves*).

2615

2616

---

restrictive

A sentence usually becomes untrue or absurd when you omit a restrictive clause.

Because a restrictive clause is very essential to the meaning of a sentence, do *not* set it off with commas.

Visitors *who stay too long* are not welcome.

Does the italicized clause require commas? (*Yes, No*)

2884

2885

Theater, Avenue, English, Italian

A crowd was gathered around a ford truck, where a man was giving away free samples of snowflake crackers.

3153

3154

subject complement	a. **The quality of the programs** *is* **excellent.** b. **The quality of the programs** *is* **improving.** In one of the sentences *is* serves as a helper to the main verb. In the other, it is a linking verb followed by a subject complement. Which sentence contains a subject complement? _____ 190
189	
b	WHY? **because, since, as, so that** **The man moved over . . . Doris and I could sit together.** The clause signal needed in this sentence would consist of (*one word, two words*).
459	460
subject	**A lie detector shows** *whether you are telling the truth.* The noun clause begins with the word _____ and ends with the word _____ .
729	730
three	**He adjusted the carburetor** *so that it would use less gas.* Fill in the infinitive phrase to which the adverb clause can be reduced: **He adjusted the carburetor** _____
999	_____ . 1000
Ann applied to two colleges, both of which accepted her.	a. **The union held a meeting, the outcome of which was not announced.** b. **I was struck by a car, and the owner was not insured.** _____ _____
1269	1270
dangling	a. *Packed in straw,* **you can ship this clock anywhere.** b. *Packed in straw,* **this clock can be shipped anywhere.** Which sentence is correct because the introductory phrase is followed closely by the word it modifies—the word that answers the question **What?** _____
1539	1540

WRONG: **Montreal is the largest of all the other cities in Canada.**

To make this comparison logical, we must omit the word

_____.

1810

A small number of verbs such as **bet, hit, put,** and **shut** have only one form for all uses. These verbs that have reached the limit of simplification are called *one-part* verbs.

see	**saw**	**(have) seen**
hit	**hit**	**(have) hit**

The one-part verb is (*see, hit*).

2079

I had (*lain, laid*) **there reading for about an hour but then had** (*rose, risen*) **to answer the telephone.**

2348

Why did the clerk put (*hisself, himself*) **in this embarrassing position?**

2617

A newspaper should not publish any news *that has not been carefully checked.*

Read this sentence again, omitting the italicized clause.

Is the clause too important to the meaning of the sentence to be set off with a comma? (*Yes, No*)

2886

Our high school will open on september 5, the day after labor day.

_____

3155

Gwen felt . . . about the tear in her jeans.

a

The missing word in this sentence would be a (*subject complement, direct object*).

190   191

---

two words
(so that)

Several clause signals can start adverb clauses that answer the question **On (*or* under) what condition?** These are **if, unless, though, although, provided that.**

        The cake might burn *unless you watch it.*

The adverb clause explains **under what condition** the cake

460   _____ _____.   461

---

whether . . . truth

        A lie detector shows *whether you are telling the truth.*

The noun clause is used as the _____
of the verb **shows.**

730   731

---

to use less gas.

Adjective clauses, too, can often be reduced to the same kind of verbal phrases. See how we change an adjective clause to a present participial phrase:
   a. **The house was built on a hill** *that overlooked a lake.*
   b. **The house was built on a hill** *overlooking a lake.*
The present participle in sentence *b* is _____.

1000   1001

I was struck
by a car, the
owner of which
was not insured.

a. **The fact that Alfonso is good-natured makes him very popular.**
b. **Miss Daly has gray hair, but that doesn't make her old.**

_____

_____

1270   1271

---

b

     After biting six children, **a police officer shot the dog.**

Since this introductory phrase is not followed by a word that sensibly answers the question **Who?** or **What?** it suggests that a _____ bit the children.

1540   1541

other	a. **Montreal is the largest of any other city in Canada.** b. **Montreal is the largest of all the other cities in Canada.** c. **Montreal is the largest of all the cities in Canada.** Which comparison is correct? _____
1810	1811

	burst	**burst**	**(have) burst**
	cost	cost	(have) cost
hit	**find**	**found**	**(have) found**
	hurt	**hurt**	**(have) hurt**
	All the above verbs are one-part verbs except _____.		
2079			2080

lain, risen	**We had (*set, sat*) a bench under a tree and had (*lain, laid*) our picnic baskets on it.**
2348	2349

himself	**Coach Fry told us that we might lose the game if we are too sure of (*our selves, ourselves*).**
2617	2618

Yes	Suppose that a druggist were to put a sign in the window to advertise for a salesperson.
	
	    a. **A salesperson is wanted.**
	    b. **A salesperson *who has a car* is wanted.**
	
	Which statement would restrict or limit the number of applicants for the job—*a* or *b*? _____

2886	2887

September, Labor Day	**Next fall Arlene plans to attend medical school in the east.**
3155	3156

subject complement 191	**We moved the . . . to the kitchen.** The missing word in this sentence would be a (*subject complement, direct object*). 192

might burn
 	
461
	The adverb clause, just like the adverb it resembles, can generally be moved from one position to another in a sentence.
	
	   a. **Lucille changed her mind** *when she saw the price.*
	   b. *When she saw the price,* **Lucille changed her mind.**
	
	The adverb clause comes first in sentence (*a, b*).
	
	462

object *or* direct object 731	**You can depend on whatever he tells you.** The noun clause begins with the word _____ and ends with the word _____. 732
overlooking 1001	**Books may be borrowed by anyone** *who has a library card.* Fill in the present participial phrase to which the adjective clause can be reduced: **Books may be borrowed by anyone** _____ _____. 1002
The fact that Miss Daly has gray hair doesn't make her old. 1271	a. **It was fortunate that the fire broke out after school.** b. **The child was traveling alone, and this seemed strange.** _____ _____ 1272
police officer 1541	a. **After biting six children, the dog was shot by a police officer.** b. **After biting six children, a police officer shot the dog.** Which sentence is wrong because it contains a dangling phrase? _____ 1542

c 1811	Now we shall look at another type of comparison. Supply the missing word that completes the comparison: **Laura earns** *as much* _____ **her brother.** 1812
find 2080	Many irregular verbs have the same form for both their past and past participles. These are called *two-part* verbs. **bring** **brought** **(have) brought** **spread** **spread** **(have) spread** One of the above verbs has one part; the other has two parts. The two-part verb is _____. 2081
set, laid 2349	**Herman moved to Appleton, where he** (*bought, buys*) **a small newspaper.** 2350
ourselves 2618	**Harvey and** (*you, yourself*) **can ride with us.** 2619
b 2887	**A salesperson** *who has a car* **is wanted.** Not anyone would apply for this job—only one *who has a car.* The clause *who has a car* is therefore a _____ clause. 2888
East 3156	**Surrounding Shady Grove park are an episcopal church, an elementary school, and a library.** 3157

direct object	**The house seemed strangely empty without the children.**
	The word **empty** is a _____ _____.
192	193

b	a. **Lucille changed her mind** *when she saw the price.*
	b. *When she saw the price,* **Lucille changed her mind.**
	A comma is needed when the adverb clause comes (*before, after*) the main statement of the sentence.
462	463

whatever . . . you	**You can depend on whatever he tells you.**
	The noun clause is used as the object of a (*verb, preposition*).
732	733

	Now we shall reduce an adjective clause to a past participial phrase:
having a library card.	**We bought some corn** *that was picked this morning.*
	Which two words in the adjective clause can be omitted without changing the meaning? _____ _____
1002	1003

	a. **The article explains that, as time has gone on, football has become more complicated.**
It seemed strange that the child was traveling alone.	b. **Mother insisted that I had to invite Martha because she is my cousin.** (Insert the adverb clause after *that*.)
	_____
	_____
1272	1273

	Of course, if your introductory word group has a subject to explain **whom** or **what** it is about, you do not need to explain this again in the main statement that follows it.
b	a. **While I was pushing the car, I ripped my coat.**
	b. **While I was pushing the car, my coat ripped.**
	Are both sentences correct? (*Yes, No*)
1542	1543

as	Supply the missing word that completes the comparison:
	Laura earns *more* _____ **her brother.**
1812	1813

bring	PRESENT	PAST	PAST PARTICIPLE
	bring	brought	(have) brought
	catch	caught	(have) caught
	swing	swung	(have) swung
2081	In two-part verbs, the past and _____ _____ forms are the same.		2082

bought	The play is about a woman who came to live with a family and (*tries, tried*) to take over.
2350	2351

you	The British and (*ourselves, we*) are united by the bond of a common language.
2619	2620

restrictive	**Dictionaries** *which are too small* **are not very useful.**
	Because a restrictive clause is essential to the meaning of a sentence, it (*should, should not*) be set off with commas.
2888	2889

Park, Episcopal	The Civil Aeronautics administration appealed to congress for new legislation.
3157	3158

subject complement	**A membership card gives one many privileges.**
	The indirect object in this sentence is the word _____ .
193	194
before	a. **Although we were tired, we finished the job.** b. **We finished the job although we were tired.**
	The adverb clause comes first in sentence (*a*, *b*).
463	464
preposition	**This tiny spring is what powers the watch.**
	The noun clause begins with the word _____
	and ends with the word _____ .
733	734
that was	**We bought some corn** *that was picked this morning.*
	Fill in the past participial phrase to which the adjective clause can be reduced:
	We bought some corn _____ .
1003	1004
Mother insisted that, because Martha is my cousin, I had to invite her.	a. **No sooner had I turned in my test paper than I realized my mistake.** b. **It began to pour as soon as we stepped out of the house.**
	_____
	_____
1273	1274
	Do you remember that an elliptical clause is an adverb clause from which the subject and part of the verb have been omitted?
Yes	a. **While I was pushing the car, . . .** b. **While pushing the car, . . .**
1543	Which is an elliptical (incomplete) clause? _____ 1544

than 1813	WRONG: **Laura earns as much,** *if not more than,* **her brother.** Omit the italicized phrase and you will see what is wrong with the above sentence. The trouble is that **as much** is followed by *than* instead of by _____. <div align="right">1814</div>
past participle 2082	Most irregular verbs have a special form for the past participle. These are the *three-part* verbs that are responsible for most verb trouble. | **see**	**saw**	**(have) seen**
catch	**caught**	**(have) caught**	 The three-part verb is (*see, catch*). <div align="right">2083</div>
tried 2351	**Johnny couldn't understand why a fourth** (*was, is*) **larger than a fifth.** <div align="right">2352</div>
we 2620	(*Those, Them*) **dishes are exactly like** (*our's, ours*). <div align="right">2621</div>
should not 2889	Less frequently, an adjective clause is used merely to provide an additional fact about the word it modifies. Such a clause may be omitted without destroying the truth or accuracy of your statement. **Hale Smith,** *who composes music,* **is a professor.** Is this sentence true without the clause? (*Yes, No*) <div align="right">2890</div>
Administration, Congress 3158	**The program is sponsored jointly by the makers of zip soap and polar bear freezers.** (Brand names are treated somewhat differently from other names. See frame 3147, page 364.) <div align="right">3159</div>

Lesson 6 One-word Modifiers: Adjectives and Adverbs

[Frames 196–237]

---

a

464

a. **Although we were tired, we finished the job.**
b. **We finished the job although we were tired.**

A comma is needed when the adverb clause comes (*before, after*) the main statement.

465

---

what . . . watch

734

This tiny spring is what powers the watch.

The noun clause in this sentence completes the meaning of the linking verb **is** and is used as a (*subject complement, direct object*).

735

---

picked this morning.

1004

An adjective clause can sometimes be reduced to an infinitive phrase.

> **You need more facts** *that will prove your argument.*
> **You need more facts** *to prove your argument.*

In the second sentence we changed the verb *will prove* to

the infinitive ————————.

1005

No sooner had we stepped out of the house than it began to pour.

1274

a. **Not only did Marta pass the course, but she also received an A.**
b. **Phil borrowed my book, and he lost it.**

————————————————————

————————————————————

1275

---

b

1544

a. **While I was pushing the car, . . .**
b. **While pushing the car, . . .**

After which clause would you need to tell **who** in order to

avoid a dangling word group? ———

1545

as
 	
1814
	In combining an "as" and a "than" comparison, first complete the "as" comparison. Then add the "if" phrase at the end, where it need not be completed.
	
	  a. **Laura earns as much, if not more than, her brother.**
	  b. **Laura earns as much as her brother, if not more.**
	
	Which sentence is correct? _____ 1815

see 2083	The main danger with three-part verbs is confusing their two past forms—the simple past and the past participle. PRESENT PAST PAST PARTICIPLE **see** **saw** **(have) seen** The past form of the verb **see** that may be used by itself without a helping verb is (*saw, seen*). 2084
is 2352	**The doctor said that too much salt** (*is, was*) **bad for people.** 2353
Those, ours 2621	**Mrs. Kemp parked** (*hers, her's*) **next to** (*theirs, their's*)**.** 2622
Yes 2890	a. **Any number** *which can be divided by two* **is an even number.** b. **Crater Lake,** *which is two thousand feet deep,* **has no inlet or outlet.** In which sentence can the clause be omitted without damaging the meaning of the sentence? _____ 2891
Zip, Polar Bear 3159	**The auditorium of the Utley high school is used for jewish religious services on saturdays and for christian services on sundays.** 3160

Until this point, we have been dealing mainly with only the framework of sentences—subjects, verbs, and sometimes complements.

Brakes cause accidents.

Does this sentence contain any words that are not a part of its framework? (*Yes, No*)

196

---

before

465

a. **Children appreciate nothing if they are given too much.**
b. **If children are given too much they appreciate nothing.**

Which sentence requires a comma—*a or b?* _____

466

---

subject
complement

735

Some of the same clause signals that start adverb and adjective clauses can also start noun clauses; for example, **if, when, where, who,** and **which.**

If the clause is an essential part of the sentence that cannot be omitted, it is (*an adverb, an adjective, a noun*) clause.

736

---

to prove

1005

We are planning a program *that will stimulate an interest in science.*

Fill in the infinitive phrase to which the adjective clause can be reduced:

We are planning a program _____

_____.

1006

Not only did Phil
borrow my book,
but he also
lost it.

1275

a. **The more one reads, the more interested one becomes in the characters.**
b. **As he argued more, he convinced me less.**

_____

_____

1276

---

b

1545

a. **While pushing the car, my coat ripped.**
b. **While pushing the car, I ripped my coat.**

Which sentence is wrong because it suggests that the coat was pushing the car? _____

1546

b

a. **The new school will be as large, if not larger, than ours.**
b. **The new school will be as large as ours, if not larger.**

Which sentence is correct? _____

1815

1816

---

saw

To avoid misusing the past and past participle forms of a verb, observe two rules:

1. Never use the past participle by itself without some form of the helping verb **have** or **be**.

  a. I *seen* **the accident.**   b. I *saw* **the accident.**

Which sentence is wrong? _____

2084

2085

---

is

Cooking is an art that always (*has appealed, appealed*) **to me.**

(*Note:* It still does.)

2353

2354

---

hers, theirs

(*Yours, Your's*) **must be in one of** (*those, them*) **drawers.**

2622

2623

---

b

A clause which merely adds a fact that is not essential to the meaning of the sentence is called a **nonrestrictive clause.**

A nonrestrictive clause is (*more, less*) important than a restrictive clause.

2891

2892

High School,
Jewish,
Saturdays,
Christian,
Sundays

Heroes of both the north and the south are buried in Arlington national cemetery.

_____

3160

3161

No

196

To supply additional information about the various parts of the sentence framework, we use *modifiers*.

Poor <u>brakes</u> <u>cause</u> many accidents.

This sentence contains two modifying words that are not part of its framework. These two words are: _____ and

_____.

197

---

b

466

a. **Mr. Tate becomes hard-of-hearing, when anyone asks him for money.**
b. **When anyone asks Mr. Tate for money, he becomes hard-of-hearing.**

In which sentence should the comma be dropped? _____

467

---

a noun

736

a. **The bus** *that the train delayed* **was an hour late.**
b. **We found** *that a train had delayed the bus.*

One clause is an adjective clause that can be omitted; the other is a noun clause that is an essential part of the sentence framework.

Which sentence contains the noun clause? _____

737

---

to stimulate an interest in science.

1006

By understanding the various types of subordinate word groups, you not only save words but also give more interesting variety to your sentences.

If you had several adjective clauses close together, would it generally be a good idea to change one of them to a participial phrase? (*Yes, No*)

1007

The more he argued, the less he convinced me.

1276

a. **The nights being cold, we took along our sweaters.**
b. **The inn was expensive, and we stayed only one day.**

_____

_____

1277

---

a

1546

a. **While pushing the car, my coat ripped.**
b. **While pushing the car, I ripped my coat.**

Which sentence is right because the elliptical clause is followed by a word that answers the question **Who?** _____

1547

b 1816	**This is one of the best,** *if not the best,* **hotel in town.** Omit the italicized phrase and you will see what is wrong with the above sentence. The trouble is that **one of the best** requires **hotels** (plural) and *the best* requires _____ (singular). 1817
a 2085	WRONG: I *seen* **the accident.** This sentence is wrong because the past participle *seen* is used without the helping verb *have.* Supply the correct form of **see:** RIGHT: I _____ **the accident.** 2086
has appealed 2354	**Uncle Raúl** (*has smoked, smoked*) **for twenty years and then suddenly quit.** 2355
Yours, those 2623	(*It's, Its*) **looking for** (*it's, its*) **nest.** 2624
less 2892	Because a nonrestrictive clause is an "extra" that may be omitted—just like parenthetical expressions, appositives, and direct address—we set it off with commas. Punctuate the following sentence: **My birthday** *which is on Christmas* **receives very little attention.** 2893
North, South, National Cemetery 3161	**The Union bank is in the Keystone building on the south side of Main street.** 3162

Poor brakes cause many accidents.

Poor, many

The word **Poor** modifies the noun _____.

The word **many** modifies the noun _____.

197

198

---

a

The maple trees are still green *after the ash trees have shed their leaves.*

If you moved the adverb clause to the beginning of the sentence, would you put a comma after *leaves*? (*Yes, No*)

467

468

---

b

We found *that a train had delayed the bus.*

The noun clause cannot be omitted because it is the (*subject, direct object*) of the verb **found.**

737

738

Yes

If you thought that you had repeated the word *because* too many times, how could you change the adverb clause in the following sentence?

I threw away the box *because I thought it was empty.*

I threw away the box, _____ *it was empty.*

1007

1008

The inn being
expensive, we
stayed only
one day.

a. **The two boys were playing together, their recent quarrel forgotten.**
b. **We looked up the old house, and its porch was still unrepaired.**

_____

_____

1277

1278

---

b

After an introductory word group that lacks a subject, do not use the possessive form of a noun or pronoun to answer the question **Who?** or **What?**

While standing in the crowd, *Pam's* **purse was stolen.**

This sentence is wrong because the person standing in the crowd was not *Pam's purse,* but _____.

1547

1548

hotel 1817	**This is one of the best, if not the best, hotel in town.** **This is one of the best hotels in town, if not the best.** We repaired this sentence as we did the others. We completed the first statement and then added the "if" phrase at the _____ of our sentence. 1818
saw 2086	2. Never use the simple past form of a three-part verb after any form of the helping verb **have** or **be**. PRESENT PAST PAST PARTICIPLE **write** **wrote** **(have) written** The form of **write** that must be used with the helping verb **have** is (*wrote, written*). 2087
smoked 2355	**Electric home appliances** (*have made, made*) **the homemaker's chores much easier.** 2356
It's, its 2624	(*It's, Its*) **quills stiffen when** (*it's, its*) **frightened.** 2625
birthday, Christmas, 2893	a. **Anyone** *who lives in Bedford* **knows Aunt May.** b. **Aunt May** *who lives in Bedford* **knows everyone in town.** In which sentence should the clause be set off with commas because it is not essential to the meaning of the sentence and is therefore nonrestrictive? _____ 2894
Bank, Building, Street 3162	Lesson **88** Further Uses of Capitals [Frames 3164–3201]

(Poor) brakes (many) accidents	Words that modify *nouns* and *pronouns* are **adjectives**. Adjectives modify _____ different classes of words. (How many?)
198	199
Yes	**This book begins where the other leaves off.** The adverb clause in this sentence starts with the clause signal _____ and ends with the word _____.
468	469
direct object	a. *Where Captain Kidd buried his treasure* **remains a mystery.** b. **No one has yet discovered the place** *where Captain Kidd buried his treasure.* Which sentence contains a noun clause? _____
738	739
thinking	If you thought that you had used too many clauses beginning with "*When you . . . ,*" how could you change the adverb clause in the following sentence? *When you train a dog,* **always use the same commands.** *In* _____, **always use the same commands.**
1008	1009
We looked up the old house, its porch still unrepaired. 1278	UNIT 6: RECOGNIZING THE SENTENCE UNIT Lesson **35** Some Typical Sentence Fragments: Clauses and Verbal Phrases [Frames 1280–1316]
Pam	a. **While standing in the crowd, Pam's purse was stolen.** b. **While standing in the crowd, Pam had her purse stolen.** Which sentence is correct because the elliptical clause is followed by a word that answers the question **Who?** _____
1548	1549

a. **Cookie is one of the smartest dogs I know, if not the smartest.**
b. **Cookie is one of the smartest, if not the smartest, dog I know.**

Which sentence is correct? _____

1819

---

written

2087

PRESENT   PAST   PAST PARTICIPLE
write   **wrote**   **(have) written**

  a. I *have wrote* **a letter.**   b. I *have written* **a letter.**

Which sentence is wrong? _____

2088

---

have made

2356

We had hoped (*to have visited, to visit*) **Williamsburg on our trip East last summer.**

2357

Its, it's

2625

Lesson **73** Keeping Person and Number Consistent

[Frames 2627–2663]

---

b

2894

a. **Rich people** *who pretend to be poor* **disgust me.**
b. **Mr. Wetherby** *who pretends to be poor* **is really very rich.**

Which sentence requires commas because the clause is nonrestrictive? _____

2895

In this lesson we complete our study of capitals.

7. Capitalize titles that show a person's profession, rank, office, or family relationship *when they are used with personal names.*

    a. **the mayor of the city**   b. **for mayor Gibson**

Mayor should be capitalized in phrase (*a, b*).

3164

An **adjective** makes the meaning of a noun or pronoun more exact by telling *what kind, which one(s),* or *how many.* Underline the adjective that tells *what kind:*

these **roads**   *wide* **roads**   *three* **roads**

200

Fred looks tall until he stands beside his father.

The adverb clause in this sentence starts with the clause signal _____ and ends with the word _____.

470

Where Captain Kidd buried his treasure **remains a mystery.**

The noun clause is the _____ of the verb **remains.**

740

As I got off the bus, I saw fire engines.

After the above sentence, which of the following sentences would offer greater variety—*a* or *b?* _____

a. **As I looked down the street, I saw clouds of smoke.**
b. **Looking down the street, I saw clouds of smoke.**

1010

To be a sentence, a word group must pass two tests:

1. Does it have a subject and verb?
2. Does it make sense by itself?

If you change your mind

This word group fails to pass test (*1, 2*).

1280

---

a. **Raised in Georgia, Sally had a Southern accent.**
b. **Raised in Georgia, Sally's accent was Southern.**

Which sentence is correct? _____

1550

Do not omit words needed to prevent ambiguity (double meaning).

a. **Andy enjoys television more than his friends.**
b. **Andy enjoys television more than he enjoys his friends.**
c. **Andy enjoys television more than his friends enjoy it.**

Could sentence *a* mean either *b* or *c*? (*Yes, No*)

a

1819

1820

WRONG: **I** *have wrote* **a letter.**

This sentence is wrong because the simple past instead of the past participle is used with the helping verb *have*.

Supply the correct form of the verb **write:**

RIGHT: **I** *have* _____ **a letter.**

a

2088

2089

---

to visit

How could Gordon ever have expected (*to have memorized, to memorize*) **his speech in one evening?**

2357

2358

Personal pronouns show by their form whether they mean the person or persons *speaking, spoken to,* or *spoken about.*

The person *speaking* refers to himself as *I* and to his group as *we.* We say that these pronouns are in the **first person.**

Underline the two pronouns in the *first person:*

you   I   he   we

2627

---

a. **It is against the law to use a stamp,** *which has been canceled.*
b. **Shakespeare died at fifty-two,** *which was considered an advanced age at that time.*

In which sentence should the comma be omitted because the clause is restrictive? _____

b

2895

2896

---

a. **Does superintendent Stern approve the plan?**
b. **A new superintendent will be selected.**

In which sentence should **superintendent** be capitalized because it is used with a personal name? _____

b

3164

3165

wide	Underline the adjective that points out *which one:*
	comfortable **chair** *one* **chair** *this* **chair**
200	201

	Poor sports do not enjoy games unless they can win.
until . . . father	The adverb clause in this sentence starts with the clause
	signal _____ and ends with the word _____.
470	471

	a. **The bike** *which I liked best* **was too expensive.**
subject	b. **I could not decide** *which I liked best.*
	Which sentence contains a noun clause? _____
740	741

	In this and the following frames, reduce each italicized clause to the type of word group indicated in parentheses:
b	*If they are overcooked,* **vegetables lose their flavor.** (elliptical clause)
	_____, **vegetables lose**
	their flavor.
1010	1011

	Tests for a sentence:
	1. Does it have a subject and verb?
2	2. Does it make sense by itself?
	A touchdown in the third quarter
1280	This word group fails to pass test (*1, 2, 1 and 2*). 1281

	In this and the following frames, circle the letter of the correct sentence—the one in which the introductory word group does *not* dangle:
a	a. **Being barefooted, the stones cut our feet.**
	b. **Because we were barefooted, the stones cut our feet.**
1550	1551

This sentence is also ambiguous:

The dealer made Dad a better offer than Ed.

Yes

Add the necessary words to mean that the dealer's offer to Dad was better than Ed's offer to Dad:

The dealer made Dad a better offer than _____ _____.

1820

1821

---

written

This and the following frames will present twenty-two three-part verbs whose past participles all end with *-n* or *-en*. Their similarity should help you to remember them. In each frame, fill in the correct forms of the verbs in parentheses. Be sure to use the past participle with any form of the helping verb **have** or **be**.   (*Turn to the next frame.*)

2089

2090

---

to memorize

Diana Nyad realized that she (*had reached, reached*) **the Florida coast.**

2358

2359

I, we

A pronoun in the **second person** is the one that the person *speaking* uses to address the person or persons *spoken to.*

Underline the one pronoun in the *second person:*

she   you   I   they

2627

2628

---

a

Occasionally, the same clause can be either restrictive or nonrestrictive, depending on what you mean to say.

Mr. Crump sold his land *which was unprofitable.*

If you mean that Mr. Crump sold only that part of his land *which was unprofitable,* you would make the clause restrictive by (*using, omitting*) a comma.

2896

2897

---

a

Wendy is staying with our Uncle Steve and Aunt Jane.

Would you capitalize **Uncle** and **Aunt** if you omitted the names **Steve** and **Jane**? (*Yes, No*)

3165

3166

this 201	Underline the adjective that tells *how many:* *modern* **houses** *these* **houses** *several* **houses** 202
unless . . . win 471	**Donna seldom eats sweets although she enjoys them very much.** The adverb clause in this sentence starts with the clause signal _____ and ends with the word _____. 472

b
 	
741
	When *that* starts an adjective clause, it is a relative pronoun. When *that* starts a noun clause, it is an "empty" word that merely signals the start of a noun clause.
	
	    a. **I have a tame crow** *that* (= *crow*) *can talk.*
	    b. **Mother said** *that she was ready.*
	
	Which sentence contains a noun clause? _____
	
	742

If overcooked, 1011	**A violin will deteriorate** *if it is not played occasionally.* (elliptical clause) **A violin will deteriorate** _____ _____. 1012
1 and 2 1281	1. Does it have a subject and verb? 2. Does it make sense by itself? If you cannot answer "Yes" to both questions, the word group is not a complete sentence but a **fragment.** A handle broken off a cup is to a cup what a fragment is to a _____. 1282

b
 	
1551
	Circle the letter of the correct sentence:
	
	    a. **Going down the drain, the chemical made a boiling sound.**
	    b. **Going down the drain, I heard the chemical make a boiling sound.**
	
	1552

Ed made (*or* did) 1821	**The dealer made Dad a better offer than Ed.** Add the necessary words to mean that the dealer's offer to Dad was better than the dealer's offer to Ed: **The dealer made Dad a better offer than** _____ _____ . 1822

2090	PRESENT PAST PAST PARTICIPLE
	  blow **blew** **(have) blown**
	  tear **tore** **(have) torn**
	
	A gale had _____ (*blow*) **down our sign, and it was badly** _____ (*tear*).
	
	2091

had reached 2359	**The campers discovered that they** (*used, had used*) **their last match.** 2360
you 2628	*You* **are my best friend.** *You* **are my three best friends.** Does the second-person pronoun **you** have different forms for singular and plural? (*Yes, No*) 2629
omitting 2897	**Mr. Crump sold his land** *which was unprofitable.* If you mean that all of Mr. Crump's land was unprofitable and that he therefore sold all of it, you would make the clause nonrestrictive by (*using, omitting*) a comma. 2898
No 3166	a. **The flowers were from my Cousin.** b. **The flowers were from my Cousin Manuel.** **Cousin** should not be capitalized in sentence (*a, b*). 3167

several

202

This sentence contains three nouns:

Three *students* **received perfect** *scores* **on this** *test.*

How many adjectives does this sentence contain? _____

203

---

although . . .
much

472

The actor hesitated as though he had forgotten his lines.

The adverb clause starts with the two-word clause signal

_____ _____ and ends with the word _____.

473

---

b

742

The "empty" word *that,* which starts many noun clauses, is often omitted when the clause is a direct object.

I knew (*that*) *we would win.* **I hope** (*that*) *you can go.*

Is the clause signal *that* a relative pronoun that stands for any noun in the other part of the sentence? (*Yes, No*)

743

---

if not played
occasionally.

1012

As I walked through the tall grass, **I suddenly heard the rattle of a snake.** (present participial phrase)

_____ ——,

I suddenly heard the rattle of a snake.

1013

---

sentence

1282

The various types of clauses and phrases you have used to subordinate ideas fail to meet the two tests of a sentence. If you detach them from the sentences with which they are grammatically connected, you have (*fragments, sentences*).

1283

---

a

1552

Circle the letter of the correct sentence:

    a. **In opening the can, Amy's finger was badly cut.**
    b. **In opening the can, Amy cut her finger badly.**

1553

he made (*or* did) to Ed 1822	**I know Sally better than Evelyn.** Add the necessary words to mean that you are better acquainted with Sally than you are with Evelyn: **I know Sally better than** _____. 1823

blown, torn 2091	PRESENT PAST PAST PARTICIPLE
	  give gave (have) given
	  fall fell (have) fallen
	
	The farmer _____ (*give*) **us the apples that had**
	
	_____ (*fall*) **from the tree.**
	
	2092

had used 2360	**If we** (*had offered, would have offered*) **Henry the nomination, he might have accepted.** 2361
No 2629	A pronoun in the **third person** indicates the person or persons *spoken about.* Underline three pronouns in the *third person:* **he** **I** **she** **they** **you** **we** 2630
using 2898	a. **Do not use string** *which is too weak.* b. **Do not use string,** *which is too weak.* Which sentence suggests that you avoid using only *certain* string—string which is too weak? _____ 2899
a 3167	**My grandmother speaks Cheyenne.** If you inserted the name **Whitedove** after **grandmother**, would you capitalize **grandmother**? (*Yes, No*) 3168

three (Three—perfect—this) 203	**Three students received perfect scores on this test.** Each adjective comes (*before, after*) the noun that it modifies. 204
as though . . . lines 473	**The dog chewed up the letter before we had read it.** The adverb clause in this sentence starts with the clause signal _____ and ends with the word _____. 474
No 743	Lesson **20** The *Who–Whom* Problem in Noun Clauses [Frames 745–784]
Walking through the tall grass, 1013	*Since I don't understand Spanish,* **I was at a serious disadvantage.** (present participial phrase) _____, **I was at a serious disadvantage.** 1014
fragments 1283	WRONG: **The class starts.** *When the bell rings.* "*When the bell rings*" is an adverb clause. Although it has a subject and verb, does it make sense by itself? (*Yes, No*) 1284
b 1553	Continue to circle the letter of the correct sentences: a. **If neatly written, more attention will be paid to your letter.** b. **If neatly written, your letter will get more attention.** 1554

I know (*or* do)
Evelyn

1823

I know Sally better than Evelyn.

Add the necessary words to mean that Evelyn is not as well-acquainted with Sally as you are:

I know Sally better than _____.

1824

---

gave, fallen

2092

PRESENT	PAST	PAST PARTICIPLE
fly	flew	(have) flown
drive	drove	(have) driven

We have _____ (*fly*) **to Miami, and we have also**

_____ (*drive*) **there.**

2093

---

had offered

2361

I would certainly have written to you from Hawaii if I (*had remembered, would have remembered*) **your address.**

2362

---

he, she, they

2630

The terms **first person, second person,** and **third person** apply to plural pronouns as well as to singular pronouns. Do not let this use of the term *person* confuse you.

I and *we* are both pronouns in the *first person.*

He, she, and *they* are all pronouns in the _____ *person.*

2631

---

a

2899

---

a. **Do not use string** *which is too weak.*
b. **Do not use string,** *which is too weak.*

Which sentence suggests that you avoid using *all* string because *all* string is too weak for the purpose? _____

2900

Yes

3168

As a mark of respect, the titles of high government officials are capitalized even when used without personal names.

a. **The President consulted the Secretary of State.**
b. **The Corporal hoped to become a Sergeant.**

The capitalization is correct in sentence (*a, b*).

3169

before 204	Besides coming right before the nouns they modify, adjectives are sometimes found in another position. **The car is blue. The eggs are fresh. The house looks new.** The adjectives in these sentences follow *linking verbs* and are therefore (*subject complements, direct objects*). 205
before . . . it 474	A sentence that contains a clause is called a **complex sentence.** It is more complex (or complicated) than a simple sentence. a. **My friend often telephones at dinnertime.** b. **My friend often telephones** *while we are eating dinner.* Which is a complex sentence—*a or b?* _____ 475
	Few people notice the *sign.* The noun *sign* is the direct object of the verb _____. 745
Not understanding Spanish, 1014	**We went to the lake** *so that we could escape the heat.* (infinitive phrase) **We went to the lake** _____. 1015
No 1284	SENTENCE: **The bell rings.** ADVERB CLAUSE: *When the bell rings* Which word in the clause makes the clause depend on something else for its full meaning? _____ 1285
b 1554	a. **To get an honor diploma, a student must maintain a B average or better.** b. **To get an honor diploma, a B average or better must be maintained.** 1555

Evelyn knows her (Sally) *or* Evelyn does 1824	In this and the following frames, put a circle around the letter of the sentence which states the comparison logically:
	
	   a. **Our traffic laws are different from Oregon's.**
	   b. **Our traffic laws are different from Oregon.**
	
	                                 1825

flown, driven 2093	PRESENT PAST PAST PARTICIPLE **choose** **chose** **(have) chosen** **draw** **drew** **(have) drawn** **The design that was** _____ (*choose*) **by the judges** **was** _____ (*draw*) **by Vera.** 2094
had remembered 2362	**In a few more months, we** (*shall live, shall have lived*) **in our present house for twenty years.** 2363
third 2631	*I* or *we* (first person) speak to *you* (second person) about *him, her,* or *them* (third person). Write *first, second,* or *third* (but not in this order) in each blank to indicate the person of each italicized pronoun: *They* (_____ person) told *us* (_____ person) about *you* (_____ person). 2632
b 2900	Participial phrases, as well as adjective clauses, can be either restrictive or nonrestrictive. a. **All cars** *leaving Lewiston* **were stopped by the police.** b. **Maxine** *excusing herself politely* **went upstairs to study.** In which sentence would you use commas because the participial phrase is not essential to the meaning? _____ 2901
a 3169	**The courageous** *captain* **was decorated by the** *governor.* Which italicized word should be capitalized? _____ 3170

The car is blue.   The eggs are fresh.   The house looks new.

When adjectives are subject complements, they come (*before, after*) the nouns they modify.

206

---

b

475

My friend often telephones *while we are eating dinner.*

We know that this is a complex sentence because it contains a

_____.

476

---

notice

745

a. **Few people notice the** *sign.*
b. **Few people notice** *who directs a movie.*

The clause *who directs a movie* in sentence *b* does the same job as the noun *sign* in sentence *a*.

Both are _____ _____ of the verb **notice.**

746

---

to escape
the heat.

1015

It is a tedious job *which requires much patience.* (present participial phrase)

It is a tedious job _____

_____.

1016

When

1285

WRONG: **The class starts.** *Promptly.*

You would never think of separating the adverb *promptly* from the sentence that contains the word it modifies.

The class starts. *When the bell rings.*

Is it correct to separate an adverb clause from the sentence that contains the verb it modifies? (*Yes, No*)

1286

---

a

1555

a. **Questioned about her campaign, Miss Whitecloud's answers were very informative.**
b. **Questioned about her campaign, Miss Whitecloud answered very informatively.**

1556

a 1825	a. **We beat North High worse than Marshall Tech.** b. **We beat North High worse than we beat Marshall Tech.** 1826
chosen, drawn 2094	PRESENT PAST PAST PARTICIPLE **freeze** **froze** **(have) frozen** **wear** **wore** **(have) worn** **If I had not** _____ (*wear*) **my sweater, I would** **have** _____ (*freeze*). 2095
shall have lived 2363	**By this time next year, you** (*will have cast, will cast*) **your first vote.** 2364
They (third) *us* (first) *you* (second) 2632	Write the word *first, second,* or *third* in each blank to indicate the person of the italicized pronouns: *You* (_____ person) told *her* (_____ person) to invite *me* (_____ person). 2633
b 2901	In this and the following frames, supply the necessary commas. If the clause is restrictive because it is essential to the meaning of the sentence, add no commas and write *None*. **Willa Cather** *who was born in Virginia* **wrote stories about the American West.** 2902
Governor 3170	Copy the words that require capitals: **The chairman of the meeting sent a telegram of congratulation to senator Hayakawa and the president.** 3171

after 206	a. **Melba Moore has an <u>excellent</u> voice.** b. **Melba Moore's voice is <u>excellent</u>.** Does the adjective **excellent** come after the noun it modifies in sentence *a* or *b?* _____ 207
clause *or* adverb clause 476	**I always drive as though everyone else were crazy.** Because this sentence contains a clause, it is called a _____ sentence. 477
direct objects 746	a. **Few people notice the** *sign.* b. **Few people notice** *who directs a movie.* Because the clause *who directs a movie* in sentence *b* is used just like the noun *sign* in sentence *a*, it is a _____ clause. 747
requiring much patience. 1016	**The union published a full-page advertisement** *which stated* *their viewpoint on the strike.* (present participial phrase) **The union published a full-page advertisement** _____ _____. 1017
No 1286	**The class starts** *when the bell rings.* Now the adverb clause makes sense because it is in the same sentence with the verb _____, which it modifies.

b
 	
1556
	a. **After winning three games, the school keeps the trophy**
	   permanently.
	b. **After winning three games, the trophy is kept permanently**
	   by the school.
	
	1557

b

1826

---

a. **Brazil has a greater area than any country in South America.**
b. **Brazil has a greater area than any other country in South America.**

(Can a country have a larger area than itself?)

1827

---

worn, frozen

2095

PRESENT	PAST	PAST PARTICIPLE
know	knew	(have) known
steal	stole	(have) stolen

The dealer must have _____ (*know*) **that the car**
was _____ (*steal*).

2096

---

will have cast

2364

Rewrite this sentence, changing the verb from passive to active:

The Segals' paper *had been left* **at our door by mistake by the newsboy.**

_____

_____

2365

You (second)
her (third)
me (first)

2633

She **and her** *dog* **were strolling down the street.**

Since a noun is something that you talk *about,* every noun—just like the pronouns *he, she, it,* and *them*—is ordinarily in the (*first, second, third*) person.

2634

Cather,
Virginia,

2902

It is the policy of our restaurant to serve no food *which we would not eat ourselves.*

2903

Senator,
President

3171

When a title is used alone, without a name, to refer to a particular person, it may be capitalized.

a. **A** *principal* **has many responsibilities.**
b. **The** *principal* **will address the parents' meeting.**

In which sentence would it be permissible to capitalize *principal?* _____

3172

b	Adjectives normally come before the nouns they modify except when they are _____ *complements.*
207	208
complex	Unlike a sentence, a clause (*does, does not*) make sense by itself.
477	478
noun	The choice between **who** and **whom,** when they start noun clauses, depends upon their use *within the clause.* *who directs a movie* The clause signal *who* is the subject of the verb _____.
747	748
stating their viewpoint on the strike.	**Every nail** *that was used in the old fort* **was made by hand.** (past participial phrase) **Every nail** _____ **was made by hand.**
1017	1018
starts	WRONG: **She went to Ohio.** *Leaving me in charge of the farm.* *"Leaving me in charge of the farm"* is a present participial phrase. Does it have a subject and verb, and does it make sense by itself? (*Yes, No*)
1287	1288
a	a. **When I was six years old, my aunt first took me sailing.** b. **When six years old, my aunt first took me sailing.**
1557	1558

b

1827

a. **Next year's team will be as good as this year's, if not better.**

b. **Next year's team will be as good, if not better, than this year's team.**

1828

---

known, stolen

2096

PRESENT	PAST	PAST PARTICIPLE
grow	**grew**	**(have) grown**
see	**saw**	**(have) seen**

How Steve has _____ (*grow*) **since I last** _____ (*see*) **him!**

2097

The newsboy (had) left the Segals' paper at our door by mistake.

2365

Rewrite this sentence, changing the verb from passive to active:

The star *could be seen* **clearly by us through the telescope.**

_____

_____

2366

---

third

2634

Underline three words (nouns or pronouns) that are in the third person:

I   team   you   it   story   we

2635

None

2903

Caffeine *which is present in both tea and coffee* **stimulates the heart and raises blood pressure.**

2904

---

b

3172

When you use *mother, father, dad,* etc., in place of personal names, you may capitalize them or not—as you prefer.

Have I told you how Mother first met Dad?
Have I told you how mother first met dad?

Are both sentences correct? (*Yes, No*)

3173

subject	**Most people are honest.** The two adjectives—**Most** and **honest**—modify the noun _____ .
208	209
does not	An adverb clause is so called because it does the work of an _____ .
478	479
directs	Use the subject form **who** for subjects and subject complements; use the object form **whom** for objects of verbs and prepositions. *who directs a movie* We use the subject form *who* because it is the (*subject, direct object*) of the verb *directs*.
748	749
used in the old fort	**Most of the articles** *that were advertised in the paper* **were sold out.** (past participial phrase) **Most of the articles** _____ **were sold out.**
1018	1019
No	RIGHT: **She went to Ohio,** *leaving me in charge of the farm.* The present participial phrase should be a part of the sentence containing the noun _____, which it modifies.
1288	1289
a	a. **Written in simple language, any child can enjoy this book.** b. **Written in simple language, this book can be enjoyed by any child.**
1558	1559

Franklin D. Roosevelt served longer than *any* _____ American president.

a	A president cannot serve longer than himself.
	To make this comparison logical, we must add the word
1828	_____.
	1829

	PRESENT	PAST	PAST PARTICIPLE
	take	took	(have) taken
grown, saw	throw	threw	(have) thrown

Someone had _____ (*take*) the letter and had

_____ (*throw*) it away.

2097	2098

Change the verb from active to passive by eliminating the present subject:

We could see the star clearly through the telescope.	**My dad** *had not paid* **our telephone bill.**
	_____
2366	_____
	2367

A shift in person confuses the viewpoint within a sentence. You begin by talking about one person and end up by talking about another.

Underline the pronoun that continues the same viewpoint:

team, it, story	**As we looked around us,** (*you, we*) **could see that spring was near.**
2635	2636

Caffeine, coffee,	**Pearl Buck** *who wrote many stories* **was one of the outstanding writers of her day.**
2904	2905

On the other hand, when you use *mother, father, dad,* etc., merely to show family relationship, always use small letters.

Yes	**His** *mother* **is a** *cousin* **of my** *father.*
	Should the italicized words be capitalized? (*Yes, No*)
3173	3174

people	We very seldom use adjectives before pronouns as we do before nouns. We say "a *pretty* girl," but not "a *pretty* she"; "a *new* book," but not "a *new* it."
	She looks very pretty. It is new.
209	In these sentences, the adjectives come (*before, after*) the pronouns they modify.
	210

adverb	Any clause that modifies a verb is an _____
	clause.
479	480

	Few people notice *who directs a movie.*
subject	Be careful to avoid the mistake of thinking that the clause signal is the direct object of the verb **notice** and therefore requires the object form *whom.*
	The direct object of the verb **notice** is not the clause signal
749	but the entire noun _____.
	750

advertised in the paper	**Frank had little money** *that he could spend on entertainment.* (infinitive phrase)
	Frank had little money _____
	_____.
1019	1020

She	a. **She went to Ohio, leaving me in charge of the farm.** b. **She went to Ohio. She left me in charge of the farm.** c. **She went to Ohio. Leaving me in charge of the farm.**
	Which one of the above three items is incorrect? _____
1289	1290

b	a. **Because the man was wearing a blue uniform, Dave mistook him for a police officer.** b. **Wearing a blue uniform, Dave mistook the man for a police officer.**
1559	1560

other

1829

---

a. **The Pacific is the largest of any other ocean in the world.**
b. **The Pacific is the largest ocean in the world.**

1830

---

taken, thrown

2098

PRESENT	PAST	PAST PARTICIPLE
shake	shook	(had) shaken
break	broke	(had) broken

The collision had _____ (*shake*) **up the box, and**

many dishes were _____ (*break*).

2099

Our telephone
bill had not
been paid.

2367

Change the verb from active to passive by eliminating the
present subject:

Bob Redwing *delivers* **our mail around ten o'clock.**

_____

2368

---

we

2636

SHIFT IN PERSON: *I* **liked this story because it kept** *you*
                 guessing until the very last page.

This sentence is faulty because *I* is in the first person and

you is in the _____ person.

2637

Buck,
stories,

2905

We seldom interrupt a person *who is praising us.*

2906

No

3174

When *father, mother, dad,* etc., are used with articles (*a, an,
the*) or possessive pronouns (*my, his, your*), they show
family relationship and should not be capitalized.

The *mother* **of one of my friends knew my** *dad* **at college.**

Should the italicized words be capitalized? (*Yes, No*)

3175

after	We have seen that adjectives answer the questions *What kind? Which one(s)?* and *How many?* about nouns and
210	_____.
	211

adverb	**Lesson 13 Expressing the Exact Relationship**
	[Frames 482–523]
480	

clause	WRONG: **Few people notice** *whom directs a movie.*
	The object form *whom* is wrong because the clause signal is not the object of the verb **notice** but the subject of the verb
750	_____ within the clause.
	751

to spend on entertainment.	**We called a meeting** *so that we could elect officers.* (infinitive phrase)
	We called a meeting _____.
1020	1021

c	WRONG: **I sent for a free booklet.** *Advertised in a magazine.*
	"*Advertised in a magazine*" is a past participial phrase. Does it have a subject and verb, and does it make sense by itself? (*Yes, No*)
1290	1291

a	**Lesson 43 Repairing Dangling Word Groups**
	[Frames 1562–1586]
1560	

b 1830	In this and the following frames, cancel or add any words or letters that are necessary to make the comparisons logical: **Our way of life is very similar to Canada.** <div align="right">1831</div>

shaken, broken
 	
2099
	PRESENT PAST PAST PARTICIPLE
	  eat ate (have) eaten
	  ride rode (have) ridden
	If we had _____ (*eat*) our lunch, we would have
	
	_____ (*ride*) further.
	<div align="right">2100</div>

Our mail is delivered around ten o'clock. 2368	UNIT 10: USING ADVERBS AND ADJECTIVES Lesson **66** Using Adverbs to Describe Action <div align="right">[Frames 2370–2408]</div>
second 2637	a. *I* liked this story because it kept *you* guessing. b. *I* liked this story because it kept *me* guessing. Which sentence is correct because the person of the pronouns is consistent? _____ <div align="right">2638</div>
None 2906	**One should be suspicious of any investment** *which offers an unusually high rate of return.* <div align="right">2907</div>
No 3175	**I want my** *dad* **and** *uncle* **Frank to meet your** *grandfather.* The only one of the italicized words that should be capitalized is _____. <div align="right">3176</div>

pronouns

211

We need another class of words to answer the questions that we might ask about the action of verbs.

George drove.   (*When? Where? How? How much? How often?*)

Are the questions in parentheses about **George** or **drove?**

_____

212

In this lesson you will study **subordination** as a way of building sentences.

Subordinate means "of lower rank." A *clerk*, for example, is subordinate to a *manager*.

In the army, a *sergeant* is subordinate to a (*private, general*).

482

---

directs

751

Now we shall change the wording of our sentence:

Few people notice *who the director was.*

The direct object of the verb **notice** is not the clause signal *who* but the entire noun _____.

752

---

to elect officers.

1021

Lesson **27** Other Types of Reduction

[Frames 1023–1063]

No

1291

RIGHT: **I sent for a free booklet** *advertised in a magazine.*

The past participial phrase should be a part of the sentence containing the noun _____, which it modifies.

1292

Don't hesitate to start your sentences with word groups that do not tell **whom** or **what** they are about. They add interest to your writing. Just remember that you owe your reader this information (*somewhere in, at the beginning of*) the main statement that follows.

1562

Canada's.
or
that of Canada.
or
Canada's way
of life.
1831

The double bass is the largest of all the other members of the violin family.

1832

---

eaten, ridden

2100

PRESENT	PAST	PAST PARTICIPLE
swear	swore	(have) sworn
speak	spoke	(have) spoken

The witness _____ (*swear*) **that he had never**

_____ (*speak*) **to the accused man.**

2101

Adjectives can modify only nouns and pronouns—no other class of words.

Adverbs modify everything else that can be modified—verbs, adjectives, and other adverbs.

A word that modifies any word except a noun or a pronoun is an _____.

2370

---

b

2638

SHIFT IN PERSON: **Whether** *you* **live in a big city or in the country, nature surrounds** *us.*

This sentence is faulty because *you* is in the second person

and *us* is in the _____ person.

2639

None

2907

It turned out that Shirley Smith *who was chosen Dairy Queen* **is allergic to milk.**

2908

---

uncle

3176

8. Capitalize the first word and all important words in titles of books, stories, movies, works of art, musical compositions, etc.

      a. *Invisible Man*   b. *Invisible man*

Which title is correctly capitalized? _____

3177

drove 212	**George drove** *safely*. Underline the question that the word *safely* answers: **When? Where? How? How much? How often?** 213
general 482	In grammar, a subordinate word group is one that is *less than a sentence*—one that *does not make sense by itself*. Phrases and clauses are examples of _____ word groups. 483
clause 752	*who the* <u>director</u> <u>was</u> Within the noun clause, the subject of the linking verb *was* is not *who* but _____. 753
	Reduction is the same principle as using a tack—and not a spike—to fasten a calendar to the wall. If either a *clause* or a *phrase* says exactly the same thing, use the _____. 1023
booklet 1292	a. **I sent for a free booklet. It was advertised in a magazine.** b. **I sent for a free booklet. Advertised in a magazine.** c. **I sent for a free booklet advertised in a magazine.** Which one of the above three items is incorrect? _____ 1293
at the beginning of 1562	When your introductory word group lacks a subject, tell **whom** or **what** it is about at the beginning of your main statement. Failure to supply this information results in an error known as a _____ word group. 1563

~~other~~	**Our gas bill was three dollars more than our neighbor.**
1832	1833

swore, spoken	Whenever you are doubtful about the past participle form of a verb, ask yourself, "Is there a form of this verb that ends with *-n* or *-en?*" If there is, use it after any form of **have** or **be**.
	Underline two verbs that have forms ending with *-n* or *-en*:
2101	**freeze** **think** **speak** **work**
	2102

adverb	Although a few adjectives end in *-ly* (*homely, manly, lonely*), the *-ly* ending usually signals an adverb.
	We can make an adverb of almost any adjective by adding *-ly* to it.
	Write the adverb form of each of the following adjectives:
2370	sad _____ prompt _____ cheerful _____
	2371

first	a. **Whether** *you* **live in a big city or in the country, nature surrounds** *you.*
	b. **Whether** *you* **live in a big city or in the country, nature surrounds** *us.*
	Which sentence is correct? _____
2639	2640

Smith, Queen,	**In our living room we don't have a single chair** *that is really comfortable.*
2908	2909

a	Do not capitalize the articles *a, an,* and *the* or short prepositions and conjunctions in a title except when they are the first word of the title.
	a. *Gone with the Wind* b. *Gone With The Wind*
3177	Which title is correctly capitalized? _____
	3178

How?	**George drove** *yesterday*.
	Underline the question that the word *yesterday* answers:
	When? Where? How? How much? How often?
213	214

subordinate	When we put an idea into a clause rather than into a sentence, we say that we *subordinate* it.
	When we subordinate an idea, we express it in a word group that is (*more, less*) than a sentence.
483	484

	who the <u>director</u> <u>was</u>
director	When we straighten out this clause by putting the subject first, we get:
	the <u>director</u> <u>was</u> who
	Since *who* completes the linking verb *was*, it is a (*subject complement, direct object*).
753	754

phrase	If either a *phrase* or an *adverb* says exactly the same thing,
	use the _____.
1023	1024

	WRONG: **Pat showed her bad manners.** *By laughing at my car.*
b	*"By laughing at my car"* is a prepositional phrase with a gerund as the object of the preposition *By*.
	Can a prepositional phrase be written as a separate sentence? (*Yes, No*)
1293	1294

	What is the difference between a *misplaced modifier* and a *dangling word group*?
dangling	A *misplaced modifier* is not in its proper place with relation to the word it modifies. A *dangling word group*, on the other hand, often has no word at all to modify and therefore appears to modify the (*right, wrong*) word.
1563	1564

neighbor's. *or* that of our neighbor. *or* neighbor's gas bill. 1833	**Death Valley, California, is hotter than any region on earth.** 1834
freeze, speak 2102	Even though you may make the mistake of saying **has broke, had spoke,** or **was froze,** you know that the words **broken, spoken,** and **frozen** exist. If there is a form of the verb ending with *-n* or *-en,* use it after any form of **have** or **be.** Underline two verbs that have forms ending with *-n* or *-en:* rang gave stole went 2103
sadly promptly cheerfully 2371	There are hundreds of modifiers that have both an adjective and an adverb form. a. **bad** **rough** **noisy** **easy** **careful** b. **badly** **roughly** **noisily** **easily** **carefully** Which group of words consists of adverbs? _____ 2372
a 2640	A pronoun should also agree with its antecedent in number. Use a singular pronoun to refer to a singular antecedent. Use a plural pronoun to refer to a _____ antecedent. 2641
None (*or* living room,) 2909	My parents *hearing of this opportunity* **moved our family to Oregon.** 2910
a 3178	Write the following title correctly: *the return of the native* _____ 3179

George drove *frequently.*

When?

Underline the question that the word *frequently* answers:

When? Where? How? How much? How often?

214   215

---

a. **The rain stopped.**
b. **when the rain stopped**

less

Which is a subordinate word group because it is less than

a sentence? _____

484   485

---

subject
complement

Few people notice (*who, whom*) *the director was.*

Because the clause signal is a subject complement, we use
the subject form (*who, whom*).

754   755

---

1. Sentence   3. Phrase (verbal, appositive, prepositional)
2. Clause   4. Single word (adjective, adverb)

adverb

As we move down this list from 1 to 4, the sentence elements
become (*simpler, more complicated*).

1024   1025

WRONG: **Pat showed her bad manners.** *By laughing at my*
car.

No

The prepositional phrase answers the question **How?** about

the verb _____ in the main statement.

1294   1295

To avoid a dangling word group, you must tell **who** or **what**
either (1) in the introductory word group itself or (2) at the
beginning of the main statement that follows it.

wrong

When a small baby, a bee stung me on the nose.

Does this sentence tell **who** in either place? (*Yes, No*)

1564   1565

other any ∧ region 1834	**The rat has been the most destructive of any other animal on this planet.** 1835
gave, stole 2103	In this and the following frames, supply the correct forms of the two verbs in parentheses. After any form of **have** or **be,** think whether the verb has an *-n* or *-en* form. If it has, use it. **It** _____ *(cost)* **ninety cents for the distance we had** _____ *(ride).* 2104
b 2372	The adverbs made by adding *-ly* to adjectives usually answer the question **How?** about the action of the verb. **Dean ate his soup** *noisily.* The adverb *noisily* answers the question **How?** about the action of the verb _____. 2373
plural 2641	SHIFT IN NUMBER: **You should train a** *dog* **before** *they* **get too old to learn.** This sentence is faulty because the plural pronoun *they* is used to refer to the singular noun _____. 2642
parents, opportunity, 2910	**This book will be valuable to anyone** *wanting to take better pictures.* 2911
The Return of the Native 3179	Write the following title correctly: *how to choose a vocation* _____ 3180

How often?

215

George drove *away.*

Underline the question that the word *away* answers:

When?   Where?   How?   How much?   How often?

216

---

b

485

a. **The rain stopped.**
b. **when the rain stopped**

We subordinated the idea in sentence *a* by adding the clause

signal _____.

486

---

who

755

WRONG: **Few people notice** *whom* **the director was.**

The object form *whom* is wrong because the clause signal is not the object of the verb **notice.**

The object of the verb **notice** is the entire _____

_____.

756

---

simpler

1025

1. Sentence   3. Phrase (verbal, appositive, prepositional)
2. Clause   4. Single word (adjective, adverb)

When we reduce a word group, we move (*up, down*) the above list of sentence elements.

1026

---

showed

1295

a. **Pat showed her bad manners. By laughing at my car.**
b. **Pat showed her bad manners by laughing at my car.**

Which sentence is right because the prepositional phrase is in the same sentence as the verb **showed,** which it modifies?

___

1296

No

1565

a. **When a small baby, I was stung on the nose by a bee.**
b. **When I was a small baby, a bee stung me on the nose.**

In which sentence is the question **Who?** answered sensibly

in the introductory word group? ___

1566

most destructive of all the animals . . . *or* most destructive animal . . .	Rewrite this sentence correctly: **I study as hard, if not harder, than Phil.** _____ _____
1835	1836
cost, ridden	Gilda was _____ (*choose*) **because she has always** _____ (*drive*) **carefully.**
2104	2105
ate	The most common error in the use of adjectives and adverbs is failing to use the adverb (-*ly*) form to describe the action of a verb. The fact that *verb* is part of the word ad*verb* will remind you always to use an adverb to modify a _____.
2373	2374
dog	a. **You should train a** *dog* **before** *they* **get too old to learn.** b. **You should train a** *dog* **before** *it* **gets too old to learn.** Which sentence is correct? _____
2642	2643
None	Lesson **81** Review: Uses of the Comma [Frames 2913–2932]
2911	
How to Choose a Vocation	9. Capitalize the names of historical events, periods, and documents. **World War II** **Monroe Doctrine** **Bill of Rights** **Colonial Period** **Battle of Gettysburg** **Ten Commandments** Copy the words that require capitals: **The crusades took place during the middle ages.** _____
3180	3181

Where? 216	Words that modify verbs are called **adverbs.** The fact that the word ad*verb* contains the word *verb* will help you to remember that adverbs modify _____. 217
when 486	**when the rain stopped** Because this type of subordinate word group answers the question **When?**—like an ordinary adverb—it is classified as an _____ clause. 487
noun clause 756	Now we shall put the same idea in a different way: **Few people pay any attention to the** *director*. The noun *director* is the object of the preposition _____. 757
down 1026	a. **We play the game** *in a different way.* b. **We play the game** *differently.* When we reduce the prepositional phrase (4 words) in sentence *a* to the adverb *differently* in sentence *b*, do we change the meaning in any way? (*Yes, No*) 1027
b 1296	a. **Pat showed her bad manners. She laughed at my car.** b. **Pat showed her bad manners by laughing at my car.** c. **Pat showed her bad manners. By laughing at my car.** Which one of the above three items is incorrect? _____ 1297
b 1566	a. **When a small baby, I was stung on the nose by a bee.** b. **When I was a small baby, a bee stung me on the nose.** In which sentence is the question **Who?** answered in the main statement? _____ 1567

I study as hard as Phil, if not harder. 1836	Rewrite this sentence correctly: **This is one of the fastest, if not the fastest, car on the road.** _____ _____ 1837
chosen, driven 2105	**The suspect had** _____ (_swear_) **that the car was not** _____ (_steal_). 2106
verb 2374	**The reward was divided** (_equal, equally_) **between the two girls.** To explain _how_ the reward **was divided,** use the adverb _____. 2375
b 2643	a. **Most things are cheaper when you buy them in large quantities.** b. **Most things are cheaper when you buy it in large quantities.** Which sentence is correct? _____ 2644
	In this and the following frames, supply the necessary commas. If no commas are required, write _None_. **Many years have passed since then and many changes of course have taken place.** 2913
Crusades, Middle Ages 3181	Copy the words that require capitals: **Twenty years after the american revolution, the louisiana purchase greatly increased the size of the new nation.** _____ 3182

verbs

217

Many adverbs—especially those that tell *how*—end with **-ly**. In fact, we form many adverbs by adding **-ly** to adjectives: **polite—politely, graceful—gracefully, fearless—fearlessly**.

> A *careful* **person drives** *carefully.*

The adverb in this sentence is _____.

218

---

adverb

487

We continued our game *when the rain stopped.*

The adverb clause *when the rain stopped* modifies the verb _____.

488

---

to

757

a. **Few people pay any attention to the** *director.*
b. **Few people pay any attention to** *who directs a movie.*

In sentence *a*, the object of the preposition **to** is the noun *director.*

In sentence *b*, the object of the preposition **to** is the noun clause _____.

758

No

1027

By reduction we do not mean eliminating words that add to the meaning or interest of a sentence.

When we reduce a word group, we make (*no, a slight*) change in the meaning.

1028

---

c

1297

WRONG: **The customer soon returned.** *To get his money back.*

"To get his money back" is an infinitive phrase. It explains *why* about the verb _____ in the main statement.

1298

---

a

1567

If your introductory word group answers the question **Who?** or **What?** do you need to answer this question again at the beginning of your main statement? (*Yes, No*)

1568

This is one of the fastest cars on the road, if not the fastest.

1837

---

sworn, stolen

2106

Any food that is not _____ (*eat*) **will be** _____ (*throw*) **out.**

2107

---

equally

2375

Noel must have done (*poor, poorly*) on his test.

To explain *how* Noel **must have done** on his test, use the adverb _____.

2376

---

a

2644

You may use **he** when a statement applies equally to either sex. The expressions **he or she** and **his or her** are awkward.

A person should wash *his* **hands before** *he* **eats.**

Does the above sentence apply to women as well as to men? (*Yes, No*)

2645

---

then, changes, course,

2913

We had to wait for the principal was busy when we arrived at his office.

2914

American Revolution, Louisiana Purchase

3182

10. Capitalize all sacred names:

God	**the Almighty**	**our Father**	**Christ**
Lord	**the Holy Ghost**	**Saviour**	**the Virgin**

Copy the words that require capitals:

The stained-glass window pictures the virgin holding the christ child. _____

3183

carefully	We have seen that adjectives have a *fixed* position in the sentence—usually before the words they modify.
	Most adverbs, by contrast, are very *movable*.
	I finally finished the final chapter.
218	The word that can be shifted to another position is the (*adjective* **final**, *adverb* **finally**). 219
continued	**We continued our game** *when the rain stopped.*
	Because the clause signal **when** starts a *subordinate* word group and also *connects* this word group with the sentence, we call it a **subordinating conjunction.**
	The subordinating conjunction in the above sentence is
488	——————. 489
who directs a movie	**Few people pay any attention to** *who directs a movie.*
	Within the noun clause, the subject of the verb *directs* is the
	clause signal —————.
758	759
no	In the previous lesson, we reduced clauses to phrases built on present and past participles, gerunds, and infinitives.
	These word groups are simpler than clauses because they (*do, do not*) contain subjects and predicates.
1028	1029
returned	a. **The customer returned to get his money back.**
	b. **The customer returned. To get his money back.**
	Which sentence is right because the infinitive phrase is in the same sentence as the verb **returned,** which it modifies?
1298	—— 1299
No	If your introductory word group *does not* answer the question **Who?** or **What?** do you need to answer this question at the beginning of your main statement? (*Yes, No*)
1568	1569

We remove deadwood from a tree because it contributes nothing to the life or productiveness of the tree. By "deadwood" in sentences, we mean empty words and phrases that add nothing to the meaning or to the interest.

Cross out two words that add nothing to the meaning of:

Mr. Lovett was an elderly man in age.

1839

---

eaten, thrown

2107

I would have _____ (*speak*) **to Mr. Price if I had** _____ (*see*) **him.**

2108

---

poorly

2376

WRONG: **Noel must have done** *poor* **on his test.**

This is wrong because the adjective *poor* cannot modify the

_____ **must have done.**

2377

Yes

2645

a. **Before a person votes, he or she should inform himself or herself about the candidates.**
b. **Before a person votes, he should inform himself about the candidates.**

Which sentence is better? _____

2646

---

wait,

2914

Before fireworks were prohibited hundreds of children were maimed blinded and killed every Fourth of July.

2915

Virgin,
Christ Child

3183

Too many capitals are as serious an error as too few. Do not capitalize—

FOODS: **spaghetti, hamburgers, brownies, angel food**

Copy the words that require capitals:

We ate chop suey at a chinese restaurant on Campus street.

_____ 3184

adverb *finally*	**Our friends** ∧ **have** ∧ **come** ∧ **for dinner** ∧ . (often)
	Can the adverb **often** be inserted in the sentence at each point indicated by a caret (∧)? (*Yes, No*)
219	220

when	**We lost our way** *because we made a wrong turn.*
	The subordinating conjunction in the above sentence is
	_____.
489	490

who	WRONG: **Few people pay any attention to** *whom directs a movie.*
	The object form *whom* is wrong because the clause signal is not the object of the preposition **to** but the subject of the
759	verb _____ within the clause. 760

do not	Here is an adjective clause that can be reduced to something even simpler—a prepositional phrase.
	The apples *that were in the window* **looked larger.**
	The apples *in the window* **looked larger.**
	By reducing the adjective clause to a prepositional phrase,
1029	we eliminate _____ words. (How many?) 1030

a	a. **The customer returned. He wanted his money back.**
	b. **The customer returned. To get his money back.**
	c. **The customer returned to get his money back.**
	Which one of the above three items is incorrect? _____
1299	1300

Yes	*While peeling onions,* **my eyes always smart.**
	Does either the introductory word group or the main statement tell **who** is *peeling the onions?* (*Yes, No*)
1569	1570

in age

1839

Some people try to impress others by using pretentious language, by repeating themselves, and by expressing themselves in a roundabout way.

  a. **Wilma Rudolph was one who was a determined person.**
  b. **Wilma Rudolph was a determined person.**

The sentence containing ''deadwood'' is sentence (*a, b*). 1840

---

spoken, seen

2108

The pipe had _____ (*burst*) because the water had _____ (*freeze*).

2109

---

verb

2377

a. **The company is always quite . . . in handling complaints.**
b. **The company always handles complaints quite . . . .**

In which sentence would you use the adjective **prompt** because it would modify the noun **company?** _____

2378

---

b

2646

WRONG: **When a *student* plays football, *you* must keep in condition.**

This sentence is wrong because the pronoun *you* disagrees with its antecedent in (*number, person*).

2647

---

prohibited, maimed, blinded(,)

2915

A bank will not hire any person who is known to gamble.

2916

Chinese, Street

3184

Do not capitalize—

  GAMES: **baseball, hockey, checkers**
  MUSICAL INSTRUMENTS: **violin, piano, saxophone**

Copy the words that require capitals:

My cousin Lisa sees every colby football game because she plays the trumpet in the college band. _____

3185

Yes

220

Because adverbs are often movable, we frequently find them several words away from the verbs they modify.

Aunt Mary talks about politics *continually.*

The adverb *continually* modifies the verb _____.

221

because

490

The grammar term for the clause signals that start adverb clauses is *subordinating* _____.

491

directs

760

Few people pay any attention to *who directs a movie.*

How do we know that the clause signal is not the object of the preposition **to?**

If the clause signal *who(m)* were the object of the preposition **to,** the clause would have no (*subject, object*).

761

two

1030

This is a matter *which is of great importance.*

Reduce the italicized adjective clause to a prepositional phrase:

This is a matter _____.

1031

b

1300

Sentence fragments can result from splitting off a clause or a phrase from the beginning of a sentence, as well as from the end.

a. **I wandered among the crowd. Looking for a familiar face.**
b. **Looking for a familiar face. I wandered among the crowd.**

The sentence fragment comes first in (*a, b*). _____

1301

No

1570

Sometimes it is difficult or awkward to tell **who** or **what** at the beginning of your main statement.

While peeling onions, ____?____

Since it would be difficult to continue this sentence, it would be best to tell **who** in the (*introductory word group, main statement*).

1571

a

1840

The way to make a theme longer is to develop your thoughts and to add ideas. Don't pack it with empty words that waste your reader's time.

_∧ **I think that the plot is weak.**

To lengthen your theme, would it be a good idea to add the words **In my opinion** at the point indicated? (*Yes, No*)

1841

---

burst, frozen

2109

Lesson **59** Another Group of Three-Part Verbs

[Frames 2111–2147]

---

a

2378

a. **The company is always quite . . . in handling complaints.**
b. **The company always handles complaints quite . . . .**

In which sentence would you use the adverb **promptly** because it would modify the verb **handles?** _____

2379

---

person

2647

WRONG: **Always reread a** *letter* **before you mail** *them.*

This sentence is wrong because the pronoun *them* disagrees with its antecedent in (*number, person*).

2648

None

2916

Reminder: After the first part of a date or an address, put a comma both before and after each additional part unless it ends the sentence.

We shall be at the Chippewa Motor Hotel 850 Laurel Street Brainerd Minnesota until Tuesday May 10.

2917

Cousin, Colby

3185

Do not capitalize—

OCCUPATIONS: **engineer, artist, lawyer, minister**
DISEASES: **measles, mumps, flu, chicken pox, polio**

Copy the words that require capitals:

Just before easter our minister got pneumonia and was taken to the Oakfield hospital. _____

3186

talks

221

Tomorrow **my cousins will drive back to Springfield.**

The adverb *Tomorrow* modifies the verb _____.

222

---

conjunctions

491

You have had much practice in using the conjunctions **and, but,** and **or** to make compound sentences.

These conjunctions, **and, but,** and **or,** are sometimes called **coordinating (co-** means *equal*) **conjunctions** because they connect words and word groups that are (*unequal, equal*) in rank.

492

---

subject

761

Now let us look at another sentence:

The producers must consider *whom a* <u>*movie*</u> <u>*might*</u> <u>*offend*</u>.

The pronoun *whom* cannot be the subject of the verb *might offend* because the verb already has a subject, the noun

_____.

762

---

of great
importance.

1031

Sometimes you can do even better by reducing the adjective clause to a single adjective.

>**The plane carries a raft** *that is made of rubber.*
>**The plane carries a** *rubber* **raft.**

Does the five-word adjective clause say any more than the one-word adjective *rubber*? (*Yes, No*)

1032

---

b

1301

>a. **Though I don't collect them. Stamps interest me.**
>b. **Stamps interest me. Though I don't collect them.**

The sentence fragment comes first in (*a, b*). _____

1302

---

introductory
word group

1571

When it is awkward to tell **who** or **what** in the main statement, change the introductory word group to a *complete adverb clause,* leaving the main statement as it is.

>a. **While peeling onions, my eyes always smart.**
>b. **While I peel onions, my eyes always smart.**

Which sentence is correct? _____

1572

"Deadwood" also results from a lack of careful revision. Keep working at a sentence until you succeed in removing all useful words and roundabout expressions.

No

a. **There is a great deal of value connected with this book.**
b. **This book has great value.**

Which sentence is better? _____

1841

1842

There are a number of irregular verbs that follow the pattern of the verb **ring**.

PRESENT	PAST	PAST PARTICIPLE
ring	**rang**	**(have) rung**

Underline the vowel in each of the above three forms of the verb **ring.** Vowels are $a, e, i, o, u.$

2111

---

b

Underline the correct word:

My sunburn hurt (*bad, badly*) **for several days.**

2379

2380

In this and the following frames, circle the N when the pronoun disagrees with its antecedent in *Number,* the P when it disagrees in *Person.* Then cross out the incorrect pronoun (and sometimes the verb, too), and write your correction above.

number

$N \ P$ **A person is expected to keep their appointment.**

2648

2649

Hotel, Street,
Brainerd,
Minnesota,
Tuesday,

The time will come however when nations will settle their differences around the conference table not on the battlefield.

2917

2918

Do not capitalize—

TREES: **elm, maple, willow, pine, birch**
FLOWERS: **rose, peony, orchid, dandelion**

Easter, Hospital

Copy the words that require capitals:

The yellow chrysanthemums with the scarlet oak leaves make the display of the Meyer flower shop very colorful.

3186

3187

will drive 222	a. **One of the windows** *occasionally* **sticks.** b. **One of the windows sticks** *occasionally.* c. *Occasionally* **one of the windows sticks.** In which sentence is the adverb farthest away from the verb it modifies? _____ 223
equal 492	Because the two parts of a compound sentence are equal in rank, they are connected by a (*coordinating, subordinating*) conjunction. 493
movie 762	*whom a movie might offend* When we straighten out this clause, we get: *a movie might offend whom* The clause signal *whom* is the (*subject, direct object*) of the verb *might offend.* 763
No 1032	**This is not a good book for people** *who are nervous.* Substitute a single adjective for the adjective clause: **This is not a good book for** _____ **people.** 1033
a 1302	a. **Juan completely overhauls each motor. Before selling the car.** b. **Before selling the car. Juan completely overhauls each motor.** The sentence fragment comes first in (*a, b*). _____ 1303
b 1572	*Sitting on the step,* **my foot fell asleep.** The introductory word group is dangling because it was not the **foot** that was *sitting on the step,* but a person. It would be easier to correct this faulty sentence by answering the question **Who?** in the (*main statement, introductory word group*). 1573

Some sentences remind us of a person who walks around the block to get to the house next door. The best sentence is one that—like an arrow—goes straight to the mark.

Before the realization of what had happened came to me, it was too late.

Could this sentence be improved by revision? (*Yes, No*)

b	1843
1842	

PRESENT	PAST	PAST PARTICIPLE
ring	**rang**	**(have) rung**

Does the vowel remain the same in any two forms of this verb? (*Yes, No*)

ring, rang, rung

2111

2112

Underline the correct word:

A family can live more (*economical, economically*) **in a small town.**

badly

2380

2381

N P **When people were in debt, you used to be put in prison.**

(Punish the innocent for the crimes of the guilty?)

his
N ~~their~~

2649

2650

For the protection of small children matches drugs and sharp objects should be kept out of their reach.

come, however,
table,

2918

2919

Do not capitalize—

    BIRDS: **robin, blue jay, crow, pheasant**
    ANIMALS AND FISH: **terrier, spaniel, elephant, catfish**

Copy the words that require capitals:

We plan to take our collie with us to Moose lake, but we shall leave our canary with grandma Voss. _____

Flower Shop

3187

3188

There are hundreds of adverbs that give information about verbs. In addition, there are some special adverbs that control the "power" of adjectives and other adverbs.

c

very **hot**   *somewhat* **hot**   *rather* **hot**   *so* **hot**
quite **hot**   *extremely* **hot**   *slightly* **hot**   *too* **hot**

The italicized adverbs modify the (*adjective, adverb*) **hot**.

223   224

---

coordinating

Conjunctions such as **because, when, if,** and **unless** are called **subordinating conjunctions** because they connect a word group of (*higher, lower*) rank than a sentence.

493   494

---

direct object

(*who, whom*) *a movie might offend*

Because the clause signal is the direct object of the verb *might offend*, we choose the object form _____.

763   764

Often the single adjective to which we reduce an adjective clause is a present or past participle.

Milk is a necessity for any child *that is growing.*
Milk is a necessity for any *growing* **child.**

nervous

In the second sentence the adjective clause has been reduced to a (*present, past*) participle.

1033   1034

In this and the following frames, one of each pair of word groups is a sentence, and the other is a fragment. Draw a circle around the letter of the complete sentence.

b

     a. **As soon as I realized my mistake.**
     b. **I soon realized my mistake.**

1303   1304

---

introductory word group

     a. **As I was sitting on the step, my foot fell asleep.**
     b. **Sitting on the step, my foot fell asleep.**

Which sentence is correct? _____

1573   1574

Yes 1843	a. **Before the realization of what had happened came to me, it was too late.** b. **Before I realized what had happened, it was too late.** How many useless words are eliminated by the revision of sentence *a?* _____ <div align="right">1844</div>
No 2112	PRESENT PAST PAST PARTICIPLE **ring** **rang** **(have) rung** Notice that the past and past participle are different. The vowel **a** in the past turns to _____ in the past participle. <div align="right">2113</div>
economically 2381	A few adverbs have two forms—one with *-ly* and another without; for example, **slow—slowly, quick—quickly, loud—loudly, fair—fairly, cheap—cheaply.** The shorter form is frequently used in brief commands and on traffic signs. a. **Drive ... !** b. **I always eat my meals ....** In which sentence is the adverb **slow** acceptable? _____ <div align="right">2382</div>
they P ~~you~~ 2650	*N P* **When a person gets angry, they should count to ten.** <div align="right">2651</div>
children, matches, drugs(,) 2919	**Grace Hopper studied and improved computer programming and communication.** <div align="right">2920</div>

Lake, Grandma
 	
3188
	11. Capitalize proper adjectives that modify common nouns.
	    Dutch apple pie **Swiss cheese** **Spanish moss**
	    Chinese checkers **Harvard beets** **American elm**
	Copy the words that require capitals:
	Our french poodle and siamese cat get along well together.
	<div align="right">3189</div>

adjective 224	*very* **awkwardly** *rather* **awkwardly** *so* **awkwardly** *quite* **awkwardly** *somewhat* **awkwardly** *too* **awkwardly** All the italicized adverbs modify the (*adjective, adverb*) **awkwardly.** 225
lower 494	Because adverb clauses are of lower rank than the sentence to which they are attached, they are connected by (*coordinating, subordinating*) conjunctions. 495
whom 764	**The producer must consider** *whom a movie might offend.* We choose the object form *whom* because it is the direct object of the verb (*must consider, might offend*). 765
present 1034	**Nothing disgusts me more than a child** *that has been spoiled.* **Nothing disgusts me more than a** *spoiled* **child.** In the second sentence the adjective clause has been reduced to a (*present, past*) participle. 1035

b
 	
1304
	Continue to draw a circle around the letter of each complete sentence:
	
	    a. **I laughed until my sides ached.**
	    b. **Laughing until my sides ached.**
	
	1305

a 1574	In this and the following frames, correct the dangling word group by changing it to a complete adverb clause. Make no change in the main statement. **Being a rainy day, the outdoor track meet was postponed.** _____, the **outdoor track meet was postponed.** 1575

four

1844

---

a. **It tells how the American people conquered the wilderness.**
b. **It tells of the American people and the way in which they conquered the wilderness.**

Which sentence is better? _____

1845

---

u

2113

Supply the missing forms of the verb **ring**:

PRESENT	PAST	PAST PARTICIPLE
ring	_____	**(have)** _____

2114

---

a

2382

---

a. **Play . . . !**   b. **The store treats all customers . . . .**

Although both **fair** and **fairly** are adverbs, in which sentence should **fairly,** rather than **fair,** be used? _____

2383

---

he
N ~~they~~

2651

N P   **Can you really judge a person's character by their handwriting?**

2652

None

2920

The newspaper praised Fran Kaslow the driver of the bus for her cool skillful handling of the emergency.

2921

French, Siamese

3189

In this and the following frames, copy only the words in each sentence to which capitals need to be added:

Among the sponsors of the Good Will club are father Cole of Trinity church, mayor Morales, a judge, a doctor, and my uncle George.

3190

adverb	**Too many people vote without sufficient information.** The adjective **many** modifies the noun **people.** What adverb modifies the adjective **many?** _____
225	226
subordinating	A sentence that contains one or more subordinate clauses is called a **complex sentence.** Any sentence that contains an adverb clause is a (*complex, compound*) sentence.
495	496
might offend	To choose between **who** and **whom** in a noun clause, see how it is used *within the clause itself.* The way in which the entire noun clause is used in the full sentence has no bearing on your choice of **who** or **whom.** (*True, False*)
765	766

past	Any adjective clause that identifies someone or something can be reduced to an appositive phrase very simply.
	
	    Corn, *which was our main crop,* **did poorly that year.**
	    Corn, *our main crop,* **did poorly that year.**
	
	This reduction eliminates two useless words: _____ and _____.

1035	1036
a	a. **It was woven from discarded scraps of cloth.** b. **Woven from discarded scraps of cloth.**
1305	1306
Because (Since, As) it was a rainy day,	Continue to follow the directions for the previous frame. **Struggling through the underbrush, the hunter's clothes were badly torn.** _____ , **the hunter's clothes were badly torn.**
1575	1576

a 1845	Avoid repeating in the same sentence the meaning already stated by another word or group of words. Cross out two repetitious words: **The modern car of today is a complicated machine.** 1846
rang, (have) rung 2114	The next seven verbs that we study follow the **ring-rang-rung** pattern. One should help you to remember the others. Supply the missing forms: **ring**　　　　　**rang**　　　　　**(have) rung** **sing**　　　　　**sang**　　　　　**(have)** _____ 2115
b 2383	When an adverb has two forms—one with *-ly* and another without—the longer form is preferred in formal usage. a. **Please come** *quick!* b. **A good executive can make important decisions** *quick.* In which sentence would it be advisable to change the adverb *quick* to *quickly?* _____ 2384
his N ~~their~~ 2652	*N P*　　Once a player takes his hand off a checker, you can't take back the move. 2653
Kaslow, bus, cool, 2921	**You know Ralph that any player who breaks the training rules is suspended for the season.** 2922
Club, Father, Church, Mayor, Uncle 3190	**Perhaps grandma Wiles will spend easter with my aunt in the east.** 3191

Lois speaks French very fluently.

Too

The adverb **fluently** modifies the verb **speaks.**

What adverb modifies the adverb **fluently?** _____

226

227

---

complex

In every complex sentence that contains an adverb clause, you can expect to find a (*coordinating, subordinating*) conjunction.

496

497

True

To decide whether to use the pronoun **who** or **whom,** you need to look only (*inside, outside*) the clause.

766

767

The next event, *which was a tug of war,* **was won by the freshmen.**

Write in the appositive phrase to which the italicized clause can be reduced:

which, was

The next event, _____, **was won by the freshmen.**

1036

1037

---

a

a. **Although the movie finally came to a happy ending.**
b. **The movie finally came to a happy ending.**

1306

1307

While (As) he struggled through the underbrush,

Unless thoroughly cooked, a person should not eat pork.

_____

_____, **a person should not eat pork.**

1576

1577

of today 1846	Reduce the following wordy sentence to only four words: **John's attitude toward his parents was that he had respect for them.** _____ _____ 1847
sung 2115	Supply the missing forms: PRESENT PAST PAST PARTICIPLE ring rang (have) rung sink _____ (have) sunk shrink shrank (have) _____ 2116
b 2384	Although we frequently hear **sure** (instead of **surely**) used as an adverb in informal conversation, to many people it sounds slangy and slipshod. He _surely_ **gave our suggestion his careful consideration.** The adverb _surely_ is required because it modifies the verb _____. 2385
he P ~~you~~ 2653	_N P_ **It's exciting to hook a sailfish because they put up a big fight.** 2654
know, Ralph, 2922	In the remaining frames, put circles around any commas that should be omitted. If all the commas in any sentence are necessary, write _Correct._ **When we finally reached the stadium, we drove around, and looked for a place to park.** 2923
Grandma, Easter, East 3191	**My dad often says that he married my mother because she was born on the fourth of July, and he therefore would not run the risk of forgetting her birthday.** _____ 3192

very

227

The lake was slightly rough.

The adverb **slightly** modifies the _____ **rough.**

228

---

subordinating

497

a. **when, as, since, where, after, as if, because, unless, so that, although,** *etc.*
b. **and, but, or**

Which one of the above groups consists of subordinating conjunctions—*a* or *b?* _____

498

---

inside

767

If the clause signal is the subject or subject complement within the clause, use the subject form (*who, whom*).

768

---

a tug of war

1037

Do you remember that a gerund is a noun formed by adding -*ing* to a verb and that a gerund can be used in any way that a noun is used?

The women raised money *by selling books.*

Here the gerund phrase *selling books* is the object of the preposition _____.

1038

---

b

1307

a. **He gave no signal to the car behind him.**
b. **Giving no signal to the car behind him.**

1308

Unless it (the pork) has been thoroughly cooked,

1577

Used for only a short time, the Sibleys expect a good price for their car.

_____

_____, **the Sibleys expect a good price for their car.**

1578

John respected his parents. 1847	In this and the following frames, improve each sentence by crossing out the number of useless words indicated in the parentheses: **It would do more harm than it would do good to your car. (3)** 1848

---

sank,
(have) shrunk

2116

Supply the missing forms:

PRESENT	PAST	PAST PARTICIPLE
ring	**rang**	**(have) rung**
spring	_____	**(have) sprung**
swim	**swam**	**(have)** _____

2117

---

gave

2385

Underline the correct word:

Young people (*sure, surely*) **appreciate a parent's interest in their activities and problems.**

2386

---

it puts
N ~~they put~~

2654

N P   **The less exercise one takes, the less food you need.**

2655

---

around ⊙

2923

Films, slides, and models, make a science course, for example, much more interesting.

2924

Fourth

3192

The president urged full support of the United nations.

_____

3193

adjective (*or* subject complement) 228	**Jack can type quite rapidly.** The adverb **quite** modifies the _____ **rapidly.** 229
a 498	a. **A serious fire broke out, and the building was empty.** b. **A serious fire broke out while the building was empty.** One sentence merely adds one fact to another. The other sentence explains *how* the two facts are related. Which sentence brings out more clearly the *relationship* between the two ideas—*a* or *b?* _____ 499
who 768	If the clause signal is the object of a verb or preposition within the clause, use the object form (*who, whom*). 769

by
 	
 1038
	An adverb clause can often be reduced to a prepositional phrase with a gerund phrase as the object of the preposition (*by, for, on, in, before, after,* etc.).
	
	    Because we took a short cut, **we saved five miles.**
	    By taking a short cut, **we saved five miles.**
	
	 The gerund phrase is the object of the preposition _____.
	
	 1039

a 1308	a. **Which makes her look much taller than she is.** b. **It makes her look much taller than she is.** 1309
Because (Since, As) it (the car) was used for only a short time, 1578	**Seeing a large crowd around the car, our curiosity was aroused.** _____ _____, **our curiosity was aroused.** 1579

it would do	**The dashboard on the inside of the car has also been improved. (3)**
1848	1849

sprang, (have) swum	Supply the missing forms, following the **ring-rang-rung** pattern:
	PRESENT PAST PAST PARTICIPLE
	begin _____ (have) _____
	drink _____ (have) _____
2117	2118

surely	If using **surely** sounds stiff and unnatural to you, you can use the adverb **certainly** in its place.
	Supply an adverb with the same meaning as **surely:**
	We _____ saved money by painting the house ourselves.
2386	2387

one (he) needs	N P **Before you take medicine, a person should always read the label.**
P ~~you need~~	(*Note:* In this frame you need to cross out a noun rather than a pronoun.)
2655	2656

models☉	**We are supposed to memorize, not read, our parts in the play.**
2924	2925

President, Nations	**Our assignment was to write an interpretation of "the Death of the Hired man" by Robert Frost, the new england poet.**
3193	3194

adverb	You have now seen that adverbs can modify *three* different classes of words.
	Besides modifying verbs, adverbs can also modify other modifiers.
229	By "other modifiers" we mean adjectives and _____.
	230

b	a. **A serious fire broke out, and the building was empty.**
	b. **A serious fire broke out while the building was empty.**
	Which sentence is a complex sentence because it contains a subordinating conjunction? _____
499	500

whom	When a noun clause begins with **whoever** or **whomever,** we make our choice in exactly the same way as we did with **who** and **whom.**
	Underline the correct word:
769	**Mrs. Torrey tells** (*whoever, whomever*) *will listen* **about her travels.**
	770

By	*When he saw his final grade,* **Ron leaped with joy.**
	Complete the following sentence by supplying a gerund phrase as the object of the preposition *On:*
1039	*On* _____, **Ron leaped with joy.**
	1040

b	In this and the following frames, write an *S* for each word group that is a *Sentence,* and an *F* for each word group that is a *Fragment.* Write your answers on the two lines in the same order as the word groups.
	This article recommends electing our Presidents. By a direct vote of the people. _____ _____
1309	1310

Because (Since, As) we saw a large crowd around the car,	**While writing my summary of** *Macbeth,* **my baby sister kept interrupting me.**
	_____
1579	_____, **my baby sister kept interrupting me.**
	1580

on the inside	We weighed the meat on a scale in order to see if we had been cheated. (5)
1849	1850
began, (have) begun drank, (have) drunk	a. **rang, sang, sank, shrank, sprang, swam, began, drank** b. **rung, sung, sunk, shrunk, sprung, swum, begun, drunk** Which group consists of simple past verbs that you would use *without* the forms of the helping verb **have** or **be**?
2118	_____ 2119
certainly	Use **really,** not **real,** as an adverb meaning **very.** Underline the correct word: **Dorothy Hamill is** (*real, really*) **serious about skating.**
2387	2388
you P ~~a person~~	From here on, supply a pronoun that agrees in number and person with its antecedent: **If a person overparks, the police tow _____ car away.**
2656	2657
Correct	**No, I should not like to meet Mr. Parker, when he is angry.**
2925	2926
"The . . . Man," New England	Among the exhibits of the Library of congress are the original declaration of independence and the constitution. _____ _____
3194	3195

adverbs 230	In this and the following frames, the position of the periods should tell you whether the missing word would be an adjective or an adverb. **Our hotel room was very . . .** The missing word (such as *small, shabby,* or *comfortable*) would be an (*adjective, adverb*). 231
b 500	a. **A serious fire broke out, and the building was empty.** b. **A serious fire broke out while the building was empty.** The relationship between the two facts is brought out more clearly by the (*complex, compound*) sentence. 501
whoever 770	**Mrs. Torrey tells** *whoever will listen* **about her travels.** *Whoever* is correct because it is the (*subject, object*) of the verb *will listen* within the clause. 771
seeing his final grade, 1040	**You can often frighten away wild animals** *if you will hit two stones together.* Supply a gerund phrase as the object of the preposition *by:* **You can often frighten away wild animals** *by* _____ _____. 1041
S F 1310	Write an *S* (for *Sentence*) or an *F* (for *Fragment*) for each of the two word groups: **Thinking that the gun was empty. He jokingly pointed it at** **his friend.** ____ ____ 1311
While (As, When) I was writing my summary of *Macbeth,* 1580	From here on, correct each sentence by answering the question **Who?** or **What?** at the beginning of the main statement. Make no change in the introductory word group. **Having studied hard, my test score disappointed me.** **Having studied hard,** _____ _____. 1581

on a scale in order 1850	**After the time that our family moved to Argyle, I did not see Uncle John very frequently from then on. (6)** 1851
a 2119	a. **rang, sang, sank, shrank, sprang, swam, began, drank** b. **rung, sung, sunk, shrunk, sprung, swum, begun, drunk** Which group consists of past participles that you would use *with* the forms of the helping verb **have** or **be?** _____ 2120
really 2388	a. **The test was** *real* **difficult.** b. **The party was a** *real* **success.** The word *real* should be changed to *really* in sentence ____. 2389
his 2657	The poster shows a person how _____ should put on a life preserver. 2658
Mr. Parker⊙ 2926	**Not a thing was broken, or lost, or mislaid as a result of our moving.** (Note that there are two *or*'s in this series.) 2927
Congress, Declaration, Independence, Constitution 3195	**At various times we have owned a collie, a police dog, an irish terrier, and a persian cat.** _____ _____ 3196

adjective	**We . . . find Skippy in a neighbor's yard.**
	The missing word (such as *often, usually,* or *sometimes*) would be an (*adjective, adverb*).
231	232

complex	a. **The dog won't eat, and it seems to be hungry.**
	b. **The dog won't eat although it seems to be hungry.**
	The relationship between the two facts is brought out more clearly by the (*compound, complex*) sentence.
501	502

subject	Underline the correct word:
	(*Whoever, Whomever*) *the country elects* **will face serious problems.**
771	772

hitting two stones together.	*Before I joined the club,* **I attended several meetings.**
	Supply a gerund phrase as the object of the preposition *Before:*
	Before _____, **I attended several meetings.**
1041	1042

F S	Write an *S* (for *Sentence*) or an *F* (for *Fragment*) for each of the two word groups:
	Although the dog is friendly to the family. It is very unfriendly to others. ____ ____
1311	1312

I was disappointed in my test score.	**When inflated with air, six people can be carried on this raft.**
	When inflated with air, _____
	_____.
1581	1582

the time that, from then on 1851	Shirley had unusual self-confidence in herself when she went shopping to buy something for herself or someone else. (5) 1852
b 2120	Underline three verbs that follow the **ring-rang-rung** pattern: **think sing sink wink spring** 2121
a 2389	Although -*ly* is used mainly to change adjectives to adverbs, it is also used to change a few nouns to adjectives; for example, **friend-ly, neighbor-ly, father-ly, order-ly.** **Our new neighbors are unusually** *friendly*. The word *friendly* is an adjective because it modifies the noun _____. 2390
he 2658	Why don't you boys help _____ to some lunch? 2659
broken⊙ lost⊙ 2927	The alligator has a thick, tough, leathery, hide. 2928
Irish, Persian 3196	The members of our latin class sent Alva an african violet after her operation for appendicitis at the Bennett hospital. 3197

adverb 232	**The fair will last for . . . days.** The missing word would be an (*adjective, adverb*). 233
complex 502	SUBORDINATING CONJUNCTIONS **when, as, since, where, after, as if, because, unless, so that, although,** *etc.* COORDINATING CONJUNCTIONS **and, but, or** The conjunctions that show *more specifically* the relationship between the two facts or ideas that they connect are the (*subordinating, coordinating*) conjunctions. 503
Whomever 772	*Whomever the country elects* **will face serious problems.** *Whomever* is correct because it is the (*subject, object*) of the verb *elects* within the clause. 773
joining the club, 1042	Here is an adjective clause, too, that can be reduced in the same way: **We have a plan** *that would improve the bus service.* Supply a gerund phrase as the object of the preposition *for:* **We have a plan** *for* _____ _____. 1043
F S 1312	**Sara Teasdale admired Christina Rossetti. Who wrote imaginative poetry.** ____ ____ 1313
this raft can carry six people. 1582	**Reaching for the sugar, the cream pitcher was overturned by my dad.** **Reaching for the sugar,** _____ _____. 1583

in herself,
to buy something

1852

Of all the hunter's articles of equipment that he uses, his rifle is the most important to him. (7)

1853

---

sing, sink, spring

2121

Underline three verbs that follow the **ring-rang-rung** pattern:

swim   fling   skin   begin   drink

2122

---

neighbors

2390

Since words such as **neighborly, fatherly,** and **orderly** are adjectives, they cannot be used to modify verbs.

WRONG: **Mr. Momaday discusses literature** *scholarly.*

This sentence is wrong because the adjective *scholarly* cannot modify the verb _____.

2391

---

yourselves

2659

Some of the customers made it difficult for the clerk by rushing _____.

2660

---

leathery⊙

2928

To tell the truth, I tried to be friendly, but Bob didn't respond.

2929

Latin, African,
Hospital

3197

Dr. Carver, the great negro agricultural chemist, refused money for his discoveries because he felt that he was doing god's work.

3198

adjective

233

We studied the road map . . . carefully.

The missing word would be an (*adjective, adverb*).

234

---

subordinating

503

We can give a sentence many different meanings merely by changing the subordinating conjunction.

I shall not tell Ruth . . . I see her.

Underline the only subordinating conjunction that does *not* fit into the above sentence:

when   until   so that   if   unless   although

504

---

object

773

Underline the correct word:

I have great admiration for (*whoever, whomever*) **wrote this article.**

774

---

improving the
bus service.

1043

The French class has a new tape recorder *on which they listen to their pronunciation.*

Change the adjective clause to a prepositional phrase with a gerund:

The French class has a new tape recorder _____

_____ *to their pronunciation.*

1044

S F

1313

Situated at the southern tip of Florida. Everglades Park is a vast wilderness of plants, birds, and animals. _____ _____

1314

---

my dad
overturned the
cream pitcher.

1583

Rolled very thin, you can make five dozen cookies from this dough.

Rolled very thin, _____

_____.

1584

articles of, that he uses, to him 1853	The reporter spent a week in the town of Belding in order to observe the differences that exist between city life and small-town life. (7) 1854
swim, begin, drink 2122	In this and the following frames, supply the correct forms of the verb in parentheses. All follow the **ring-rang-rung** pattern. **After the bell had _____ three times, it _____ once again.** (*ring*) 2123
discusses 2391	**neighborly fatherly scholarly lovely** Since these adjectives already end in -*ly*, can we make adverbs of them by adding another -*ly*? (*Yes, No*) 2392
him 2660	**Don't judge a person entirely by _____ clothes.** 2661
Correct 2929	**When we hit the wet, and slippery pavement, our car skidded badly.** 2930
Negro, God's 3198	A boys' chorus from Ralph Bunche high school sang "Joy to the world" and several french christmas carols at the december meeting. _____ _____ 3199

adverb	**The room looks very . . . without the piano.**
	The missing word would be an (*adjective, adverb*).
234	235

	Think of the meaning of each sentence before you select the clause signal.
so that	**The boys greeted each other . . .** *nothing had happened.*
	Underline the clause signal you would use to explain **how** the boys greeted each other:
504	**unless** **as if** **although** **so that** 505

whoever	Underline the correct word:
	Scholars have argued about (*who, whom*) **wrote Shakespeare's plays.**
774	775

	A prepositional phrase can sometimes be replaced by a single adjective or adverb.
	The cashier looked at the check *in a suspicious way.*
for listening	Substitute an adverb for the italicized prepositional phrase:
	The cashier looked at the check_____.
1044	1045

F S	**I have more than two thousand stamps. All of which are different.** ____ ____
1314	1315

this dough will (can) make five dozen cookies.	**While waiting for a bus, a passing car splashed me.**
	While waiting for a bus, _____
	_____.
1584	1585

the town of, in order, that exist 1854	When he had his examination, it showed that he needed dental work to be done in his mouth by a dentist. (13) 1855
rung, rang 2123	The shirt _____ more than it should have _____. (*shrink*) 2124
No 2392	lovely neighborly fatherly scholarly To make adverbial modifiers of these -*ly* adjectives, we must put them in prepositional phrases that can modify verbs: for example, **in a fatherly way, in an orderly manner.** **Mr. Momaday discusses literature** *in a scholarly manner.* The italicized phrase modifies the verb _____. 2393
his 2661	Once a customer has worn a dress,_____ cannot return it. 2662
wet⊙ 2930	The Springfield Electric Company, which employs many young people, will not hire anyone, who has not completed high school. 2931
High School, World, French, Christmas, December 3199	Our pastor told about the four chaplains of the catholic, jewish, and protestant faiths who went down with linked arms when their ship was sunk by the germans in world war II. _____ _____ 3200

adjective	**It is . . . hot at the equator.** The missing word would be an (*adjective, adverb*).
235	236
as if	**Bob studies at night . . .** *he completes his work in the after-noon.* Underline the clause signal you would use to explain **on what condition** Bob studies at night: **until although because unless**
505	506
who	Underline the correct word: **The jury could not decide** (*who, whom*) **they could believe.**
775	776
suspiciously.	**You can buy a film at the store** *on the corner.* Substitute an adjective for the italicized prepositional phrase: **You can buy a film at the** _____ **store.**
1045	1046
S F	**Many college students help to pay their expenses. By doing odd jobs in their spare time.** ____ ____
1315	1316
I was splashed by a passing car.	**By sitting around and talking, our work will never get done.** **By sitting around and talking,** _____ _____.
1585	1586

When he had, it, to be done in his mouth by a dentist	My handicap that I have is in not being able to pronounce the sound of new words that I am not familiar with. (13)
1855	1856
shrank, shrunk	All of us _____ more cider than we should have _____. (*drink*)
2124	2125
discusses	WRONG: **Mr. Dale spoke to Earl** *fatherly.* This sentence is wrong because the adjective *fatherly* cannot modify the verb **spoke.** Supply a prepositional phrase that will include the adjective *fatherly:* **Mr. Dale spoke to Earl** _____.
2393	2394
she	The graduate should choose a college that is outstanding in the field of _____ choice.
2662	2663
anyone ☉	Don't yawn, or look at your watch, when you are entertaining guests.
2931	2932
Catholic, Jewish, Protestant, Germans, World War	The zinnias bloom in august, but the asters do not bloom until fall.
3200	3201

adverb 236	An adjective can modify only two classes of words: nouns and pronouns. An adverb, however, can modify _____ classes of words. (How many?) 237
unless 506	**María applied for the job . . .** *she read the advertisement in the newspaper.* Underline the clause signal you would use to explain **when** María applied for the job: **if as soon as although where** 507
whom 776	Underline the correct word: **The jury could not decide** (*who, whom*) **was telling the truth.** 777
corner 1046	In this and the following frames, reduce each italicized word group to the construction indicated in parentheses: **The author** *who wrote this story* **knows a lot about sports.** (prepositional phrase) **The author** _____ **knows a lot about sports.** 1047
S F 1316	Lesson **36** Other Types of Sentence Fragments [Frames 1318–1355]
we will never get our work done. *or* we will never finish our work. 1586	Lesson **44** Parallel Construction for Parallel Ideas [Frames 1588–1618]

that I have, in,
the sound of,
that I am not
familiar with

1856

In the remaining frames, rewrite each sentence to express the idea more directly. (If your answer differs from that in the key, count your answer right if you have eliminated useless words.)

The meal that I receive the most enjoyment out of is breakfast. _____

1857

---

drank, drunk

2125

We _____ where we had never _____

before. (*swim*)

2126

---

in a fatherly
way (manner).

2394

Correct the following sentence:

Mrs. Cornelius, our grocer, treats all her customers very *neighborly*.

Mrs. Cornelius, our grocer, treats all her customers _____

_____.

2395

---

his

2663

Lesson **74** Pronouns That Mean One

[Frames 2665–2703]

---

yawn⊙
watch⊙

2932

Lesson **82** How to Use Semicolons,
Colons, and Dashes

[Frames 2934–2974]

August

3201

Lesson **89** Review: The Principles
of Graphics

[Frames 3203–3232]

three	Lesson 7 The Prepositional Phrase as a Modifier [Frames 239–282]
237	

---

as soon as	**Our guide tied the canoe to a tree** . . . *it would not drift away.* Underline the clause signal you would use to explain **why** the guide tied the canoe to a tree: **as if where since so that**
507	508

---

who	Underline the correct word: (*Who, Whom*) **contributed this money is a deep and dark secret.**
777	778

---

of this story	**The employee must state the reason** *why he was absent.* (prepositional phrase) **The employee must state the reason** _____
1047	_____. 1048

	Don't let an appositive phrase become a fragment. WRONG: **The home run was hit by Baker.** *The first man at bat.* *"The first man at bat"* is an appositive phrase. Does the appositive phrase have a subject and a verb? (*Yes, No*)
	1318

	When you dress in the morning, you may select any shoes you please as long as they make a matching pair. Similarly, when you express two or more similar ideas, you may use any type of word group you wish as long as they (*match, differ*).
	1588

I enjoy (my) breakfast most.

1857

Judy started going with another boy, and this boy that she started going with was very popular.

_____

_____

1858

swam, swum

2126

The game had already _____ when it _____ to rain. (*begin*)

2127

in a very neighborly way (manner).

2395

Do not use **kind of** and **sort of** as adverbial modifiers meaning **rather** or **somewhat** except in relaxed conversation. They are out of place in formal writing or speaking.

a. **I felt** *kind of* **embarrassed about my mistake.**
b. **The public is** *kind of* **dubious about campaign promises.**

In which sentence is *kind of* inappropriate? _____

2396

The pronouns **everyone** and **everybody** are peculiar words. They are often singular and plural at the same time. They are singular in form because they are built upon the words **one** and **body,** which are (*singular, plural*).

2665

SEMICOLONS
His car was out of gas, and mine had two flat tires.

This is a compound sentence. Its two main clauses are connected by the conjunction _____.

2934

a. **Bert pulled over to the side of the road, and the oil truck passed him.**
b. **Bert pulled over to the side of the road, and let the oil truck pass.**

Omit the comma in sentence (*a, b*).

3203

The picture . . . the cover is amusing.

Is the **picture** *on, in, near, over,* or *behind* the **cover?**

We need a word to show the *relationship* between the noun **cover** and the noun _____.

239

---

so that

Mr. Hart put in a pinch of grass seed . . . *he pulled out a weed.*

Underline the clause signal you would use to explain **where** Mr. Hart put in grass seed:

after   so that   if   wherever

508

509

Who

Underline the correct word:

The newspaper would not reveal (*who, whom*) **their informant was.**

(*Note:* Take into account that the subject of the linking verb **was** is **informant.** If you are puzzled, look back to frame 754, page 427.)

778

779

---

for his absence.

The article offers many suggestions *that are practical.* (adjective)

The article offers many _____ **suggestions.**

1048

1049

No

The home run was hit by Baker. *The first man at bat.*

Does the appositive phrase make sense by itself? (*Yes, No*)

1318

1319

---

match

The principle of expressing similar ideas in a similar or parallel way is known as **parallel construction.**

This principle means that if you put one idea into a prepositional phrase, you should also put a parallel idea into (*a prepositional phrase, an adverb clause*).

1588

1589

Judy started going with another boy who was very popular.

1858

The reason that I got up early was that I had work that needed to be done.

_____

_____

1859

---

begun, began

2127

The chorus _____ the same numbers that they had _____ at their spring concert. (*sing*)

2128

---

b

2396

In more formal speech and writing, use the adverb **rather** or **somewhat** instead of **kind of** or **sort of**.

Correct the following sentence:

The public is *kind of* **dubious about campaign promises.**

The public is _____ dubious about campaign promises.

2397

---

singular

2665

Everyone *is* **ready.**   **Everybody** *was* **impatient.**

Do the pronouns **Everyone** and **Everybody** take singular or plural verbs? _____

2666

---

and

2934

A semicolon may be used in place of the conjunction **and, but,** or **or** to connect the main clauses in a compound sentence.

His car was out of gas; mine had two flat tires.

The two main clauses of this compound sentence are not connected by a conjunction but by a _____. 2935

---

b

3203

You may omit the comma and the conjunction in a compound sentence and replace them with a _____.

3204

picture 239	**The picture** *on* **the cover is amusing.** The word that now shows the relationship between **cover** and **picture** is _____. 240
wherever 509	**Fear is good . . .** *it leads you to protect yourself.* Underline the clause signal you would use to explain **under what condition** fear is good: **though** **if** **although** **unless** 510
who 779	Underline the correct word: **The orchestra extends an invitation to** (*whoever, whomever*) **can play a musical instrument.** 780
practical 1049	**People** *who are irritable* **do not make good clerks.** (adjective) _____ **people do not make good clerks.** 1050
No 1319	**The home run was hit by Baker,** *the first man at bat.* Now the appositive phrase makes sense because it is in the same sentence with the noun _____, which it explains. 1320
a prepositional phrase 1589	If you put one idea into an infinitive phrase, you should also put a parallel idea into (*a participial, an infinitive*) phrase. 1590

I got up early because I had work to do. 1859	I sent a defective pen to you approximately a month or so ago to have a repair job done on it for me. _____ _____ 1860
sang, sung 2128	The ship _____ where several other ships had _____ before. (*sink*) 2129
rather *or* somewhat 2397	a. **It made us** *sort of* **sad to leave the old farm.** b. **Jefferson was** *sort of* **fearful of centralized government.** In which sentence is *sort of* inappropriate? _____ 2398
singular 2666	**Everyone** *is* **ready.** **Everybody** *was* **impatient.** Although **everyone** and **everybody** are singular in form and always take singular verbs, we tend to think of them as meaning a number of persons, rather than a single person. Although **everyone** and **everybody** are *singular* in form, they are somewhat _____ in meaning. 2667
semicolon 2935	**I tried to explain; he was too angry to listen.** In this compound sentence the semicolon takes the place of the conjunction (*and, but*). 2936
semicolon 3204	*Fortunately* **the tornado missed our town.** *Occasionally* **Mr. Baxter forgot to give an assignment.** Putting commas after the italicized adverbs would give them (*more, less*) emphasis. 3205

Jerry strolled . . . the park.

Did Jerry stroll *through, past, around,* or *toward* the park?

We need a word to show the *relationship* between the noun **park** and the verb _____ .

on

240

241

See how simple it is to combine two sentences by using an adverb clause.

As

ʌ *The man came closer.* **I noticed a scar on his cheek.**

We change the italicized sentence to an adverb clause by adding the subordinating conjunction **As.** Then we change the period after the first sentence to a _____ .511

if

510

Underline the correct word:

Margaret Mead, the famous anthropologist, became a friend to (*whoever, whomever*) **she studied.**

whoever

780

781

These toys were made of materials *which had been dis-carded.* (past participle)

These toys were made of _____ **materials.**

Irritable

1050

1051

---

a. **The home run was hit by Baker. He was the first man at bat.**
b. **The home run was hit by Baker. The first man at bat.**
c. **The home run was hit by Baker, the first man at bat.**

Which one of the above three arrangements is incorrect—

a, b, or *c?* _____

Baker

1320

1321

Bert's parents promised *to buy a new car.*

In the above sentence, what Bert's parents promised is expressed in an (*infinitive phrase, adverb clause*).

an infinitive

1590

1591

I sent you a pen approximately a month ago for repair. 1860	**The reason for my having been absent is that my chemistry class visited a factory where they make glass.** _____ _____ 1861
sank, sunk 2129	The five common irregular verbs that follow often cause errors that give the impression of uneducated speech. PRESENT PAST PAST PARTICIPLE **do** **did** (not **done**) **(have) done** Fill in the correct forms of **do:** I _____ **what anyone else would have** _____. 2130
b 2398	Correct the following sentence: **Jefferson was** _sort of_ **fearful of centralized government.** **Jefferson was** _____ **fearful of centralized government.** 2399
plural 2667	**everyone everybody** Shall we use singular pronouns to refer to these words because of their singular form, or shall we use plural pronouns because of their plural meaning? Those who consider form more important than meaning would use (_singular, plural_) pronouns. 2668

but
 	
2936
	A semicolon can also take the place of the clause signal **because** in a complex sentence.
	    a. **The bird couldn't fly; its wing was broken.**
	    b. **The streets were icy; traffic moved slowly.**
	In which sentence does the semicolon take the place of the clause signal **because?** _____
	
	2937

more 3205	a. _For the first time in many years_ **we won every game of the season.** b. _For the first time_ **we won every game of the season.** Because of the length of the introductory expression, a comma would more commonly be used in sentence (_a, b_). 3206

strolled 241	**Jerry strolled** *through* **the park.** The word that now shows the relationship between **park** and **strolled** is _____. 242
comma 511	**The man came closer. I noticed a scar on his cheek.** *As the man came closer,* **I noticed a scar on his cheek.** We have combined the two sentences by making a (*compound, complex*) sentence. 512
whomever 781	Underline the correct word: (*Whoever, Whomever*) **wrote this courageous editorial deserves a lot of admiration.** 782
discarded 1051	**I was kept awake by the faucet** *that was dripping.* (present participle) **I was kept awake by the** _____ **faucet.** 1052
b 1321	Now look at another cause of sentence fragments—the sentence with a compound predicate. **We climbed the tower and looked at the scenery.** The above sentence has a compound predicate that makes (*one, two*) statement(s) about the subject **We** in the first word group. 1322
infinitive phrase 1591	**Bert's parents promised** *to buy a new car.* *To buy a new car* is an infinitive phrase. If you wanted to state a second promise that Bert's parents made, it would be better, for the sake of parallel construction, to use an (*adverb clause, infinitive phrase*). 1592

I was absent because my chemistry class visited a glass factory. 1861	**Lesson 52** **Review: Problems of Sentence Construction** [Frames 1863–1883]

did, done
 	
2130
	PRESENT PAST PAST PARTICIPLE
	    go **went** **(have) gone** (not *went*)
	
	Fill in the correct forms of **go**:
	
	Joan _____ **to say good-by to Iris, but Iris had**
	
	already _____ **.**
	
	                                          2131

rather *or* somewhat
 	
2399
	In this and the following frames, underline the correct modifier or, in some cases, the word appropriate for formal usage:
	
	    Clarence types fast but not very (*accurate, accurately*).
	
	                                          2400

singular 2668	**Nearly everyone** *likes* **to see** *his* **name in print.** In this sentence, both the verb and the pronoun that refers to **everyone** are (*singular, plural*). 2669
a 2937	A comma by itself cannot connect two main clauses. Only a semicolon has the power to hold main clauses together without the help of the conjunction **and, but,** or **or.** a. **I shook the branches, the apples came tumbling down.** b. **I shook the branches; the apples came tumbling down.** Which sentence is correct? _____ 2938
a 3206	a. **Before we bought our new car, we got prices from several dealers.** b. **We got prices from several dealers, before we bought our new car.** Omit the comma in sentence (*a, b*). 3207

through 242	A word that shows the relationship of the noun or pronoun that follows it to some other word in the sentence is called a **preposition.** A preposition shows _____ship. 243
complex 512	**The man came closer, and I noticed a scar on his cheek.** *As the man came closer,* **I noticed a scar on his cheek.** The relationship between the two facts is brought out more clearly by the (*compound, complex*) sentence. 513
Whoever 782	In conversational English, **who** and **whoever** are often used in place of the object forms. In formal speech or writing, however, **whom** and **whomever** are the correct object forms. a. INFORMAL: **I wonder . . . Peggy will invite.** b. FORMAL: **The public wonders . . . the mayor will blame.** The pronoun **who** would be considered an error in (*a, b*). 783
dripping 1052	**Dr. Rosalyn Yalow,** *who was the winner of the Nobel Prize for Medicine,* **is a renowned physicist.** (appositive phrase) **Dr. Rosalyn Yalow,** _____, **is a renowned physicist.** 1053
two 1322	A careless writer sometimes creates a fragment by cutting off the last part of a compound predicate. WRONG: **We climbed the tower.** *And looked at the scenery.* The italicized word group lacks a (*subject, verb*). 1323
infinitive phrase 1592	a. **My parents promised** *to buy a new car* **and** *that they would let me drive it.* b. **My parents promised** *to buy a new car* **and** *to let me drive it.* _____ 1593

Here is a letter written by a father to his son's camp counselors at Camp Michiwaki. Each sentence contains one of the errors studied in this unit. At the top of each frame, circle the letter of the error found in that frame. Then revise the sentence correctly.   (*Turn to the next frame.*)

1863

---

went, gone	PRESENT **run**	PAST **ran**	PAST PARTICIPLE **(have) run**

Fill in the correct forms of **run:**

Cathy _____ **for the same office for which her**

mother had _____ **.**

2131

2132

---

accurately

Ron (*sure, surely*) **understood that I needed this money** (*badly, bad*).

2400

2401

---

singular

When the pronoun that refers to **everyone** or **everybody** is possessive (*his, her*), the singular pronoun sounds sensible and is preferred in formal writing and speaking.

Underline the pronoun preferred in formal usage:

Everybody **has the right to state** (*his, their*) **mind.**

2669

2670

---

b

When there are other commas in a compound sentence, the important comma that breaks the sentence into two parts gets lost among the others.

My Cousin Nan was popular, good-looking, and athletic, and, to tell the truth, I was a little jealous of her.

The *compound sentence* comma follows the word _____.

2938

2939

---

b

a. **While we discuss the teacher sits among the class and listens.**
b. **While we eat we often listen to the TV evening news program.**

To avoid misunderstanding, it would be advisable to use a comma after the short introductory clause in sentence (*a, b*).

3207

3208

page 486

relationship 243	Many prepositions show relationships in **position.** POSITION: *in, on, by, under, below, beneath, above, over, beside, behind, across, against,* etc. Underline the preposition that shows position: **box of crackers man from Mars car behind us** 244
complex 513	Combine each pair of sentences by changing the italicized sentence to an adverb clause. Write the full sentence, keeping the ideas in the same order. *Veal is not my favorite meat.* **I sometimes eat it.** _____ _____ 514
b 783	a. **The Senate is likely to approve . . . the President appoints.** b. **You can vote for . . . you want.** In which sentence would **whoever** be more acceptable as conversational usage? _____ 784
winner of the Nobel Prize for Medicine 1053	**Steve's General Store,** *which is the only store in the village,* **sells everything from lollipops to washing machines.** (appositive phrase) **Steve's General Store,** _____ _____, **sells everything from lollipops to washing machines.** 1054
subject 1323	**We climbed the tower.** *And looked at the scenery.* *"And looked at the scenery"* is a predicate that makes a statement about the subject _____ of the first word group. 1324
b 1593	**The company wants a driver** *who knows the city.* In the above sentence the qualification for the driver is expressed in (*a prepositional phrase, an adjective clause*). 1594

Never having been away from home before, we hope that you will give our son special attention.

_____,

we hope that you will give him special attention.

1864

PRESENT	PAST	PAST PARTICIPLE
come	**came** (not **come**)	**(have) come**

ran, run

Fill in the correct forms of **come**:

Earl _____ **home an hour ago, but Allen hasn't**

_____ **home yet.**

2132

2133

---

surely, badly

No teacher could have been more (_patient, patiently_) **than Annie Sullivan, Helen Keller's teacher.**

2401

2402

---

his

Though we hear the plural pronoun _their_ widely used to refer to **everyone** and **everybody** in informal English, it is likely to be criticized in formal writing or speaking.

    Has _everybody_ **turned in** _their_ **paper?**

This sentence is acceptable as (_informal, formal_) usage.

2670

2671

---

athletic

When other commas are present, it is a good idea to change the _compound sentence_ comma to a semicolon.

My Cousin Nan was popular, good-looking, and athletic; and, to tell the truth, I was a little jealous of her.

Using a semicolon instead of a comma after **athletic** makes the main break in the sentence (_more, less_) conspicuous.

2939

2940

---

a

When people are at home, do they strew papers, tin cans, and bottles, around their yards?

Omit the comma after the word _____.

3208

3209

behind 244	Some prepositions show **direction**. DIRECTION: *to, from, toward, down, up, at* **The rock rolled down the mountain.** The preposition **down** shows the _____ in which the rock rolled. 245
Although veal is not my favorite meat, I sometimes eat it. 514	Follow the directions given in the previous frame: **Skippy hid under the sofa.** *He was afraid of the storm.* _____ _____ 515
b 784	UNIT 4: OTHER DEVICES OF SUBORDINATION Lesson **21** **Subordination by Present Participles** [Frames 786–827]
the only store in the village 1054	*After he had saved all this money,* **Jones lost it.** (prepositional phrase with gerund) _____, **Jones lost it.** 1055
We 1324	**We climbed the tower and looked at the scenery.** This sentence is right because a predicate belongs in the same sentence with its _____. 1325
an adjective clause 1594	**The company wants a driver** *who knows the city.* *Who knows the city* is an adjective clause. If you want to state a second qualification for the driver, it would be better, for the sake of parallel construction, to use (*an adjective clause, a prepositional phrase*). 1595

page 489

a Since (Because, As) our son has never been away from home before, 1864	a. misplaced modifier b. nonparallel construction c. incorrect omission of words **We will telephone daily to inquire whether he is happy, comfortable, and his health is good.** **We will telephone daily to inquire whether he is** _____ _____. 1865

came, come 2133	PRESENT PAST PAST PARTICIPLE **come** **came** **(have) come** **run** **ran** **(have) run** To avoid a very common error, notice that **come** and **run** are two-part, not one-part, verbs. The form that is different from the other two is the _____ form. 2134

patient 2402	**In those days people lived** (*simpler, more simply*) **than they do today.** 2403

informal 2671	a. *Everyone* **should wash** *their* **hands before touching food.** b. *Everyone* **should wash** *his* **hands before touching food.** Which sentence would be more acceptable in formal speech or writing? _____ 2672

more 2940	**The mature reader enjoys a novel for its ideas, its portrayal of character, and its literary style, but the youthful reader, generally speaking, looks for excitement, suspense, and sudden surprises.** To make the sentence break more conspicuous, substitute a semicolon for the comma after the word _____. 2941

bottles 3209	**An old sailor and his dog and his cat lived in this lonely weather-beaten shack.** One comma is required after the word _____. 3210

direction
 	
245
	A few prepositions show relationships in **time**.
	
	TIME: *before, during, after, until, till*
	
	    a. **Brush your teeth . . . meals.**
	    b. **Park your car . . . the corner.**
	
	Which sentence requires a preposition that will show a *time* relationship? _____
	
	246

Skippy hid under the sofa because (since, as) he was afraid of the storm. 515	*You are the oldest.* **It was your responsibility.** _____ _____ (*Note:* Count your sentence right if it makes good sense, even if you did not use the same clause signal given in the answer.) 516
	In this unit we study other useful devices for subordination that will help us to write more mature sentences. When we subordinate a fact or an idea, we express it in a word group that is (*more, less*) than a sentence. 786
After saving all this money, 1055	*If you will make notes of important facts,* **you will make reviewing easier.** (prepositional phrase with gerund) _____ _____, **you will make reviewing easier.** 1056

subject
 	
1325
	a. **We climbed the tower. We looked at the scenery.**
	    b. **We climbed the tower and looked at the scenery.**
	    c. **We climbed the tower. And looked at the scenery.**
	
	Which one of the above three arrangements is incorrect—*a, b,* or *c?* _____
	
	1326

an adjective clause 1595	a. **The company wants a driver** *who knows the city* **and** *who has a good safety record.* b. **The company wants a driver** *who knows the city* **and** *with a good safety record.* In which sentence are the italicized word groups parallel? _____ 1596

b
happy,
comfortable,
and healthy.

1865

Do not force him to eat salad, which he never has and never will eat.

Do not force him to eat salad, _____

_____ .

1866

---

past

2134

PRESENT	PAST	PAST PARTICIPLE
come	**came**	**(have) come**
run	**ran**	**(have) run**

The past forms of **come** and **run** are _____ and

_____ .

2135

---

more simply

2403

It was (*rather, kind of*) **surprising that the public accepted the news so** (*calm, calmly*).

2404

---

b

2672

So far we have been dealing with the possessive pronoun *his*.

The situation is somewhat different when we use the nominative pronoun *he* or *she* or the _____ pronoun *him* or *her*.

2673

---

style

2941

COLONS

A colon says to the reader, "Look ahead. Here it comes," and directs his attention to what follows.

a. **I am taking five courses.**
b. **I am taking five courses:**

You expect the courses to be listed after (*a, b*).

2942

---

lonely

3210

Gwendolyn Brooks, a black writer, won the Pulitzer Prize for Poetry, on May 1, 1950.

Omit the comma after the word _____ .

3211

a
 	
246
	Still other prepositions, such as *of, for, about, with, except,* and *but* (when it means *except*), show many different kinds of relationships between the words they relate.
	
	EXAMPLES: **a pound of tea** **a story about war**
	                 a letter for me **a cake with frosting**
	
	Each of the underlined words is a _____.
	
	                                                                   247

Since you are the oldest, it was your responsibility. 516	**Mr. Doyle decided to buy our car.** *We had already sold it.* (In other words, Mr. Doyle made up his mind too late.) _____ _____ 517
less 786	Prepositional phrases and adverb, adjective, and noun clauses are **subordinate** word groups because they (*do, do not*) make complete sense apart from a sentence. 787
By making notes of important facts, 1056	**There seemed to be no way** *in which we could reduce our expenses.* (prepositional phrase with gerund) **There seemed to be no way** _____ _____. 1057

c
 	
1326
	A noun-participle (absolute) phrase consists of a noun followed by a present or past participle that modifies it.
	
	        a. **Dripping with rain**
	        b. **His raincoat dripping**
	
	Which item is a noun-participle phrase? _____
	
	                                                                   1327

a 1596	a. **It was cruel** *to catch the bird* **and** *keeping it in a cage.* b. **It was cruel** *to catch the bird* **and** *to keep it in a cage.* Which sentence is better? _____ 1597

c which he never has eaten and never will eat. 1866	a. misplaced modifier b. nonparallel construction c. faulty pronoun reference **Also, if there is any skin on chicken, he will refuse to eat it.** **Also, he will refuse** _____ _____. 1867
came, ran 2135	Notice the similarity between **come** and **become**: PRESENT PAST PAST PARTICIPLE **come** **came** **(have) come** **become** **became** **(have) become** Fill in the correct forms of **become**: **Howard** _____ **a draftsman although he could** 2136 **have** _____ **an engineer.**
rather, calmly 2404	**In spite of the customer's bad manners, the clerk conducted himself** (*gentlemanly, in a gentlemanly manner*). 2405
objective 2673	When the pronoun that refers to **everyone** or **everybody** is nominative (*he, she*) or objective (*him, her*), we are often forced to use the plural pronoun *their* (or *them*) to prevent absurdity. *Everybody* **had warned me, but I didn't believe** *him*. Does the singular pronoun *him* make good sense in this sentence? (*Yes, No*) 2674

b
 	
2942
	Use a colon (:) before an item or a series of items introduced by a statement that is grammatically complete.
	
	      a. **My favorite courses are . . .**
	      b. **These are my favorite courses . . .**
	
	After which statement would you use a colon because the statement is grammatically complete? _____
	2943

Poetry 3211	A *restrictive* clause is essential to the meaning of a sentence. A *nonrestrictive* clause merely adds a fact that is unessential to the meaning of a sentence. The clause that should be set off with commas from the rest of the sentence is the (*restrictive, nonrestrictive*) clause. 3212

preposition

The noun or pronoun that follows a preposition is called its **object.**

The man in the next seat was a doctor.

The preposition is **in;** the object of the preposition is the noun _____.

248

Mr. Doyle decided to buy our car after we had already sold it.
517

Peaches are plentiful. **They are very poor.**

(*Note:* **Because** or **when** would not make good sense here.)

518

---

do not

787

Verbals are also useful devices for subordination.

A **verbal** is a verb that has crossed the boundary line and become another class of word without completely losing its identity as a verb.

A word that functions as both a verb and an adjective would be classified as a _____.

788

---

of reducing our expenses.

1057

Unfortunately, the family has never been fully responsible *in financial matters.* (adverb)

Unfortunately, the family has never been fully responsible

_____.

1058

---

b

1327

A noun-participle phrase is often mistaken for a complete sentence.

        a. **His raincoat** dripped.
        b. **His raincoat** *dripping.*

Which item is a complete sentence? _____

1328

---

b

1597

a. **Ammonia is used** *for softening water* **and** *for dissolving grease.*
b. **Ammonia is used** *for softening water* **and** *to dissolve grease.*

Which sentence is better? _____

1598

page 495

c to eat chicken if there is any skin on it. *or* to eat any skin that is . . . 1867	a. misplaced modifier b. *is when* or *is where* error c. faulty comparison **Be especially careful not to serve any food to our child that is spoiled.** **Be especially careful not to serve** _____ _____. 1868
became, become 2136	In this and the following frames, supply the correct forms of the verbs in parentheses. Be sure to use the past participle after any form of **have** or **be**. Several verbs follow the **ring-rang-rung** pattern. **Miss Doyle had** _____ (*go*) **to the office to see why the bell had been** _____ (*ring*). 2137
in a gentlemanly manner 2405	**Some of the umpire's decisions** (*sure, certainly*) **seemed** (*unfair, unfairly*) **to most of the fans.** 2406
No 2674	a. **We hope** *everyone* **will attend, but** *he* **never does.** b. **We hope** *everyone* **will bring** *his* **parents to the meeting.** In both sentences, a singular pronoun is used, according to rule, to refer to *everyone*. In which sentence does following the rule result in absurdity? —— 2675

b
 	
2943
	You would not write—
	       My favorite course is: math.
	So don't make the same mistake by writing—
	       My favorite courses are: math, history, and biology.
	Colons should not be used after statements that are grammatically (*complete, incomplete*).
	
	2944

nonrestrictive 3212	a. **The Presidents** *who accomplished most* **were the most severely criticized.** b. **My mother** *who used to be a track star* **gave me valuable advice.** The italicized clause should be set off with commas in sentence (*a, b*). 3213

seat 248	A group of words that begins with a preposition and ends with its object is a **prepositional phrase**. **The cause of this sudden explosion remains a mystery.** The prepositional phrase begins with the preposition **of** and ends with its object _____. 249
Although peaches are plentiful, they are very poor. 518	In this and the following frames, convert each *compound* sentence to a *complex* sentence by changing the italicized statement to an adverb clause: *I opened the cabinet,* **and a jar fell out.** _____ _____ 519
verbal 788	The three kinds of verbals that we study in this unit are all "double-duty" words that have some of the characteristics of both a verb and another class of words—sometimes a noun, sometimes an adverb or an adjective. Look at the word *verbal*. As its name suggests, every verbal is formed from a _____. 789
financially. 1058	**Some children have unusual talent** *in music.* (adjective) **Some children have unusual** _____ **talent.** 1059
a 1328	a. **His raincoat** *dripped.* b. **His raincoat** *dripping.* Which item is *not* a sentence because it contains a present participle rather than a verb? ____ 1329
a 1598	When similar ideas are expressed in a similar way, we say that the construction is _____. 1599

a (to) our child any food that is spoiled. 1868	a. dangling word group b. nonparallel construction c. incorrect omission of words **While eating his meals, no one should hurry him.** _____ , **no one should hurry him.** 1869
gone, rung 2137	**We quickly _____ (_do_) the dishes and _____ (_run_) up to our room.** 2138
certainly, unfair 2406	**Three can sit very (_comfortably, comfortable_) in the front seat.** 2407
a 2675	When following the rule does not lead to absurdity, it is better —especially in formal usage—to refer to **everyone** or **everybody** with a (_singular, plural_) pronoun. 2676
incomplete 2944	The statements that require colons often contain the words _following, as follows, these,_ or _there are._ a. **The ingredients of waffles are: flour, milk, eggs. . . .** b. **Waffles contain the following ingredients: flour, milk, eggs. . . .** The colon is used correctly in sentence (_a, b_). 2945
b 3213	**The child feared many things; for example, electrical storms and the dark.** Instead of using the semicolon, you could use (_a dash, a period followed by a capital letter_). 3214

explosion
 	
249
	We need prepositional phrases to express meanings that cannot be expressed by a single adjective or adverb.
	
	      a glass *for water* **a** *water* **glass**
	      a glass *for milk* **a** *milky* **glass**
	
	Which adjective is not the equivalent of the corresponding prepositional phrase—*water* or *milky?* _____ 250

When I opened the cabinet, a jar fell out. 519	Follow the directions given in the previous frame: **Jim insisted on changing the tire, and** *he had on his best suit.* _____ _____ 520
verb 789	**a** *cold* **wind** Because the word *cold* modifies the noun **wind**, it is an _____. 790
musical 1059	**Mr. Hollis listens** *in a patient way* **to all complaints.** (adverb) **Mr. Hollis listens** _____ **to all complaints.** 1060
b 1329	**His raincoat** *dripping.* Does a present participle by itself have the power to make a complete statement about a subject? (*Yes, No*) 1330
parallel 1599	Suppose that we should wish to enumerate the various duties of office secretaries: **The duties of secretaries are** *to receive visitors, opening the mail,* **and** *they type letters.* Is each of the three duties expressed in the same type of word group? (*Yes, No*) 1600

a While he is eating his meals, 1869	**Eating slowly is better for him than not to eat at all.** **Eating slowly is better for him than** _____ _____. 1870
did, ran 2138	**Water** _____ (*become*) **a serious problem after the well had** _____ (*run*) **dry.** 2139
comfortably 2407	**It was** (*somewhat, sort of*) **surprising that the strike should end as** (*sudden, suddenly*) **as it began.** 2408
singular 2676	Underline the pronoun that would be more appropriate in formal writing and speaking: **Under a democracy, everybody has the right to express** (*his, their*) **opinions.** 2677
b 2945	a. **These are the primary colors: red, blue, yellow.** b. **The primary colors are as follows: red, blue, yellow.** c. **The primary colors are: red, blue, yellow.** d. **The following are the primary colors: red, blue, yellow.** In which sentence is the colon incorrect because it does not follow a grammatically complete statement? _____ 2946
a dash 3214	**We have many aunts, uncles, and cousins, and all, of course, must be invited to the wedding.** To make the main break in this compound sentence more conspicuous, change the comma after the word **cousins** to a _____. 3215

milky 250	We walked *with care.* **We walked** *carefully.* **We traveled** *by train.* **We traveled** *trainly.* The adverb *carefully* can be substituted for the prepositional phrase *with care.* Is there a proper adverb that can take the place of the phrase *by train?* (*Yes, No*) 251
Jim insisted on changing the tire although he had on his best suit. 520	*You wait long enough,* **and everything comes back into style again.** —————————————————————— —————————————————————— 521
adjective 790	a *stinging* **wind** Because the word *stinging* modifies the noun **wind**, it is also an _____. 791
patiently 1060	**Remember not to leave things such as mops and pails on the stairs** *to the basement.* (adjective) **Remember not to leave things such as mops and pails on the** _____ **stairs.** 1061
No 1330	a. **His raincoat** *dripping.* b. **His raincoat** *was dripping.* In sentence *b*, we have made the present participle part of a verb by adding to it the helping verb _____. 1331
No 1600	a. **The duties of secretaries are** *to receive visitors, opening the mail,* **and** *they type letters.* b. **The duties of the secretary are** *to receive visitors, to open the mail,* **and** *to type letters.* Which sentence is correct because the italicized word groups match? ____ 1601

a. misplaced modifier   b. nonparallel construction
c. faulty comparison

b not eating at all. 1870	Do not force him to play childish games, because his interests are just like a grownup. Do not force him to play childish games, because his interests are just like _____. 1871
became, run 2139	When my sweater _____ (*come*) back from the cleaner, I noticed that it had _____ (*shrink*) a great deal. 2140
somewhat, suddenly 2408	Lesson **67** **Choosing Modifiers After *Sense* Verbs** [Frames 2410–2446]
his 2677	anyone anybody each someone somebody each one no one nobody either Can these pronouns mean either a boy or a girl, a man or a woman? (*Yes, No*) 2678
c 2946	a. The rent includes the following items: gas, electricity, and water. b. The rent includes: gas, electricity, and water. In which sentence is the colon used correctly? _____ 2947
semicolon 3215	a. The three basic rights mentioned in the Declaration of Independence are: life, liberty, and the pursuit of happiness. b. The Declaration of Independence mentions three human rights: life, liberty, and the pursuit of happiness. The colon is correctly used in sentence (*a, b*). 3216

No 251	Most prepositional phrases are used as modifiers—either as an adjective or as an adverb. A prepositional phrase which—like an adjective—modifies a noun or pronoun is called an **adjective phrase.** An adjective phrase does the work of an _____. 252
If you wait long enough, everything comes back into style again. 521	**I'll set the alarm, and** *I'll be sure to get up early.* (Keep the word groups in the same order.) _____ _____ 522
adjective 791	**a** *cold, stinging* **wind** Which adjective was formed from a verb—*cold* or *stinging?* _____. 792
basement 1061	a. *There are curtains in the kitchen.* **They need washing.** b. **The curtains** *that are in the kitchen* **need washing.** c. **The curtains** *hanging in the kitchen* **need washing.** d. **The curtains** *in the kitchen* **need washing.** e. **The** *kitchen* **curtains need washing.** Which sentence states the idea in the fewest words? _____ 1062

was
 	
1331
	To serve as a verb, a present participle must be combined with some form of the verb *be.*
	
	      a. **His raincoat was dripping.**
	      b. **His raincoat dripping.**
	
	Which item is a sentence because the present participle is combined with a form of *be?* _____
	
	1332

b 1601	a. **The duties of secretaries are** *to receive visitors, to open the mail,* **and** *to type letters.* b. **The duties of secretaries are** *receiving visitors, opening the mail,* **and** *typing letters.* Are both sentences correct? (*Yes, No*) 1602

c
a grownup's.
or those of a
grownup. *or* a
grownup's
interests.
1871

a. nonparallel construction   b. faulty pronoun reference
c. faulty comparison

He has, by the way, read more books than any boy or girl in his class.

He has, by the way, read more books than _____

_____

1872

---

came, shrunk

2140

We had _____ (*sing*) **only a few songs when the**

lights _____ (*begin*) **to flicker.**

2141

---

look   smell   taste   feel   hear (sound)

These verbs that relate to our senses have two different meanings. One requires an adverb, the other an adjective.

  a. **Joey** *looked* **at the cake.**
  b. **The cake** *looked* **delicious.**

Looked means an action of the eyes in sentence (*a, b*).

2410

Yes

2678

Although a pronoun such as **anyone, anybody, someone, somebody** can mean either sex, we can use the masculine pronoun *his, he,* or *him* to refer to such pronouns.

Anyone **who never changes** *his* **mind has stopped learning.**

Does this statement, as it is worded, apply to either sex? (*Yes, No*)

2679

---

a

2947

a. **Scandinavia consists of three countries: Norway, Sweden, and Denmark.**
b. **Scandinavia consists of: Norway, Sweden, and Denmark.**

The colon is used incorrectly in sentence (*a, b*).

2948

---

b

3216

Many of Bach's relatives, *brothers, uncles, and cousins,* **were also musicians.**

To make it clear that the italicized nouns are used as appositives, change the commas after **relatives** and *cousins* to (*semicolons, colons, dashes*).

3217

adjective 252	**the** *corner* **house** Because *corner* modifies the noun **house,** it is an *adjective.* **the house** *on the corner* Because the prepositional phrase *on the corner* also modifies the noun **house,** it is an _____ *phrase.* 253
I'll set the alarm so that I'll be sure to get up early. 522	*Sally smells roses,* **and she begins to sneeze.** _____ _____ 523
stinging 792	**a** *stinging* **wind** The adjective *stinging* was formed by adding _____ to the verb *sting.* 793
e 1062	a. *There are curtains in the kitchen.* **They need washing.** b. **The curtains** *that are in the kitchen* **need washing.** c. **The curtains** *hanging in the kitchen* **need washing.** d. **The curtains** *in the kitchen* **need washing.** e. **The** *kitchen* **curtains need washing.** These sentences illustrate the process of _____. 1063
a 1332	a. **Columbo walked into the living room. His raincoat was dripping.** b. **Columbo walked into the living room. His raincoat dripping.** The noun-participle phrase which is written as a fragment is found in (*a, b*). 1333
Yes 1602	The basic idea of parallel construction is this: If your first item begins with a participle, then all should begin with participles. If your first item is a clause, then all the others should be _____. 1603

c
any other boy
or girl in his
class.

1872

a. *is when* or *is where* error   b. faulty pronoun reference
c. faulty comparison

Our son plans to become a scientist because it is his greatest interest.

Our son plans to become a scientist because _____

_____.

1873

---

sung, began

The bone had _____ (*spring*) **back into place before the doctor** _____ (*come*).

2141

2142

---

a

a. **The water** *felt* **cold.**
b. **The customer** *felt* **the material.**

In which sentence does *felt* mean an action of the hands?

____

2410

2411

It is generally better to use the pronoun *his* to refer to both sexes than to use *his or her,* which is clumsy.

a. **Somebody has forgotten to put** *his* **name on** *his* **paper.**
b. **Somebody has forgotten to put** *his or her* **name on** *his or her* **paper.**

Yes

Which sentence is preferable? ____

2679

2680

A colon may be used before a single item that is introduced by a complete statement.

Only one thing stopped me from going: my lack of money.

b

a. **Eva had only one ambition: to win the music prize.**
b. **Eva's only ambition was: to win the music prize.**

The colon is used correctly in sentence (*a, b*).

2948

2949

Dad predicted that I would change my mind, and I did.

dashes

To make the end of this sentence more forceful, change the comma to a _____.

3217

3218

adjective 253	**the** *corner* **house** **the house** *on the corner* The *adjective* comes before the noun it modifies. The *adjective phrase* comes (*before, after*) the noun it modifies. 254
Whenever (*or* when) Sally smells roses, she begins to sneeze. 523	Lesson **14** Understanding Adjective Clauses [Frames 525–564]
ing 793	An adjective that is formed by adding -*ing* to a verb is called a **present participle.** We can turn any verb into a present participle by adding -*ing* to it (sometimes making a minor change in the spelling). The present participle form of the verb *lose* is _____. 794
reduction 1063	UNIT 5: ACHIEVING SENTENCE VARIETY Lesson **28** Shifting Word Order in the Sentence [Frames 1065–1098]
b 1333	**His knee bandaged,** This noun-participle phrase contains a (*present, past*) participle. 1334
clauses 1603	If your first item is an adjective, then all the others should be _____. 1604

b science is his greatest interest. 1873	a. misplaced modifier b. *is when* or *is where* error c. faulty comparison **Do not let him watch violent television shows before he goes to bed, which are likely to give him nightmares.** _____ _____. 1874
sprung, came 2142	The *Titanic* had _____ (*run*) **into an iceberg and** had _____ (*sink*). 2143
b 2411	a. **The cook** *tasted* **the soup.** b. **The medicine** *tasted* **bitter.** In which sentence does *tasted* mean an action performed by the subject's tongue? _____ 2412
a 2680	Because some people feel uncomfortable in using the masculine pronoun *his* in statements that refer to both sexes, they fall back on the plural pronoun *their*, which is acceptable as informal usage. If *anyone* **should call, take** *their* **number.** This sentence is acceptable as (*informal, formal*) usage. 2681
a 2949	DASHES The dash is not a general punctuation mark that may be used for all purposes. Its uses are just as exact as those of any other punctuation mark. May a dash be used to take the place of any comma or period? (*Yes, No*) 2950
dash 3218	a. **The coach said, "This is our last chance to win."** b. **The coach said, "this is our last chance to win."** Which sentence is correct? _____ 3219

after	Adjective phrases—just like adjectives—are often used after linking verbs as subject complements.
	
	    a. **The lilacs are beautiful.**
	    b. **The lilacs are in full bloom.**
	
	In which sentence is an adjective phrase used as a subject complement? _____

254	255
	We have just studied adverb clauses—clauses that are used as adverbs. Now we turn our attention to the **adjective clause.** As its name suggests, an adjective clause is a clause that is used as an _____.
	525
losing	The present participle form of the verb *win* is _____.
794	795
	Sentences are usually parts of a paragraph—with other sentences before and after them. In a particular position, one sentence pattern might suit your purpose much better than another. Should the pattern of any preceding sentences influence a sentence that you might, at the moment, be writing? (*Yes, No*)
	1065
past	a. **His knee bandaged.** b. **His knee was bandaged.** Which item is *not* a sentence because it contains a past participle rather than a verb? _____
1334	1335
adjectives	In expressing parallel ideas, it doesn't matter which pattern you use at the beginning so long as you follow through with (*the same, a different*) pattern.
1604	1605

a

Before he goes to bed, do not . . . shows, which are likely to give him nightmares.

1874

---

a. dangling word group   b. nonparallel construction
c. incorrect omission of words

Please look in, now and then, during the night to keep him covered and seeing that he doesn't fall out of bed.

Please look in, now and then, during the night to keep him covered and _____

_____ .1875

---

run, sunk

2143

The police had _____ (*become*) **suspicious when the boy** _____ (*run*) **away from home.**

2144

---

look   smell   taste   feel   hear (sound)

When these verbs mean actions of the body, use adverbs to describe these actions—just as you use adverbs to describe any other actions.

Underline the correct word:

We smelled gas very (*distinct, distinctly*) **in the kitchen.**

a

2412

2413

Although you may use in conversation whatever forms seem natural to you, use only singular pronouns to refer to antecedents such as **anyone, anybody, someone,** and **somebody** in all careful speech and formal writing.

Underline the proper pronoun for formal usage:

Nobody can escape the consequences of (*his, their*) **actions.**

informal

2681

2682

To some extent dashes are used like commas, but they are stronger, more forceful marks that interrupt a sentence more abruptly.

a. **Rice's hit, a line drive to center field, won the game.**
b. **Rice's hit—a line drive to center field—won the game.**

Which sentence makes the appositive more forceful? _____

No

2950

2951

---

a. **"Is anybody hurt?" asked the police officer.**
b. **"Is anybody hurt," asked the police officer?**

Which sentence is correct? _____

a

3219

3220

b 255	In all but one of these sentences, the linking verb is followed by an adjective phrase used as a subject complement. a. **The plane** *was* **on time.** c. **The crops** *were* **dry.** b. **The piano** *seems* **in tune.** d. **The ring** *is* **of no value.** The one sentence in which the linking verb is not completed by an adjective phrase is sentence _____. 256
adjective 525	An adjective modifies a noun or pronoun. **I just read an *interesting* article.** The word *interesting* is an adjective because it modifies the noun _____. 526
winning 795	a. **We have a *good* team.** b. **We have a *winning* team.** In which sentence does a present participle modify the noun **team?** _____ 796
Yes 1065	You may wish to avoid repeating a word or a sentence pattern. You may consider that one pattern sounds better than another in a particular situation, or that it gives an idea more needed emphasis. Could a sentence be good in itself but poor at a particular point in a paragraph? (*Yes, No*) 1066
a 1335	a. **His knee bandaged.** b. **His knee was bandaged.** In sentence *b*, we have made the past participle part of the verb by adding it to the helping verb _____. 1336
the same 1605	In the following exercise, each sentence contains three parallel ideas arranged in columns to make comparison easier. You will find that one of the ideas does not match the other two. Your job is to rewrite this "misfit" so as to bring it in line with the other two ideas, thus making the construction _____. 1606

b to see that he doesn't fall out of bed. 1875	a. misplaced modifier b. dangling word group c. incorrect omission of words **If he coughs, sneezes, or any other symptom of a cold, wire us at once.** **If he coughs, sneezes, _____** **_____, wire us at once.** 1876
become, ran 2144	**We had _____ (_swim_) for only a few minutes** **when it _____ (_begin_) to rain.** 2145
distinctly 2413	a. **Our costumes _looked_ rather curious.** b. **Everyone _looked_ at our costumes curiously.** In which sentence does _looked_ mean an action of the eyes? _____ 2414
his 2682	a. **If that is _someone_ for me, ask _them_ to wait.** b. **If _someone_ is falsely accused, _they_ have the right to defend _themselves_.** In which sentence would the use of the plural pronoun(s) be acceptable because the situation is informal? _____ 2683
b 2951	a. **This horse—high-spirited and nervous—was hard to control.** b. **This horse, high-spirited and nervous, was hard to control.** Which sentence makes the adjectives more forceful? _____ 2952
a 3220	a. **"People matter," said Eleanor Roosevelt, "we are here to help one another."** b. **"People matter," said Eleanor Roosevelt. "We are here to help one another."** Because the quotation consists of two separate sentences, which is correctly punctuated—_a_ or _b_? _____ 3221

c 256	A prepositional phrase can also be used as an adverb. **spoke** *proudly* Because *proudly* modifies the verb **spoke**, it is an *adverb*. **spoke** *with pride* Because the phrase *with pride* also modifies the verb **spoke**, it is an ＿＿＿＿＿＿＿＿ *phrase*. 257
article 526	a. **I just read an** *interesting* **article.** b. **I just read an article** *which interested* me. The clause in sentence *b* does the same job as the adjective *interesting* in sentence *a*. The clause *which interested me* is therefore called an ＿＿＿＿＿＿＿＿＿＿ *clause.* 527
b 796	Besides being formed from a verb, a present participle resembles a verb in still another way: It may take a direct object or a subject complement, as no ordinary adjective can do. **I found Roy** *reading a magazine.* (Roy read a magazine.) The present participle *reading* is completed by the direct object ＿＿＿＿＿＿＿＿＿＿. 797
Yes 1066	In furnishing a room, you can't say whether a particular chair is good or bad without considering the other furnishings with which it must fit in. Can the same be said of a particular sentence pattern? (*Yes, No*) 1067
was 1336	a. **Namath returned to the game, his knee bandaged.** b. **Namath returned to the game. His knee bandaged.** Which arrangement is correct? ＿＿＿＿ 1337
parallel 1606	Rewrite only the "misfit" on the corresponding line at the side to make it parallel with the other two: **The new cars are tested for** a. **speed,** ＿＿＿＿＿＿＿＿＿＿＿＿＿＿＿ b. **comfort, and** ＿＿＿＿＿＿＿＿＿＿＿＿＿＿＿ c. **if they are safe.** ＿＿＿＿＿＿＿＿＿＿＿＿＿＿＿ 1607

c or shows (has, develops) any other symptom of a cold 1876	a. dangling word group b. faulty pronoun reference c. *is when* or *is where* error **In your camp bulletin, it says that parents may not visit during the first two weeks.** _____ that **parents may not visit during the first two weeks.** 1877
swum, began 2145	**When Dick** _____ (*come*) **over, Earl had already** _____ (*go*) **to bed.** 2146
b 2414	**Everyone** *looked* **at our costumes (curious, curiously).** In this sentence, *looked* means an action of the eyes. To describe this action, we should choose the adverb (*curious, curiously*). 2415
a 2683	Underline the proper pronoun for formal usage: *Anyone* **who fails to report a crime is shirking** (*his, their*) **moral duty.** 2684
a 2952	A dash gives more force to an added idea than a comma. a. **Only one person knew the combination to the safe, and he was out of town.** b. **Only one person knew the combination to the safe—and he was out of town.** Which sentence is more forceful? _____ 2953
b 3221	a. **"Where all men think alike," said Walter Lippmann, "no one thinks very much."** b. **"Where all men think alike," said Walter Lippmann, "No one thinks very much."** Which sentence is correct? _____ 3222

adverb 257	Like the adverbs they resemble, adverb phrases answer the questions *When? Where?* and *How?* about verbs. **The car turned** *at the next intersection.* Underline the question that the adverb phrase answers: **When?** **Where?** **How?** 258
adjective 527	**I just read an article** *which interested me.* Now look at just the adjective clause. Does it have a subject and a verb? (*Yes, No*) 528
magazine 797	**I found Roy** *feeling lonesome.* (Roy felt lonesome.) The present participle *feeling* is completed by the subject complement _____. 798
Yes 1067	Because English is a subject-first language, we naturally begin most of our sentences with the subject. a. **The whole pile of dishes went down.** b. **Down went the whole pile of dishes.** In which sentence does the subject come first? _____ 1068
a 1337	a. **Our engine was repaired. We continued on our way.** b. **Our engine repaired, we continued on our way.** c. **Our engine repaired. We continued on our way.** Which one of the above three arrangements is incorrect? _____ 1338
c. safety. 1607	**Rick's theme was not accepted because** a. **of its lateness,** _____ b. **it was too short, and** _____ c. **it was written in pencil.** _____ 1608

a. nonparallel construction   b. faulty pronoun reference
c. faulty comparison

Therefore, if he gets homesick or any special food is wanted, tell him to telephone us immediately.

Therefore, _____

_____, tell him to telephone us immediately.

1878

---

came, gone

2146

Walter _____ (*drink*) the milk that his little brother should have _____ (*drink*).

2147

---

curiously

2415

a. I *felt* **my pocket . . . to see if my wallet was there.**
b. I *felt* **very . . . about my test score.**

In which sentence would you use the adverb **anxiously** because *felt* means an action and the adverb **anxiously** would describe this action? _____

2416

---

his

2684

The same problem arises when you use the words **a person** or **any person** to make a statement that applies to either sex.

INFORMAL: **Can** *any person* **park** *their* **car here?**
FORMAL: *Any person* **can improve** *his* **speech if** *he* **tries.**

Formal usage requires a (*singular, plural*) pronoun.

2685

---

b

2953

Supply a missing punctuation mark that will give more force to the added idea:

Ann said that nothing could stop her from going to college and she meant it.

2954

---

a

3222

Insert any necessary apostrophes:

Myra hurts peoples feelings and then wonders why she isnt popular.

(*Note:* The feelings belong to the **people,** not to the **peoples.**)

3223

Where?	*During the night* **it snowed.** Underline the question that the adverb phrase answers: **When?** **Where?** **How?**
258	259

Yes	**I just read an article** *which interested me.* Although the adjective clause has a subject and a verb, does it make sense by itself apart from the sentence? (*Yes, No*)
528	529

---

lonesome	Like the verb from which it is made, a present participle may be modified by an adverb. **The lawyer defended her client,** *believing firmly in his innocence.* The present participle *believing* is modified by the adverb
798	_____. 799

---

a	Another way of achieving sentence variety is to begin a sentence, now and then, with an adverbial modifier—an adverb, an adverb phrase, or an adverb clause. Underline the adverb phrase that can be put ahead of the subject: **I never trusted ladders after that experience.**
1068	1069

---

c	a. **Tuesday being Election Day. The banks will be closed.** b. **Tuesday is Election Day. The banks will be closed.** c. **Tuesday being Election Day, the banks will be closed.** Which one of the above three arrangements is incorrect?
1338	—— 1339

---

a. it was late,	**In cooking class, we learned** a. **to prepare meat,** _____ b. **baking cakes, and** _____ c. **to make salads.** _____
1608	1609

a
if he gets
homesick or
wants any
special food
1878
	a. misplaced modifier b. faulty comparison
	       c. faulty pronoun reference
	
	Be sure that they don't tease him, for he often develops temper tantrums.
	
	_____,
	for he often develops temper tantrums.
	                                 1879

drank, drunk
 	
2147
	Lesson **60** Three Tricky Pairs of Verbs:
	                    Lie–Lay, Sit–Set, Rise–Raise
	                      ·[Frames 2149–2191]

a
 	
2416
	look smell taste feel hear (sound)
	Much more commonly, these same verbs are used as _linking_ verbs that express no action at all. They link an adjective in the predicate with the subject it describes.
	        The cake looked _delicious._
	The adjective _delicious_ modifies the subject _____.
	                                 2417

singular **2685**	Underline the proper pronoun for formal usage: _Any person_ **can train** (_himself, themselves_) **to concentrate.** **2686**
college—and **2954**	**The three women, Walker, Wheatley, and Giovanni, are all well-known poets.** Is it possible to interpret the subject of this sentence as meaning either _three_ or _six_ people? (_Yes, No_) **2955**

people's, isn't
 	
3223
	Remember that possessive pronouns show possession without the use of apostrophes.
	
	    a. _Yours_ **is the same color as** _theirs._
	    b. **The** _Dunns_ **car is the same color as the** _Clarks._
	
	Apostrophes are required only in sentence (_a, b_).
	                                 3224

When?

259

We mended the picture *with paste.*

Underline the question that the adverb phrase answers:

When?   Where?   How?

260

No

529

---

a. **A tree surgeon removed the** *dead* **branches.**
b. **A tree surgeon removed the branches** *that were dead.*

Both the adjective *dead* in sentence *a* and the adjective clause *that were dead* in sentence *b* modify the noun

_____.

530

---

firmly

799

Participles—with their related words—form useful phrases known as **participial phrases.** These phrases are used as adjectives to modify nouns and pronouns.

The dog, *shivering with cold,* **came into the house.**

The participial phrase modifies the noun _____.

800

---

after that
experience

1069

---

a. **I never trusted ladders after that experience.**
b. **After that experience, I never trusted ladders.**

Which sentence would it be better to use after you had

written a number of subject-first sentences? _____

1070

---

a

1339

If both word groups are sentences, add a period and a capital, or a semicolon. If one word group is a fragment, make no change except to add a comma if needed. Write only the word before and after the space between the word groups.

The lake was choppy   no small boats ventured out.

_____

1340

---

b. to bake
cakes, and

1609

All our neighbors are

a. **kind,**   _____

b. **friendly, and**   _____

c. **give help.**   _____

1610

a. nonparallel construction   b. *is when* or *is where* error
c. faulty comparison

A temper tantrum, as you know, is when a child holds his breath and turns blue from anger.

In a temper tantrum, as you know, _____

_____.

1880

To lie means "to rest in a flat position" or "to be in place."

To lay means "to put (down) or to place something."

Underline the correct word or words:

You ought (*to lie, to lay*) **down and rest for a while.**

2149

---

cake

2417

When used as linking verbs, "sense" verbs serve much the same purpose as the linking verb **be** (*is, am, are—was, were, been*).

The water *felt* (= *was*) **cold.**

The verb *felt* serves as a linking verb—like *was*—to show that the adjective **cold** modifies the subject _____.

2418

---

himself

2686

Underline the proper pronoun for formal usage:

A person **should have the courage of** (*their, his*) **convictions.**

2687

Yes

2955

Use dashes to set off a series of appositives that might be confused with the nouns they explain.

The three women—Walker, Wheatley, and Giovanni—are all well-known poets.

The dashes make it clear that you are talking about (*three, six*) people.

2956

---

b

3224

Insert any necessary apostrophes:

Freds injuries were slight, but hers were more serious.

3225

How?
 	
260
	An adverb phrase can also answer the question *Why?* about a verb.
	
	    a. **I often read science fiction** *for a change.*
	    b. **I often read science fiction** *for a few days.*
	
	In which sentence does the adverb phrase explain *Why?* in regard to the verb? _____
	
	    261

branches
 	
530
	a. **A tree surgeon removed the** *dead* **branches.**
	    b. **A tree surgeon removed the branches** *that were* *dead.*
	
	The adjective *dead* in sentence *a* comes *before* the noun it modifies.
	
	The adjective clause *that were dead* comes (*before, after*) the noun it modifies.
	
	    531

dog
 	
800
	A participial phrase can often be shifted about.
	
	    Shivering with cold, **the dog came into the house.**
	    The dog, *shivering with cold,* **came into the house.**
	    The dog came into the house, *shivering with cold.*
	
	Can a participial phrase be some distance away from the noun it modifies? (*Yes, No*) 801

b
 	
1070
	Underline the adverb clause that you could put ahead of the subject:
	
	    Our sales increased as soon as we lowered our price.
	
	    1071

choppy. No
or
choppy; no
 	
1340
	Continue to follow the directions for the previous frame:
	
	    The lake was choppy no small boats venturing out.
	
	_____
	
	    1341

c. helpful. 1610	**Iris spent the afternoon** a. **lying on the sofa,** _____ b. **reading a novel, and** _____ c. **she ate chocolates.** _____ 1611

b a child holds his breath and turns blue from anger. 1880	**Please remind him to write us every day and that he should brush his teeth after every meal.** **Please remind him to write us every day and** _____ _____. 1881
to lie 2149	Of the two verbs **lie** and **lay, lie** causes most of the trouble. PRESENT PAST PAST PARTICIPLE **lie** (to rest) **lay** **(have) lain** Notice especially that the past form of **lie** is _____. 2150

water
 	
2418
	Whenever a "sense" verb is used as a linking verb, you can generally put a form of **be** in its place.
	
	    a. **The sky** *looks* **cloudy.**
	    b. **The sailor** *looks* **at the sky.**
	
	In which sentence is *looks* used as a linking verb because you can put *is* in its place? _____
	2419

his 2687	anyone anybody each someone somebody each one no one nobody either In formal writing or speaking, refer to these words by using (*singular, plural*) pronouns. 2688
three 2956	Supply the missing punctuation: **Several pieces of equipment a file, a typewriter, and a duplicator were contributed by the Men's Club.** 2957
Fred's 3225	Insert three necessary apostrophes. (This is a high-error frame. Be sure to put each apostrophe after the noun or the part of the noun that names the owner or owners.) **This girls job is to check the mens and ladies wraps.** 3226

a	An adverb phrase—just like an adverb—can often be moved from one position to another in the sentence.
	My friend takes a nap *after dinner.*
	After dinner **my friend takes a nap.**
	The fact that a prepositional phrase can be moved shows
261	that it is an _____ *phrase.* **262**

after	It is easy to see why an adjective clause must come *after* the word it modifies.
	A tree surgeon removed the branches *that were dead.*
	If we put the adjective clause before the noun *branches,* which it modifies, the sentence would be very (*smooth,*
531	*clumsy).* **532**

Yes	**The train roared past,** *leaving a trail of smoke.*
	The participial phrase is separated by several words from the word it modifies, the noun _____.
801	**802**

as soon as	a. **The fish jumped the hook** *as I pulled in my line.*
we lowered	b. *As I pulled in my line,* **the fish jumped the hook.**
our price	Which sentence arouses more suspense by keeping you
	guessing until the end? _____
1071	**1072**

choppy, no	**Our job was to watch for forest fires and report any sign of smoke.**
	(Do you recall that no comma is used before the conjunction when it connects the two parts of a compound predicate?)
	_____
1341	**1342**

c. eating chocolates.	**We traded in our car because**
	a. **the engine burned oil,** _____
	b. **the smooth tires, and** _____
	c. **the body was rusty.** _____
1611	**1612**

a. dangling word group   b. *is when* or *is where* error
c. incorrect omission of words

b
(to) brush his
teeth after
every meal.

1881

We would appreciate your keeping a watchful eye on the companions whom he associates.

We would appreciate your keeping a watchful eye on _____

_____.

1882

PRESENT	PAST	PAST PARTICIPLE
lie (to rest)	**lay**	**(have) lain**

Use these rhymes to remember the forms of this verb:

lay

2150

"Yes-ter-day
In bed he lay."

"In pain
He has lain."

The past participle of **lie** is _____.

2151

---

look   smell   taste   feel   sound

When these verbs show no action but are used as linking verbs, they are followed by adjectives that describe the subject.

a

2419

Underline the correct word:

Our garden looks (*beautiful, beautifully*) **in the spring.**

2420

In this and the following frames, underline the pronoun (and sometimes the verb, too) that is appropriate for formal writing or speaking. Watch out for one sentence in which the sense makes the use of a plural pronoun necessary to refer to *everyone* or *everybody*.

singular

2688

A person cannot select (*their, his*) **own ancestors.**

2689

Use a dash to indicate hesitation in speech or a broken-off sentence.

equipment—
duplicator—

2957

a. **"She—she broke my wagon," sobbed little Linda.**
b. **"If he ever asks to borrow my car again—"**

In which sentence does the dash indicate hesitation in speech? _____

2958

---

girl's, men's,
ladies'

3226

Copy the correct words:

(*They're, Their*) **testing** (*it's, its*) **engines before taking off.**

3227

adverb 262	a. **They have improved the design** *of the car.* b. **A crowd was standing** *around the car.* In one sentence the phrase can be moved; in the other it can't. Which sentence contains an adverb phrase? ____ 263
clumsy 532	In a previous lesson, you saw that an *adverb clause* can often be shifted from one position to another. **I watched television** *after I studied.* Can the adverb clause *after I studied* be moved to another position? (*Yes, No*) 533
train 802	We have now become acquainted with three kinds of word groups that are used like adjectives to modify nouns. ADJECTIVE PHRASE: **a girl** *with a dog* ADJECTIVE CLAUSE: **a girl** *who was walking her dog* PARTICIPIAL PHRASE: **a girl** *walking her dog* All three word groups modify the noun _____. 803
b 1072	Putting an adverbial modifier, now and then, ahead of the subject adds variety to your writing. It also creates a greater feeling of (*suspense, confusion*). 1073
fires and 1342	**The circus is a national institution a part of our national tradition.** _____ 1343
b. the tires were smooth, and 1612	**Fish jump out of the water** a. **to shake off parasites,** _____ b. **to catch flies, and** _____ c. **escaping enemies.** _____ 1613

c the companions with whom he associates. *or* ...whom he associates with. 1882	a. dangling word group b. nonparallel construction c. faulty comparison **We trust that you will find her one of the best, if not the best, camper at Michiwaki.** **We trust that you will find him one of the best** _____ _____ 1883

(have) lain
 	
2151
	Complete these memory rhymes:
	
	   "Yes-ter-day **"In pain**
	      In bed he _____**."** **He has** _____**."**
	
	2152

beautiful 2420	**A field of sweet clover** *smells* **very pleasant.** In this sentence, the "sense" verb *smells* is used as (*an action, a linking*) verb. 2421
his 2689	**I believe that everyone should set a reasonable goal for** (*themselves, himself*). 2690

a
 	
2958
	Use a dash to indicate a sudden turn in the thought before an idea is completed.
	   "We stopped at—what was the name of that town?"
	Supply the missing punctuation:
	   "That car well, I just can't describe it."
	
	2959

They're, its 3227	Copy the correct words: (*Your, You're*) **the only one** (*who's, whose*) **not going.** 3228

b 263	An adverb phrase can usually be shifted about. Therefore it can be several words away from the verb it modifies. a. *On the first automobiles,* **solid rubber tires were used.** b. **Solid rubber tires were used** *on the first automobiles.* The adverb phrase is farthest from the verb it modifies in sentence _____. 264
Yes 533	**The teacher scolded the little girl** *who wandered away from the group.* Can the adjective clause *who wandered away from the group* be moved to another position? (*Yes, No*) 534

girl
 	
803
	To change a sentence to a participial phrase is simple.
	
	    (*We*) *heard a loud crash.* **We rushed to the window.**
	    ↓
	    Hearing a loud crash, **we rushed to the window.**
	
	To change the italicized sentence to a participial phrase, drop the subject *We* and change the verb *heard* to the present participle _____. 804

suspense . 1073	Another reason for departing from the usual subject-first word order is to give emphasis to a particular idea. On entering your room, you would be more likely to notice a piece of furniture if it (*were, were not*) in its usual position. 1074
institution, a 1343	**You can't change your face** **you can change your expression.** _____ 1344
c. to escape enemies. 1613	**Rosemary does her work** a. **with willingness,** _____ b. **quickly, and** _____ c. **accurately.** _____ 1614

Lesson 53 Keeping Your Mind on the Subject

[Frames 1885-1927]

---

c
campers at Michiwaki, if not the best.

1883

PRESENT: *Lie* **down. Don't** *lie* **in the sun. The rug** *lies* **on the floor. Your letter is** *lying* **on the desk.**

lay, lain

Fill in the correct words:

I asked Mother to _____ down, but she was already

2152

_____ down.

2153

---

a linking

A field of sweet clover *smells* **very pleasant.**

Because *smells* is used as a linking verb, it is followed by the (*adjective, adverb*) **pleasant.**

2421

2422

---

himself

No one must be made to feel that (*he is, they are***) forced to contribute.**

2690

2691

---

car—well

Use dashes to set off a sharp interruption in the thought of a sentence.

Once—and once was enough—I investigated a hornet's nest.

Insert the sentence **that's our dog** on the blank line, and punctuate it:

Patty _____ first noticed the flames.

2959

2960

You're, who's

In each of the remaining frames, you will find four phrases, in one of which the capitalization is incorrect. Copy this *one* phrase only, making the necessary corrections.

a. **her new spring outfit**   c. **read "the thing in the pond"**
b. **in a Buick car**   d. **at the Overton High School**

3228

_____

3229

A pot *of stew* **was simmering** *on the stove.*

This sentence contains both an adjective phrase and an adverb phrase.

The adverb phrase is the (*first, second*) phrase.

a

264

265

An adjective clause must always follow the noun or pronoun it modifies.

Can an adjective clause ever come at the very beginning of a sentence? (*Yes, No*)

No

534

535

I picked up the hot pan. (*I*) *thought it was cold.*

↓

I picked up the hot pan, *thinking it was cold.*

To change the italicized sentence to a participial phrase, drop the subject *I* and change the verb *thought* to the present participle _____.

hearing

804

805

In the very same way, a word that has been moved from its usual position attracts more attention.

The normal word order of an English sentence is—

Subject—Verb—Complement

If we put the complement first, it would attract (*more, less*) attention.

were not

1074

1075

Suspected of being a spy   the man was shadowed day and night.

_____

face. You
or
face; you

1344

1345

Curt Flood has spent time

a. **playing ball,** _____

b. **a business was run, and** _____

c. **broadcasting.** _____

a. willingly,

1614

1615

A singular subject requires a singular verb; a plural subject requires a plural verb. This is what we mean when we say that the subject and verb must agree in number.

We Washes Cars

This sign, seen on a garage, looks absurd because the subject **We** is plural, but the verb **Washes** is _____.

1885

---

lie, lying

2153

PAST: **Yesterday I** *lay* **in bed until noon. Dad** *lay* **back in his chair and took a nap. The food** *lay* **on the table all day.**

Lay is the past form of the verb _____.

2154

---

adjective

2422

Underline the correct word:

The old house smells (*musty, mustily*).

2423

---

he is

2691

Each girl is encouraged to join a club of (*their, her*) **own choice.**

2692

—that's our dog—

2960

Use either a dash or a semicolon before the words **for example** when they follow a complete statement.

Many words imitate sounds—for example, *crash, bang, splash.*

Would a semicolon serve equally as well as a dash in this sentence? (*Yes, No*)

2961

---

c. read "The Thing in the Pond"

3229

a. **a great author**
b. **a shot for the Flu**

c. **my father's uncle**
d. **at Niagara Falls**

3230

second

265

We saw *through the telescope* **the outline** *of a ship.*

The adverb phrase is the (*first, second*) phrase.

266

No

535

a. **The chair collapsed** *when I sat down.*
b. **I sat on a chair** *which was broken.*

In which sentence can the clause *not* be moved to another

position? _____

536

---

thinking

805

(*Bob*) *needed a haircut.* **He looked for a barber shop.**
↓
Needing a haircut, **he looked for a barber shop.**

In changing the italicized sentence to a participial phrase,

we lost the subject _____.

806

---

more

1075

Terry would not accept this money.

The noun **money** is the (*subject complement, direct object*)
of the verb **would accept.**

1076

---

spy, the

1345

Telephone operators wear headsets   leaving their hands free
to operate the switchboard.

_____

1346

---

b. running a
business, and

1615

The Owens want a house

a. **with a fireplace,**   _____

b. **having a garage, and**   _____

c. **with a screened porch.**   _____

1616

singular 1885	If all agreement errors sounded as bad as **"We Washes Cars,"** we would have no problem. However, we cannot always trust our ears in selecting a verb to match the subject. Without stopping to think, underline the verb which sounds right to your ear. (Don't score your answer right or wrong.) **One of you** (*is, are*) **always teasing the other.** 1886
lie 2154	PAST PARTICIPLE: **She** *has lain* **in bed most of the day. The dog must** *have lain* **down in the mud. This rug** *has lain* **there for years.** The past participle of **lie** that should be used after any form of **have** or **be** is _____. 2155
musty 2423	**The old house smells** *musty.* The adjective *musty* is correct because it modifies the noun _____. 2424
her 2692	**We should elect someone who can give all** (*his, their*) **time to the organization.** 2693
Yes 2961	a. **Our dog has several bad habits for example, chasing cars.** b. **Our dog has several bad habits for example, chasing cars.** In each sentence, insert a different punctuation mark before **for example.** 2962
b. a shot for the flu 3230	a. **for Mother's Day** c. **south of the park** b. **a college football star** d. **a school in the south** 3231

When we have two (or more) prepositional phrases in a row, each phrase can modify a different word.

We put a drop of water under the microscope.

The phrase **of water** modifies the noun **drop**.

Which word does the adverb phrase **under the microscope** modify? _____

first

266 | 267

---

a. **The chair collapsed** *when I sat down.*
b. **I sat on a chair** *which was broken.*

Which sentence contains an adjective clause? _____

b

536 | 537

(*Bob*) *needed a haircut.* **He looked for a barber shop.**
Bob
Needing a haircut, ~~he~~ **looked for a barber shop.**

To let the reader know the name of the person you're writing about, you must substitute **Bob** for the pronoun _____ in the main statement.

Bob

806 | 807

---

a. **Terry would not accept this money.**
b. **This money Terry would not accept.**

Which sentence gives greater emphasis to the direct object **money?** _____

direct object

1076 | 1077

The textile mill closing   hundreds of employees were thrown out of work.

_____

headsets, leaving

1346 | 1347

We shall need a board

a. **six feet in length,**   _____

b. **two feet wide, and**   _____

c. **one inch thick.**   _____

b. with a
garage, and

1616 | 1617

page 533

If *are* (wrong) sounded right, you will see why you can't always trust your ear. 1886	a. <u>One</u> <u>is</u> stuck. b. <u>One</u> (of the wheels) <u>is</u> stuck. Sentence *a* doesn't indicate whether **One** means a key, a window, a seat, or a wheel. We therefore add the prepositional phrase **of the wheels** to make our meaning clear. The subject in both *a* and *b* is the pronoun _____. 1887
lain 2155	Fill in the missing forms of **lie**: PRESENT PAST PAST PARTICIPLE **lie** (to rest) _____ **(have)** _____ 2156
house 2424	When a sentence states that something has a certain *look, taste, smell, feel,* or *sound,* the "sense" verb is then used as (*an action, a linking*) verb. 2425
his 2693	**Any girls interested in this job should see Miss Cruz as soon as** (*they, she*) **can.** 2694
a. ; *or* — b. — *or* ; 2962	The frames that complete this lesson provide good opportunities for using semicolons, colons, and dashes effectively. In several sentences, either one of two marks would be considered correct. Do not add any commas. **Before retirement, María worked steadily after retirement, she traveled around the world.** 2963
d. a school in the South 3231	a. **the Hale drug company** c. **a French horn** b. **next Tuesday night** d. **his idea of God** 3232

put	Two (or more) prepositional phrases can also modify the same word.
	Dad flew to Houston on Friday.
	The phrase **to Houston** modifies the verb **flew.**
	Which word does the phrase **on Friday** modify? _____
267	268

	a. **The bank discharged the employee** *who gambled.*
	b. **The bank discharged the employee** *because he gambled.*
b	In one sentence the clause can be shifted; in the other, it can't.
	Which sentence contains the adjective clause? _____
537	538

	If you lose a noun when making a participial phrase, put this noun back at the *beginning* of your main statement.
	Aunt Mae lives alone. **She is often lonesome for company.**
he	Fill in the blank space:
	Living alone, _____ **is often lonesome for**
807	**company.** 808

	Jackie Robinson certainly was a hero.
b	The noun **hero** follows the linking verb **was** and is therefore a (*subject complement, direct object*).
1077	1078

	The water level was dropping all danger of a flood was past.
closing, hundreds	_____
1347	1348

	A real friend is
	a. **considerate,** _____
a. six feet long,	b. **helpful, and** _____
	c. **sympathizes with you.** _____
1617	1618

	One of the wheels **is** stuck.
One	The noun **wheels** is not the subject of the above sentence.
	It is the object of the preposition _____.
1887	1888

	To lay means "to put down or to place something."
	You *lay* a book on the table, money on the counter, a package on the floor.
lay, (have) lain	PRESENT PAST PAST PARTICIPLE
	lay (to put) **laid** **(have) laid**
2156	The past and past participle forms are (*alike, different*). 2157

	The use of **badly,** instead of **bad,** after the linking verb **feel** is widespread in informal usage, even though it violates our general rule.
a linking	I feel (*bad, badly*) **about it.**
	Since **feel** is used as a linking verb in this sentence, the adjective (*bad, badly*) is correct in formal writing or speaking.
2425	2426

they	**Every applicant is asked whether** (*they have, he has*) **had any experience.**
2694	2695

steadily;	**Their lemon chiffon pie** **well, I just can't find words to describe it.**
2963	2964

a. the Hale Drug Company	
3232	

flew 268	A prepositional phrase can modify the object of the preceding prepositional phrase. **The family lived on the edge of a great forest.** The phrase **on the edge** modifies the verb **lived.** Which word does the phrase **of a great forest** modify? _____ 269
a 538	There are only a small number of *clause signals* that generally start adjective clauses: **who (whose, whom), which, that** These adjective clause signals are (*the same as, different from*) those that start adverb clauses. 539

Aunt Mae
 	
808
	Which of two sentences you subordinate depends on which idea you prefer to put in the background of the sentence.
	
	  a. *Reaching for the sugar,* **I knocked over a glass.**
	  b. **I reached for the sugar,** *knocking over a glass.*
	
	Which of the two sentences emphasizes the accident that occurred? _____ 809

subject complement 1078	a. **A hero Jackie Robinson certainly was.** b. **Jackie Robinson certainly was a hero.** Which sentence gives greater emphasis to the subject complement **hero?** _____ 1079
dropping. All *or* dropping; all 1348	**Ellen gets angry over trifles but forgives and forgets quickly.** _____ 1349
c. sympathetic. 1618	Lesson **45** Putting Sentences into Parallel Construction [Frames 1620–1647]

of

1888

One of these steaks . . . enough for a meal.

The verb has been omitted from this sentence.

The verb we choose should agree in number with the word (*One, steaks*).

CONTINUED ON PAGE 2   1889

---

alike

2157

PRESENT	PAST	PAST PARTICIPLE
lay (to put)	**laid**	**(have) laid**

Use the verb **lay** only when the sentence tells *what* was **laid** (put) somewhere.

George *had laid* **his cards on the table.**

What *was laid* on the table? _____

CONTINUED ON PAGE 2   2158

---

bad

2426

We feel *unhappy* **about losing the game.**
We feel *bad* **about losing the game.**

In both sentences the verb **feel** is followed by an adjective.

Are both sentences correct? (*Yes, No*)

CONTINUED ON PAGE 2   2427

---

he has

2695

Everybody was happy, and I didn't want to spoil (*their, his*) **fun.**

CONTINUED ON PAGE 2   2696

---

pie—

2964

Campers are expected to supply the following items   sheets, blankets, pillowcases, and towels.

CONTINUED ON PAGE 2   2965

edge

269

Remember—

A prepositional phrase that modifies a noun or a pronoun is called an *adjective phrase.*

A prepositional phrase that modifies a verb is called an

_____ *phrase.*

CONTINUED ON PAGE 1 270

---

different from

539

a. **while, when, as if, because, unless, although,** etc.
b. **who (whose, whom), which, that**

In which group are the clause signals that are used to start adjective clauses? _____

CONTINUED ON PAGE 1 540

---

a

809

a. *Reaching for the sugar,* **I knocked over a glass.**
b. **I reached for the sugar,** *knocking over a glass.*

Which sentence emphasizes the action that led to the accident? _____

CONTINUED ON PAGE 1 810

---

a

1079

His *strong, calloused* **hands were no strangers to work.**

The most common position of adjectives is (*before, after*) the nouns they modify.

CONTINUED ON PAGE 1 1080

---

trifles but

1349

Cheap paper is made from wood pulp   high-grade paper is made from rags.

_____

CONTINUED ON PAGE 1 1350

Parallel construction is a way of streamlining your writing— of giving your sentences smooth, clean lines. It is based on a very simple idea: Say similar things in a (*different, similar*) way.

CONTINUED ON PAGE 2 1620

INDEX

Each entry is indexed by frame number, followed by the page number, in parentheses, on which the frame appears. The frames indexed here are definitive, illustrative, or pivotal. Additional information and related exercises may be found in the frames preceding and following those listed. Complete review exercises for major topics are listed in the table of contents.